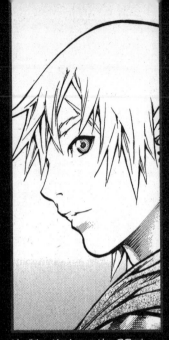

Norihiro Yagi won the 32nd
Akatsuka Award for his debut
work, *UNDEADMAN*, which
appeared in *Monthly Shonen
Jump* magazine and produced
two sequels. His first serialized
manga was his comedy *Angel
Densetsu* (Angel Legend),
which appeared in *Monthly
Shonen Jump* from 1992
to 2000. His epic saga,
Claymore, is running in
Monthly Jump Square
magazine.

In his spare time, Yagi enjoys
things like the Japanese
comedic duo Downtown, martial
arts, games, driving, and hard
rock music, but he doesn't
consider these actual hobbies

CLAYMORE VOL. 15
SHONEN JUMP ADVANCED Manga Edition

STORY AND ART BY
NORIHIRO YAGI

English Adaptation & Translation/Arashi Productions
Touch-up Art & Lettering/Sabrina Heep
Design/Courtney Utt
Editor/Leyla Aker

VP, Production/Alvin Lu
VP, Publishing Licensing/Rika Inouye
VP, Sales & Product Marketing/Gonzalo Ferreyra
VP, Creative/Linda Espinosa
Publisher/Hyoe Narita

Printed in the U.S.A.

Published by VIZ Media, LLC
P.O. Box 77010
San Francisco, CA 94107

10 9 8 7 6 5 4 3 2 1
First printing, November 2009

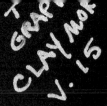

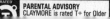

THE WORLD'S MOST
CUTTING-EDGE MANGA

SHONEN JUMP ADVANCED Manga Edition

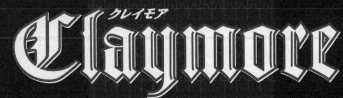

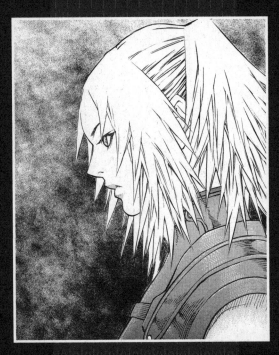

Vol. 15
Genesis of War

Story and Art by **Norihiro Yagi**

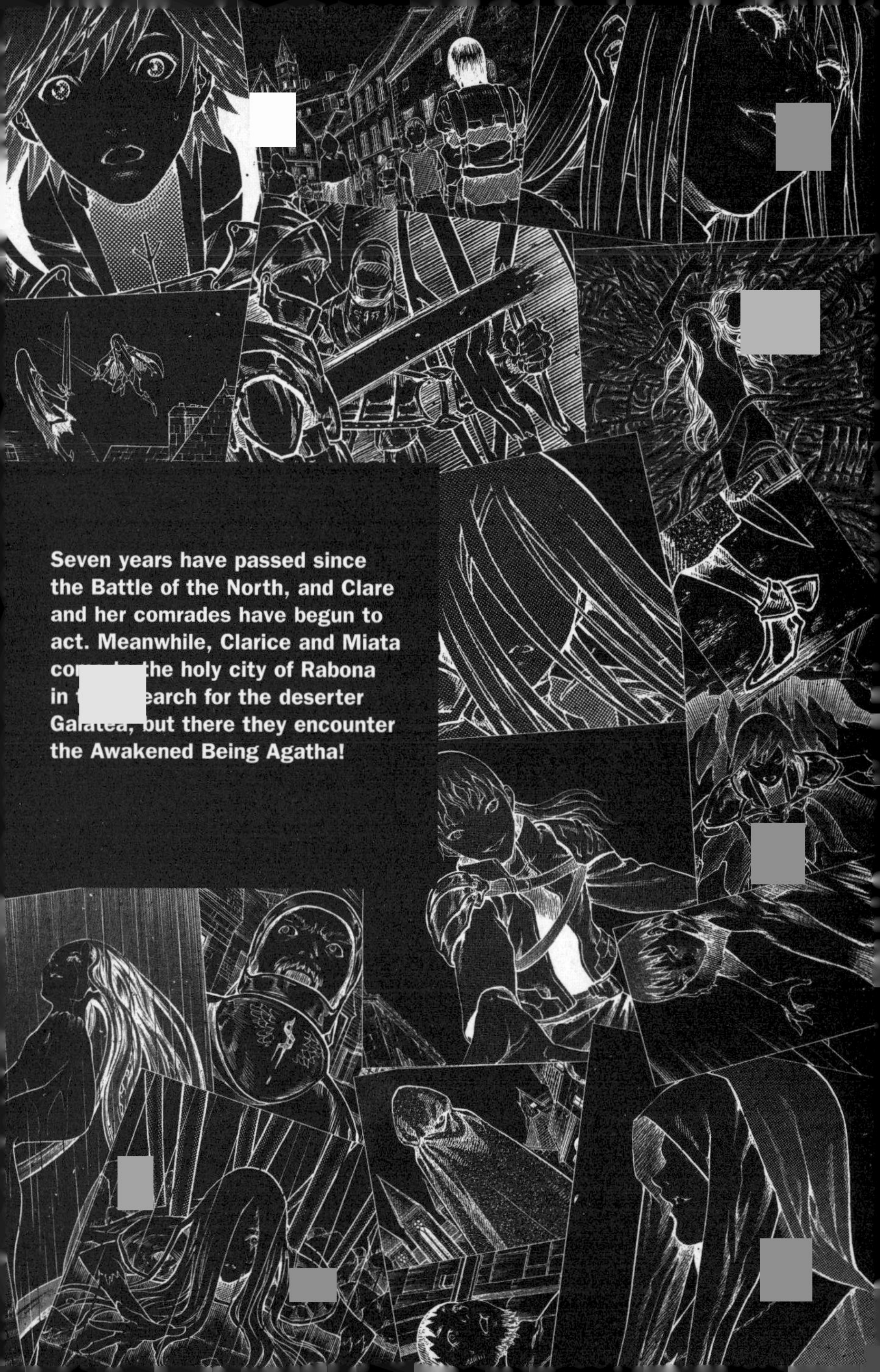

Seven years have passed since the Battle of the North, and Clare and her comrades have begun to act. Meanwhile, Clarice and Miata co[redacted]the holy city of Rabona in t[redacted]earch for the deserter Galatea, but there they encounter the Awakened Being Agatha!

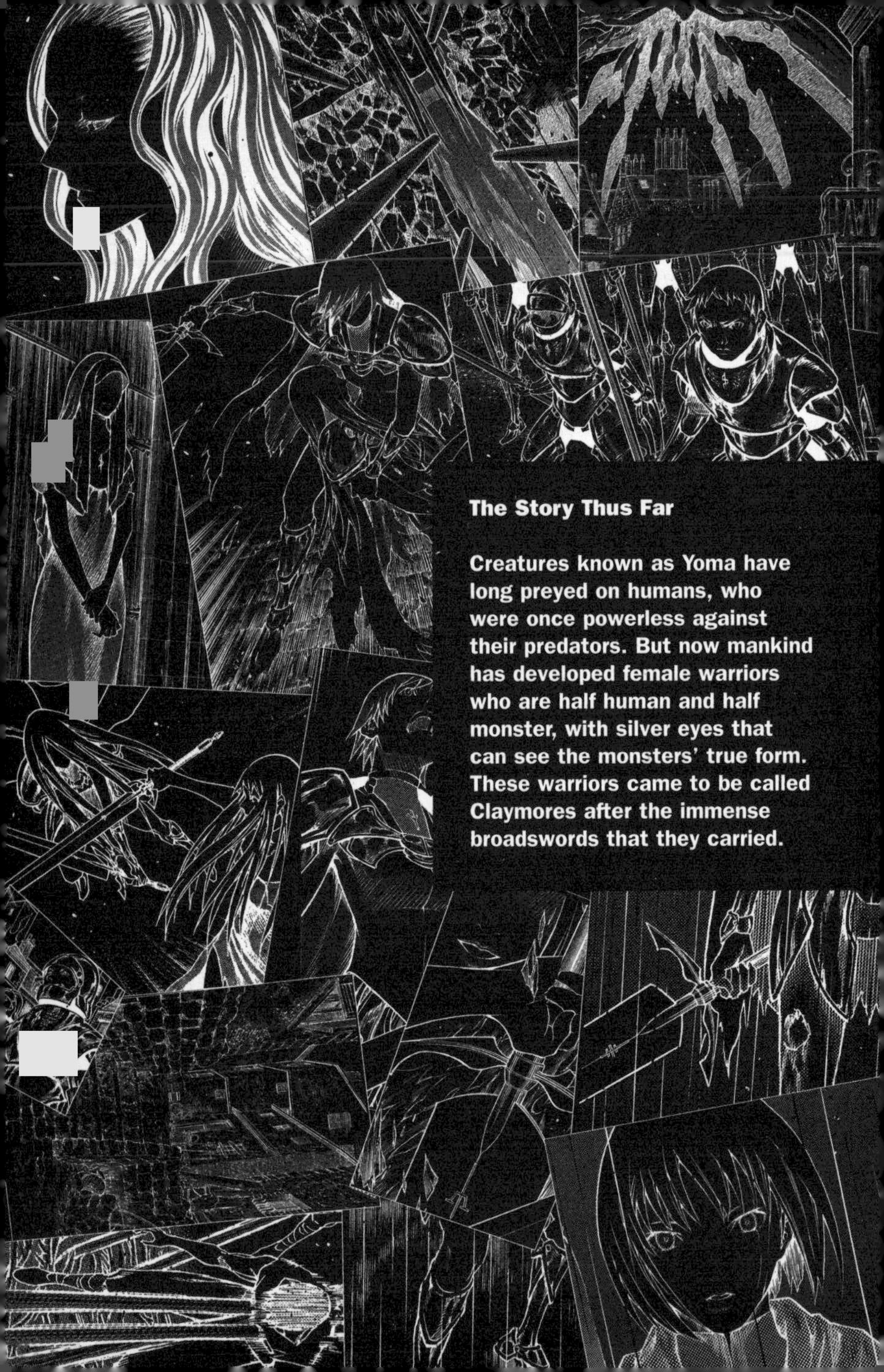

The Story Thus Far

Creatures known as Yoma have long preyed on humans, who were once powerless against their predators. But now mankind has developed female warriors who are half human and half monster, with silver eyes that can see the monsters' true form. These warriors came to be called Claymores after the immense broadswords that they carried.

クレイモア Claymore

Vol. 15

CONTENTS

Scene 78: Genesis of War, Part 1

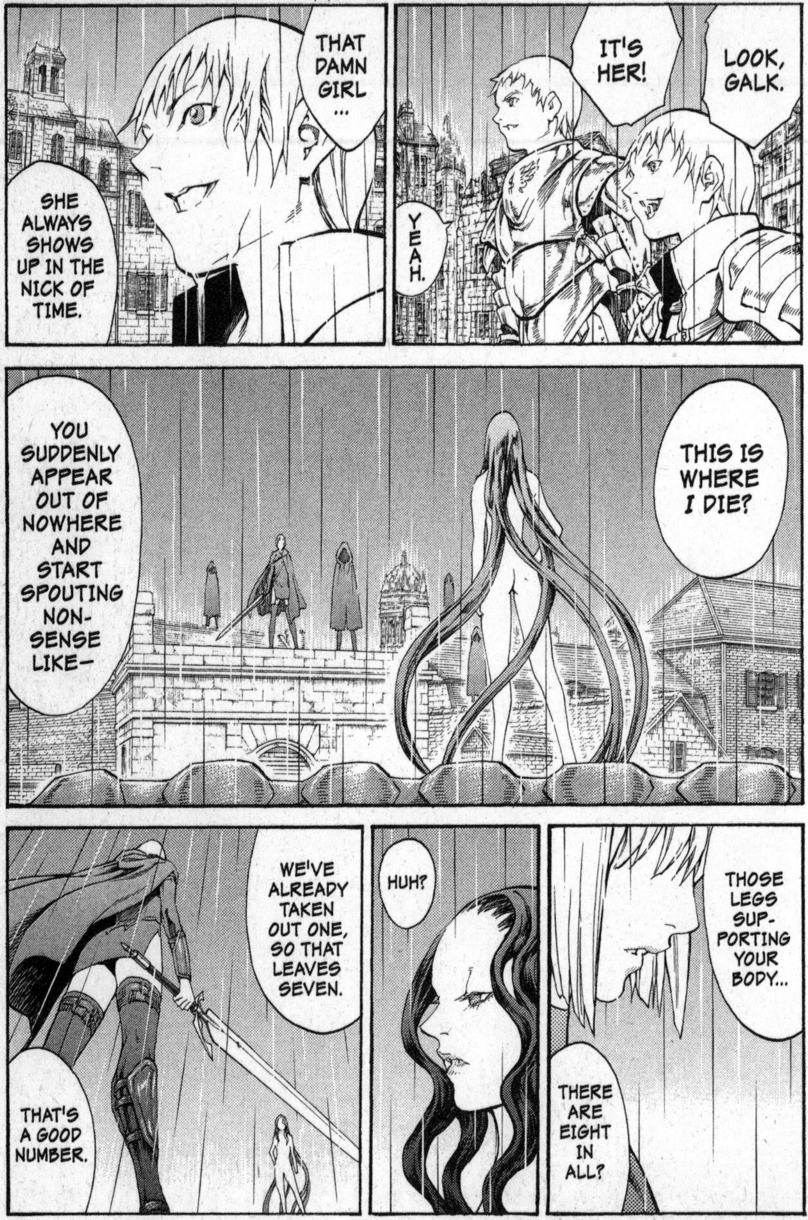
LOOK, GALK.
IT'S HER!
YEAH.
THAT DAMN GIRL...
SHE ALWAYS SHOWS UP IN THE NICK OF TIME.
THIS IS WHERE I DIE?
YOU SUDDENLY APPEAR OUT OF NOWHERE AND START SPOUTING NON-SENSE LIKE—
THOSE LEGS SUP-PORTING YOUR BODY...
THERE ARE EIGHT IN ALL?
HUH?
WE'VE ALREADY TAKEN OUT ONE, SO THAT LEAVES SEVEN.
THAT'S A GOOD NUMBER.

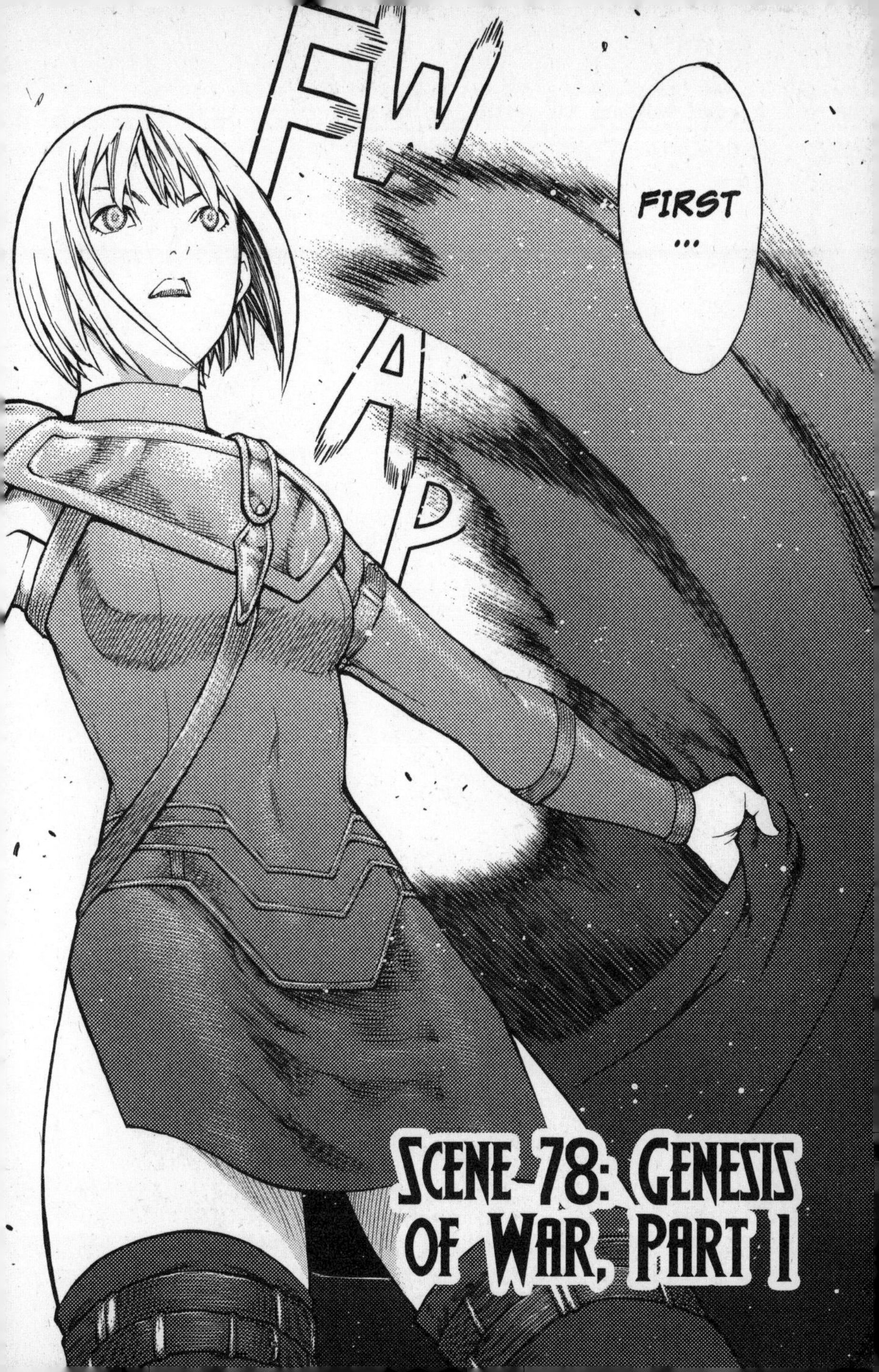
FWAP
FIRST ...
SCENE 78: GENESIS OF WAR, PART 1

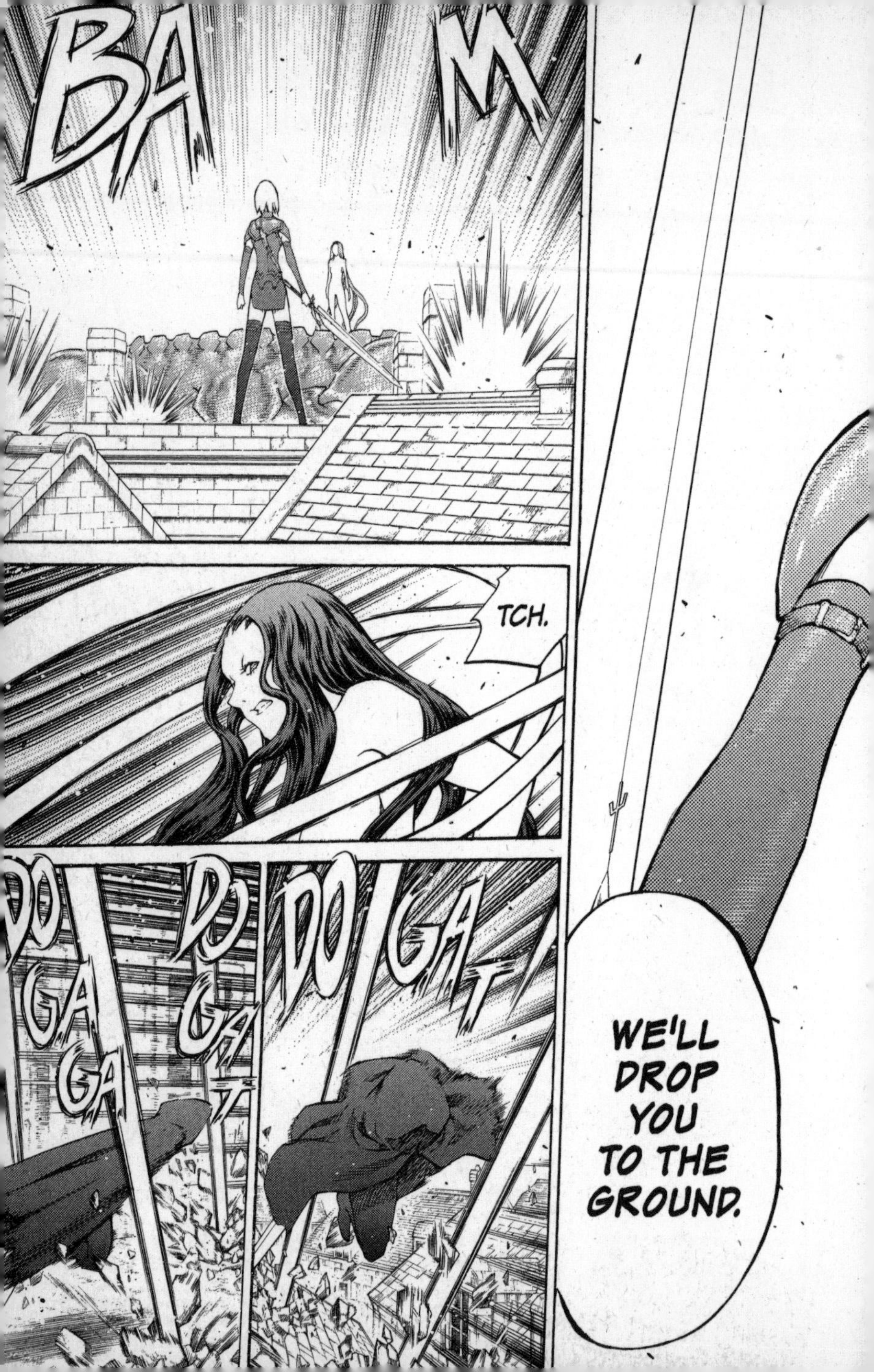
WE'LL DROP YOU TO THE GROUND.
BAM
TCH.
DO GAT
DO GA GAT
DO GA GA

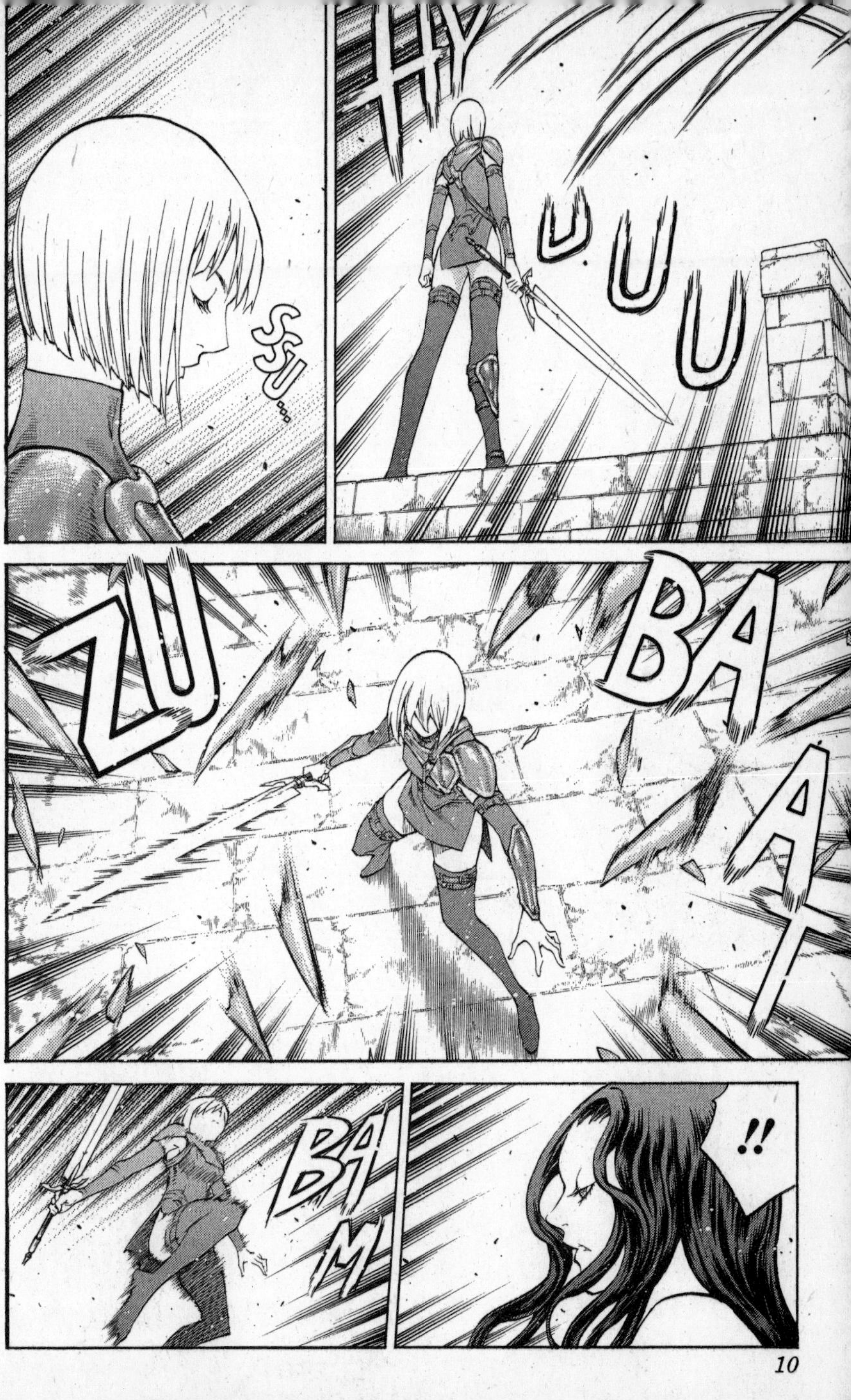
HYUUUU
SSU...
ZUBAAT
!!
BAM

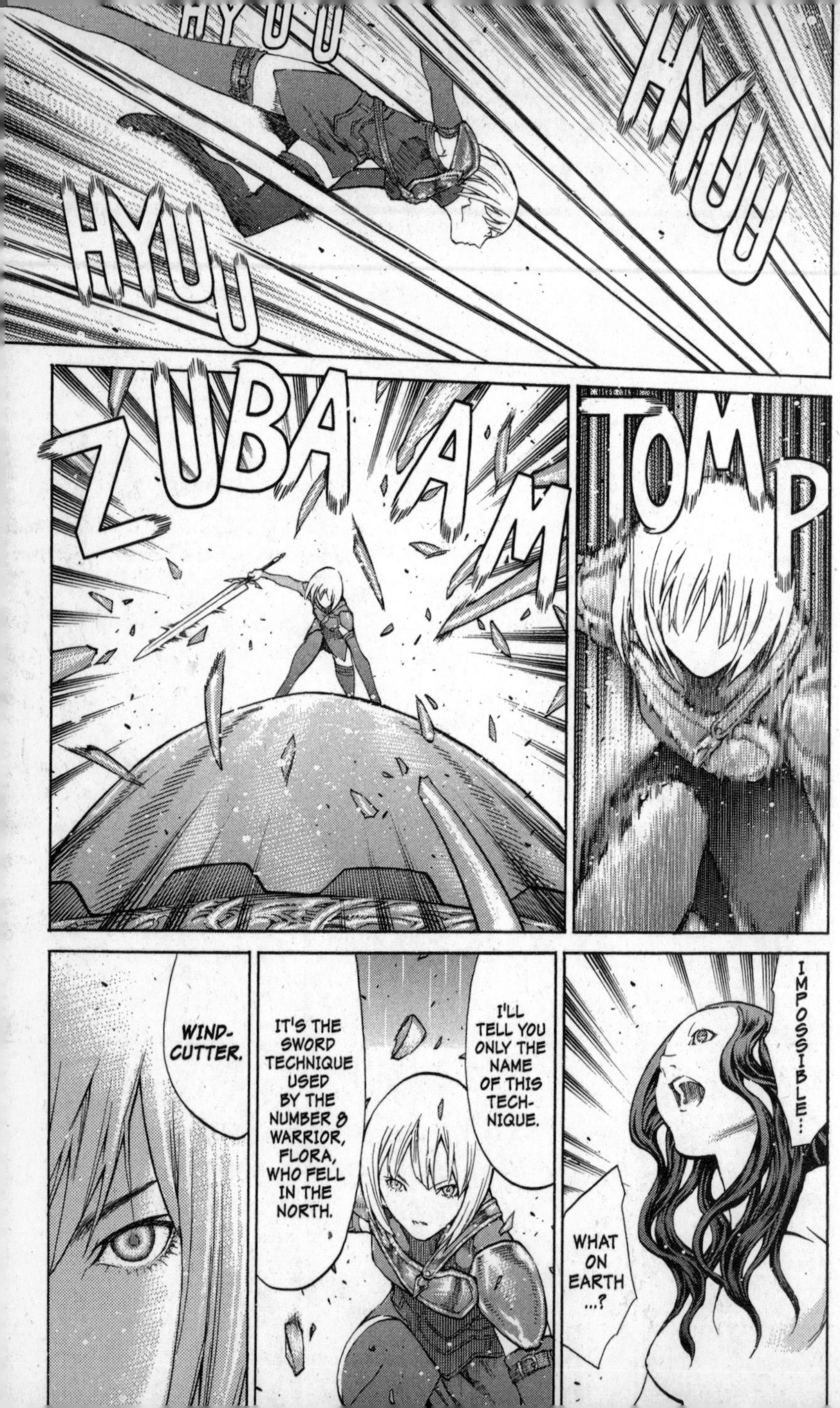
HYUU
HYUU
HYUU
TOMP
ZUBAAM
IMPOSSIBLE...
WHAT ON EARTH ...?
I'LL TELL YOU ONLY THE NAME OF THIS TECHNIQUE.
IT'S THE SWORD TECHNIQUE USED BY THE NUMBER 8 WARRIOR, FLORA, WHO FELL IN THE NORTH.
WIND-CUTTER.

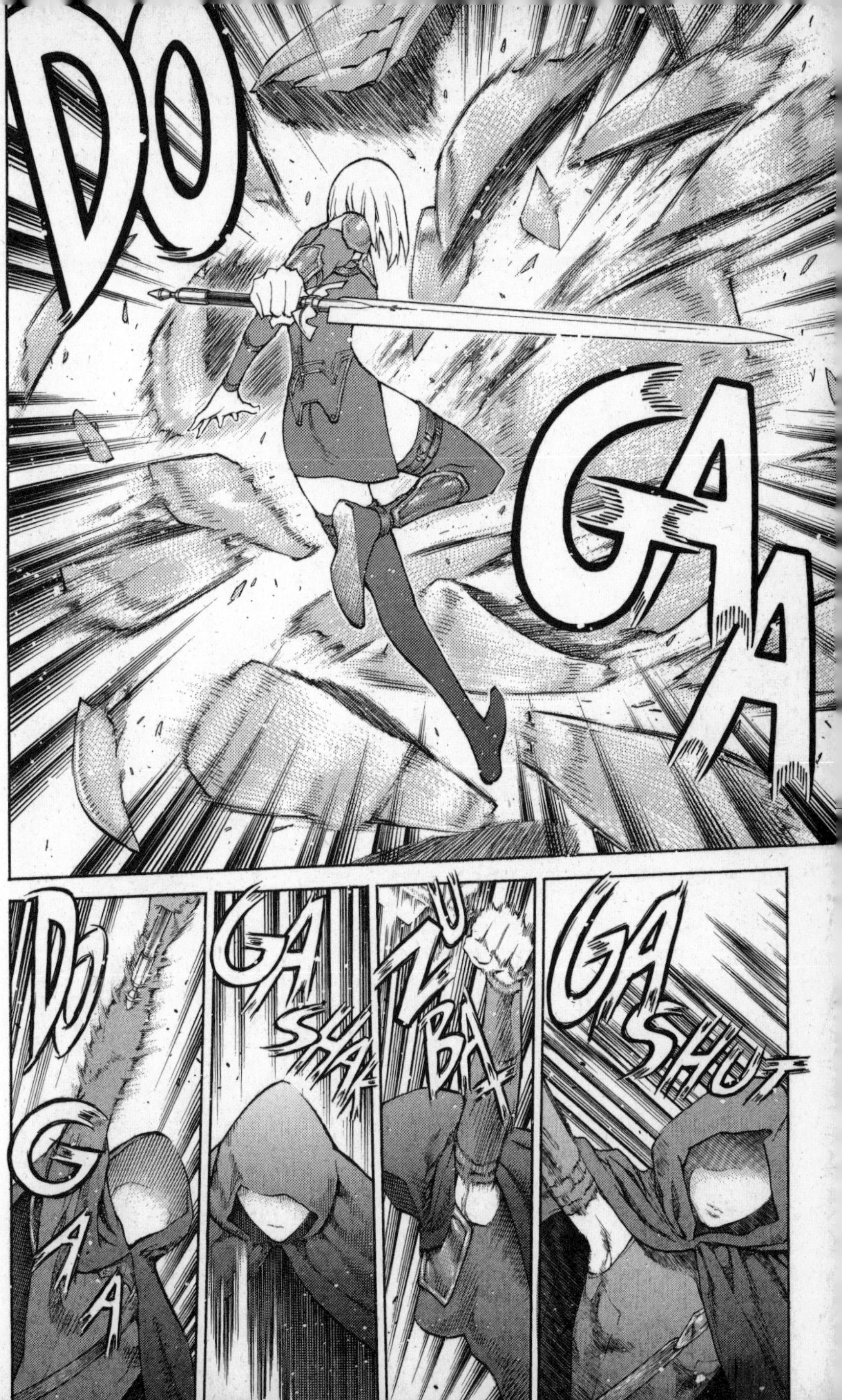
DO
GAA
GA
SHUT
ZU
BA
GA
SHAK
DO
GAA

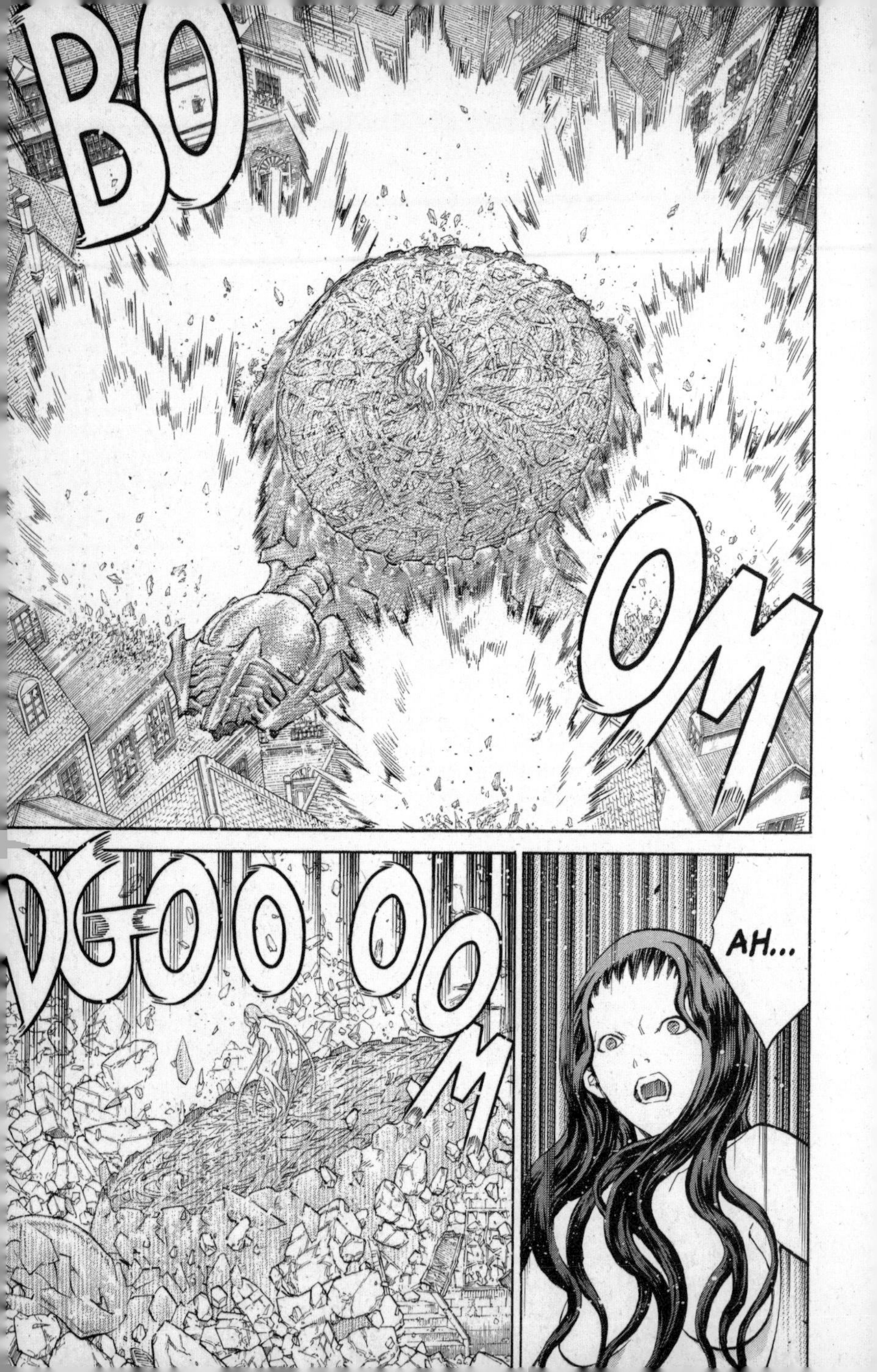
BOOM
AH...
DGOOOOM

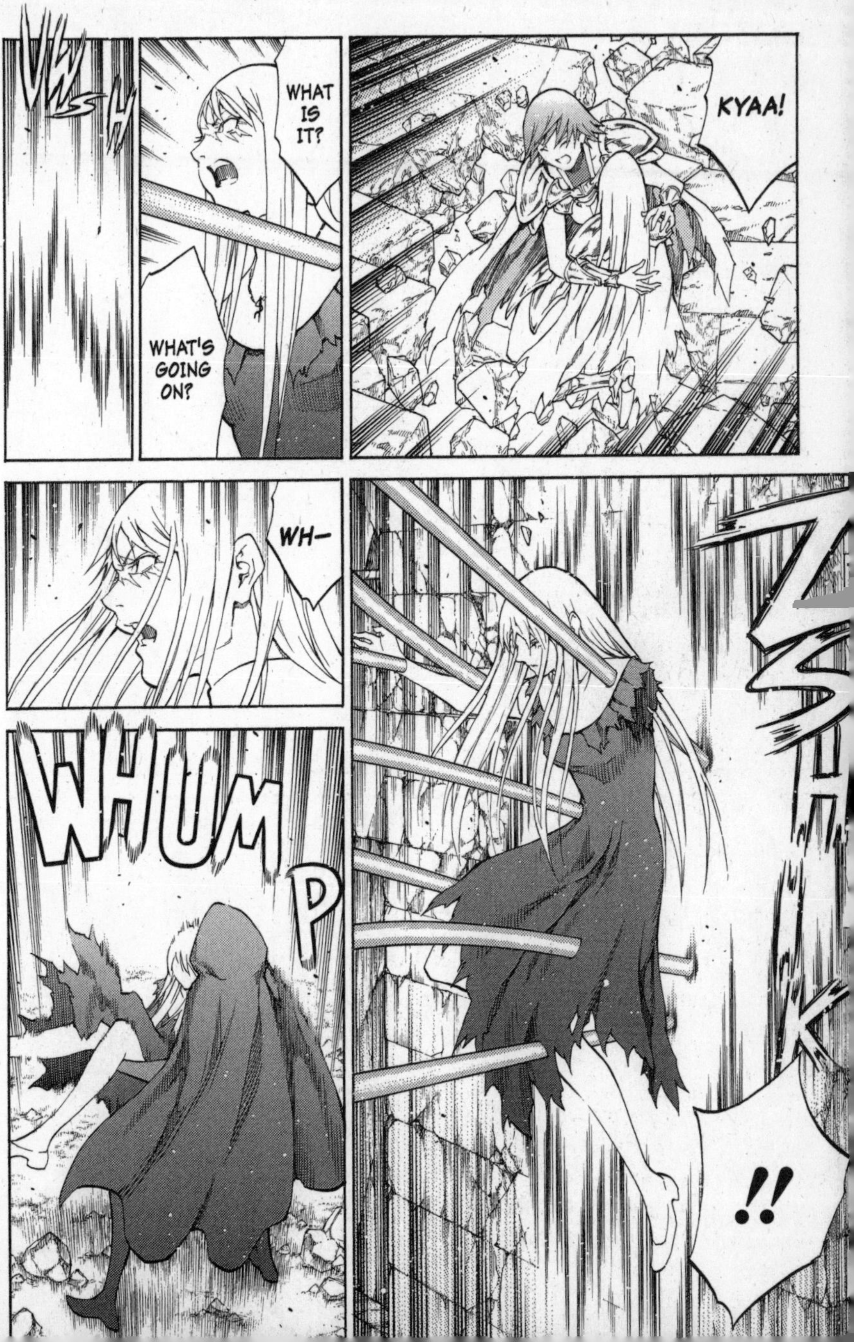
KYAA!
WHAT IS IT?
WHAT'S GOING ON?
VWSH
!!
WH-
WHUMP

READ THIS WAY

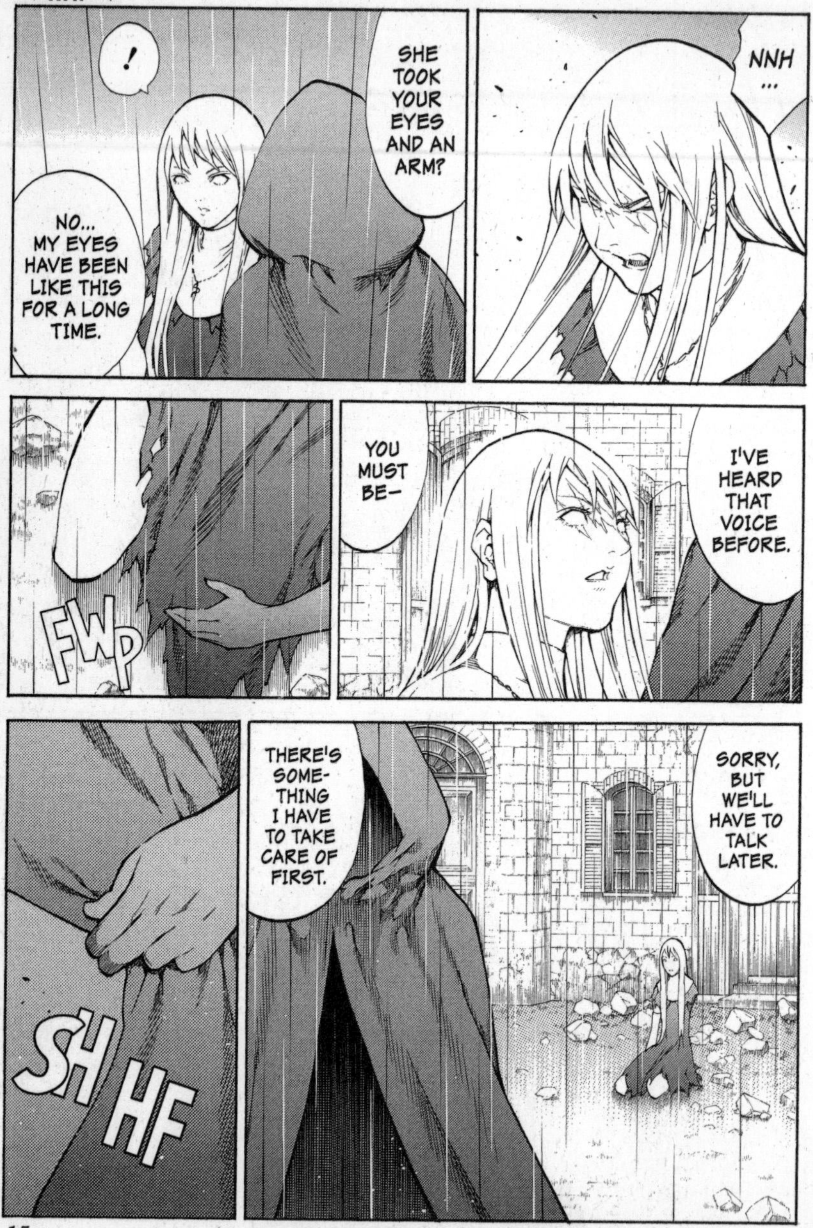
NNH ...
SHE TOOK YOUR EYES AND AN ARM?
!
NO... MY EYES HAVE BEEN LIKE THIS FOR A LONG TIME.
I'VE HEARD THAT VOICE BEFORE.
YOU MUST BE—
FWP
SORRY, BUT WE'LL HAVE TO TALK LATER.
THERE'S SOME-THING I HAVE TO TAKE CARE OF FIRST.
SHHF

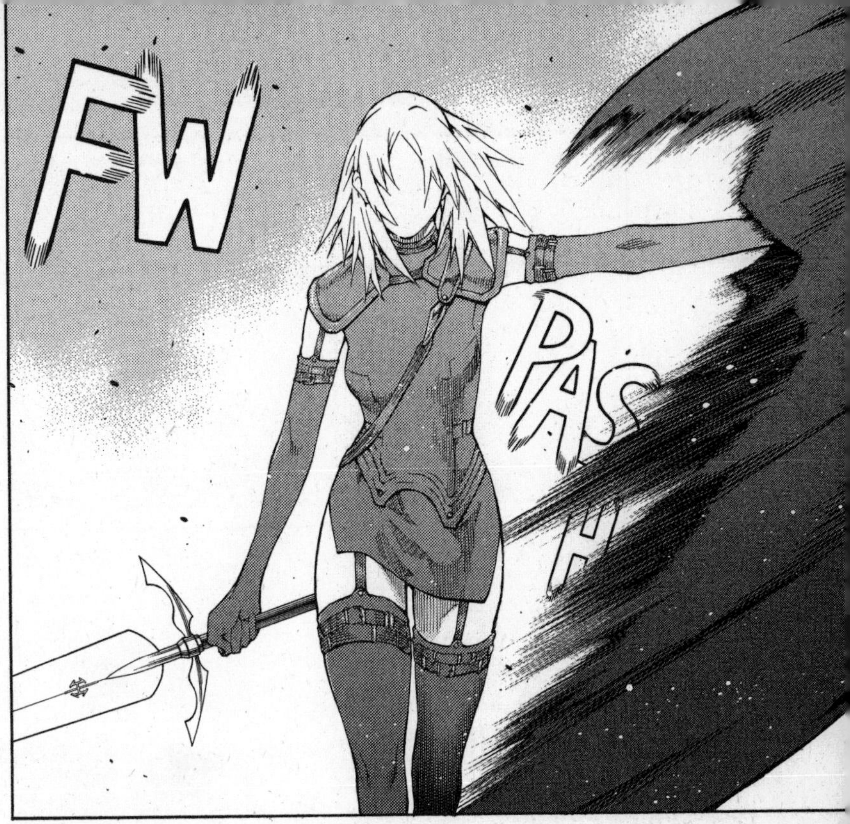
PASHH
FW

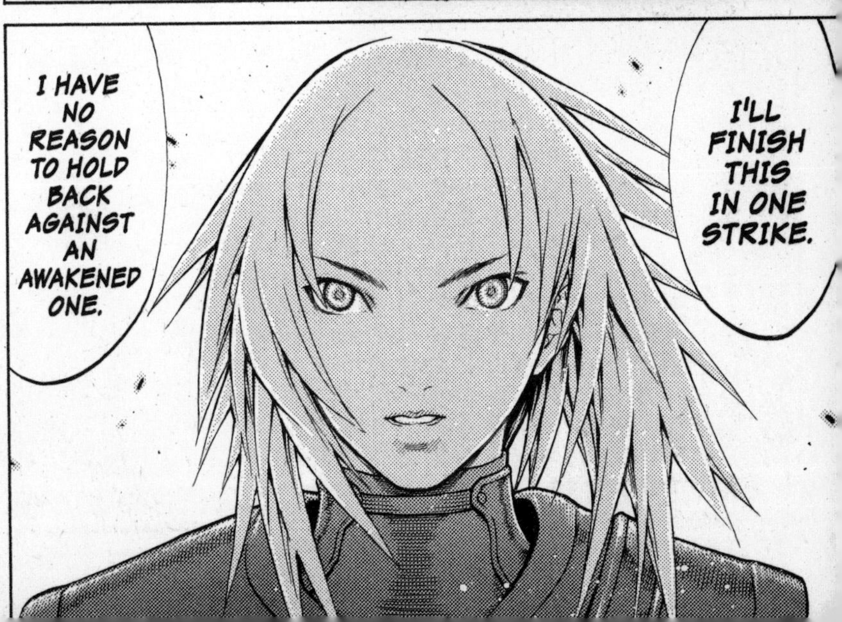
I'LL FINISH THIS IN ONE STRIKE.
I HAVE NO REASON TO HOLD BACK AGAINST AN AWAKENED ONE.

READ THIS WAY

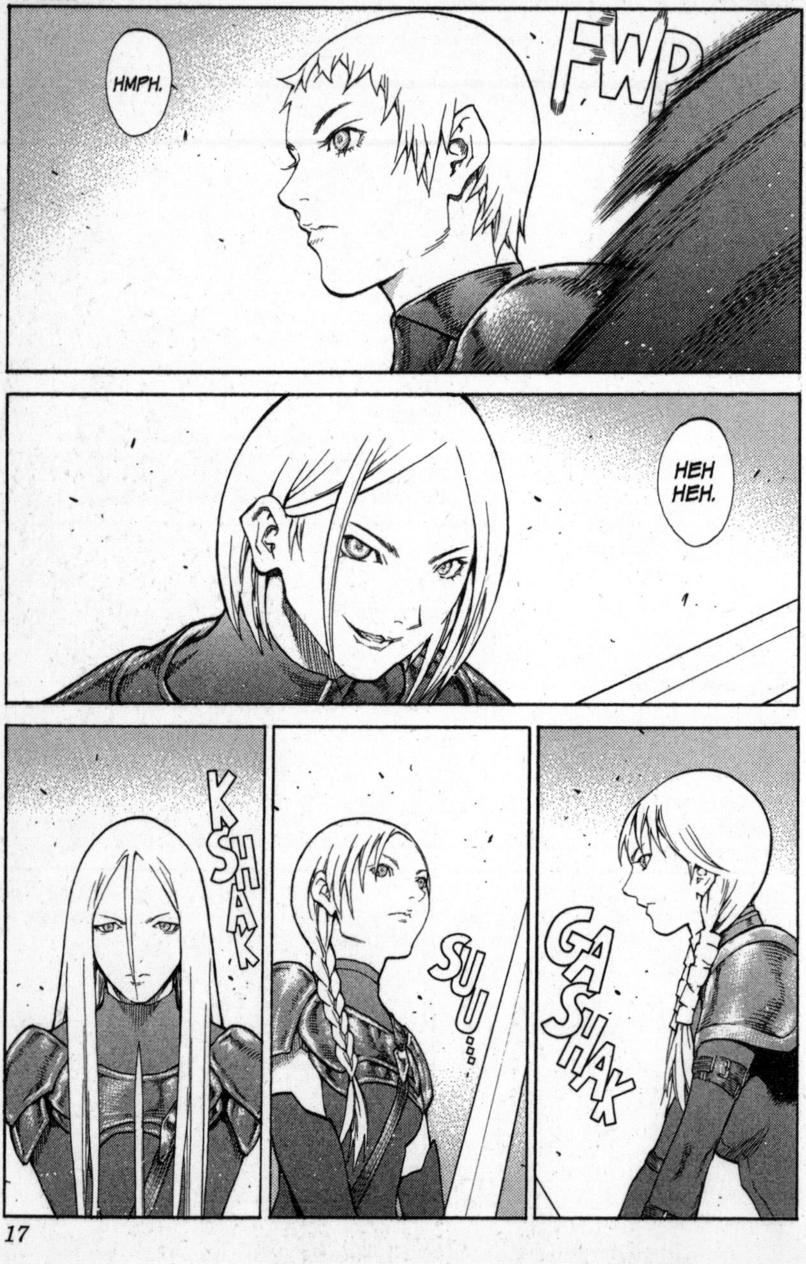
FWP
HMPH.
HEH HEH.
GASHAK
SUU...
KSHAK

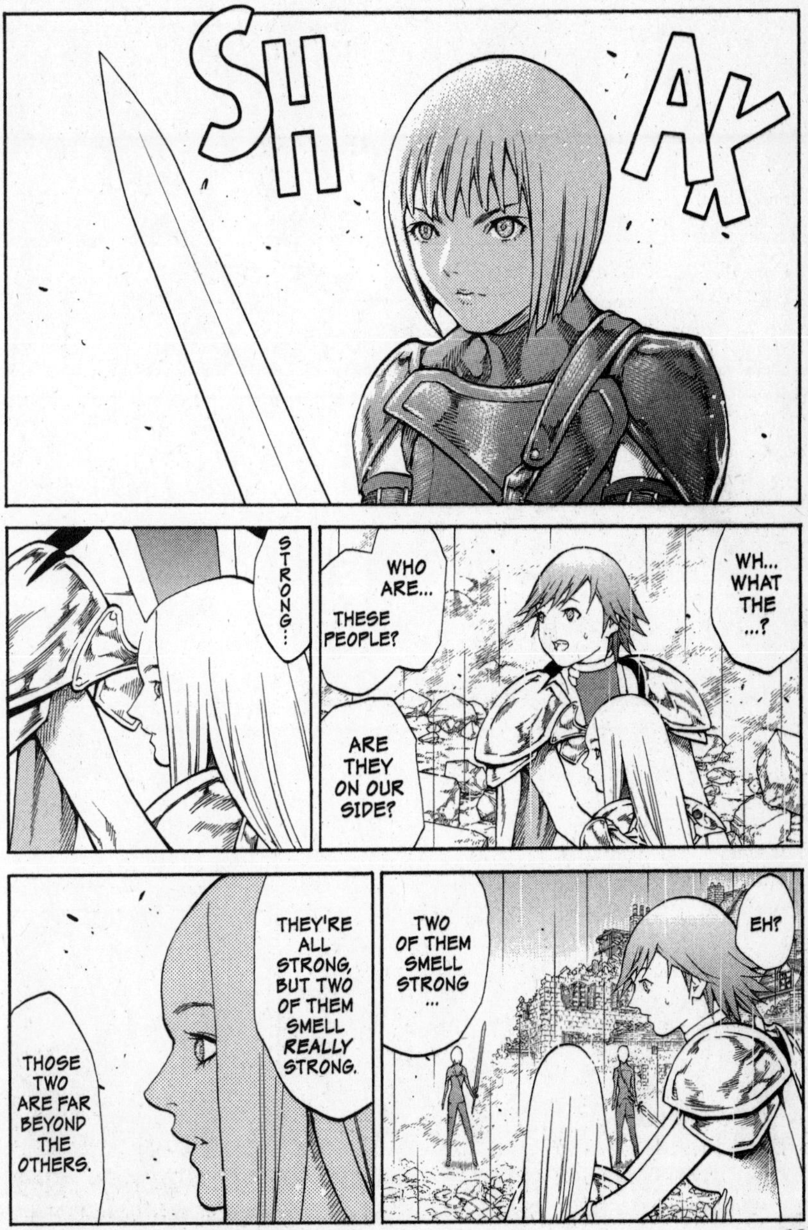
SHAK
WH... WHAT THE ...?
WHO ARE... THESE PEOPLE?
ARE THEY ON OUR SIDE?
STRONG...
EH?
TWO OF THEM SMELL STRONG ...
THEY'RE ALL STRONG, BUT TWO OF THEM SMELL REALLY STRONG.
THOSE TWO ARE FAR BEYOND THE OTHERS.

READ THIS WAY

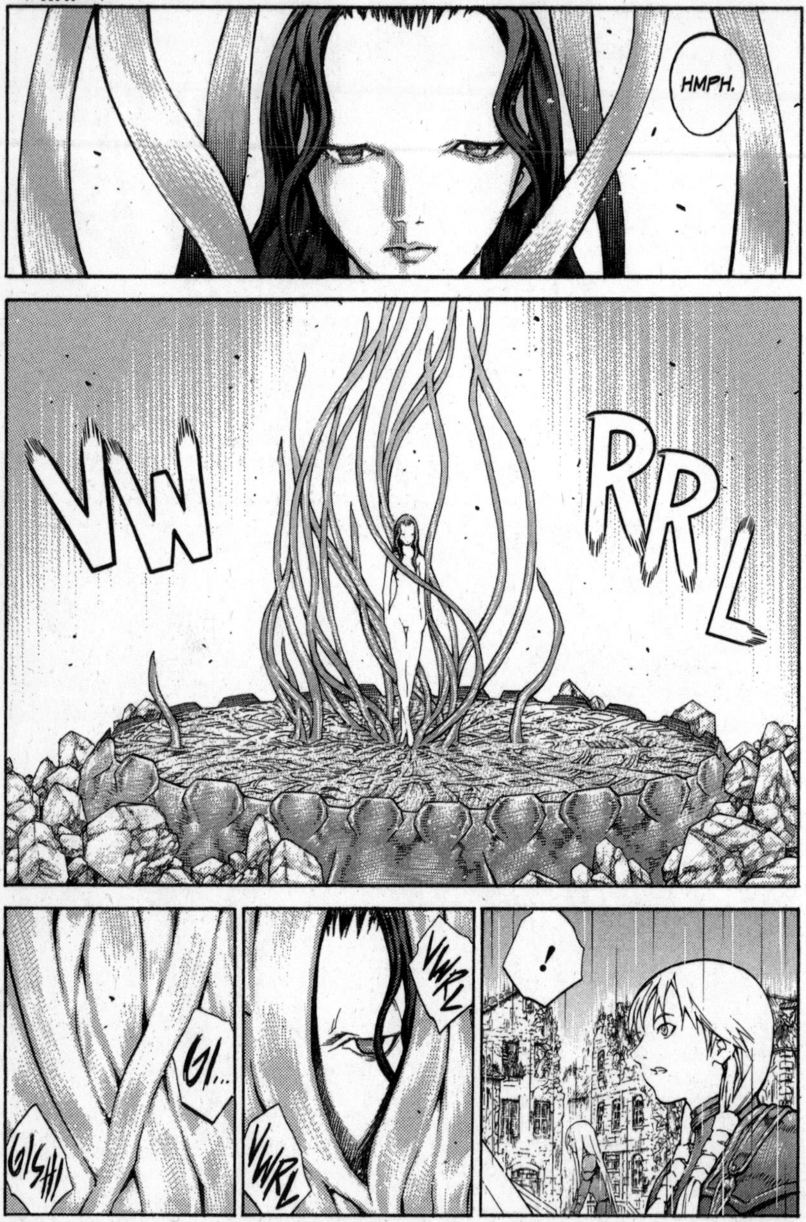

HMPH.
VW
RRL
!
VWRL
VWRL
GI...
GISHI

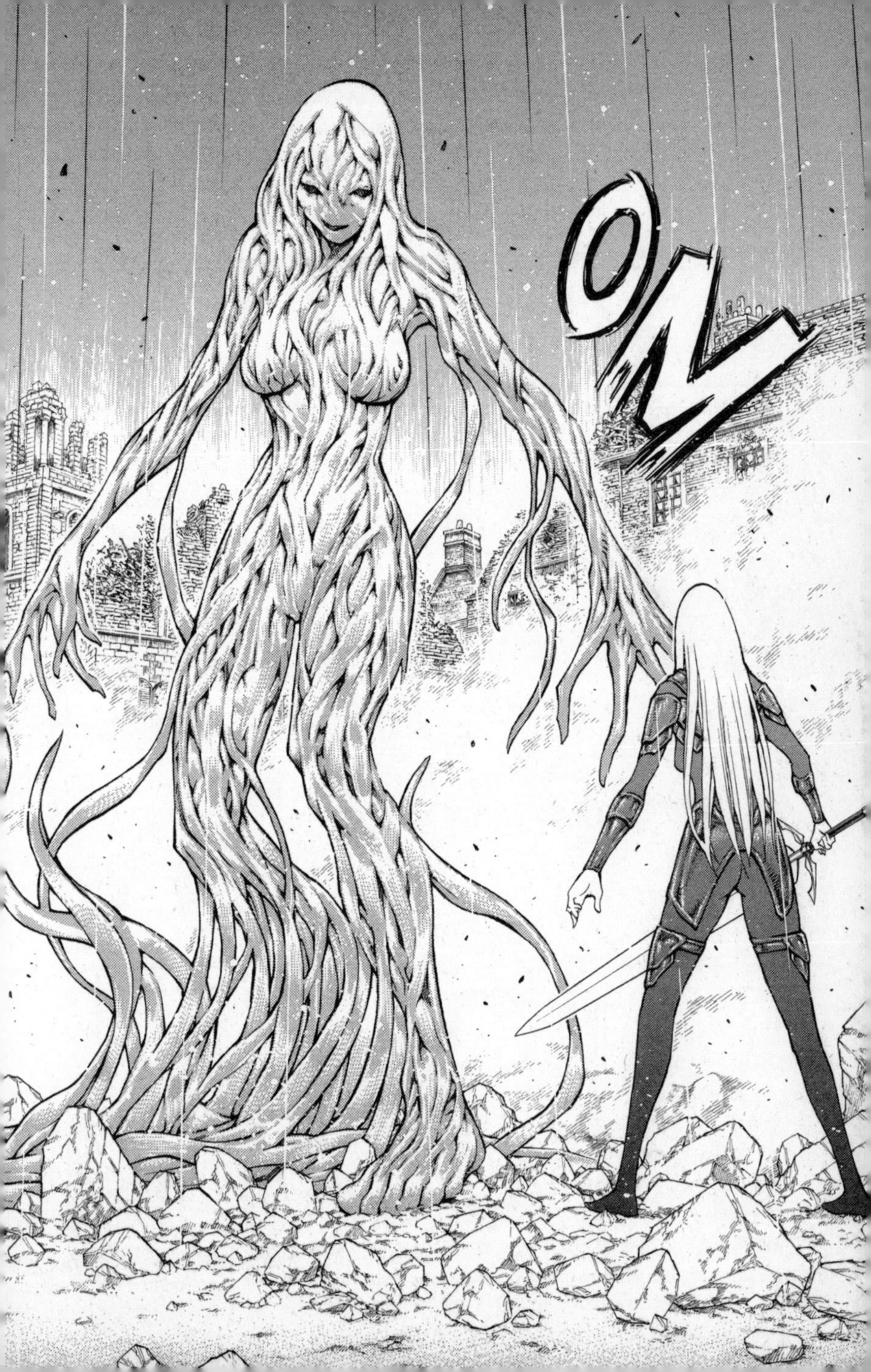
OM

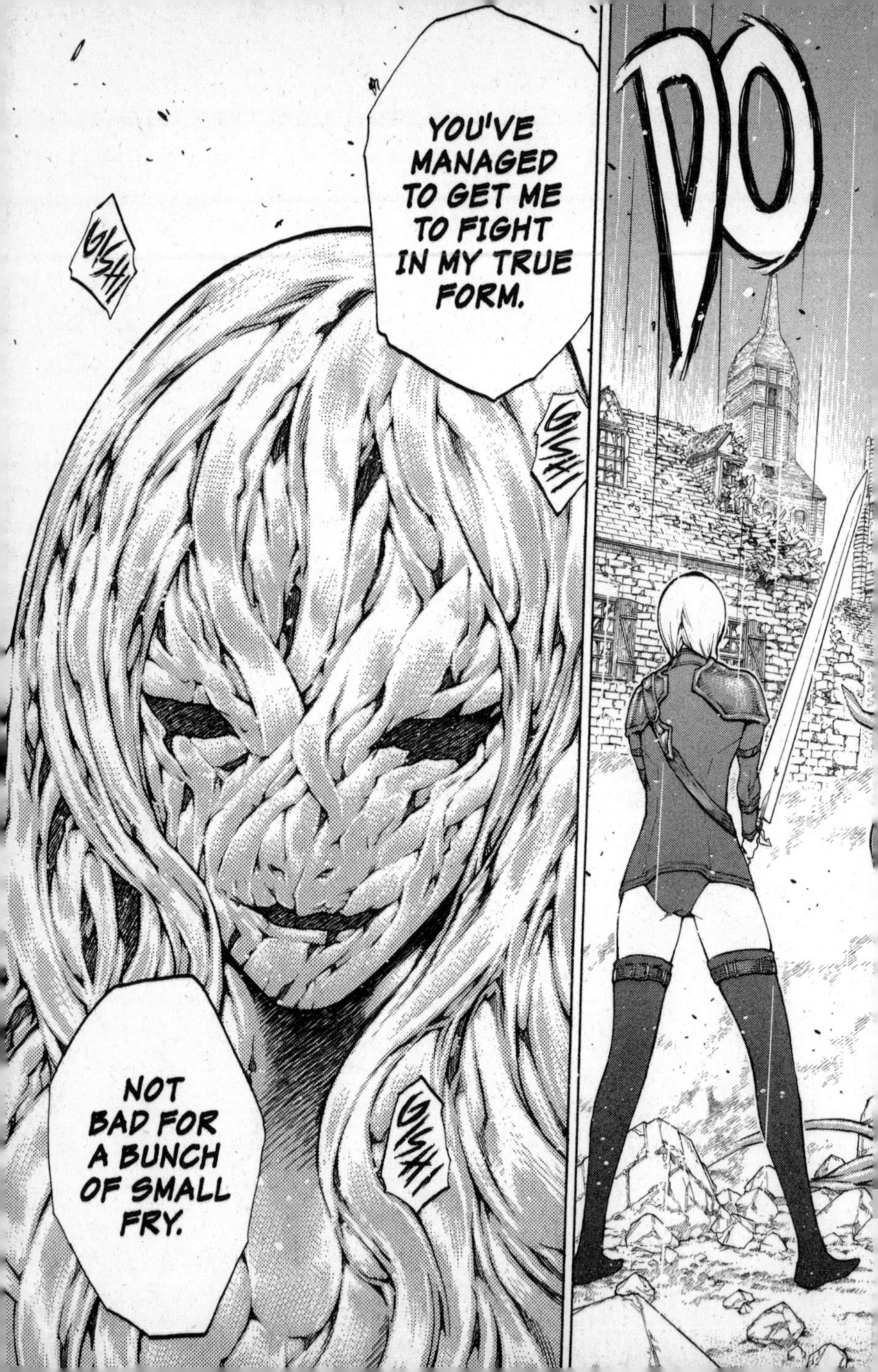
DO
YOU'VE MANAGED TO GET ME TO FIGHT IN MY TRUE FORM.
GISHI
GISHI
NOT BAD FOR A BUNCH OF SMALL FRY.
GISHI

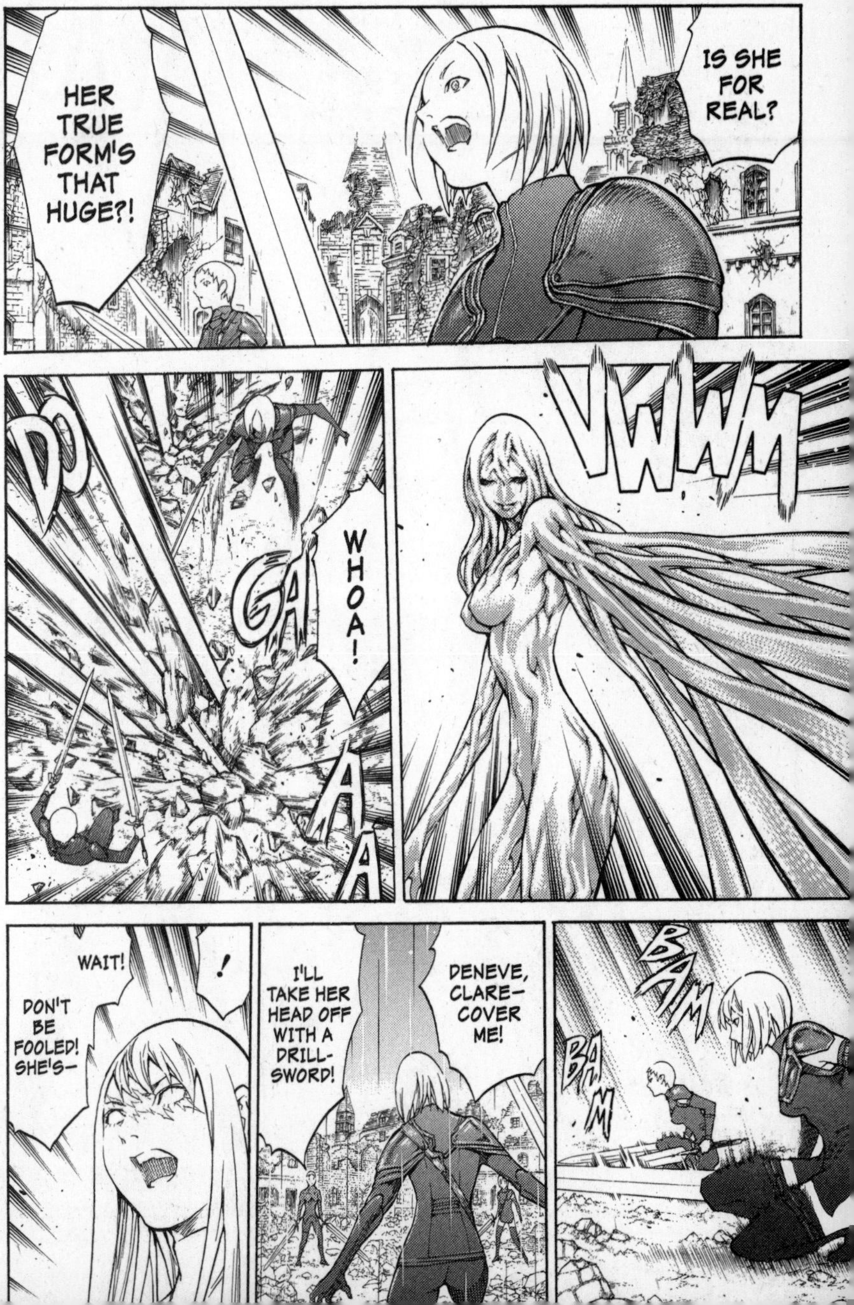
IS SHE FOR REAL?
HER TRUE FORM'S THAT HUGE?!
VWWM
DO
GA
WHOA!
AAA
BAM
BAM
DENEVE, CLARE—COVER ME!
I'LL TAKE HER HEAD OFF WITH A DRILL-SWORD!
!
WAIT!
DON'T BE FOOLED! SHE'S—

READ THIS WAY

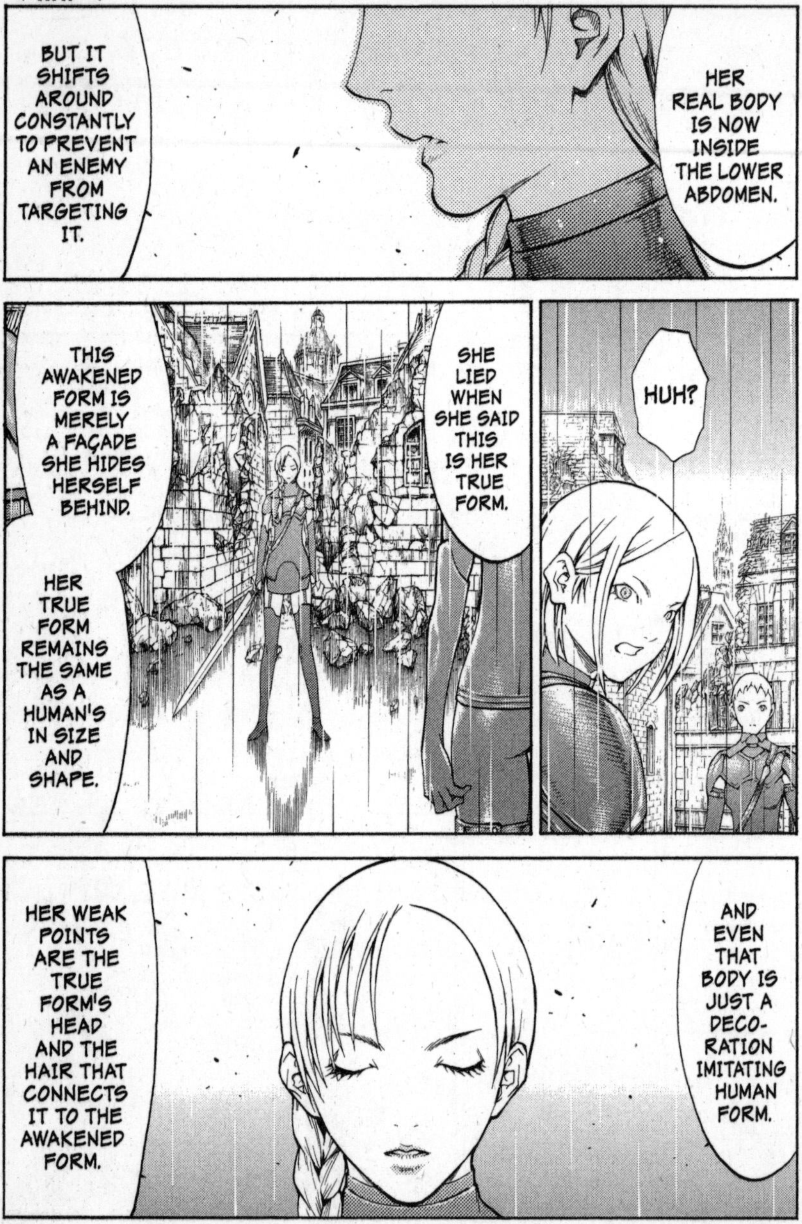

HER REAL BODY IS NOW INSIDE THE LOWER ABDOMEN.
BUT IT SHIFTS AROUND CONSTANTLY TO PREVENT AN ENEMY FROM TARGETING IT.
HUH?
SHE LIED WHEN SHE SAID THIS IS HER TRUE FORM.
THIS AWAKENED FORM IS MERELY A FAÇADE SHE HIDES HERSELF BEHIND.
HER TRUE FORM REMAINS THE SAME AS A HUMAN'S IN SIZE AND SHAPE.
AND EVEN THAT BODY IS JUST A DECO-RATION IMITATING HUMAN FORM.
HER WEAK POINTS ARE THE TRUE FORM'S HEAD AND THE HAIR THAT CONNECTS IT TO THE AWAKENED FORM.

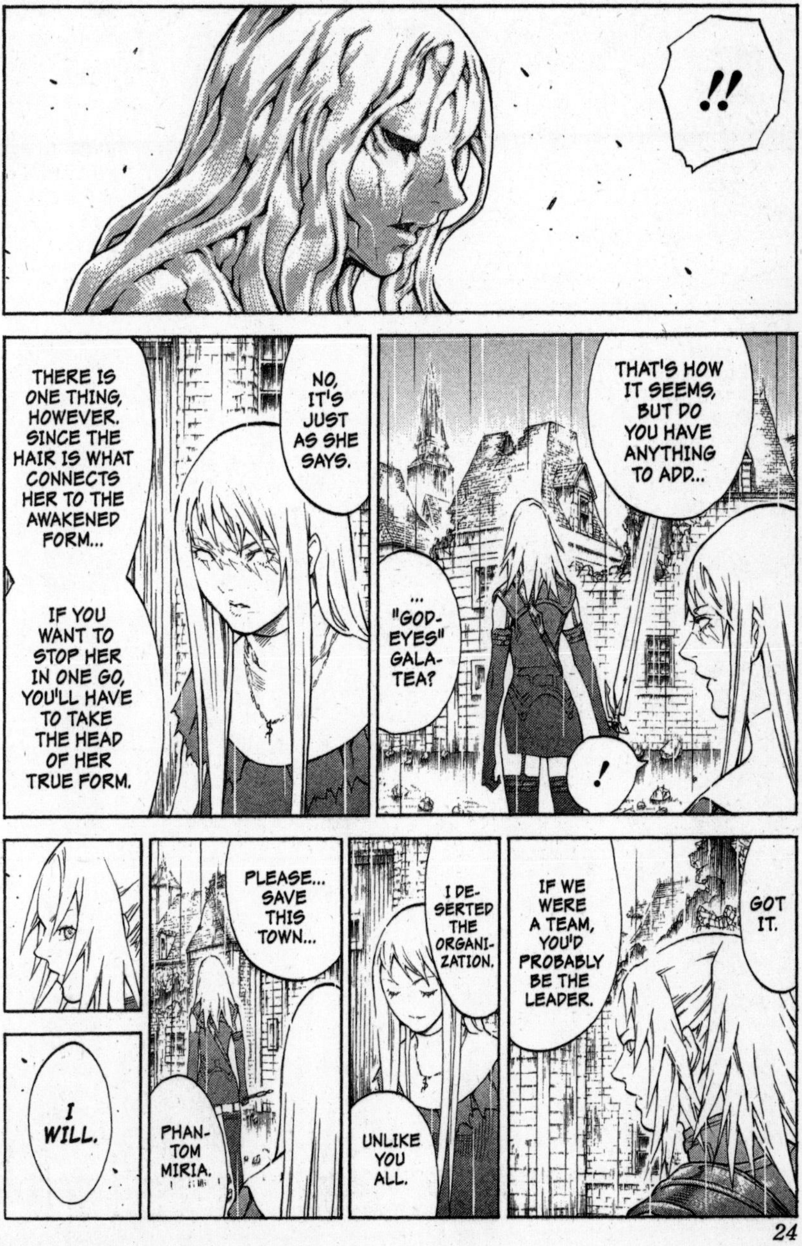
!!
THAT'S HOW IT SEEMS, BUT DO YOU HAVE ANYTHING TO ADD...
... "GOD-EYES" GALATEA?
!
NO, IT'S JUST AS SHE SAYS.
THERE IS ONE THING, HOWEVER. SINCE THE HAIR IS WHAT CONNECTS HER TO THE AWAKENED FORM...
IF YOU WANT TO STOP HER IN ONE GO, YOU'LL HAVE TO TAKE THE HEAD OF HER TRUE FORM.
GOT IT.
IF WE WERE A TEAM, YOU'D PROBABLY BE THE LEADER.
I DESERTED THE ORGANIZATION.
UNLIKE YOU ALL.
PLEASE... SAVE THIS TOWN...
PHANTOM MIRIA.
I WILL.

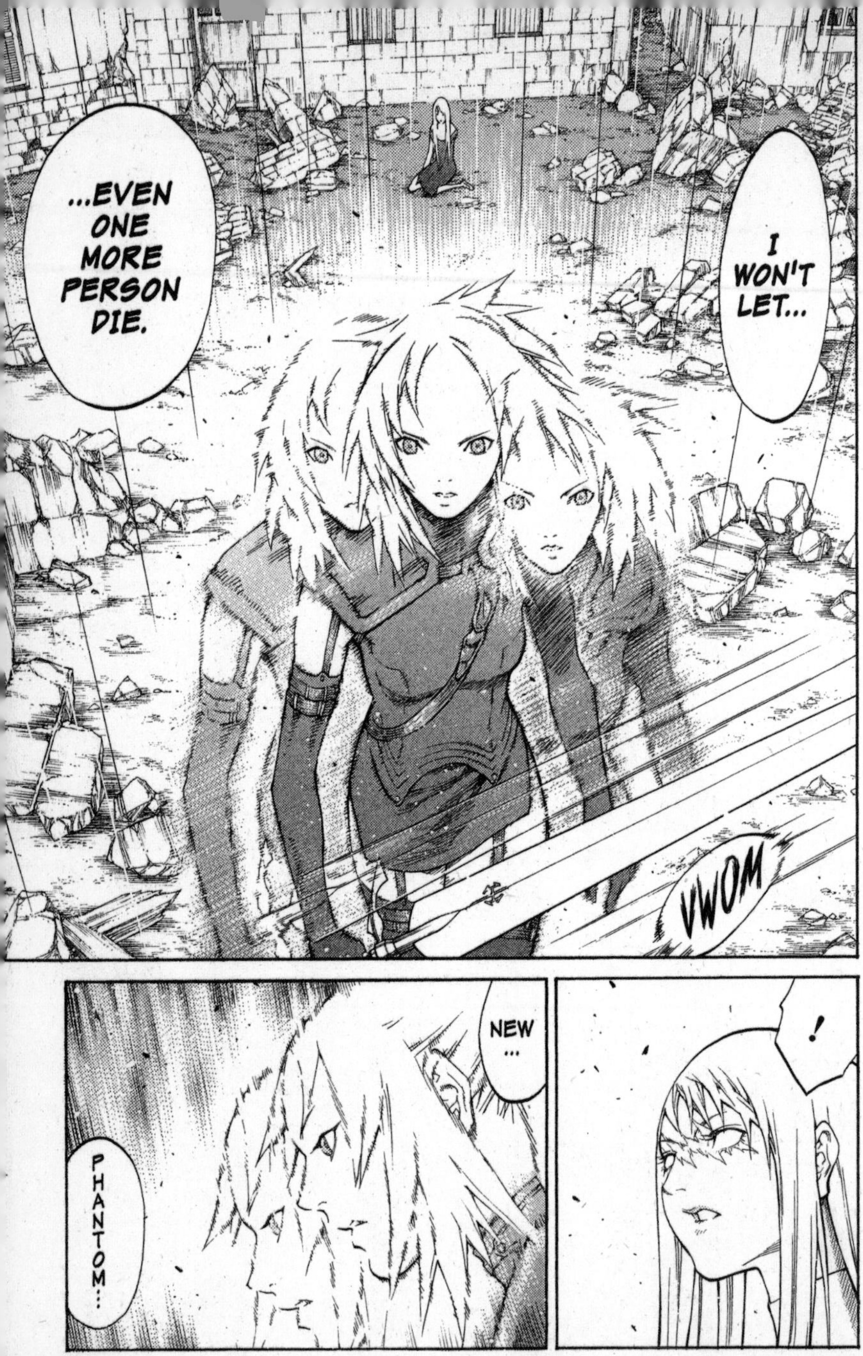
I WON'T LET...
...EVEN ONE MORE PERSON DIE.
VWOM
!
NEW ...
PHANTOM...

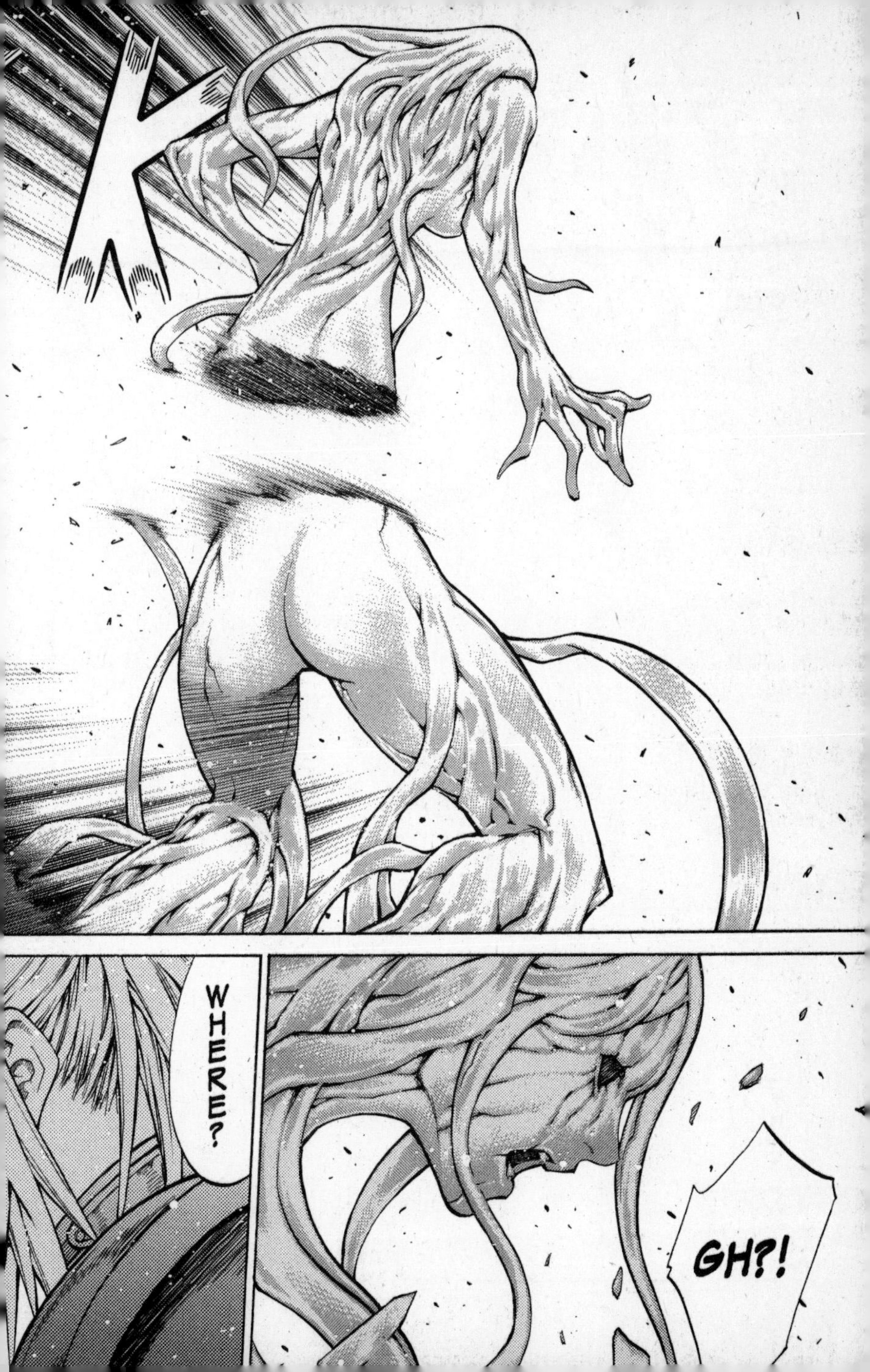
GH?!
WHERE?

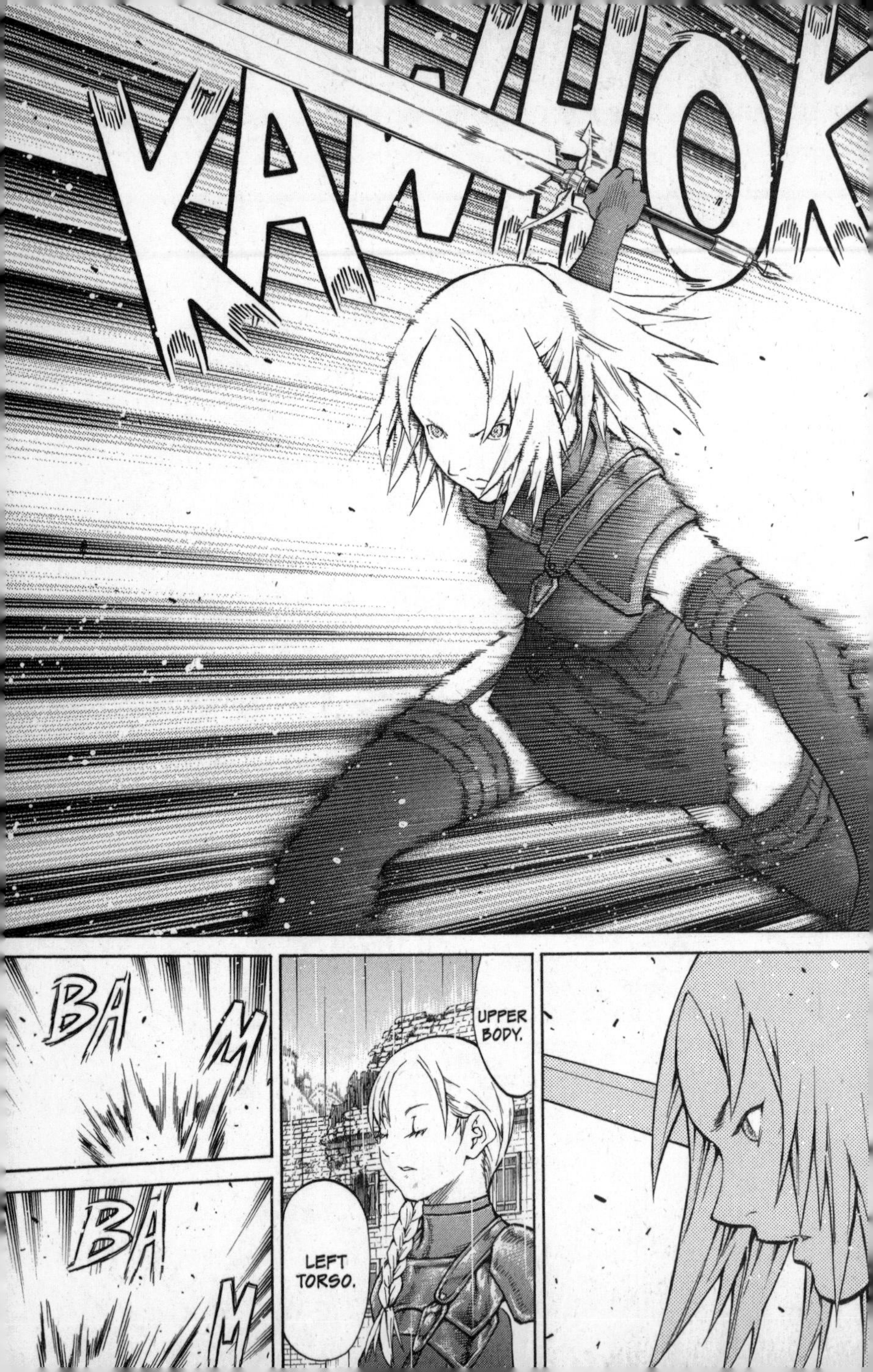
KAWHOK
UPPER BODY.
LEFT TORSO.
BAM
BAM

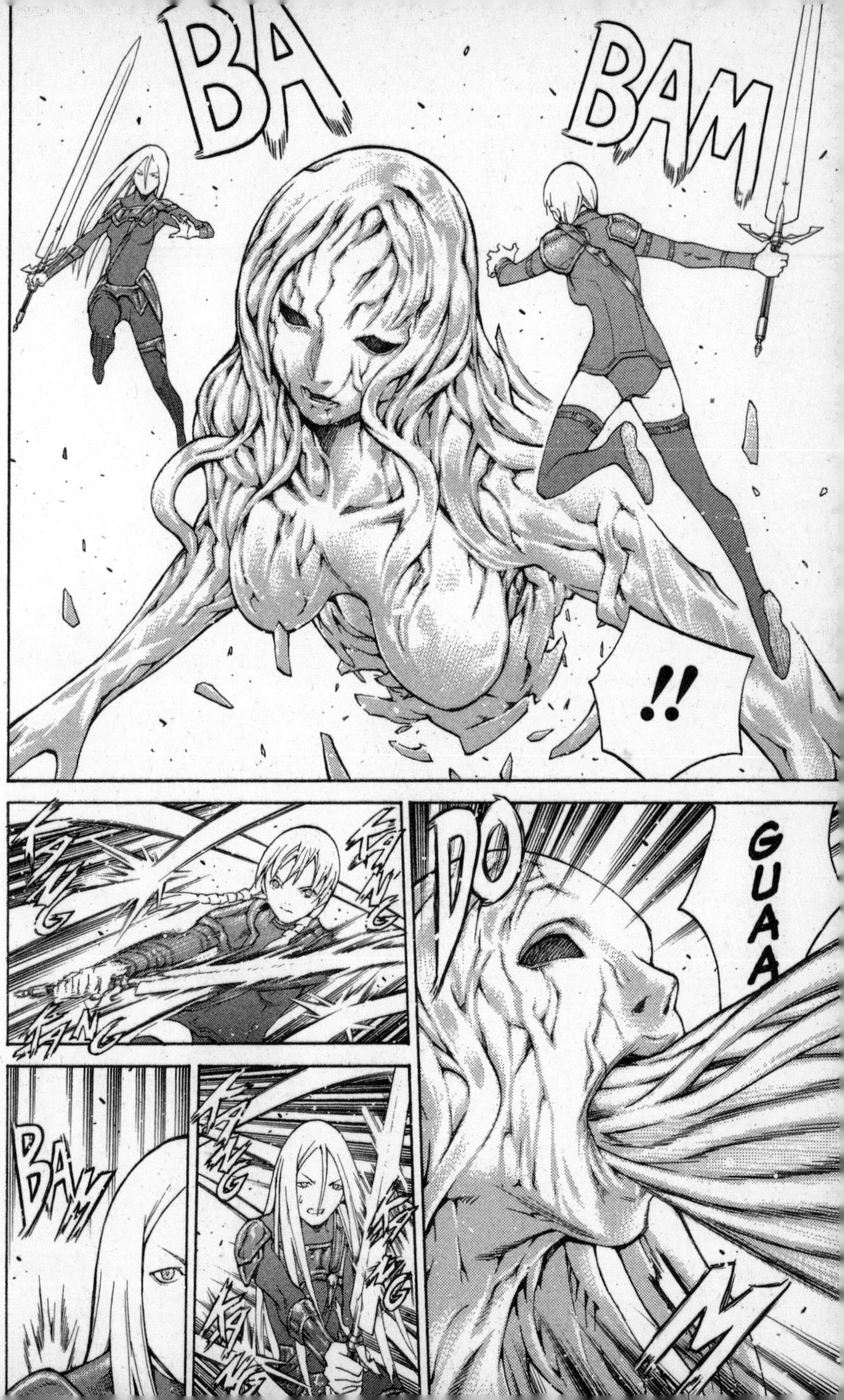

BA BAM
!!
DO
GUAA
M
KANG
KANG
KANG
KANG
KANG
KANG
BAM

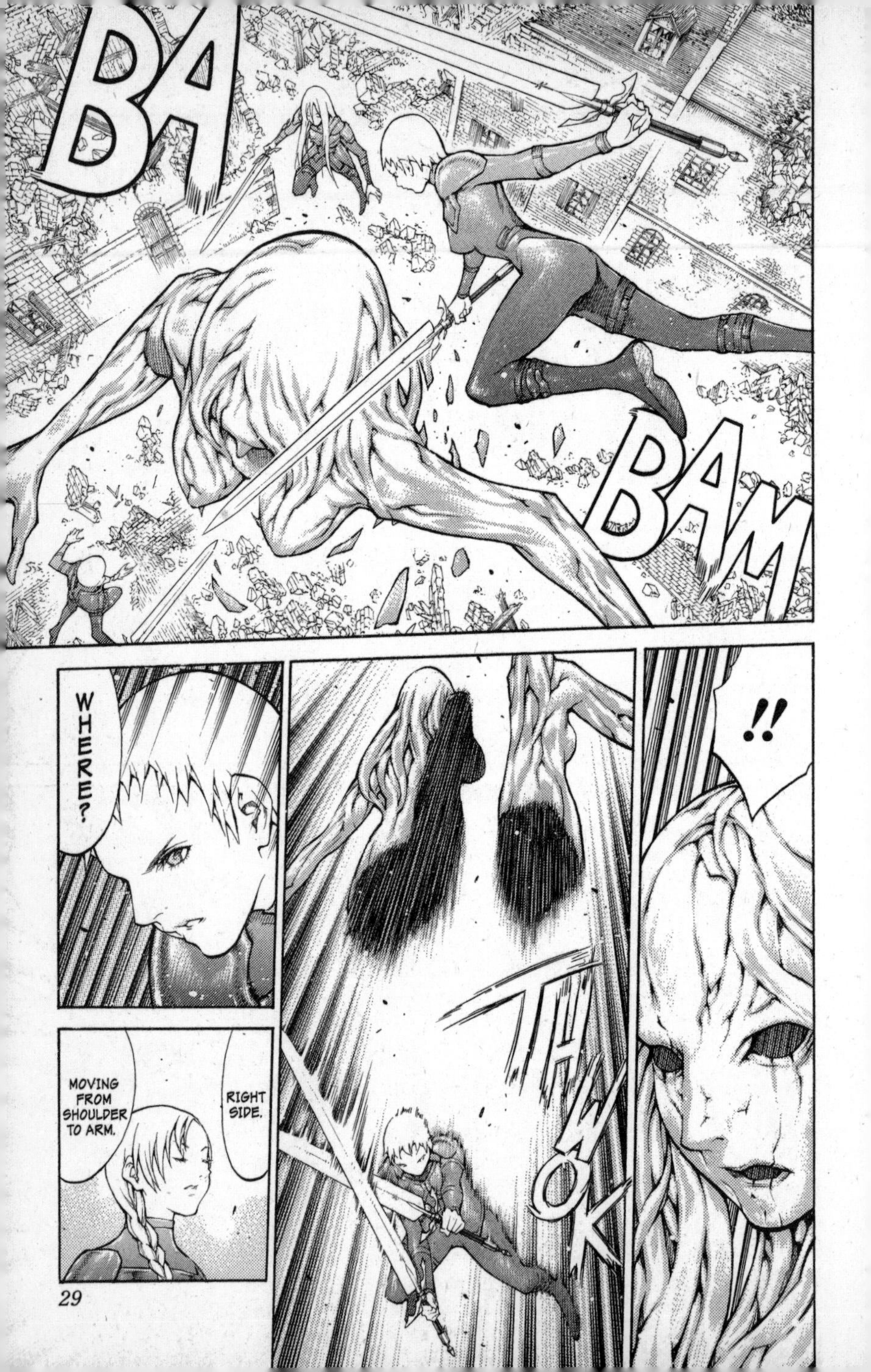
BA
BAM
!!
THWOK
WHERE?
RIGHT SIDE.
MOVING FROM SHOULDER TO ARM.

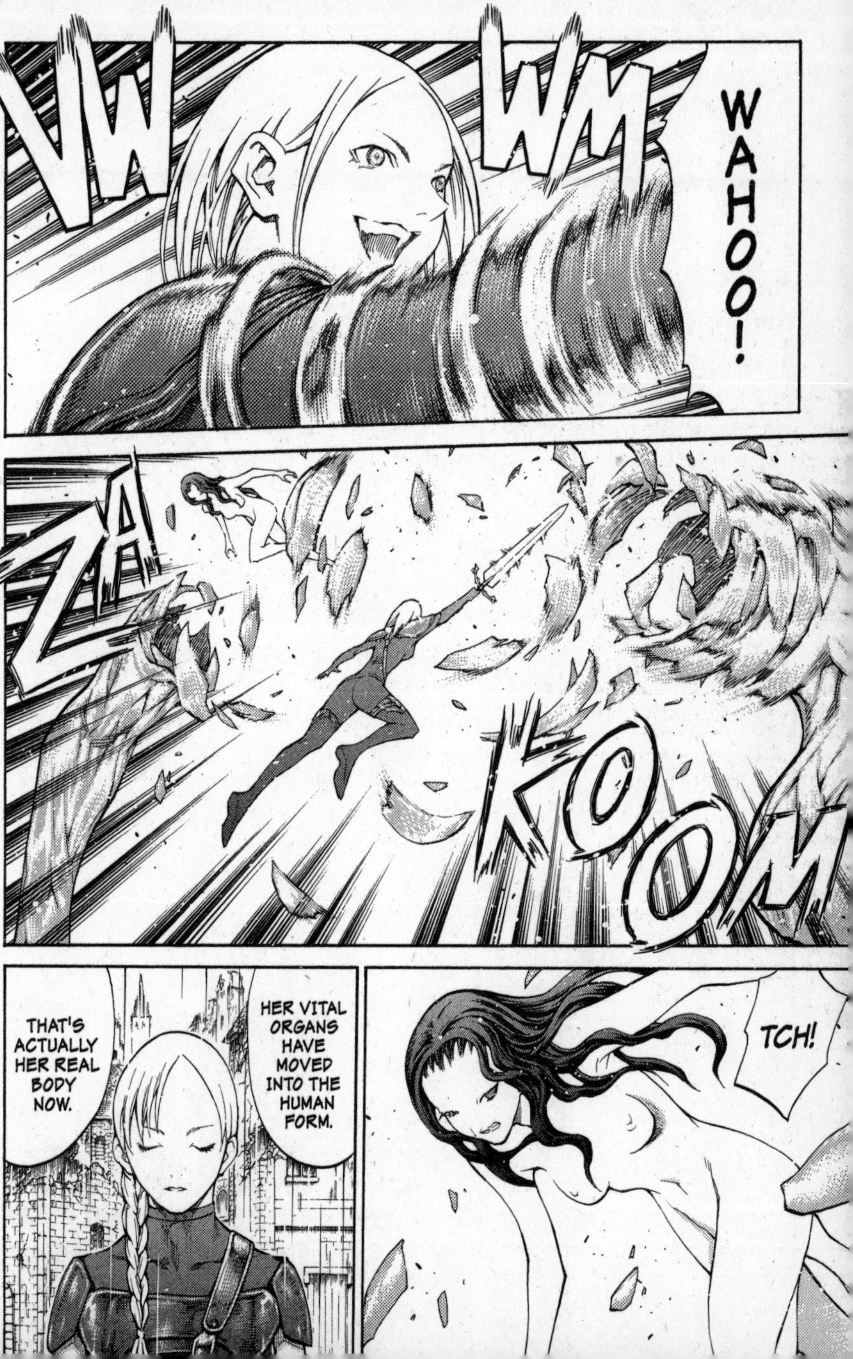
VWWM
WAHOO!
ZA
KOOOM
TCH!
HER VITAL ORGANS HAVE MOVED INTO THE HUMAN FORM.
THAT'S ACTUALLY HER REAL BODY NOW.

READ THIS WAY

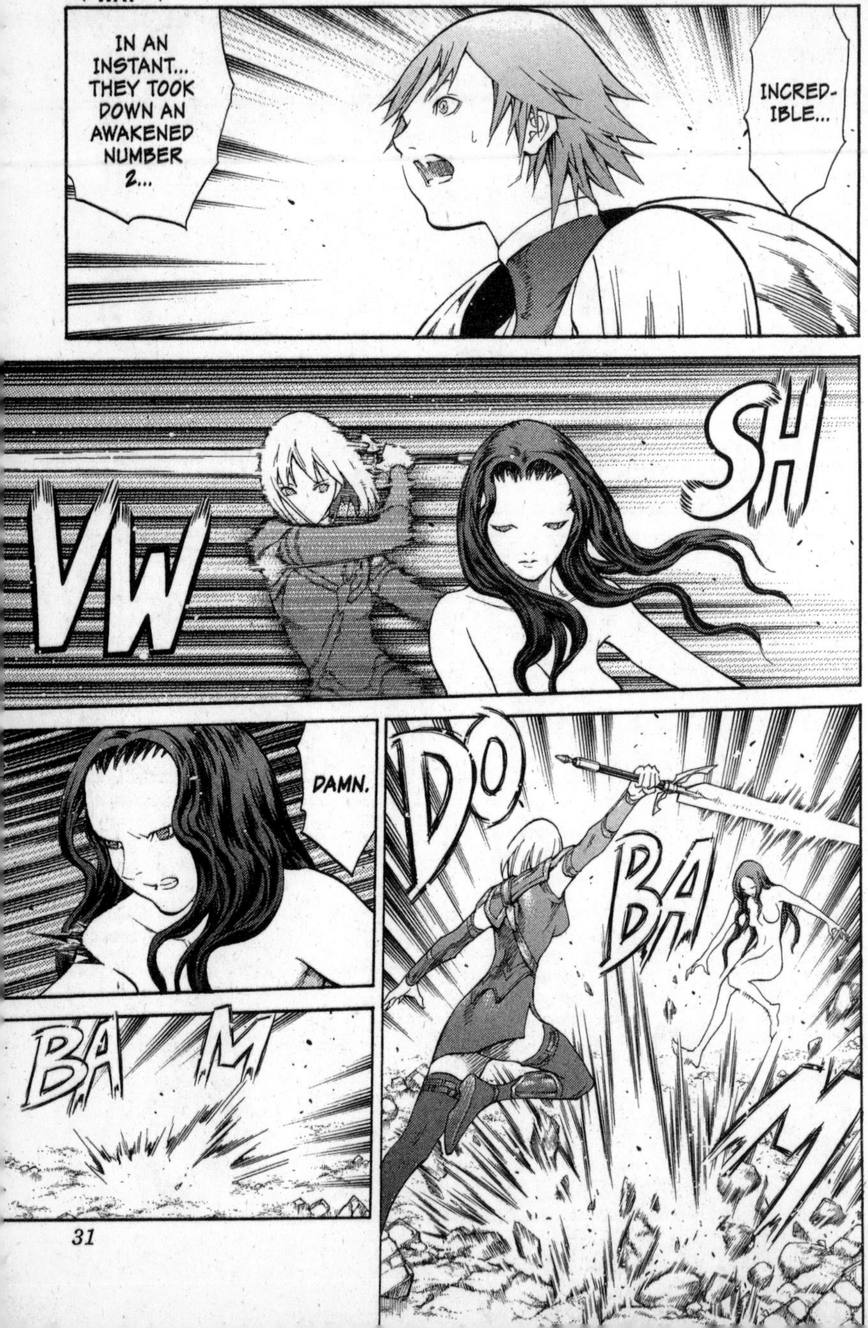
INCRED-IBLE...
IN AN INSTANT... THEY TOOK DOWN AN AWAKENED NUMBER 2...
SH
VW
DO
BA
M
DAMN.
BA M

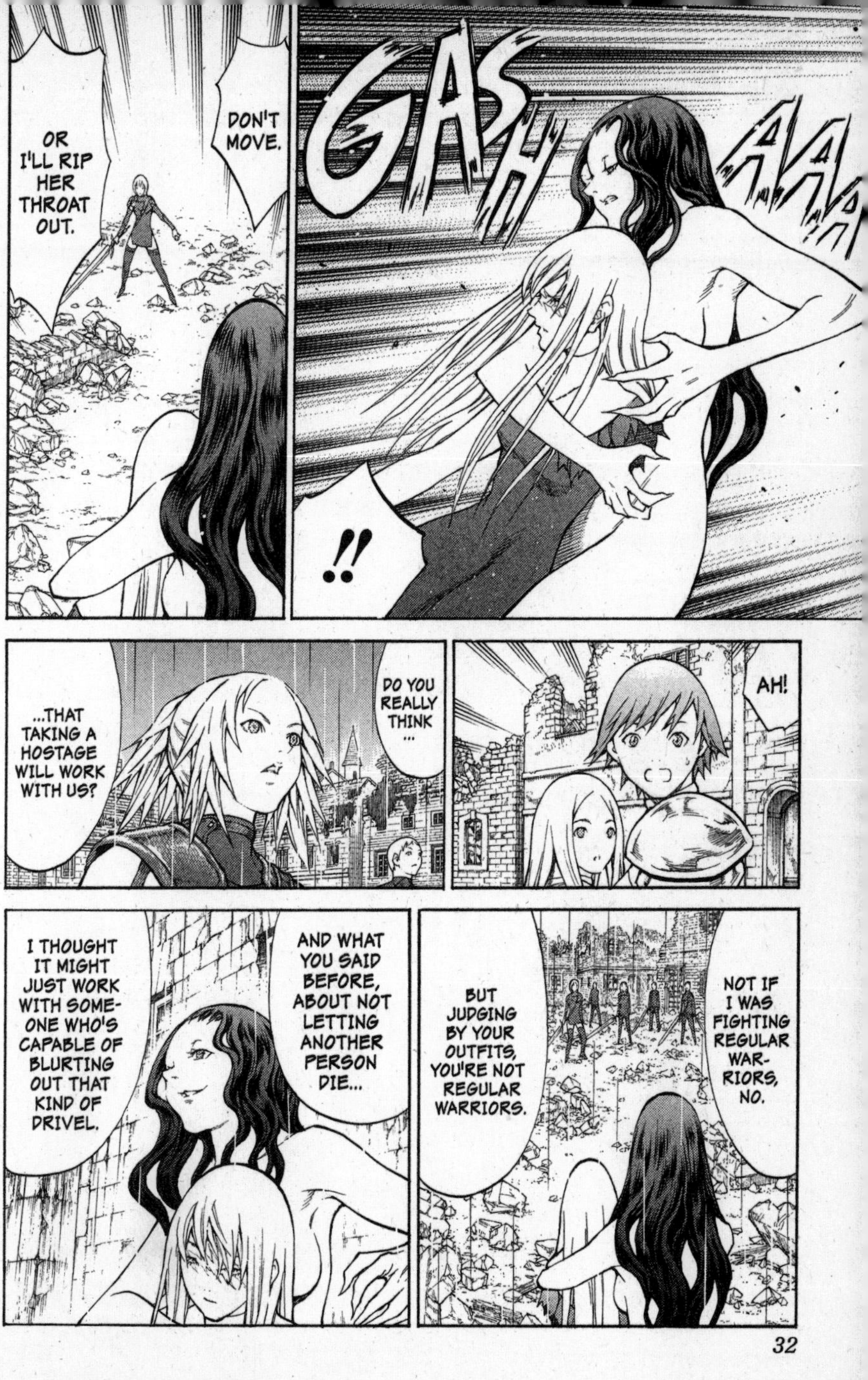
AAAA
GASH
!!
DON'T MOVE.
OR I'LL RIP HER THROAT OUT.
AH!
DO YOU REALLY THINK ...
...THAT TAKING A HOSTAGE WILL WORK WITH US?
NOT IF I WAS FIGHTING REGULAR WARRIORS, NO.
BUT JUDGING BY YOUR OUTFITS, YOU'RE NOT REGULAR WARRIORS.
AND WHAT YOU SAID BEFORE, ABOUT NOT LETTING ANOTHER PERSON DIE...
I THOUGHT IT MIGHT JUST WORK WITH SOME-ONE WHO'S CAPABLE OF BLURTING OUT THAT KIND OF DRIVEL.

READ THIS WAY

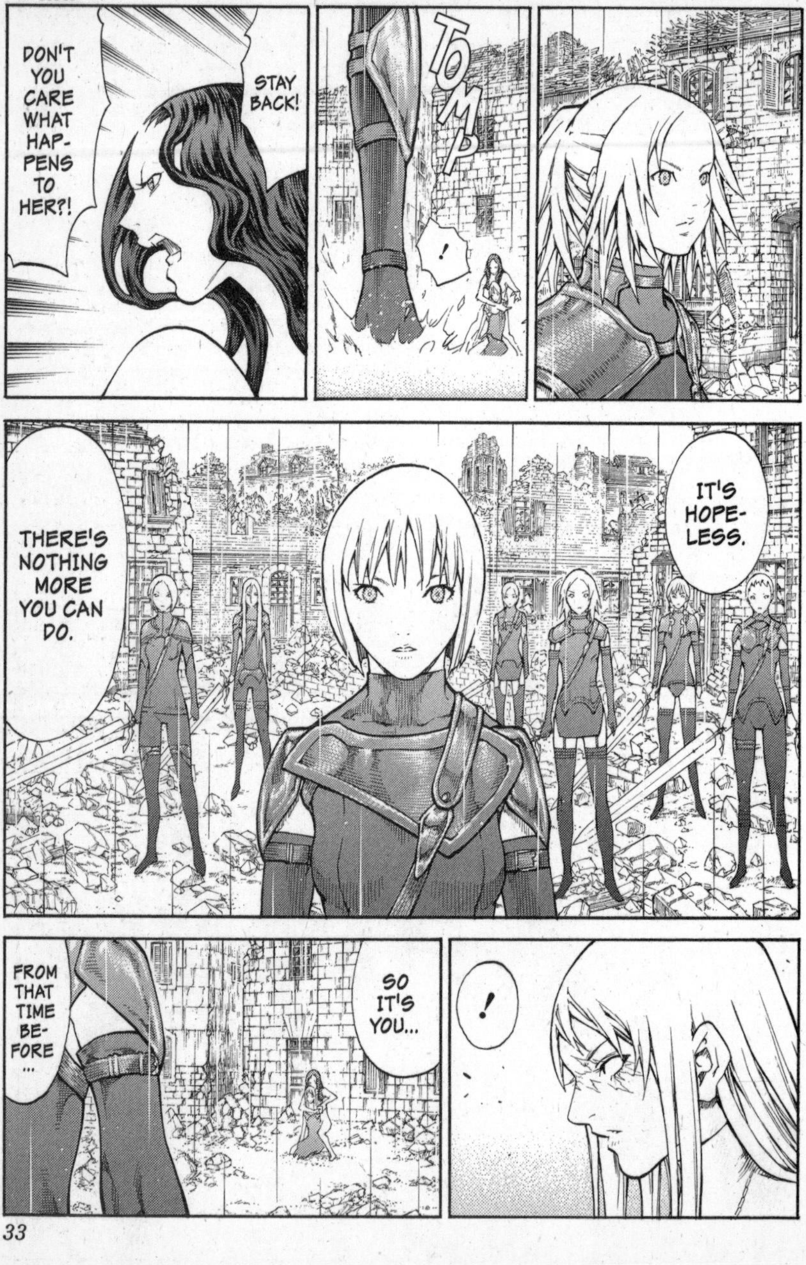
TOMP
!
STAY BACK!
DON'T YOU CARE WHAT HAP-PENS TO HER?!
IT'S HOPE-LESS.
THERE'S NOTHING MORE YOU CAN DO.
!
SO IT'S YOU...
FROM THAT TIME BE-FORE ...

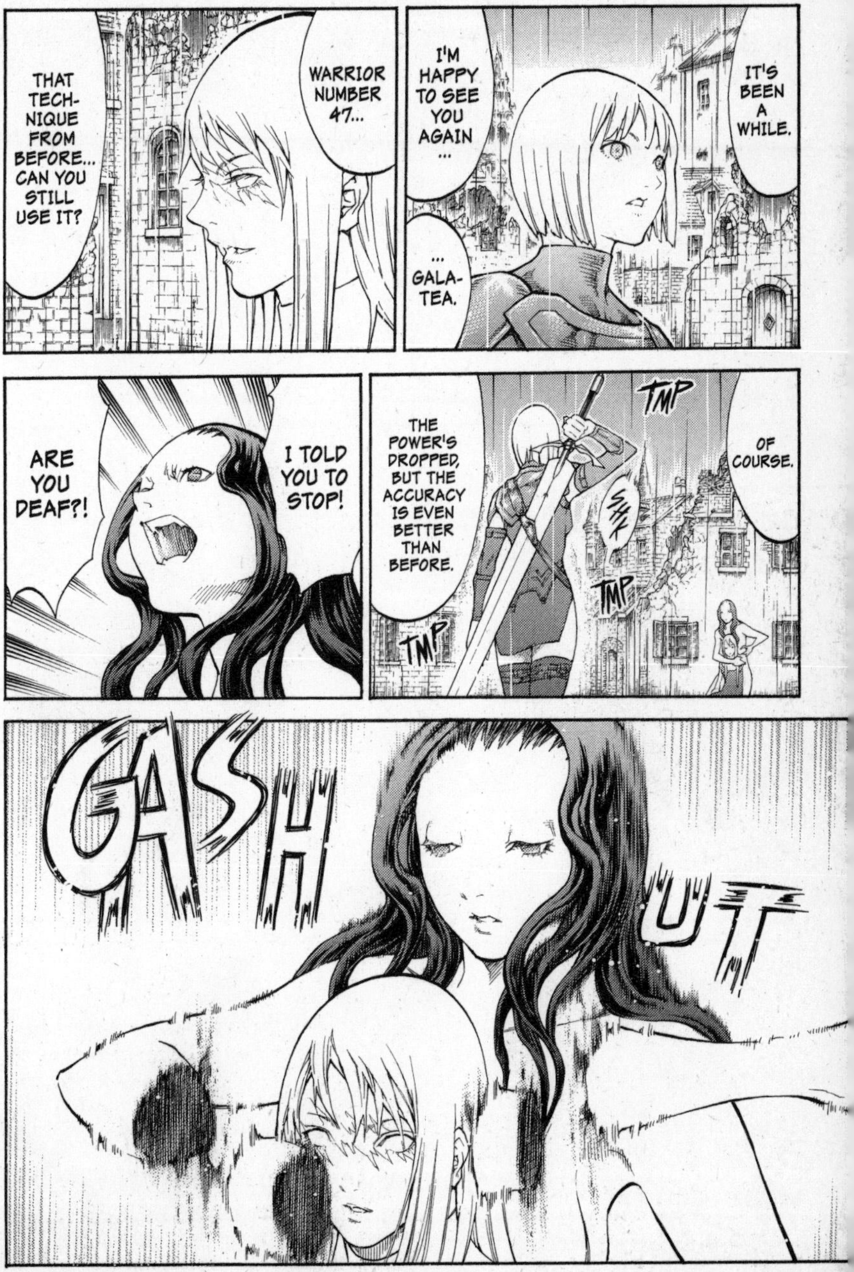
IT'S BEEN A WHILE.
I'M HAPPY TO SEE YOU AGAIN ...
... GALA-TEA.
WARRIOR NUMBER 47...
THAT TECH-NIQUE FROM BEFORE... CAN YOU STILL USE IT?
OF COURSE.
TMP
SHK
THE POWER'S DROPPED, BUT THE ACCURACY IS EVEN BETTER THAN BEFORE.
TMP
TMP
I TOLD YOU TO STOP!
ARE YOU DEAF?!
GASH
UT

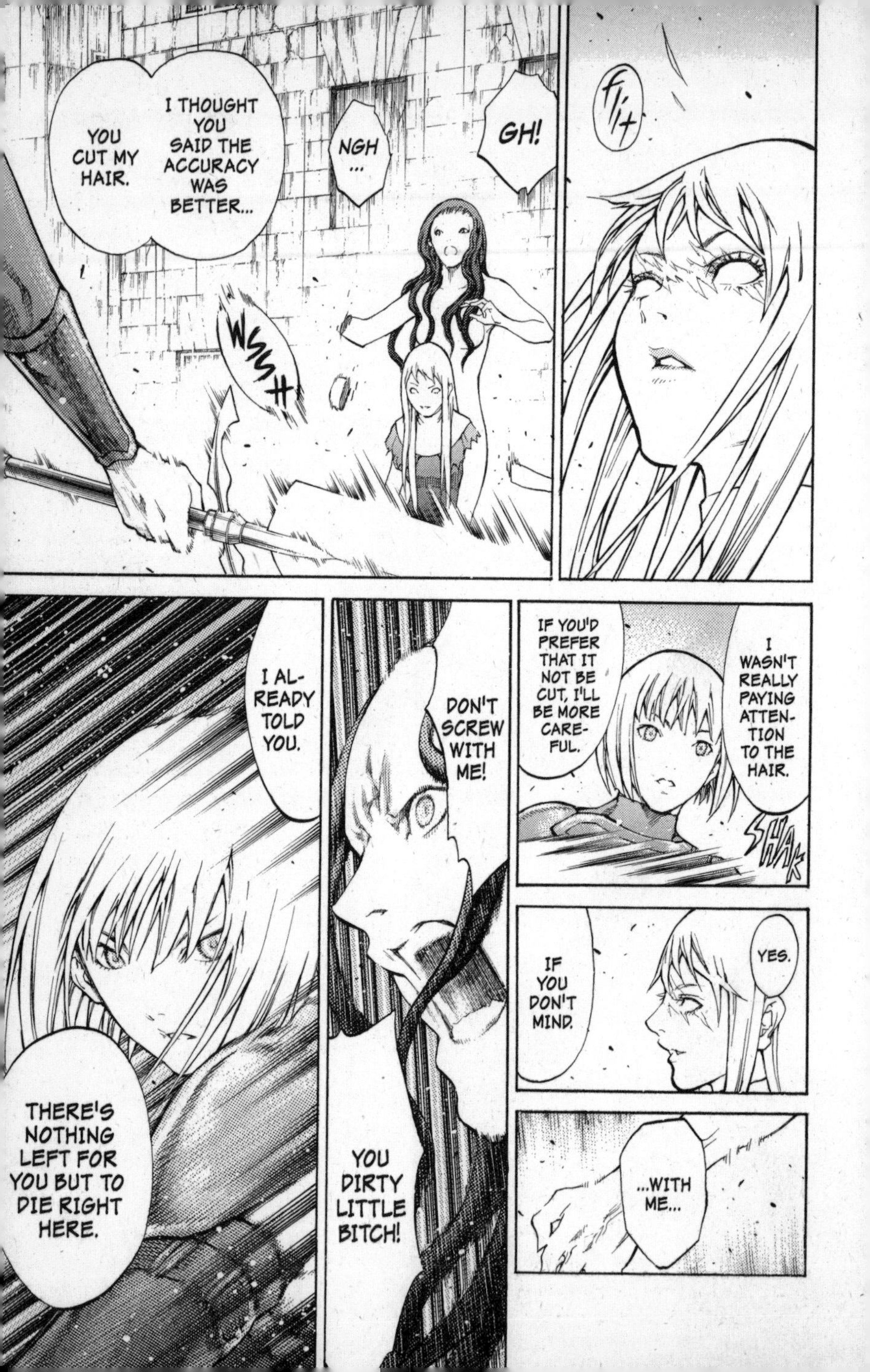
FLIT
GH!
NGH ...
I THOUGHT YOU SAID THE ACCURACY WAS BETTER...
YOU CUT MY HAIR.
WSSH
I WASN'T REALLY PAYING ATTEN-TION TO THE HAIR.
IF YOU'D PREFER THAT IT NOT BE CUT, I'LL BE MORE CARE-FUL.
SHAK
YES.
IF YOU DON'T MIND.
...WITH ME...
DON'T SCREW WITH ME!
YOU DIRTY LITTLE BITCH!
I AL-READY TOLD YOU.
THERE'S NOTHING LEFT FOR YOU BUT TO DIE RIGHT HERE.

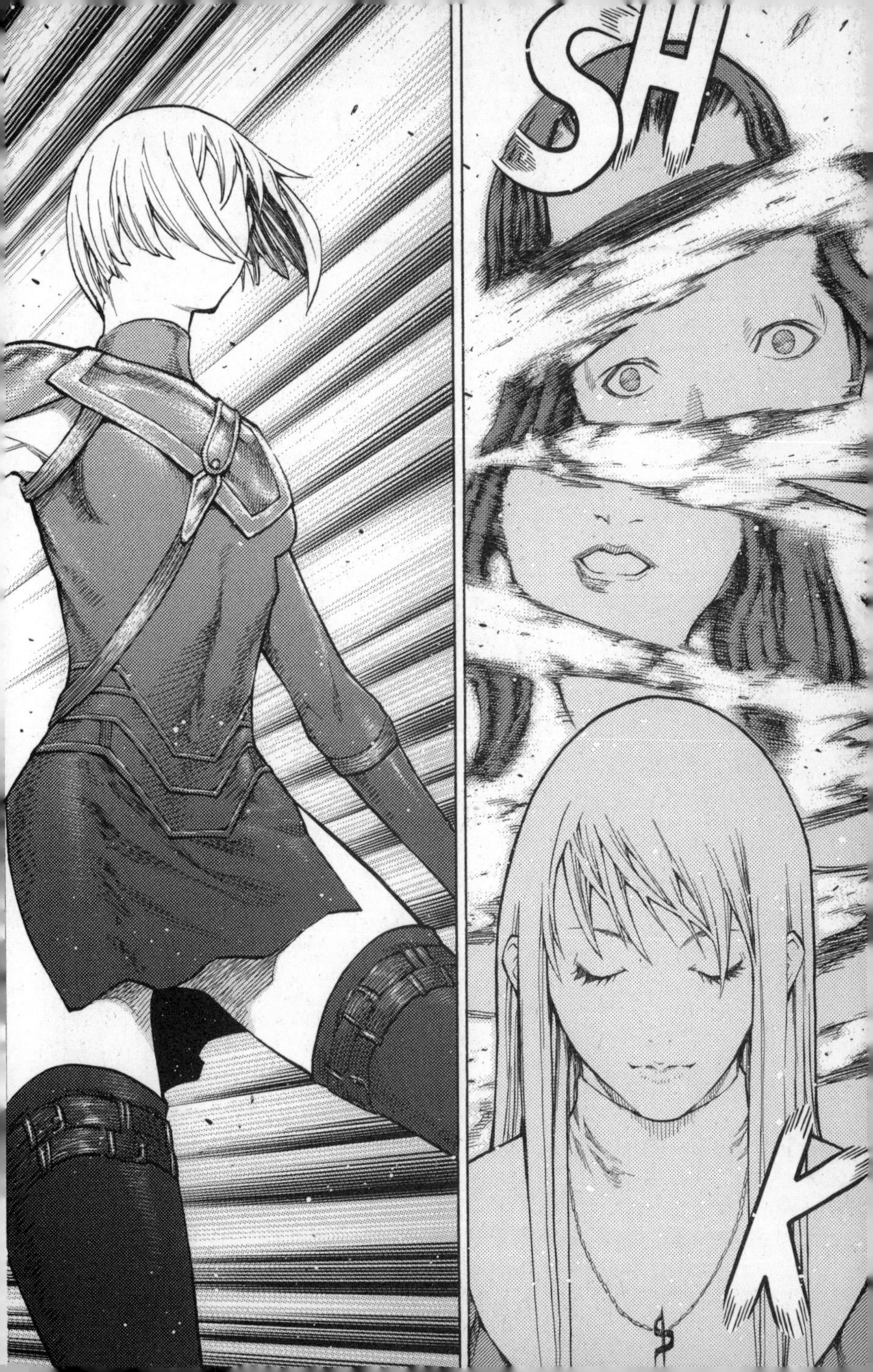
SH

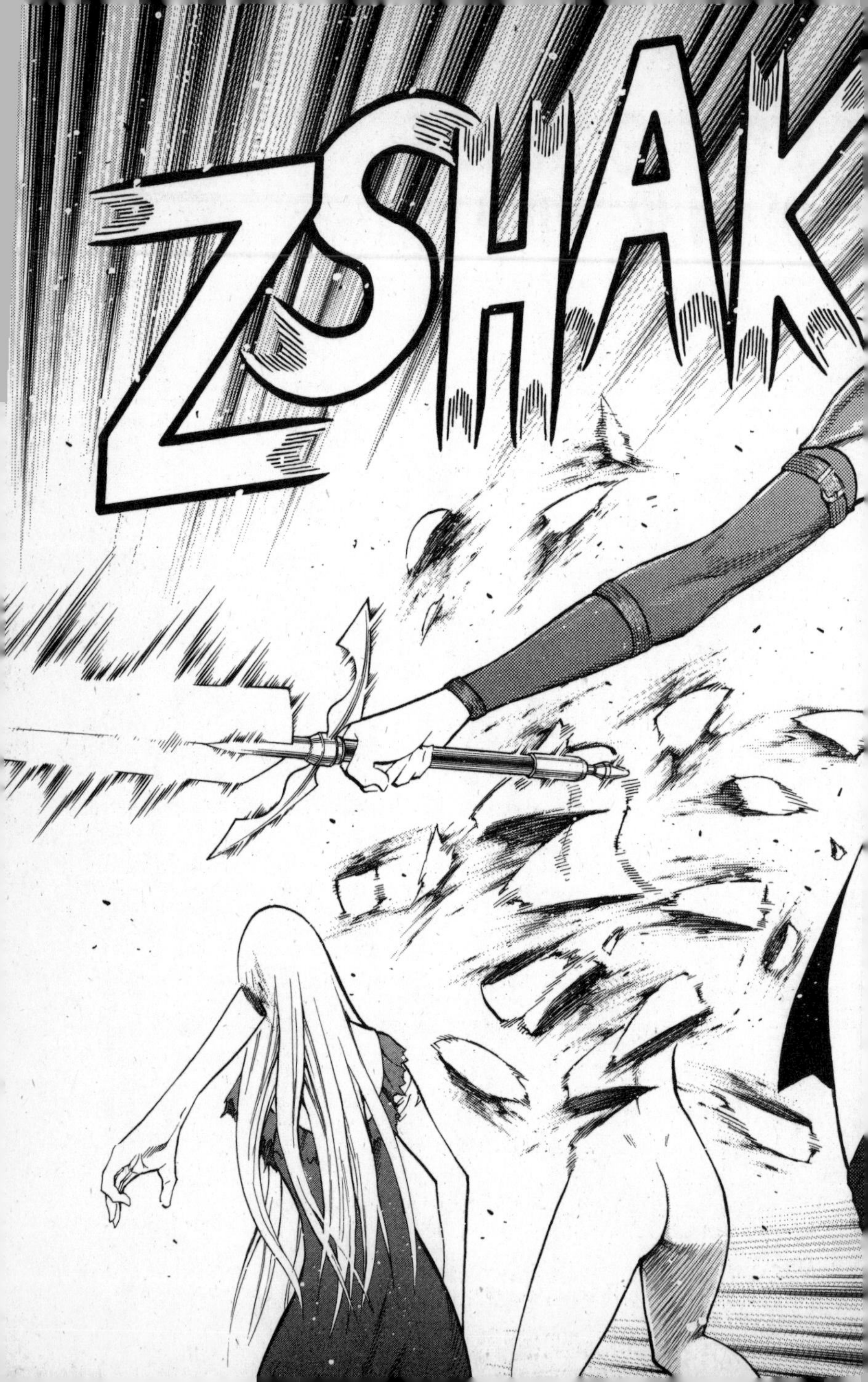
ZSHAK

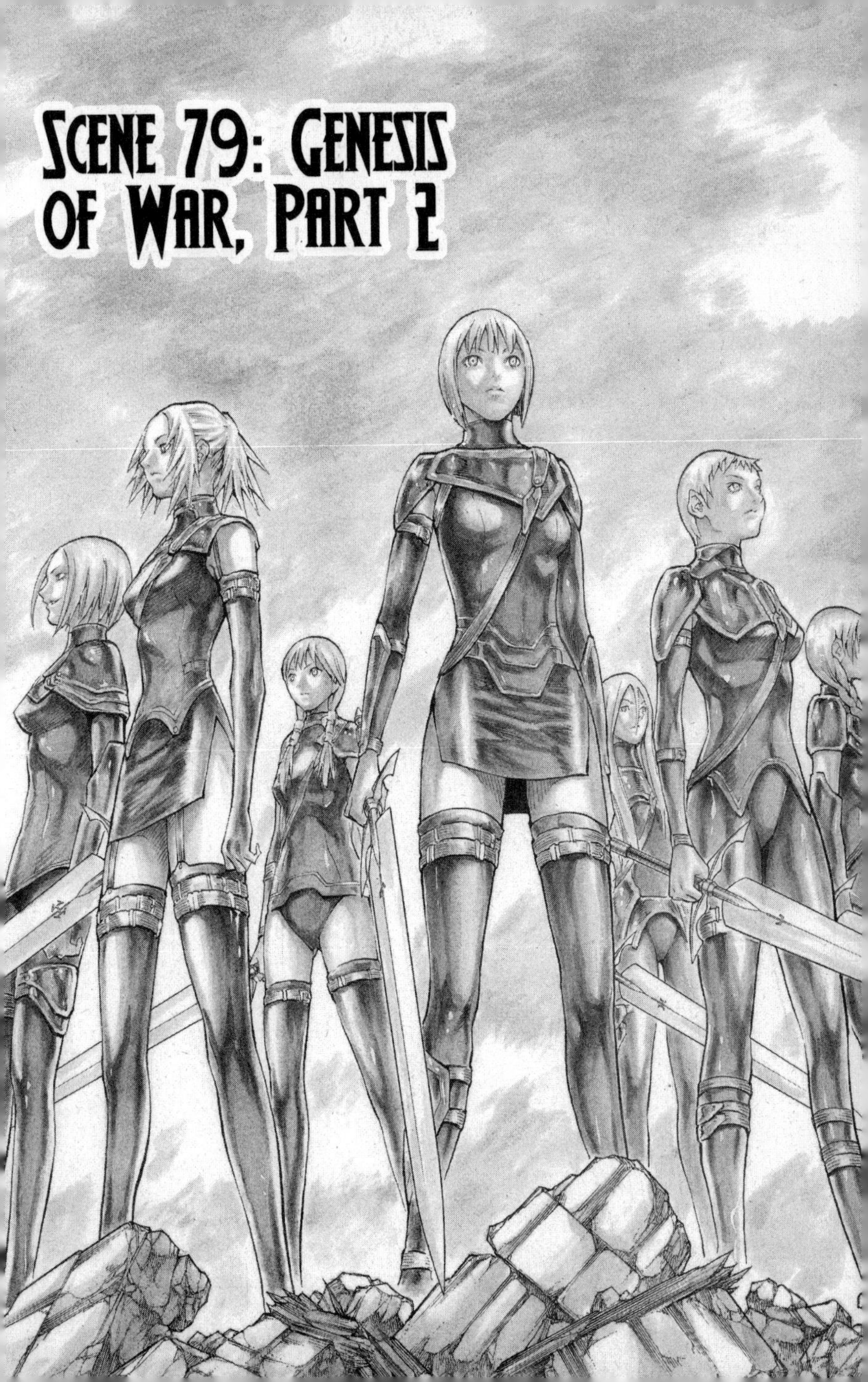
Scene 79: Genesis of War, Part 2

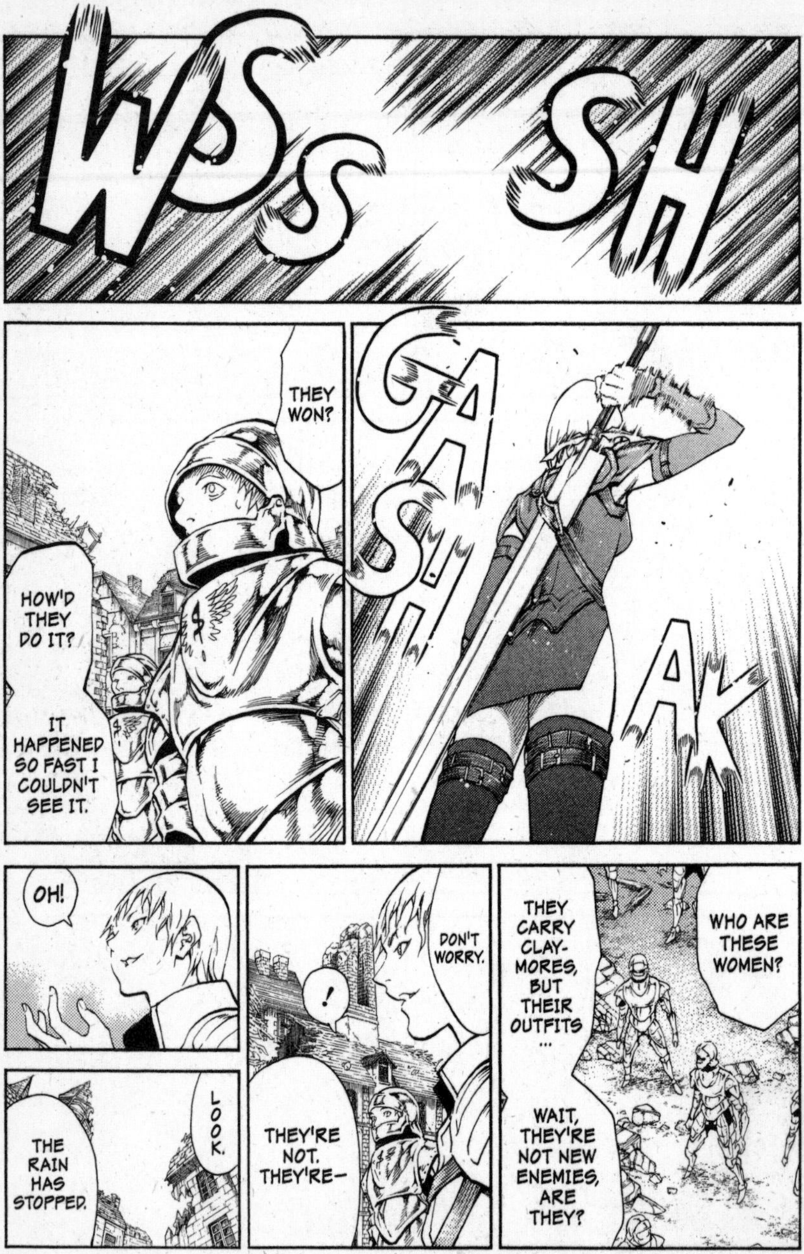
WSSSH
GASH
AK
THEY WON?
HOW'D THEY DO IT?
IT HAPPENED SO FAST I COULDN'T SEE IT.
WHO ARE THESE WOMEN?
THEY CARRY CLAYMORES, BUT THEIR OUTFITS...
WAIT, THEY'RE NOT NEW ENEMIES, ARE THEY?
DON'T WORRY.
!
THEY'RE NOT. THEY'RE–
OH!
LOOK.
THE RAIN HAS STOPPED.

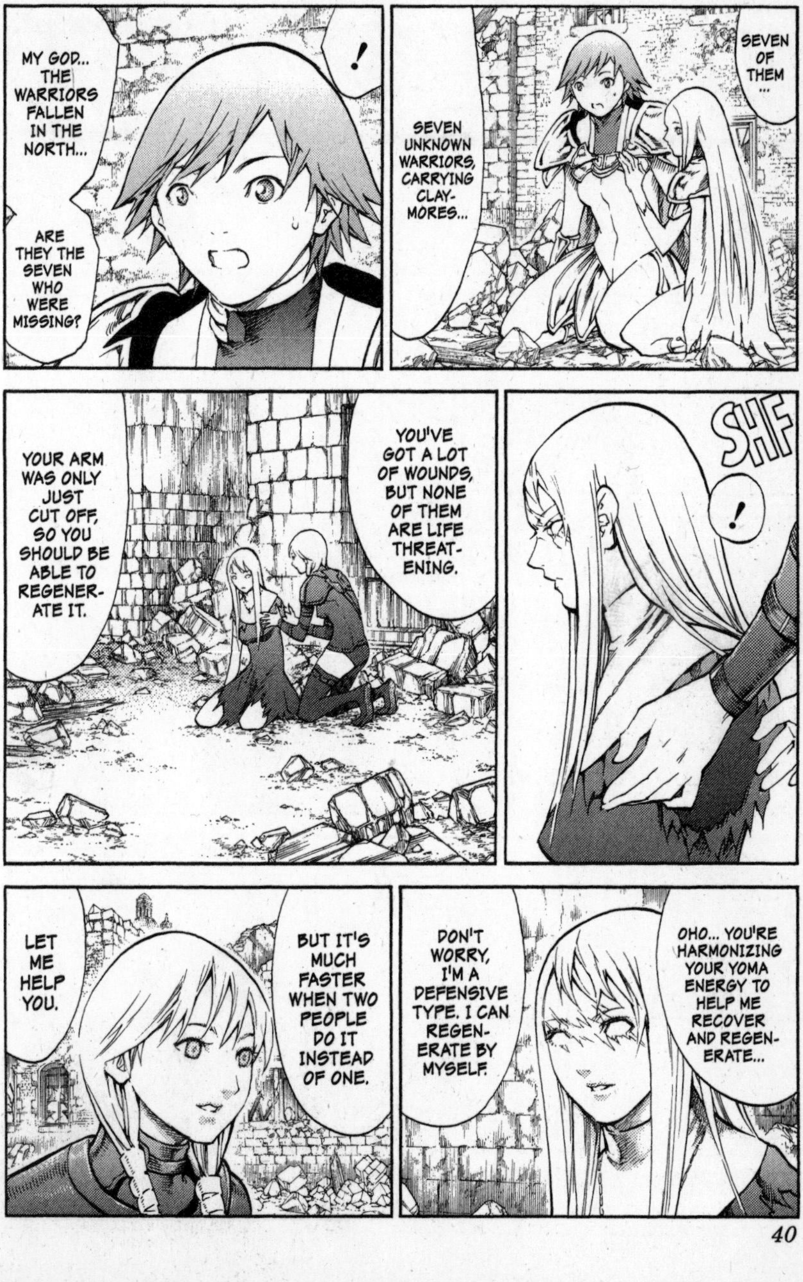
SEVEN OF THEM ...
SEVEN UNKNOWN WARRIORS, CARRYING CLAY-MORES...
!
MY GOD... THE WARRIORS FALLEN IN THE NORTH...
ARE THEY THE SEVEN WHO WERE MISSING?
SHF
!
YOU'VE GOT A LOT OF WOUNDS, BUT NONE OF THEM ARE LIFE THREAT-ENING.
YOUR ARM WAS ONLY JUST CUT OFF, SO YOU SHOULD BE ABLE TO REGENER-ATE IT.
OHO... YOU'RE HARMONIZING YOUR YOMA ENERGY TO HELP ME RECOVER AND REGEN-ERATE...
DON'T WORRY, I'M A DEFENSIVE TYPE. I CAN REGEN-ERATE BY MYSELF.
BUT IT'S MUCH FASTER WHEN TWO PEOPLE DO IT INSTEAD OF ONE.
LET ME HELP YOU.

READ THIS WAY

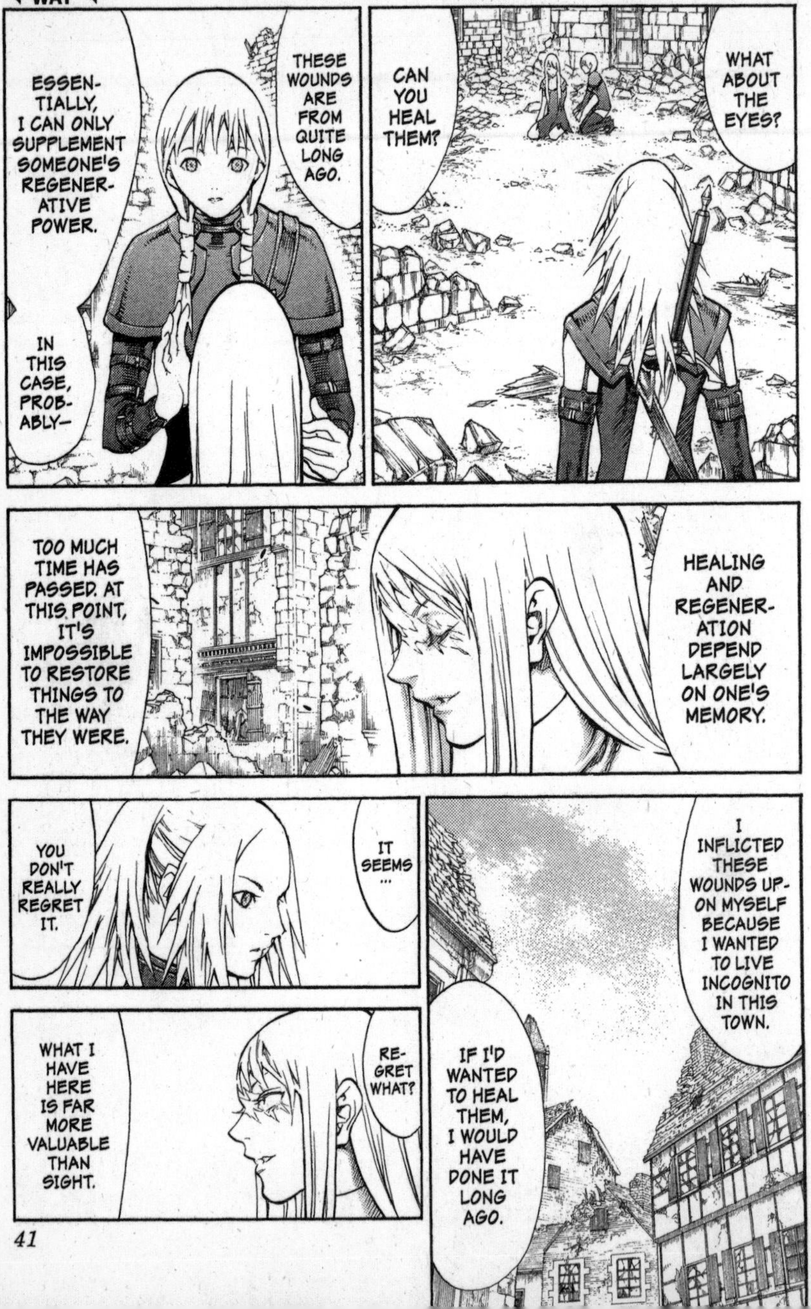

WHAT ABOUT THE EYES?
CAN YOU HEAL THEM?
THESE WOUNDS ARE FROM QUITE LONG AGO.
ESSENTIALLY, I CAN ONLY SUPPLEMENT SOMEONE'S REGENERATIVE POWER.
IN THIS CASE, PROBABLY—
HEALING AND REGENERATION DEPEND LARGELY ON ONE'S MEMORY.
TOO MUCH TIME HAS PASSED. AT THIS POINT, IT'S IMPOSSIBLE TO RESTORE THINGS TO THE WAY THEY WERE.
I INFLICTED THESE WOUNDS UPON MYSELF BECAUSE I WANTED TO LIVE INCOGNITO IN THIS TOWN.
IF I'D WANTED TO HEAL THEM, I WOULD HAVE DONE IT LONG AGO.
IT SEEMS...
YOU DON'T REALLY REGRET IT.
REGRET WHAT?
WHAT I HAVE HERE IS FAR MORE VALUABLE THAN SIGHT.

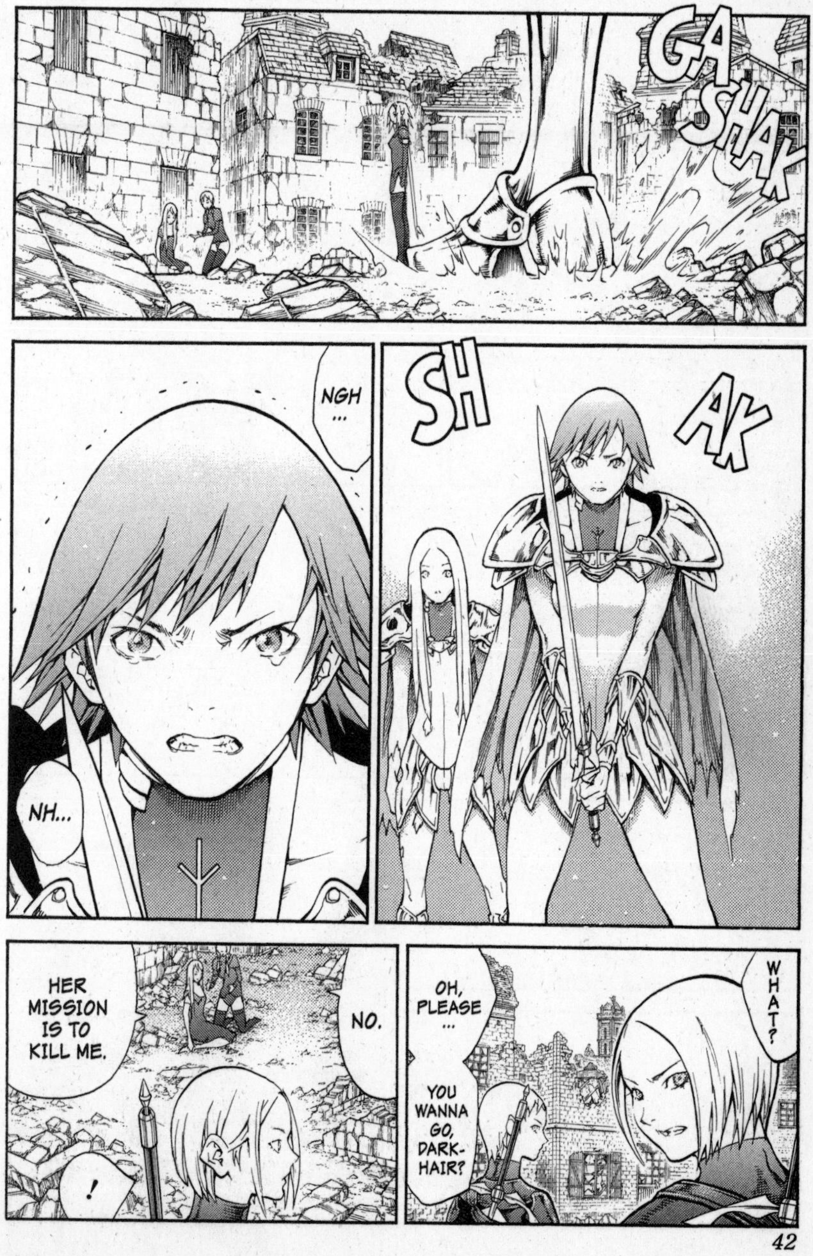
GASHAK
SHAK
NGH ...
NH...
WHAT?
OH, PLEASE ...
YOU WANNA GO, DARK-HAIR?
NO.
HER MISSION IS TO KILL ME.
!

READ THIS WAY

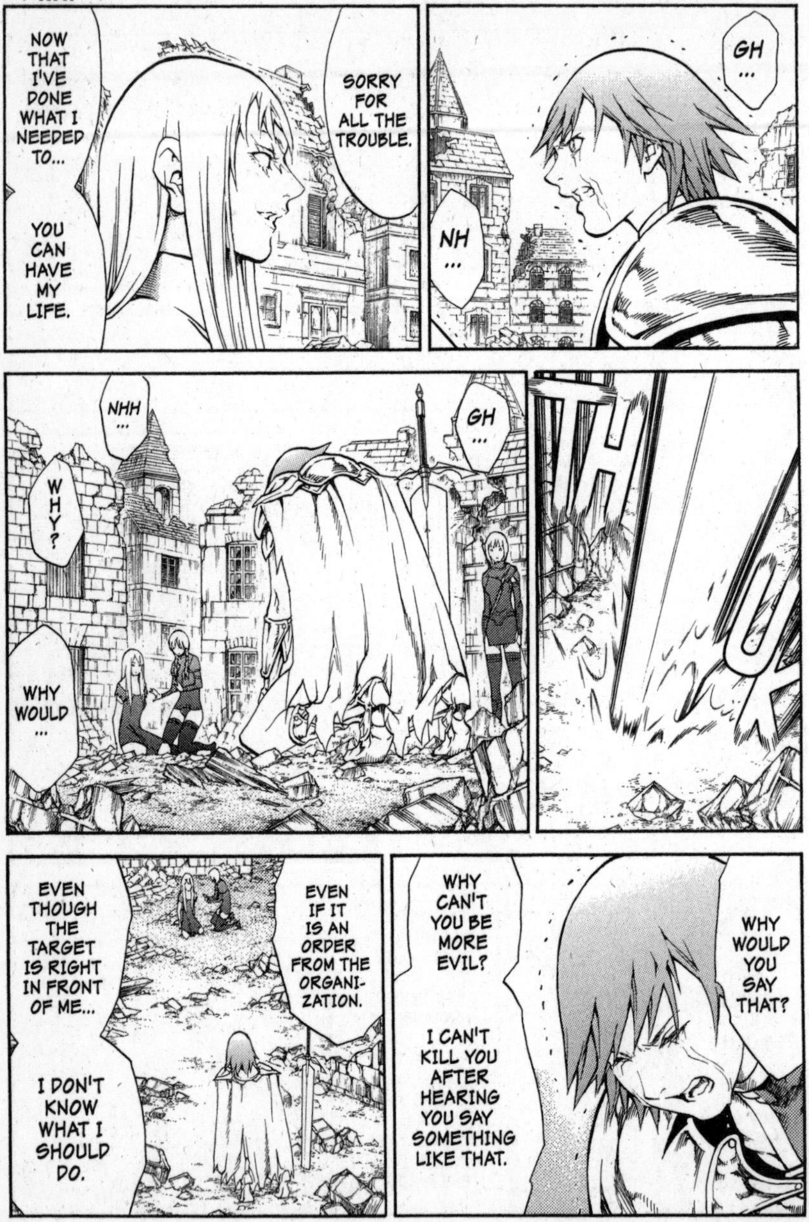
GH ...
NH ...
SORRY FOR ALL THE TROUBLE.
NOW THAT I'VE DONE WHAT I NEEDED TO...
YOU CAN HAVE MY LIFE.
GH ...
NHH ...
WHY?
WHY WOULD ...
WHY WOULD YOU SAY THAT?
WHY CAN'T YOU BE MORE EVIL?
I CAN'T KILL YOU AFTER HEARING YOU SAY SOMETHING LIKE THAT.
EVEN IF IT IS AN ORDER FROM THE ORGANIZATION.
EVEN THOUGH THE TARGET IS RIGHT IN FRONT OF ME...
I DON'T KNOW WHAT I SHOULD DO.

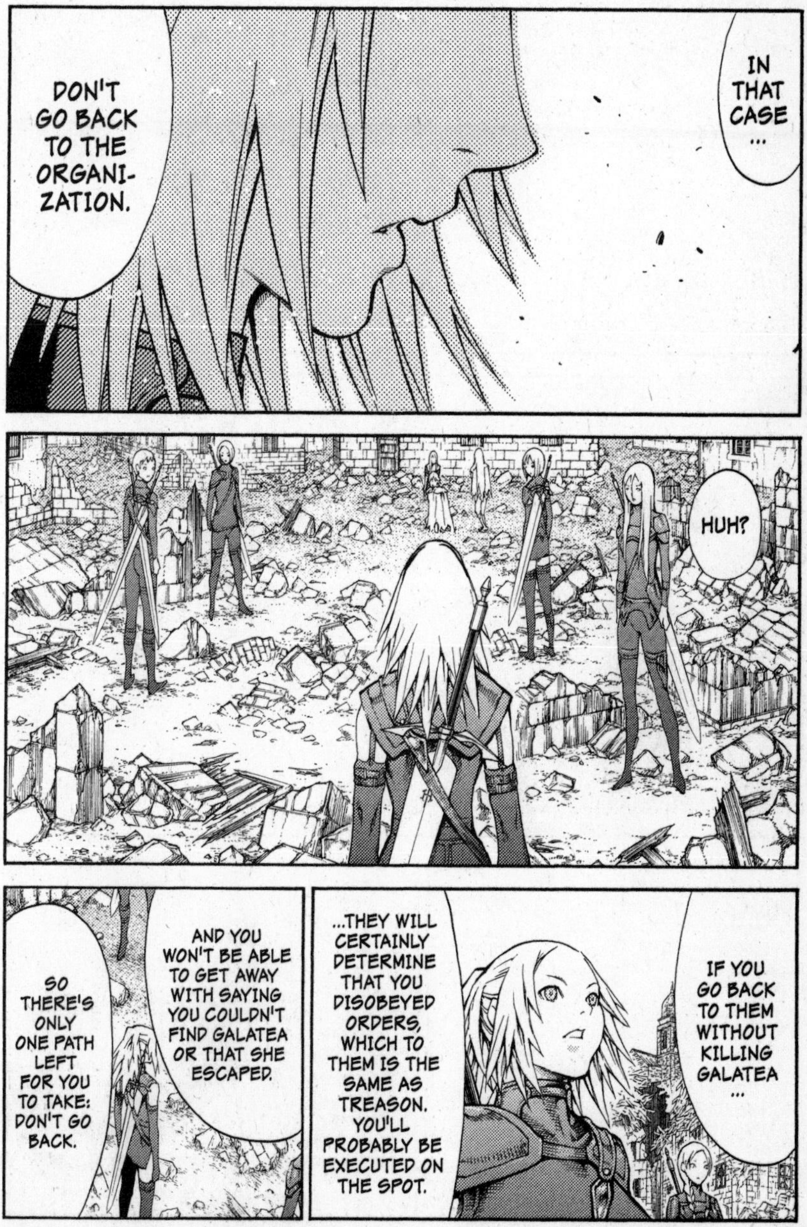
IN THAT CASE...
DON'T GO BACK TO THE ORGANIZATION.
HUH?
IF YOU GO BACK TO THEM WITHOUT KILLING GALATEA...
...THEY WILL CERTAINLY DETERMINE THAT YOU DISOBEYED ORDERS, WHICH TO THEM IS THE SAME AS TREASON. YOU'LL PROBABLY BE EXECUTED ON THE SPOT.
AND YOU WON'T BE ABLE TO GET AWAY WITH SAYING YOU COULDN'T FIND GALATEA OR THAT SHE ESCAPED.
SO THERE'S ONLY ONE PATH LEFT FOR YOU TO TAKE: DON'T GO BACK.

READ THIS WAY

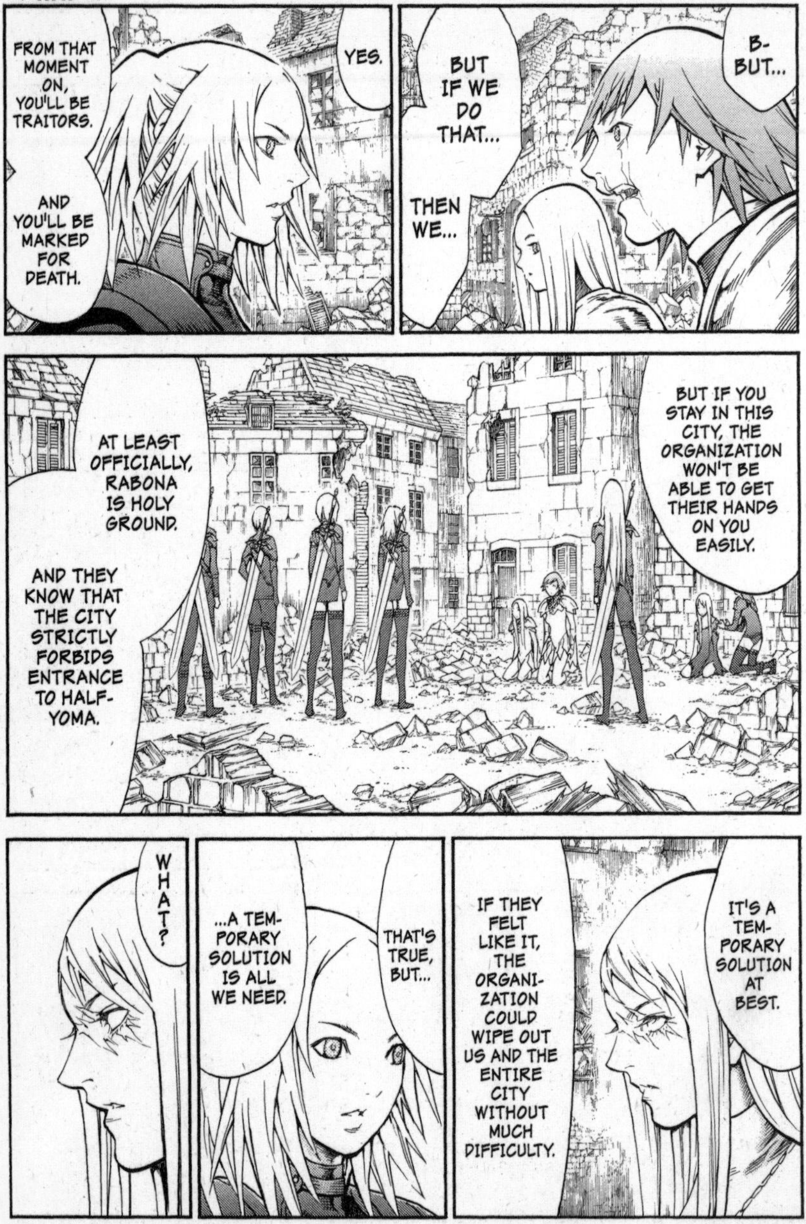
B- BUT...
BUT IF WE DO THAT...
THEN WE...
YES.
FROM THAT MOMENT ON, YOU'LL BE TRAITORS.
AND YOU'LL BE MARKED FOR DEATH.
BUT IF YOU STAY IN THIS CITY, THE ORGANIZATION WON'T BE ABLE TO GET THEIR HANDS ON YOU EASILY.
AT LEAST OFFICIALLY, RABONA IS HOLY GROUND.
AND THEY KNOW THAT THE CITY STRICTLY FORBIDS ENTRANCE TO HALF-YOMA.
IT'S A TEM-PORARY SOLUTION AT BEST.
IF THEY FELT LIKE IT, THE ORGANI-ZATION COULD WIPE OUT US AND THE ENTIRE CITY WITHOUT MUCH DIFFICULTY.
THAT'S TRUE, BUT...
...A TEM-PORARY SOLUTION IS ALL WE NEED.
WHAT?

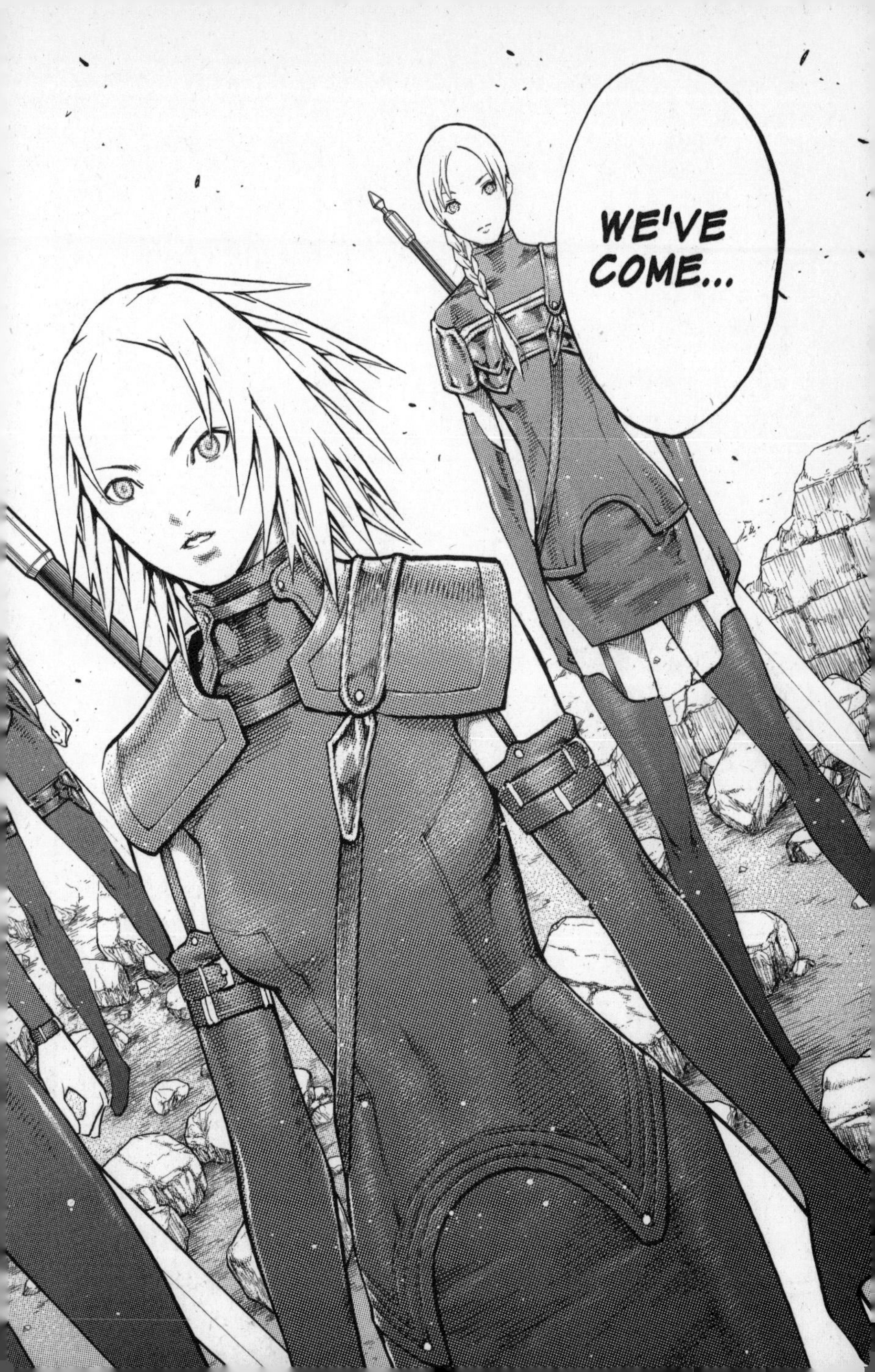
WE'VE COME...

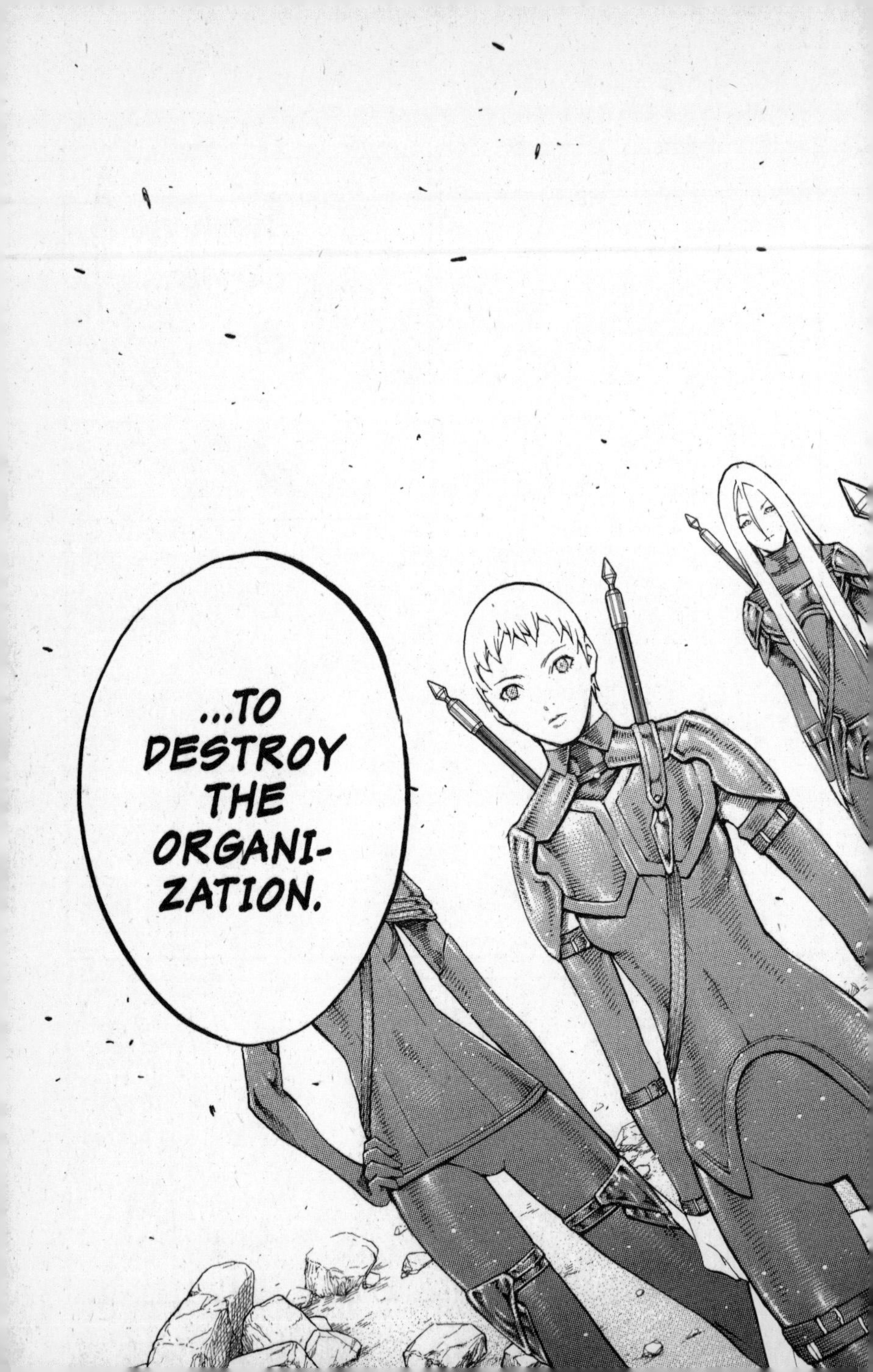
...TO DESTROY THE ORGANI- ZATION.

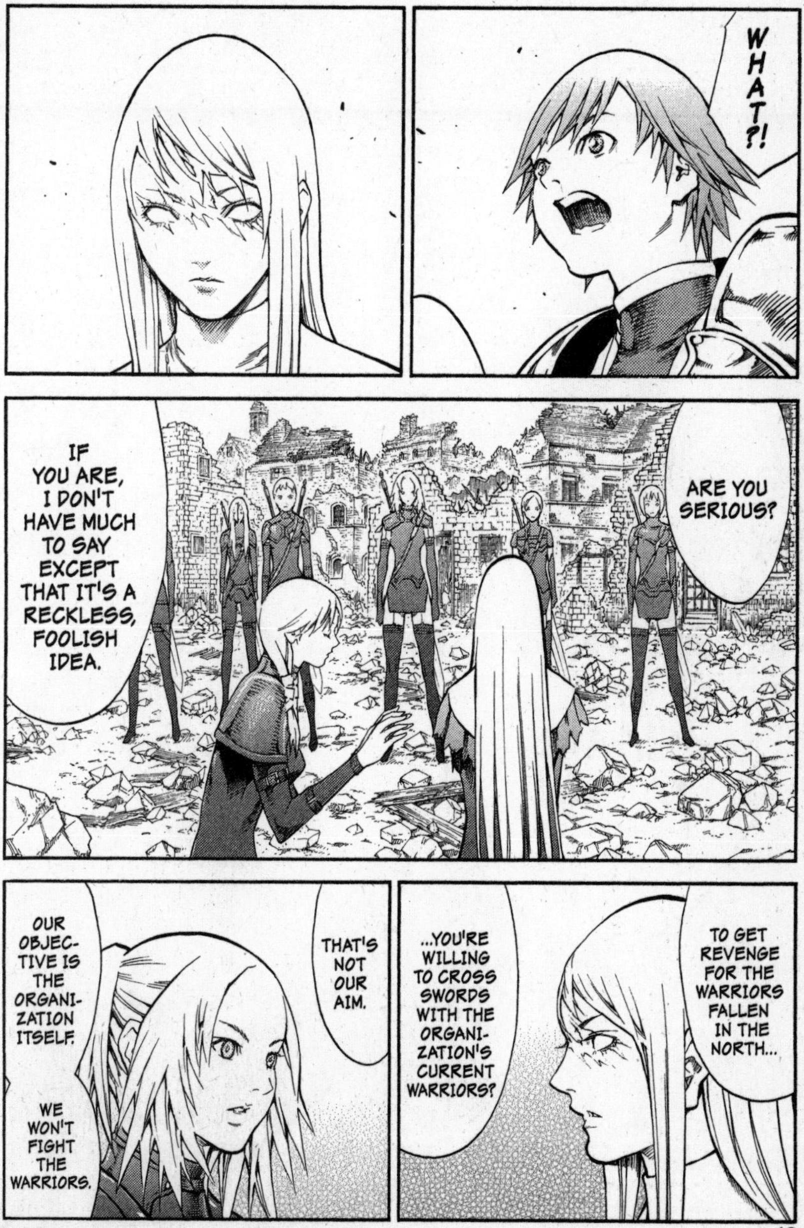
WHAT?!
ARE YOU SERIOUS?
IF YOU ARE, I DON'T HAVE MUCH TO SAY EXCEPT THAT IT'S A RECKLESS, FOOLISH IDEA.
TO GET REVENGE FOR THE WARRIORS FALLEN IN THE NORTH...
...YOU'RE WILLING TO CROSS SWORDS WITH THE ORGANIZATION'S CURRENT WARRIORS?
THAT'S NOT OUR AIM.
OUR OBJECTIVE IS THE ORGANIZATION ITSELF.
WE WON'T FIGHT THE WARRIORS.

READ THIS WAY

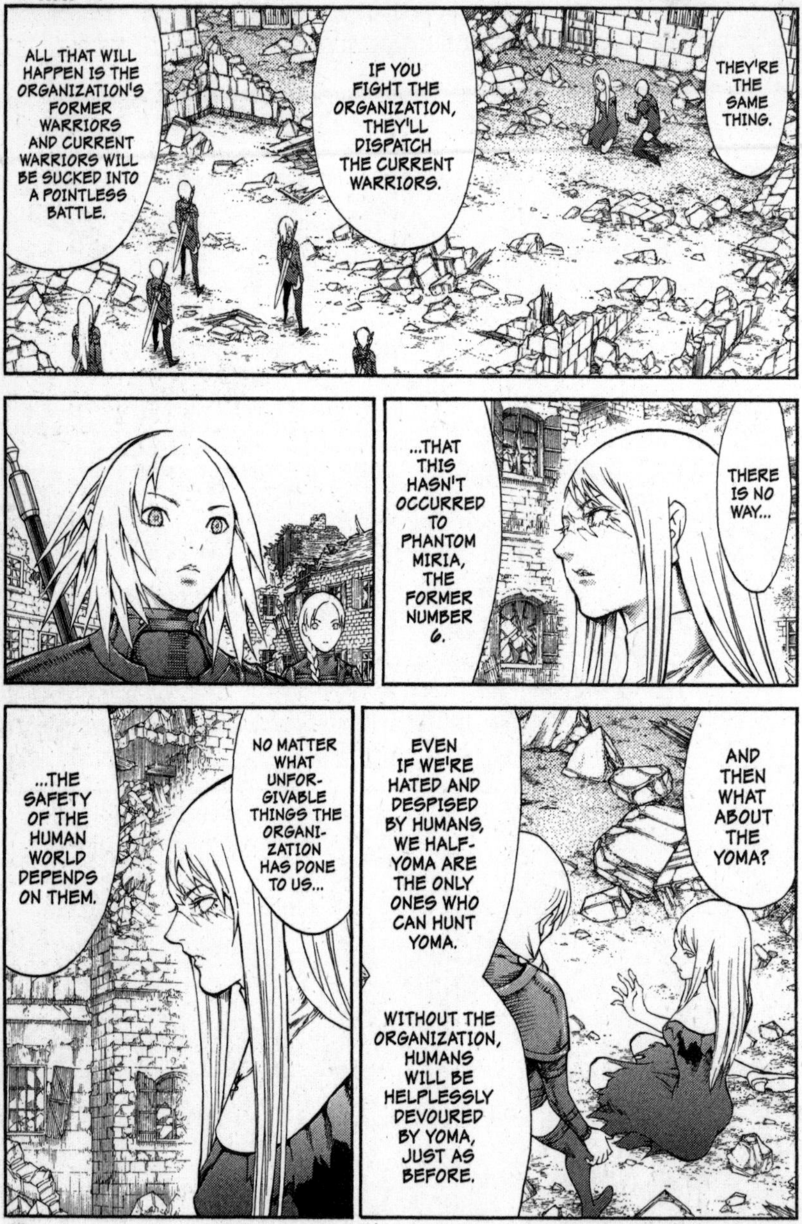
THEY'RE THE SAME THING.
IF YOU FIGHT THE ORGANIZATION, THEY'LL DISPATCH THE CURRENT WARRIORS.
ALL THAT WILL HAPPEN IS THE ORGANIZATION'S FORMER WARRIORS AND CURRENT WARRIORS WILL BE SUCKED INTO A POINTLESS BATTLE.
THERE IS NO WAY...
...THAT THIS HASN'T OCCURRED TO PHANTOM MIRIA, THE FORMER NUMBER 6.
AND THEN WHAT ABOUT THE YOMA?
EVEN IF WE'RE HATED AND DESPISED BY HUMANS, WE HALF-YOMA ARE THE ONLY ONES WHO CAN HUNT YOMA.
WITHOUT THE ORGANIZATION, HUMANS WILL BE HELPLESSLY DEVOURED BY YOMA, JUST AS BEFORE.
NO MATTER WHAT UNFORGIVABLE THINGS THE ORGANIZATION HAS DONE TO US...
...THE SAFETY OF THE HUMAN WORLD DEPENDS ON THEM.

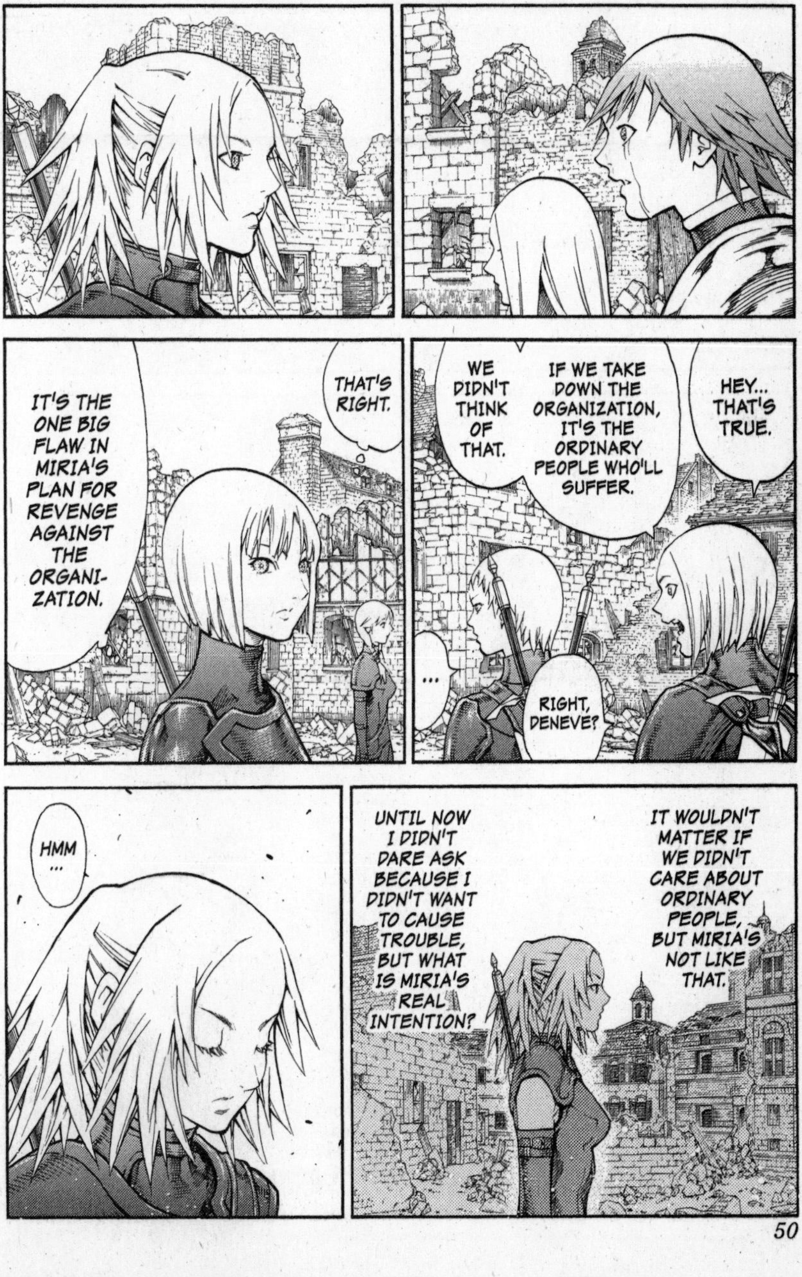
HEY... THAT'S TRUE.
IF WE TAKE DOWN THE ORGANIZATION, IT'S THE ORDINARY PEOPLE WHO'LL SUFFER.
WE DIDN'T THINK OF THAT.
RIGHT, DENEVE?
...
THAT'S RIGHT.
IT'S THE ONE BIG FLAW IN MIRIA'S PLAN FOR REVENGE AGAINST THE ORGANIZATION.
IT WOULDN'T MATTER IF WE DIDN'T CARE ABOUT ORDINARY PEOPLE, BUT MIRIA'S NOT LIKE THAT.
UNTIL NOW I DIDN'T DARE ASK BECAUSE I DIDN'T WANT TO CAUSE TROUBLE, BUT WHAT IS MIRIA'S REAL INTENTION?
HMM ...

READ THIS WAY

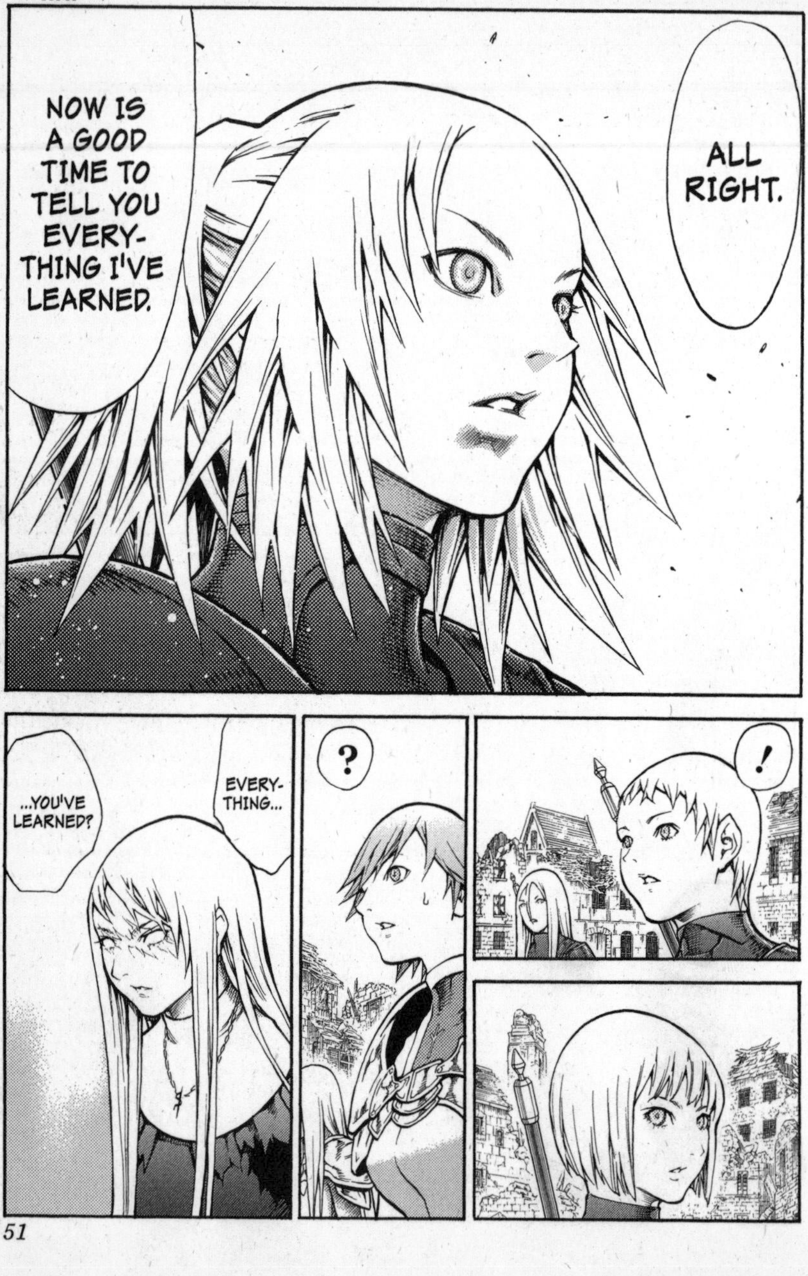

ALL RIGHT.
NOW IS A GOOD TIME TO TELL YOU EVERY-THING I'VE LEARNED.
!
?
EVERY-THING...
...YOU'VE LEARNED?

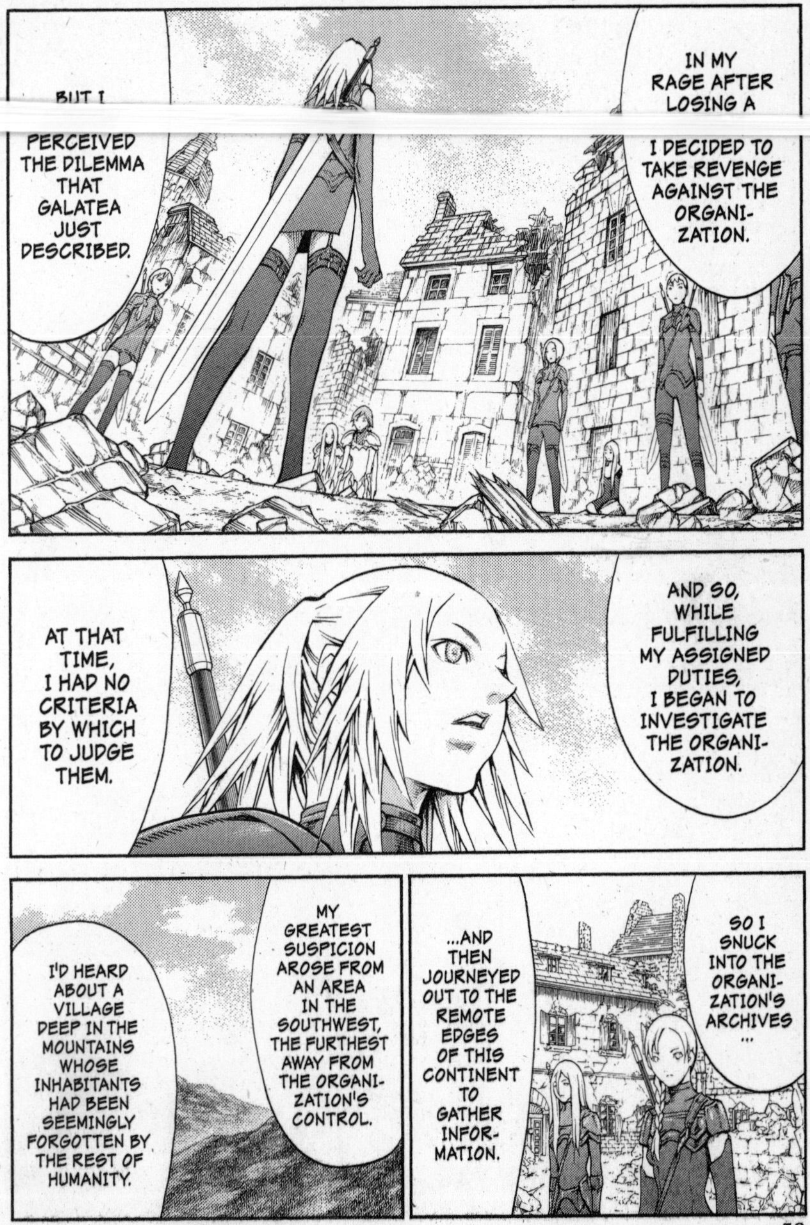
IN MY RAGE AFTER LOSING A
I DECIDED TO TAKE REVENGE AGAINST THE ORGANIZATION.
BUT I
PERCEIVED THE DILEMMA THAT GALATEA JUST DESCRIBED.
AND SO, WHILE FULFILLING MY ASSIGNED DUTIES, I BEGAN TO INVESTIGATE THE ORGANIZATION.
AT THAT TIME, I HAD NO CRITERIA BY WHICH TO JUDGE THEM.
SO I SNUCK INTO THE ORGANIZATION'S ARCHIVES...
...AND THEN JOURNEYED OUT TO THE REMOTE EDGES OF THIS CONTINENT TO GATHER INFORMATION.
MY GREATEST SUSPICION AROSE FROM AN AREA IN THE SOUTHWEST, THE FURTHEST AWAY FROM THE ORGANIZATION'S CONTROL.
I'D HEARD ABOUT A VILLAGE DEEP IN THE MOUNTAINS WHOSE INHABITANTS HAD BEEN SEEMINGLY FORGOTTEN BY THE REST OF HUMANITY.

READ THIS WAY

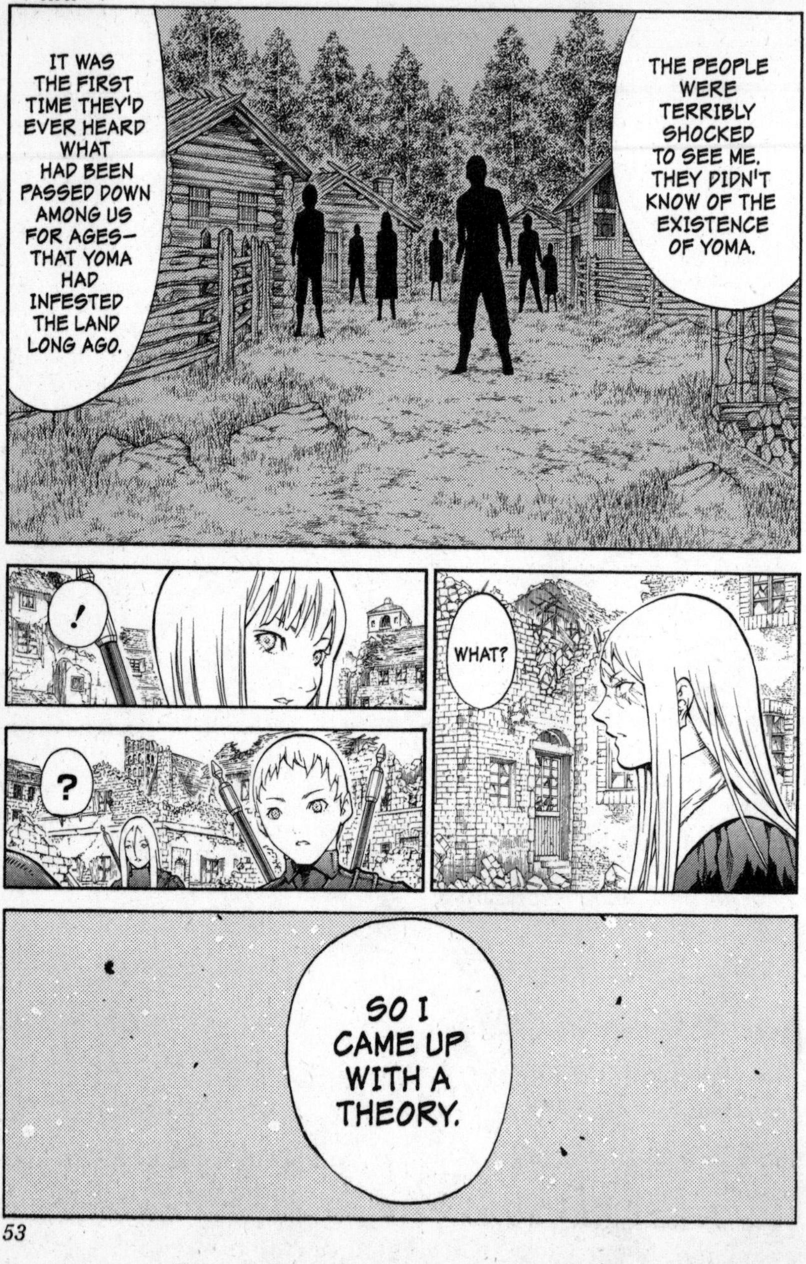
THE PEOPLE WERE TERRIBLY SHOCKED TO SEE ME. THEY DIDN'T KNOW OF THE EXISTENCE OF YOMA.
IT WAS THE FIRST TIME THEY'D EVER HEARD WHAT HAD BEEN PASSED DOWN AMONG US FOR AGES— THAT YOMA HAD INFESTED THE LAND LONG AGO.
WHAT?
!
?
SO I CAME UP WITH A THEORY.

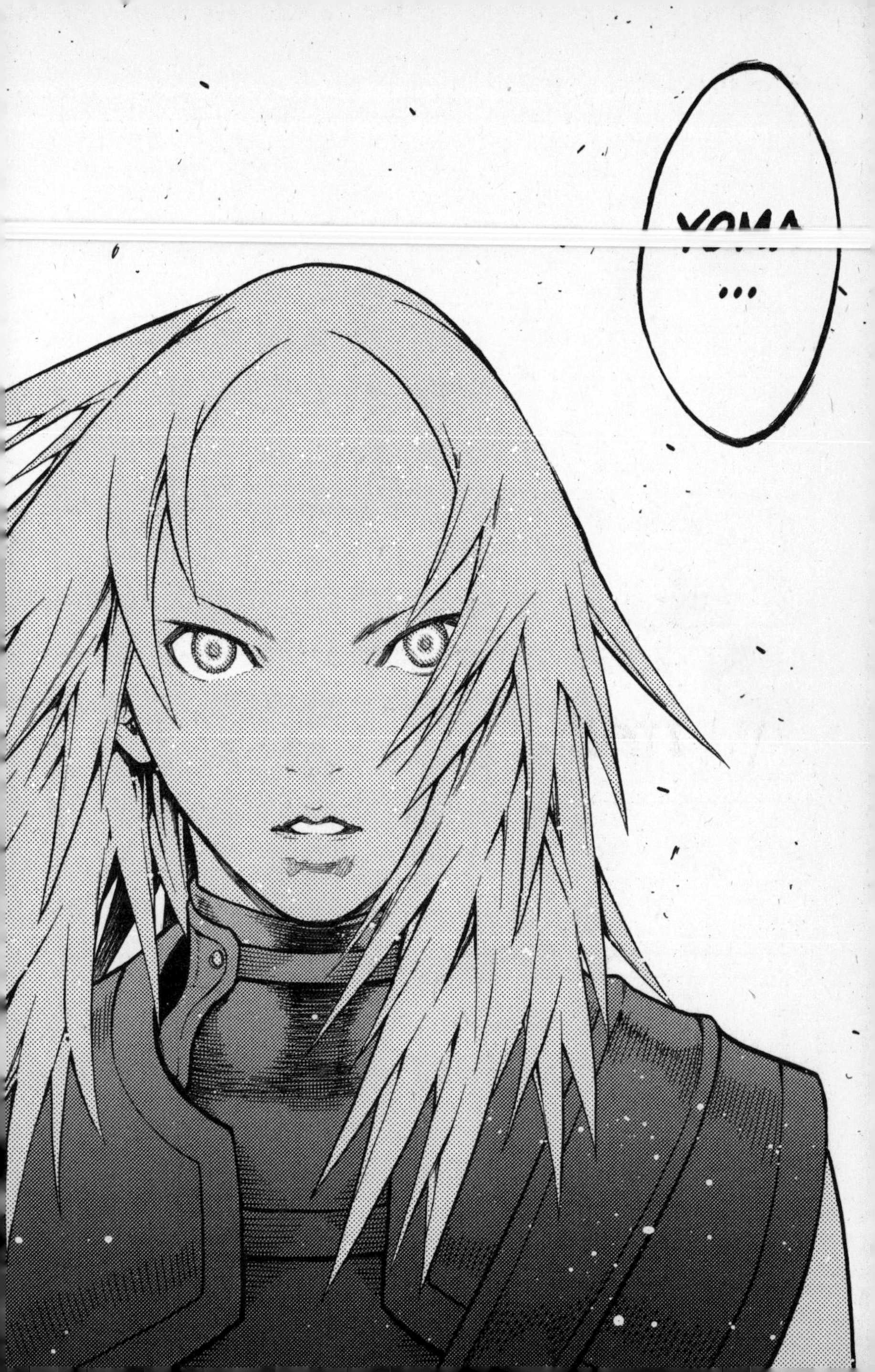
YOMA
...

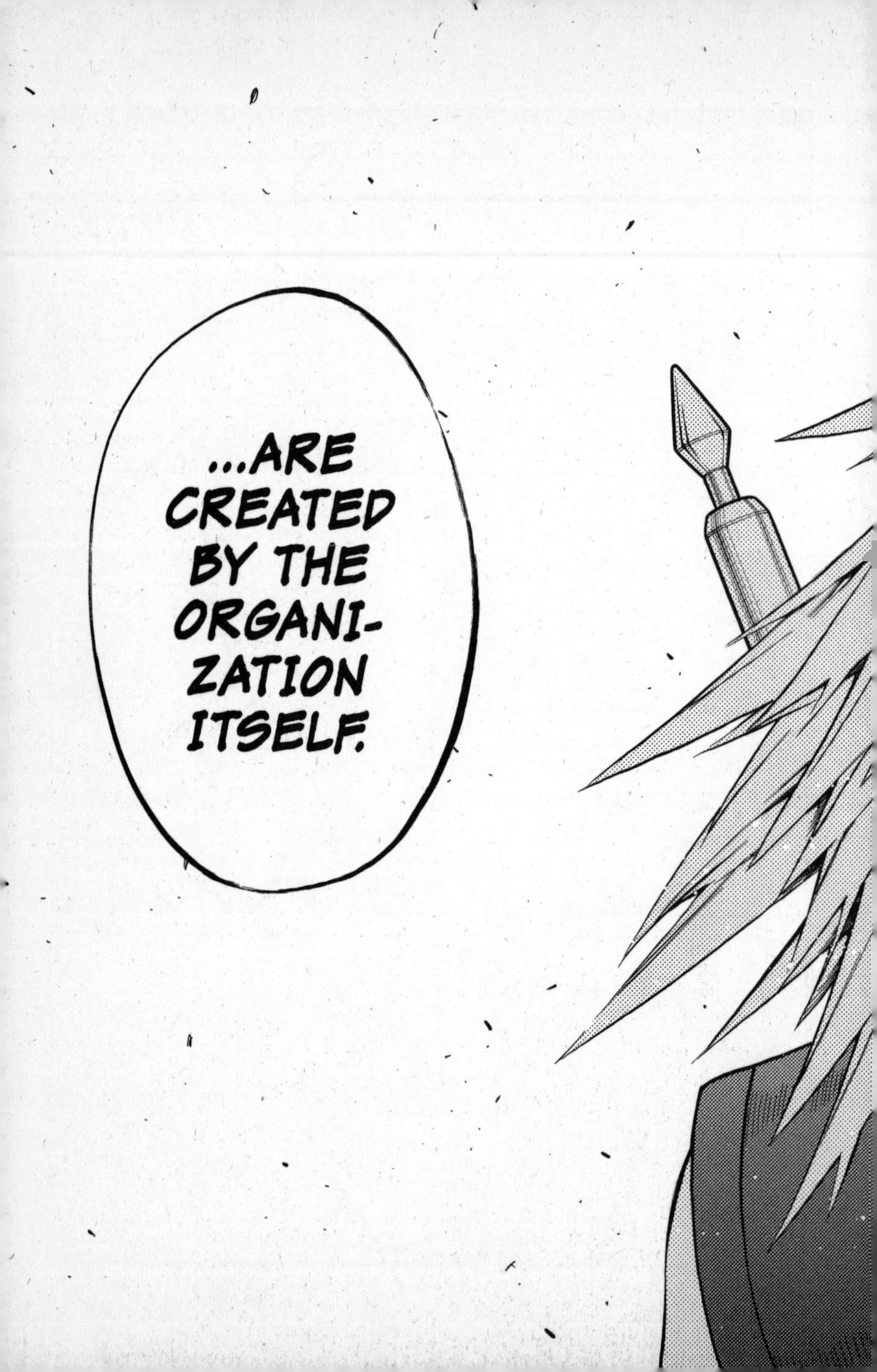
...ARE CREATED BY THE ORGANI- ZATION ITSELF.

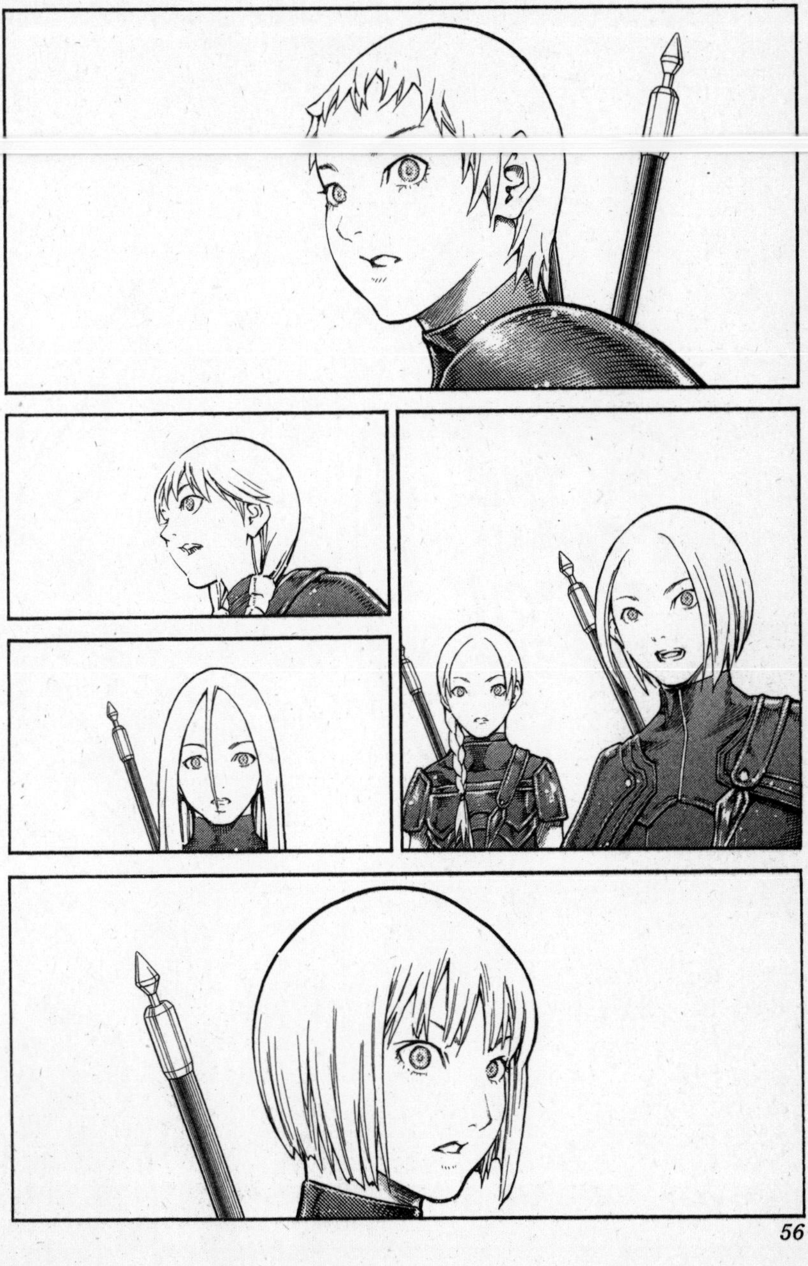

READ THIS WAY

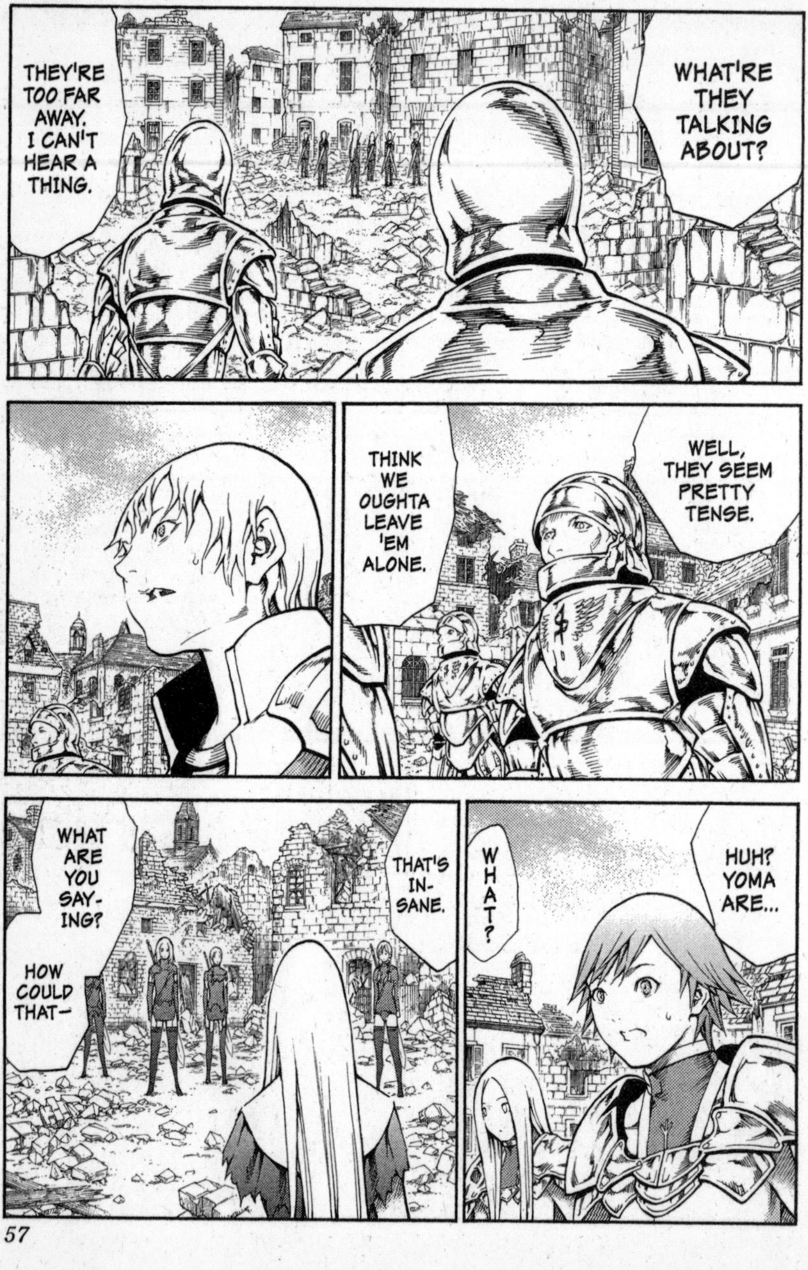
WHAT'RE THEY TALKING ABOUT?
THEY'RE TOO FAR AWAY. I CAN'T HEAR A THING.
WELL, THEY SEEM PRETTY TENSE.
THINK WE OUGHTA LEAVE 'EM ALONE.
HUH? YOMA ARE...
WHAT?
THAT'S IN-SANE.
WHAT ARE YOU SAY-ING?
HOW COULD THAT—

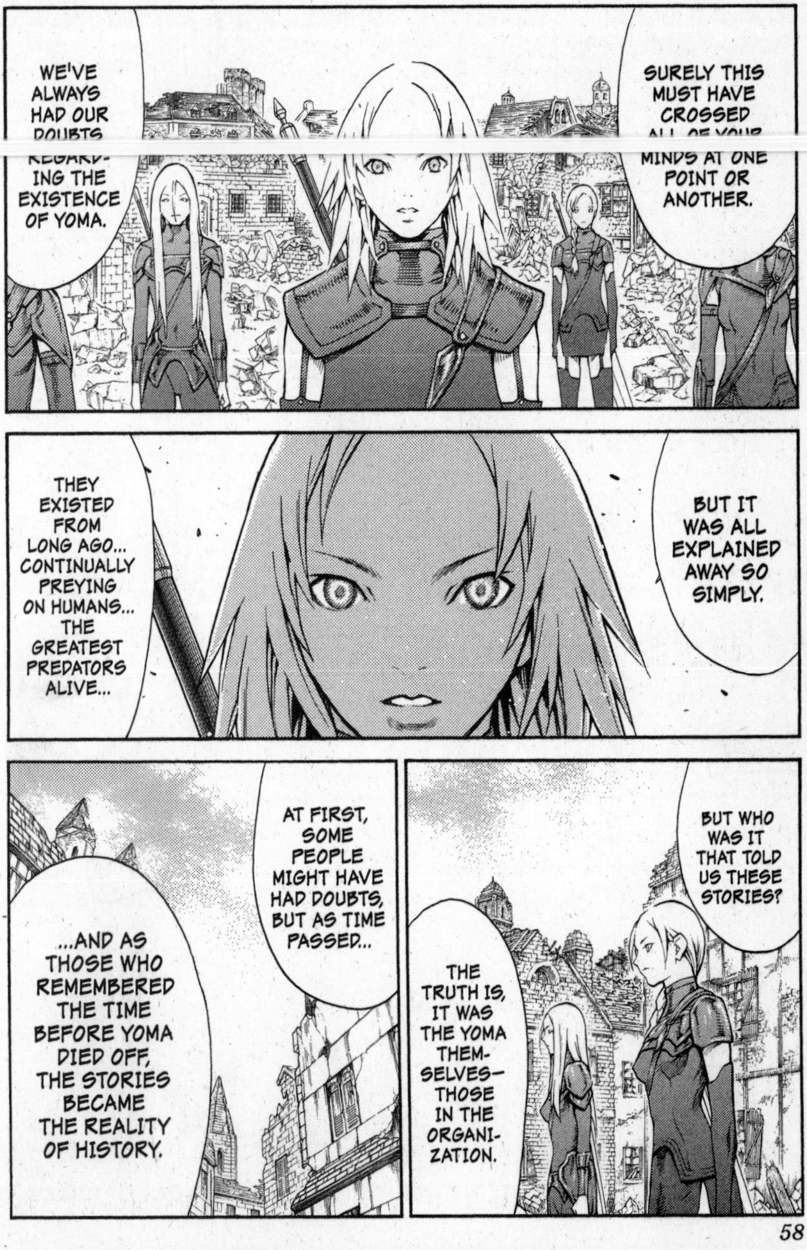
WE'VE ALWAYS HAD OUR DOUBTS REGARD-ING THE EXISTENCE OF YOMA.
SURELY THIS MUST HAVE CROSSED ALL OF YOUR MINDS AT ONE POINT OR ANOTHER.
THEY EXISTED FROM LONG AGO... CONTINUALLY PREYING ON HUMANS... THE GREATEST PREDATORS ALIVE...
BUT IT WAS ALL EXPLAINED AWAY SO SIMPLY.
AT FIRST, SOME PEOPLE MIGHT HAVE HAD DOUBTS, BUT AS TIME PASSED...
...AND AS THOSE WHO REMEMBERED THE TIME BEFORE YOMA DIED OFF, THE STORIES BECAME THE REALITY OF HISTORY.
BUT WHO WAS IT THAT TOLD US THESE STORIES?
THE TRUTH IS, IT WAS THE YOMA THEM-SELVES—THOSE IN THE ORGANI-ZATION.

READ THIS WAY

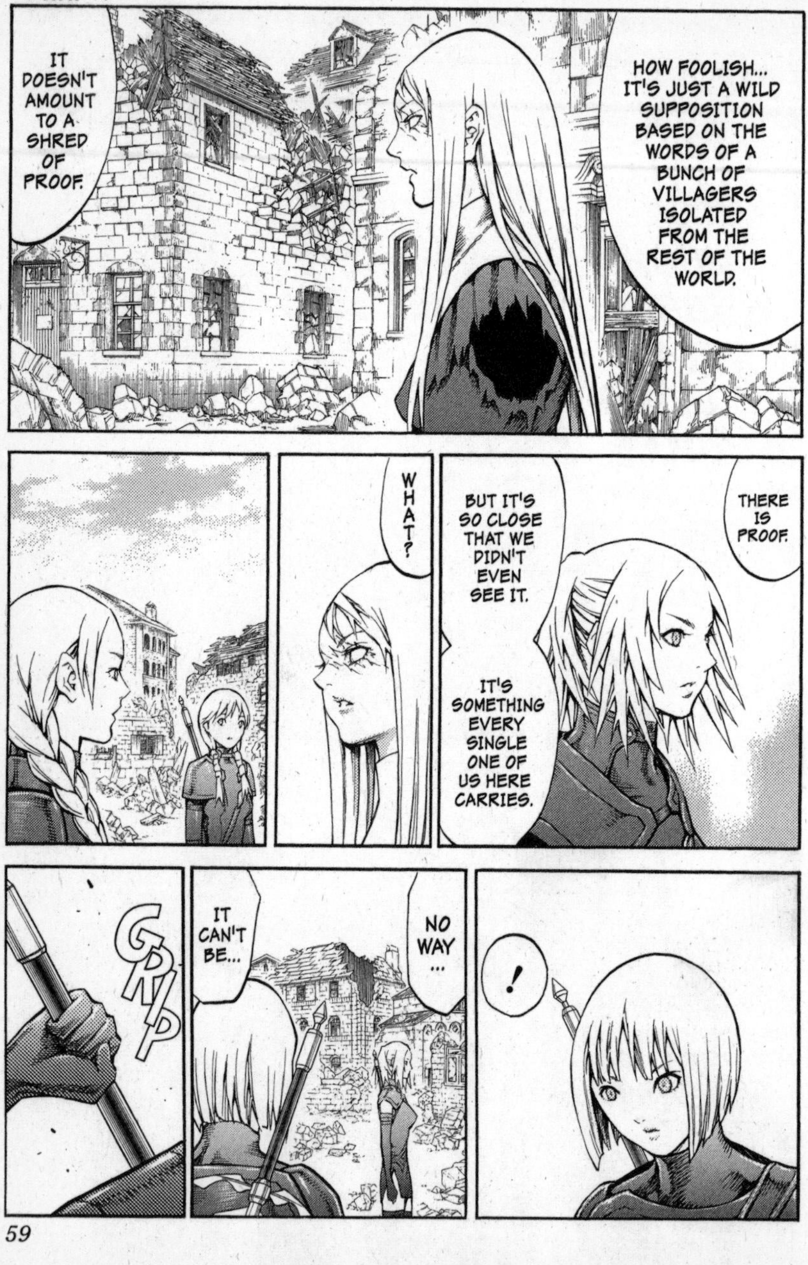
HOW FOOLISH... IT'S JUST A WILD SUPPOSITION BASED ON THE WORDS OF A BUNCH OF VILLAGERS ISOLATED FROM THE REST OF THE WORLD.
IT DOESN'T AMOUNT TO A SHRED OF PROOF.
THERE IS PROOF.
BUT IT'S SO CLOSE THAT WE DIDN'T EVEN SEE IT.
IT'S SOMETHING EVERY SINGLE ONE OF US HERE CARRIES.
WHAT?
!
NO WAY...
IT CAN'T BE...
GRIP

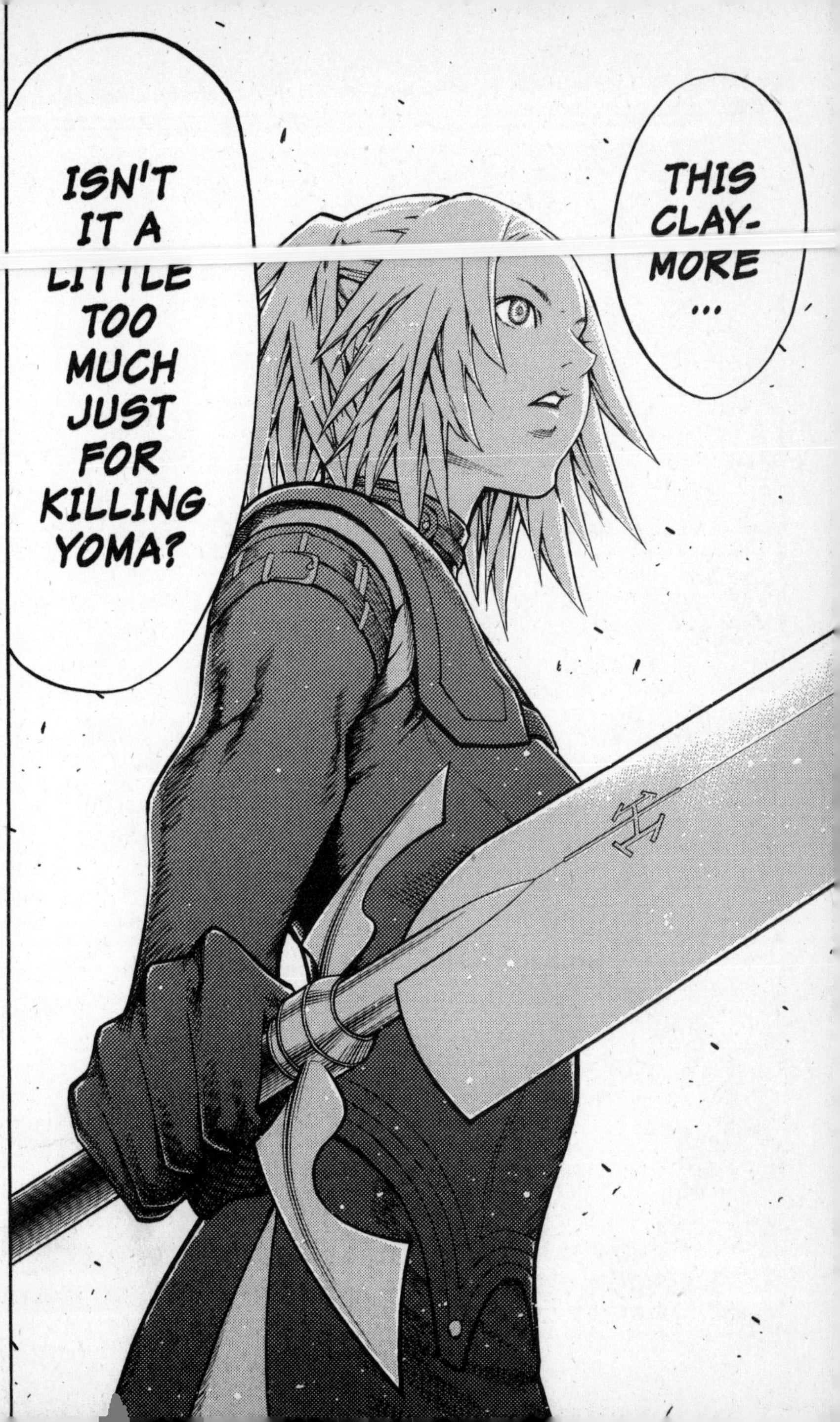
THIS CLAY-MORE...
ISN'T IT A LITTLE TOO MUCH JUST FOR KILLING YOMA?

READ THIS WAY

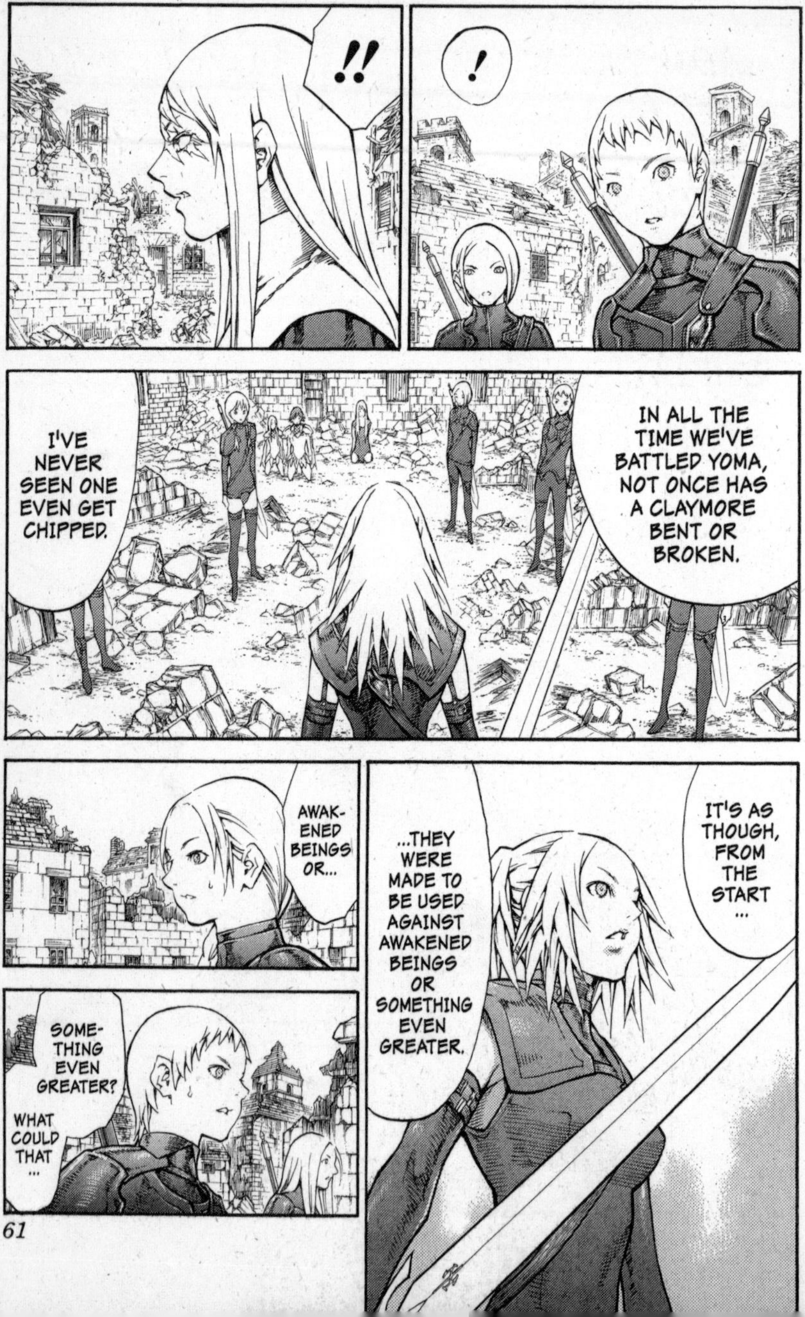
!
!!
IN ALL THE TIME WE'VE BATTLED YOMA, NOT ONCE HAS A CLAYMORE BENT OR BROKEN.
I'VE NEVER SEEN ONE EVEN GET CHIPPED.
IT'S AS THOUGH, FROM THE START ...
...THEY WERE MADE TO BE USED AGAINST AWAKENED BEINGS OR SOMETHING EVEN GREATER.
AWAKENED BEINGS OR...
SOMETHING EVEN GREATER?
WHAT COULD THAT ...

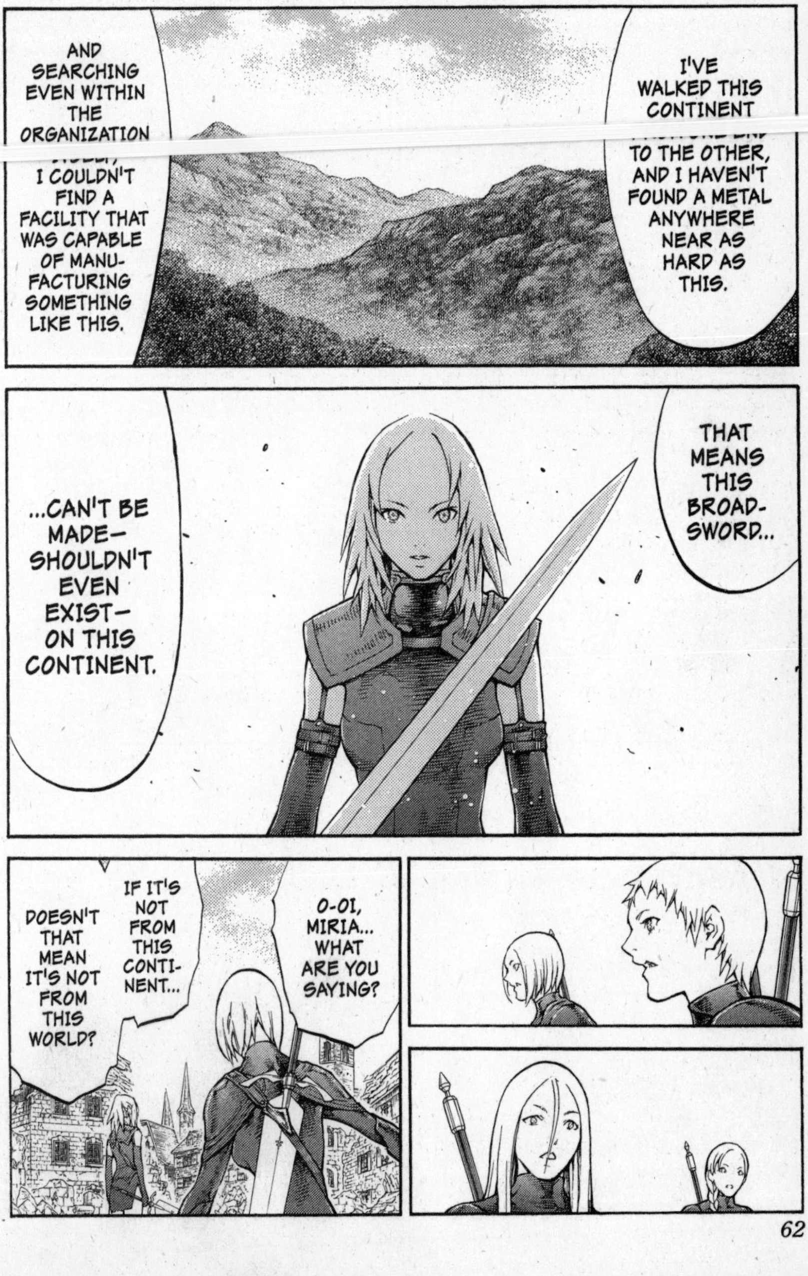
I'VE WALKED THIS CONTINENT
TO THE OTHER, AND I HAVEN'T FOUND A METAL ANYWHERE NEAR AS HARD AS THIS.
AND SEARCHING EVEN WITHIN THE ORGANIZATION
I COULDN'T FIND A FACILITY THAT WAS CAPABLE OF MANU-FACTURING SOMETHING LIKE THIS.
THAT MEANS THIS BROAD-SWORD...
...CAN'T BE MADE—SHOULDN'T EVEN EXIST—ON THIS CONTINENT.
O-OI, MIRIA... WHAT ARE YOU SAYING?
IF IT'S NOT FROM THIS CONTI-NENT...
DOESN'T THAT MEAN IT'S NOT FROM THIS WORLD?

READ THIS WAY

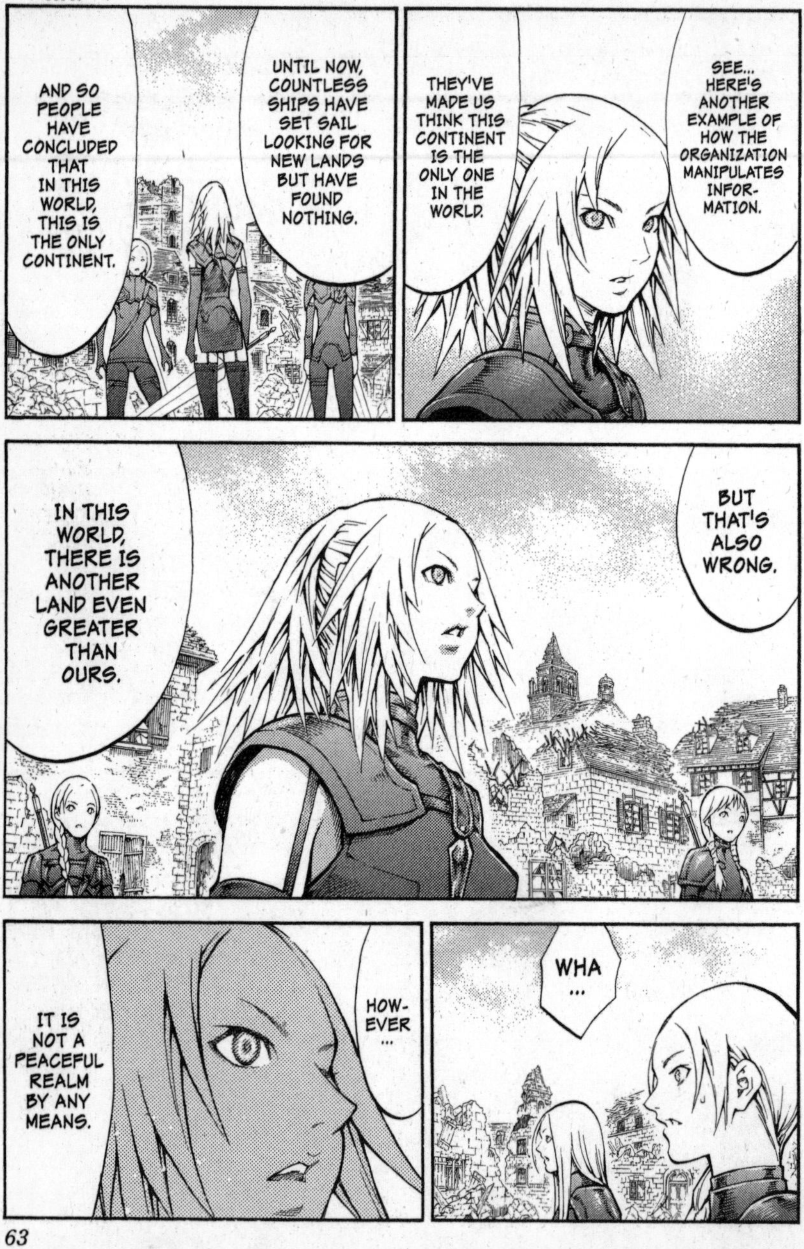
SEE... HERE'S ANOTHER EXAMPLE OF HOW THE ORGANIZATION MANIPULATES INFORMATION.
THEY'VE MADE US THINK THIS CONTINENT IS THE ONLY ONE IN THE WORLD.
UNTIL NOW, COUNTLESS SHIPS HAVE SET SAIL LOOKING FOR NEW LANDS BUT HAVE FOUND NOTHING.
AND SO PEOPLE HAVE CONCLUDED THAT IN THIS WORLD, THIS IS THE ONLY CONTINENT.
BUT THAT'S ALSO WRONG.
IN THIS WORLD, THERE IS ANOTHER LAND EVEN GREATER THAN OURS.
WHA ...
HOW-EVER ...
IT IS NOT A PEACEFUL REALM BY ANY MEANS.

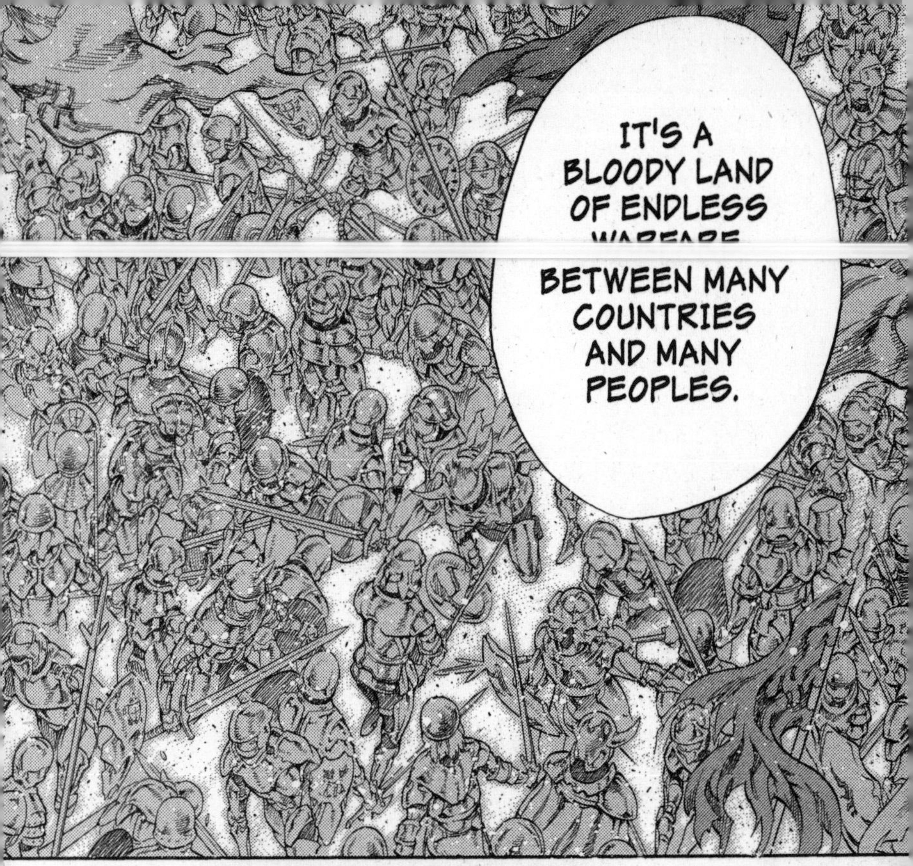
IT'S A BLOODY LAND OF ENDLESS
BETWEEN MANY COUNTRIES AND MANY PEOPLES.
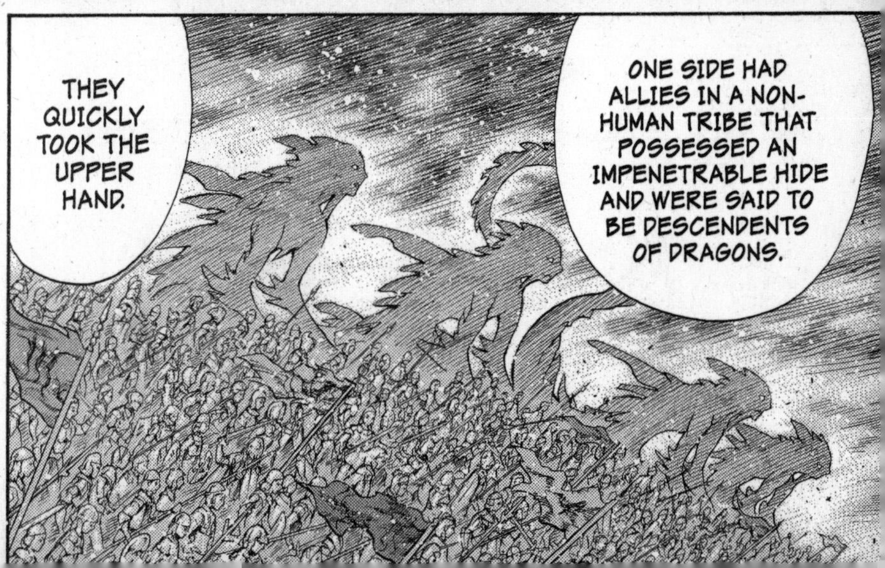
ONE SIDE HAD ALLIES IN A NON-HUMAN TRIBE THAT POSSESSED AN IMPENETRABLE HIDE AND WERE SAID TO BE DESCENDENTS OF DRAGONS.
THEY QUICKLY TOOK THE UPPER HAND.

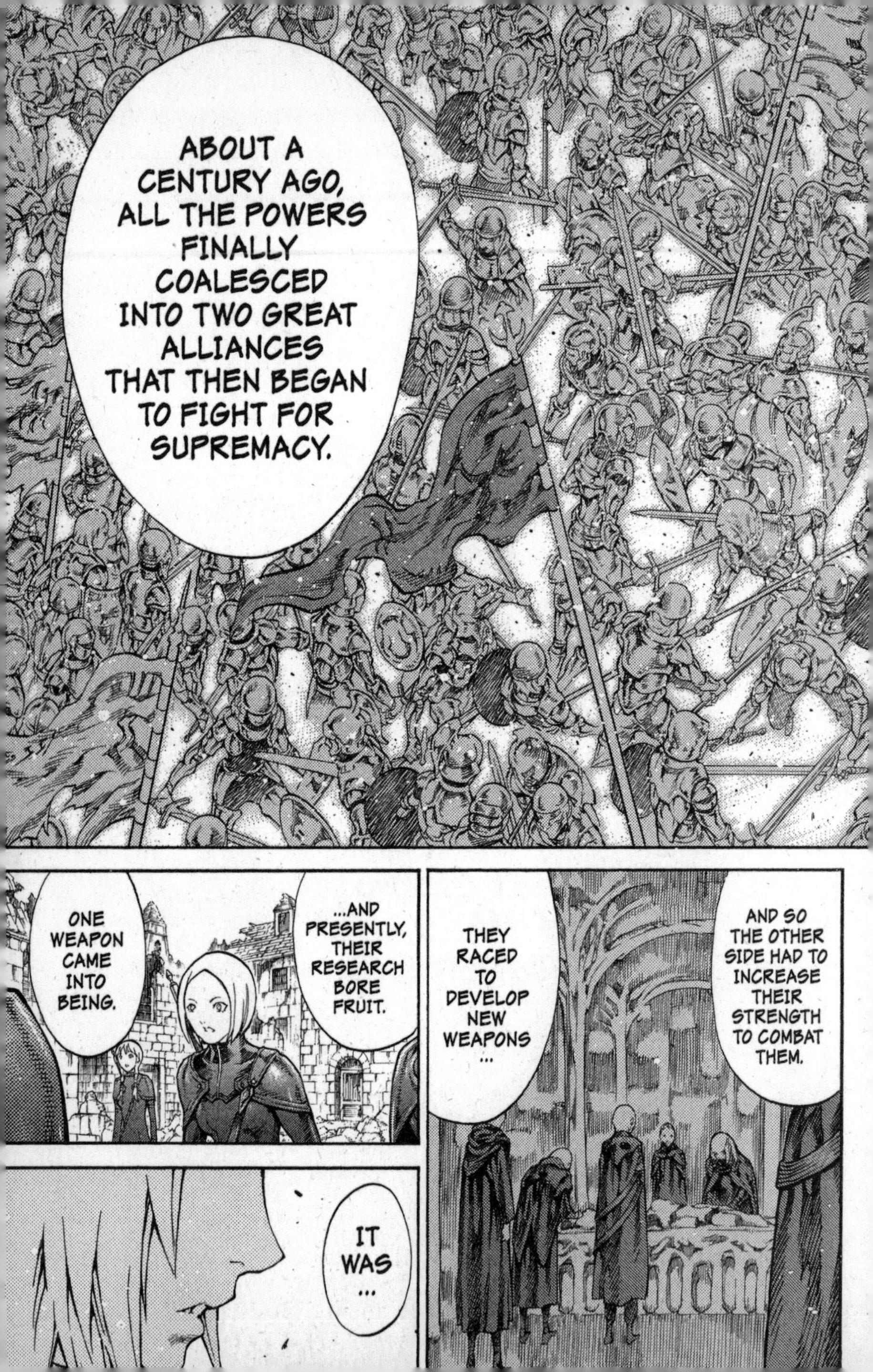
ABOUT A CENTURY AGO, ALL THE POWERS FINALLY COALESCED INTO TWO GREAT ALLIANCES THAT THEN BEGAN TO FIGHT FOR SUPREMACY.
AND SO THE OTHER SIDE HAD TO INCREASE THEIR STRENGTH TO COMBAT THEM.
THEY RACED TO DEVELOP NEW WEAPONS ...
...AND PRESENTLY, THEIR RESEARCH BORE FRUIT.
ONE WEAPON CAME INTO BEING.
IT WAS ...

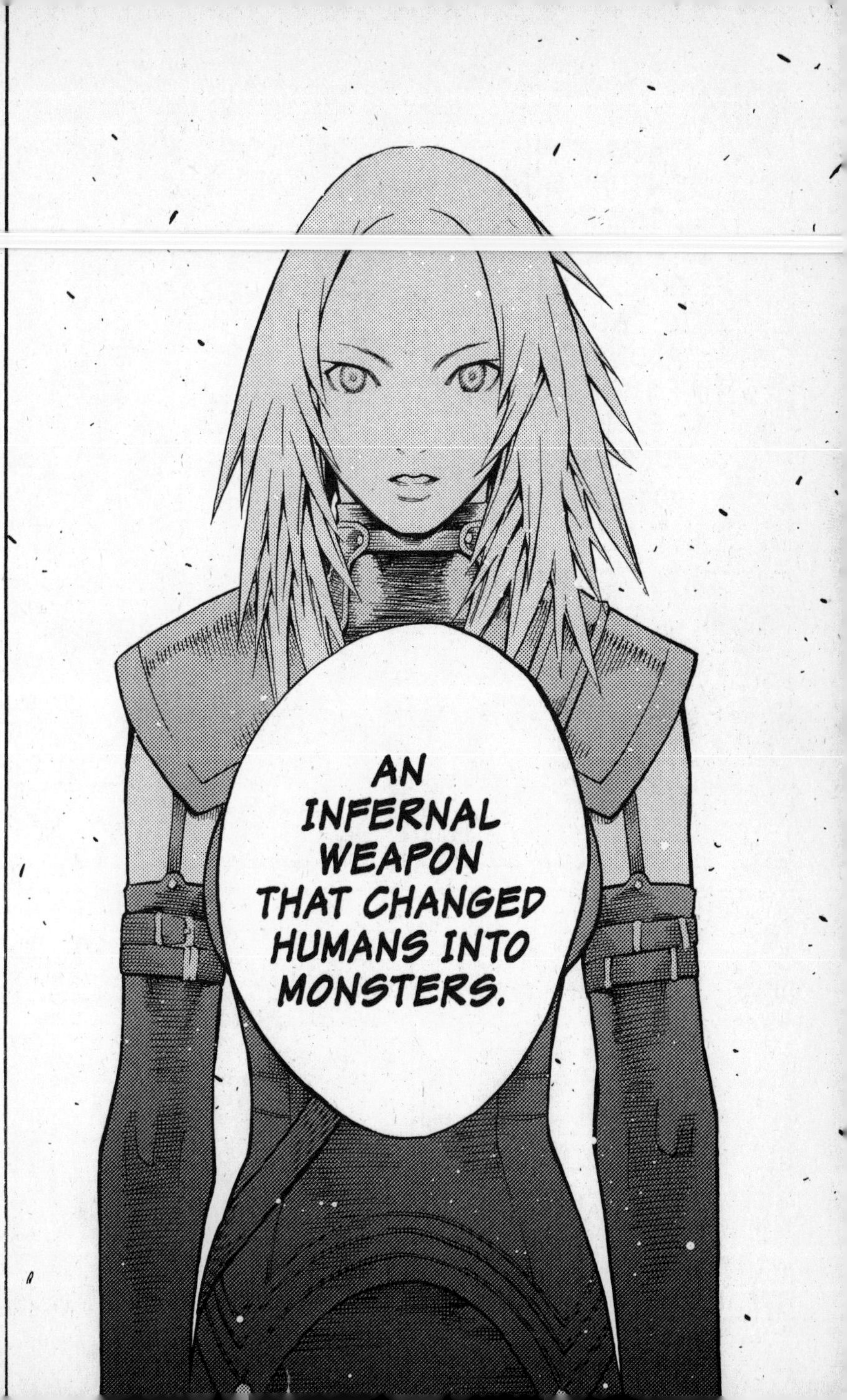
AN INFERNAL WEAPON THAT CHANGED HUMANS INTO MONSTERS.

READ THIS WAY

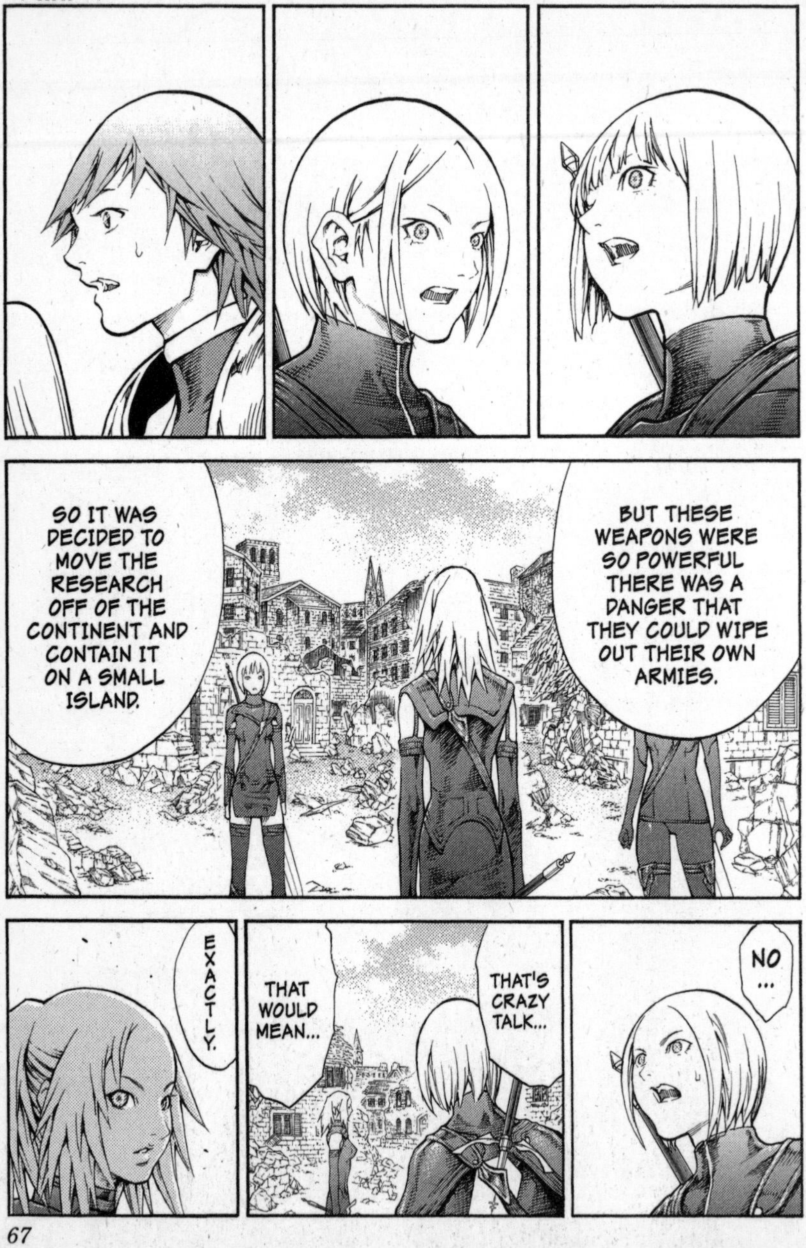

BUT THESE WEAPONS WERE SO POWERFUL THERE WAS A DANGER THAT THEY COULD WIPE OUT THEIR OWN ARMIES.
SO IT WAS DECIDED TO MOVE THE RESEARCH OFF OF THE CONTINENT AND CONTAIN IT ON A SMALL ISLAND.
NO...
THAT'S CRAZY TALK...
THAT WOULD MEAN...
EXACTLY.

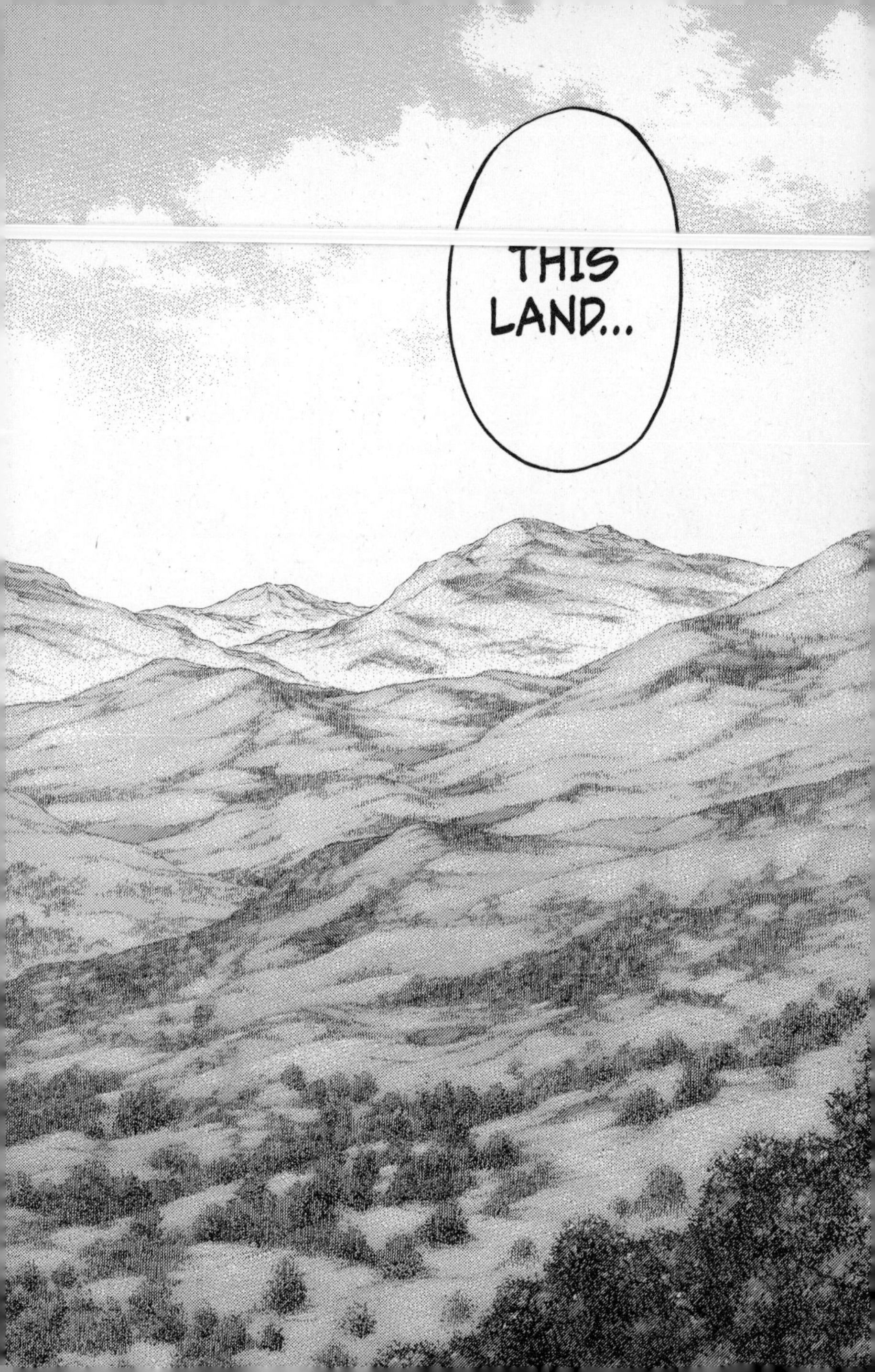
THIS LAND...

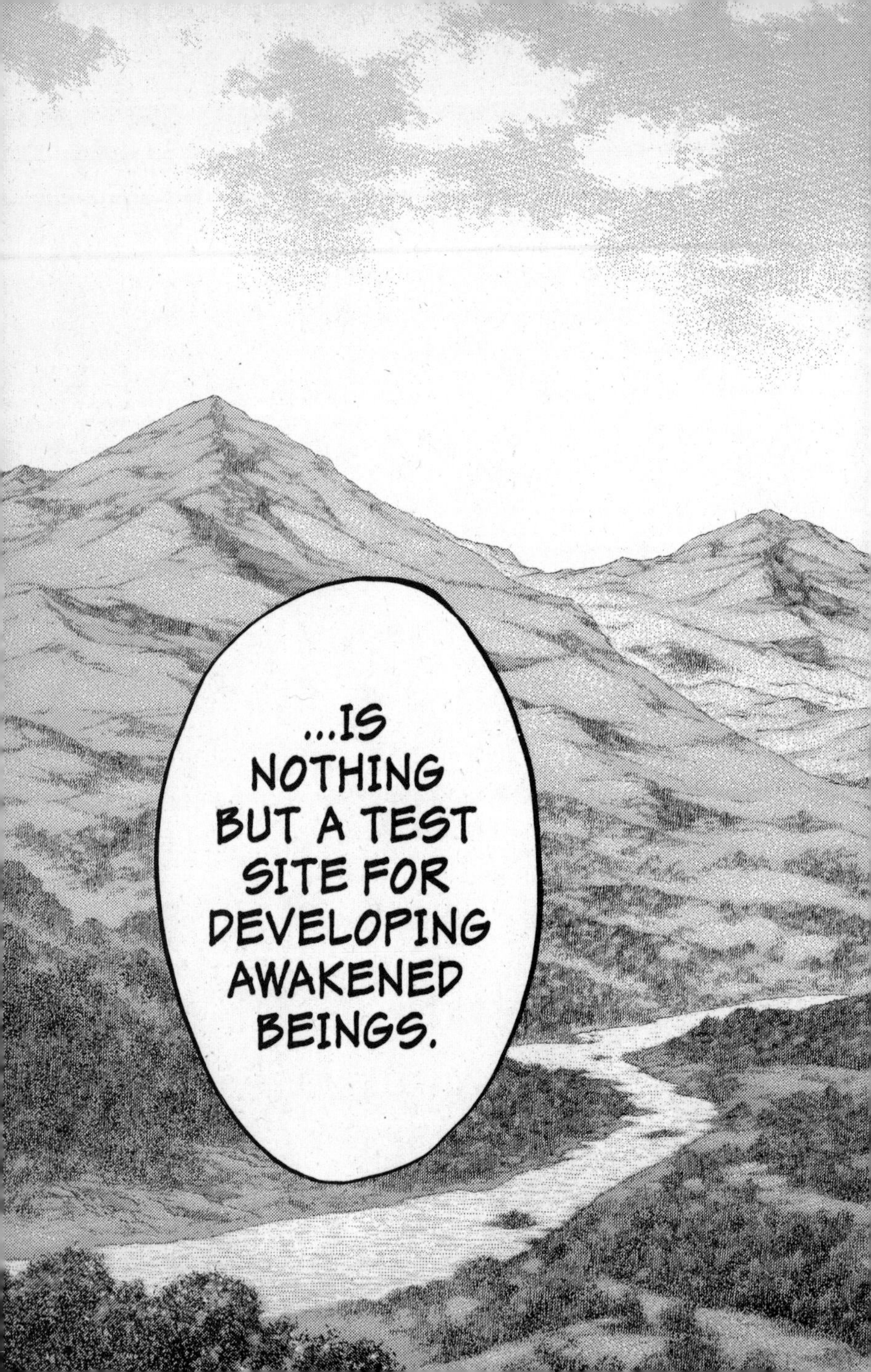
...IS NOTHING BUT A TEST SITE FOR DEVELOPING AWAKENED BEINGS.

クレイモア
Claymore

Scene 80: Genesis of War, Part 3

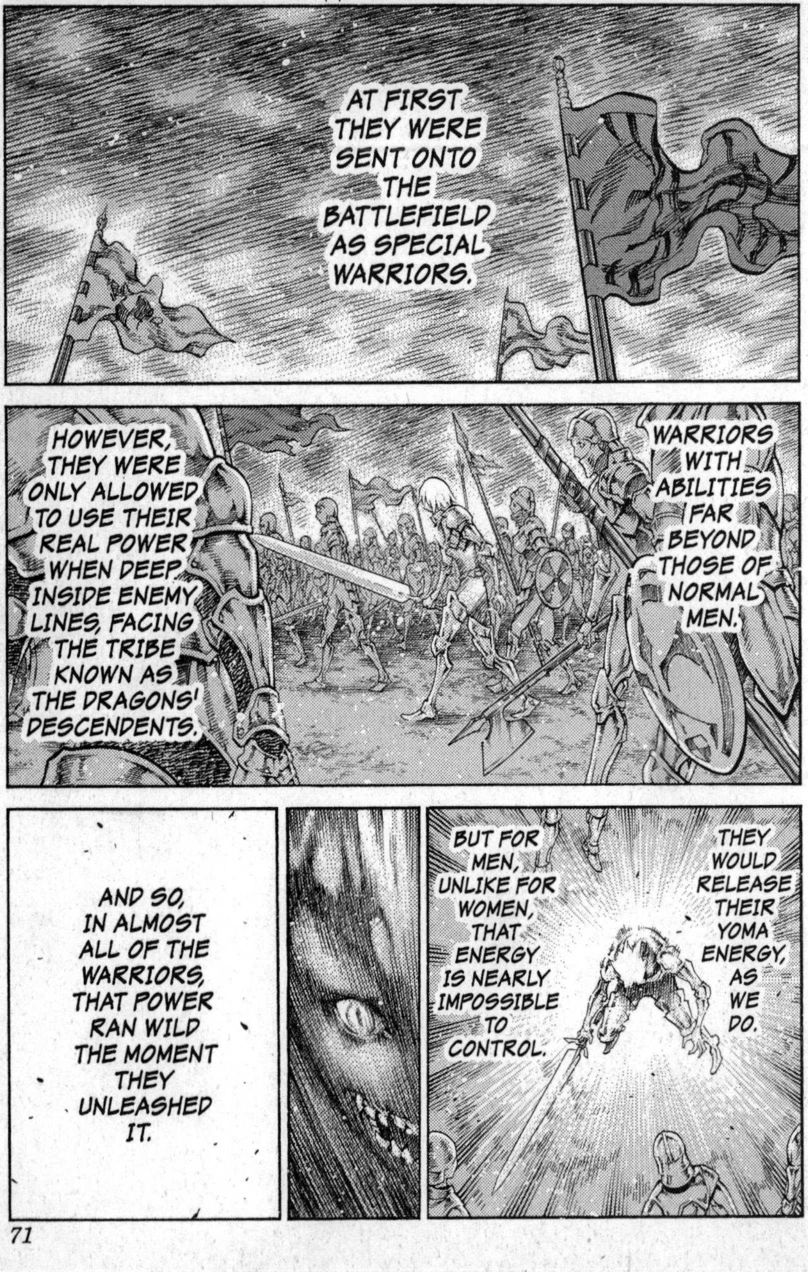
AT FIRST THEY WERE SENT ONTO THE BATTLEFIELD AS SPECIAL WARRIORS.
WARRIORS WITH ABILITIES FAR BEYOND THOSE OF NORMAL MEN.
HOWEVER, THEY WERE ONLY ALLOWED TO USE THEIR REAL POWER WHEN DEEP INSIDE ENEMY LINES, FACING THE TRIBE KNOWN AS THE DRAGONS' DESCENDENTS.
THEY WOULD RELEASE THEIR YOMA ENERGY, AS WE DO.
BUT FOR MEN, UNLIKE FOR WOMEN, THAT ENERGY IS NEARLY IMPOSSIBLE TO CONTROL.
AND SO, IN ALMOST ALL OF THE WARRIORS, THAT POWER RAN WILD THE MOMENT THEY UNLEASHED IT.

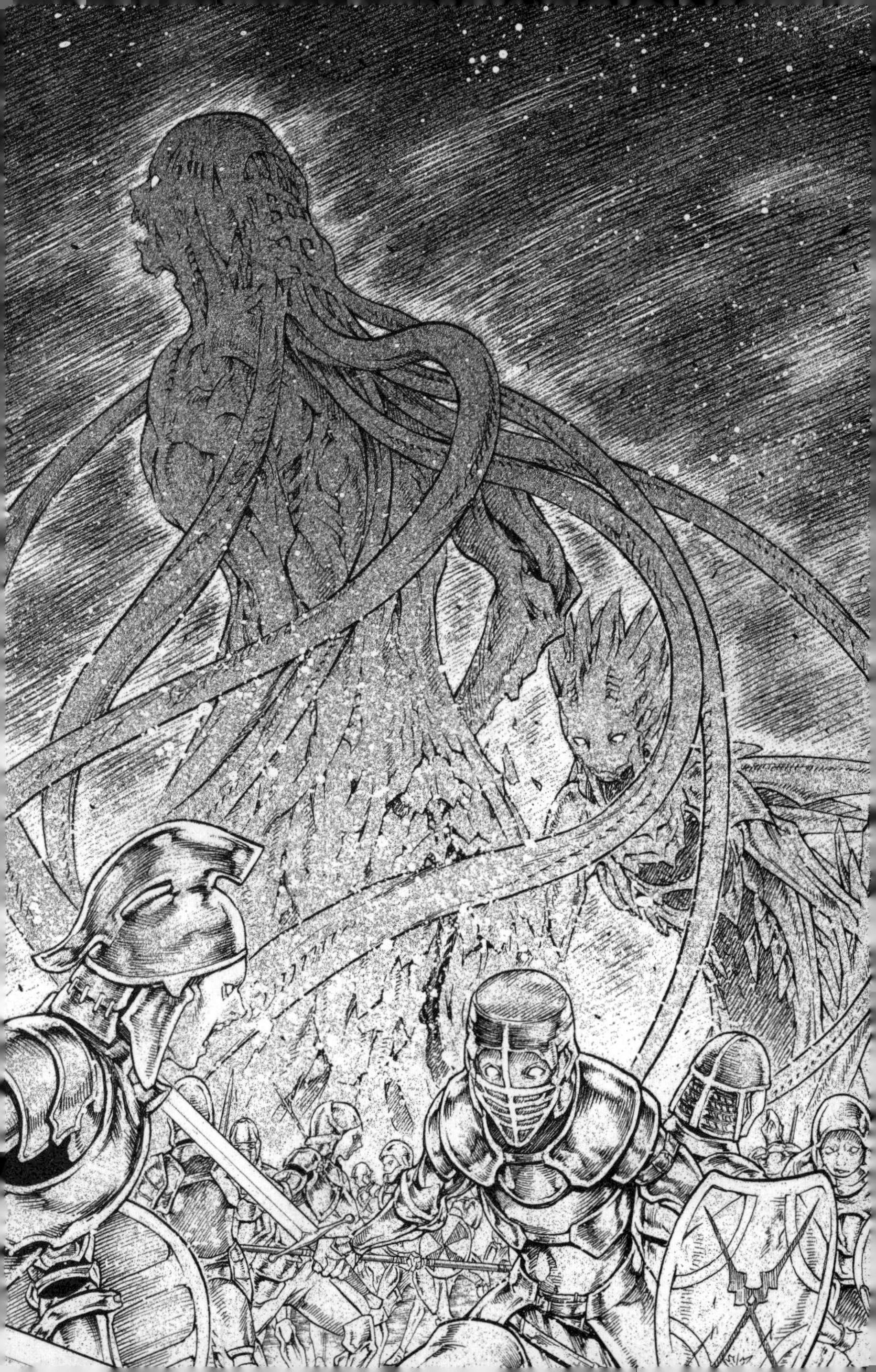

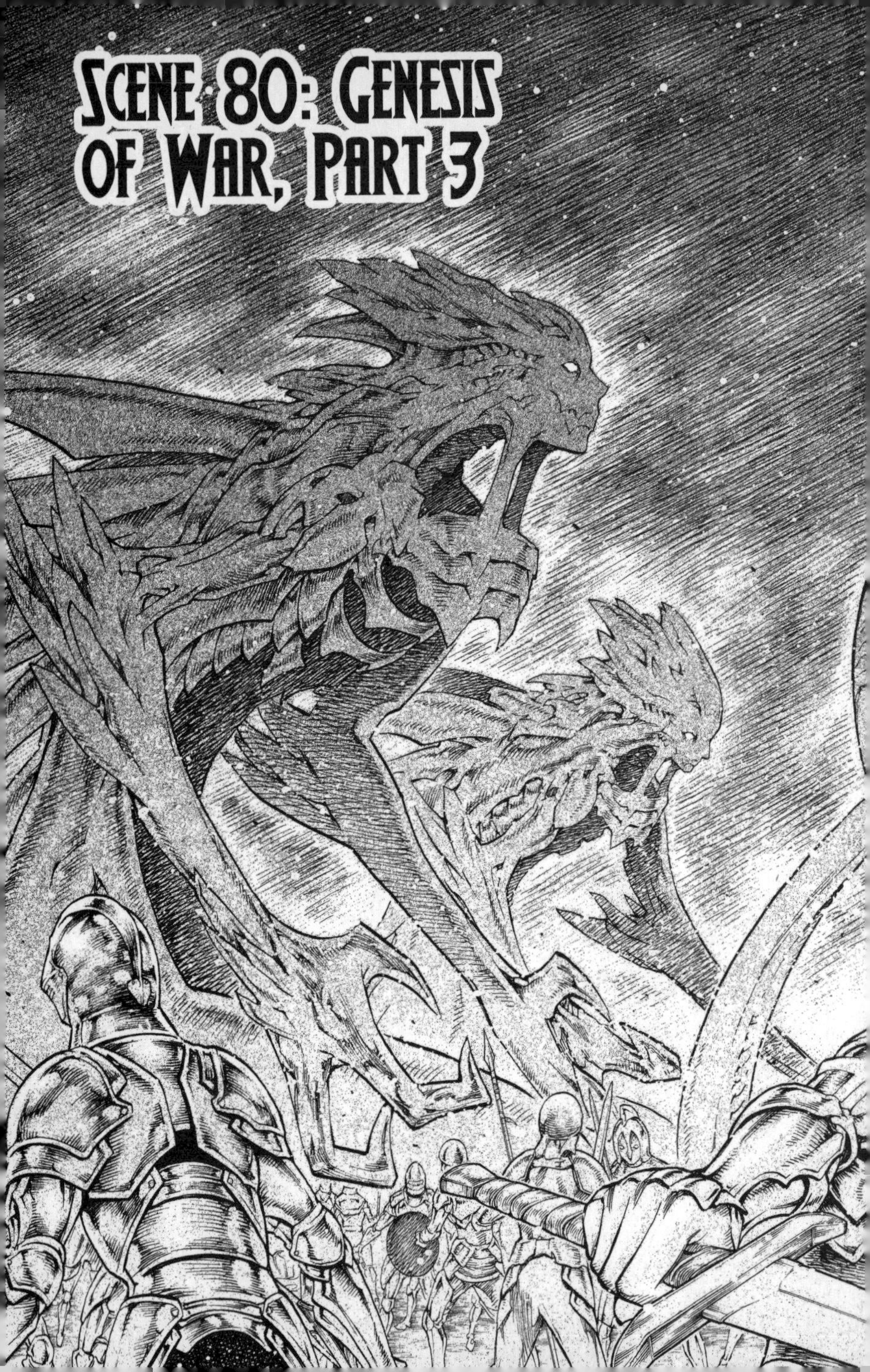
Scene 80: Genesis of War, Part 3

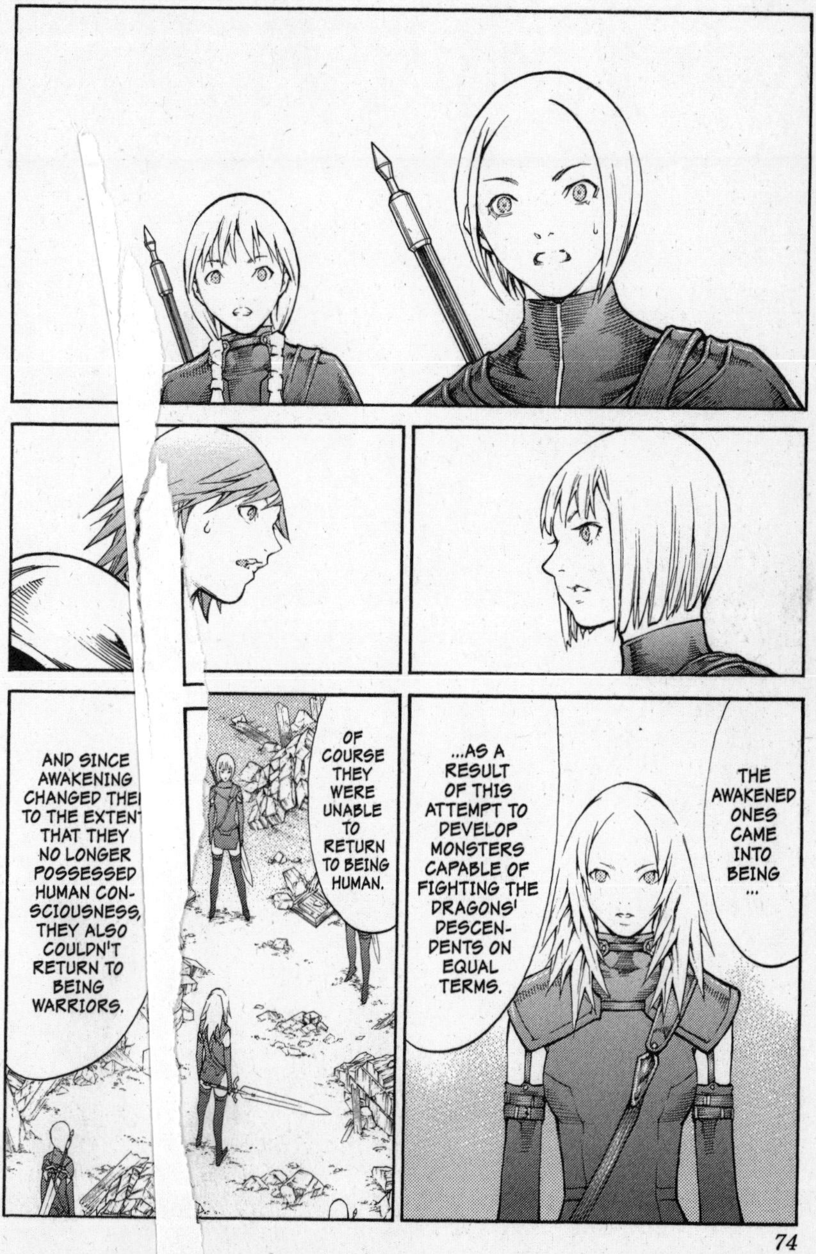
THE AWAKENED ONES CAME INTO BEING ...
...AS A RESULT OF THIS ATTEMPT TO DEVELOP MONSTERS CAPABLE OF FIGHTING THE DRAGONS' DESCEN-DENTS ON EQUAL TERMS.
OF COURSE THEY WERE UNABLE TO RETURN TO BEING HUMAN.
AND SINCE AWAKENING CHANGED THE TO THE EXTENT THAT THEY NO LONGER POSSESSED HUMAN CON-SCIOUSNESS, THEY ALSO COULDN'T RETURN TO BEING WARRIORS.

READ THIS WAY

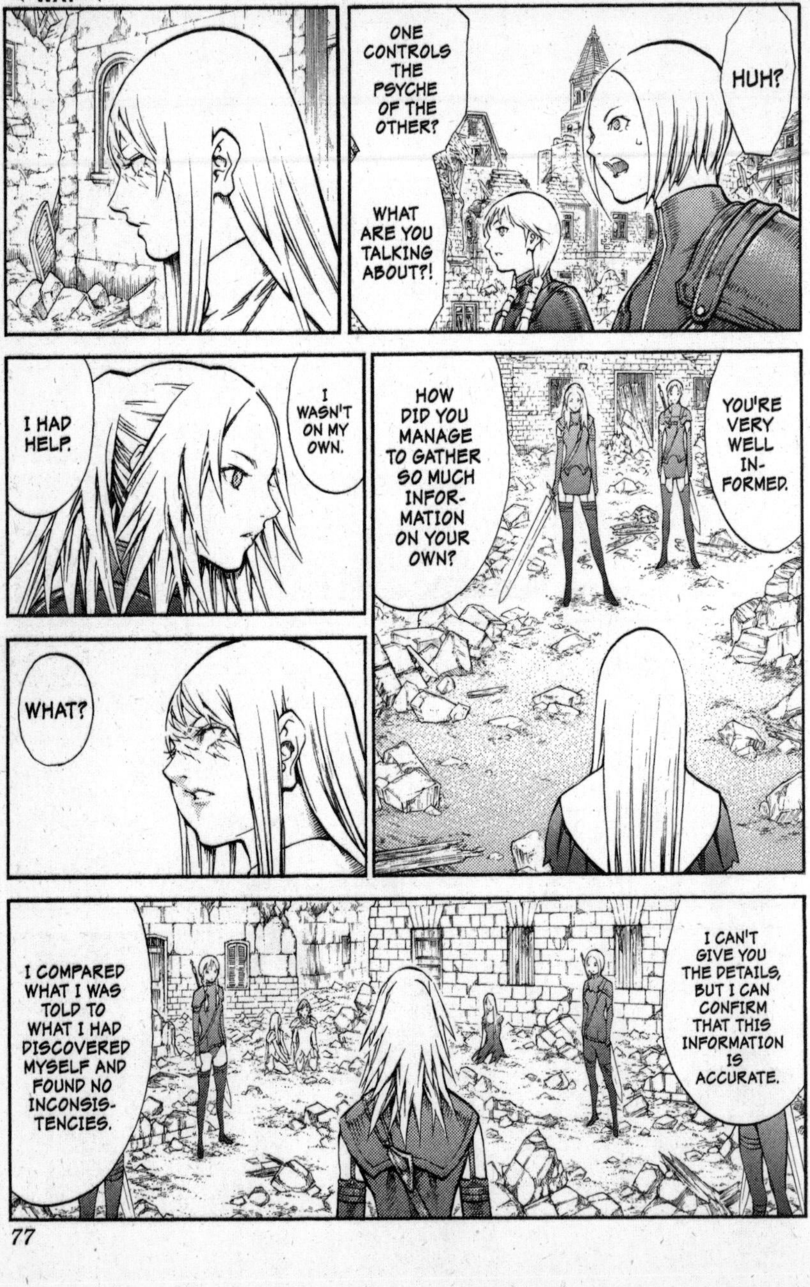
HUH?
ONE CONTROLS THE PSYCHE OF THE OTHER?
WHAT ARE YOU TALKING ABOUT?!
YOU'RE VERY WELL IN-FORMED.
HOW DID YOU MANAGE TO GATHER SO MUCH INFOR-MATION ON YOUR OWN?
I WASN'T ON MY OWN.
I HAD HELP.
WHAT?
I CAN'T GIVE YOU THE DETAILS, BUT I CAN CONFIRM THAT THIS INFORMATION IS ACCURATE.
I COMPARED WHAT I WAS TOLD TO WHAT I HAD DISCOVERED MYSELF AND FOUND NO INCONSIS-TENCIES.

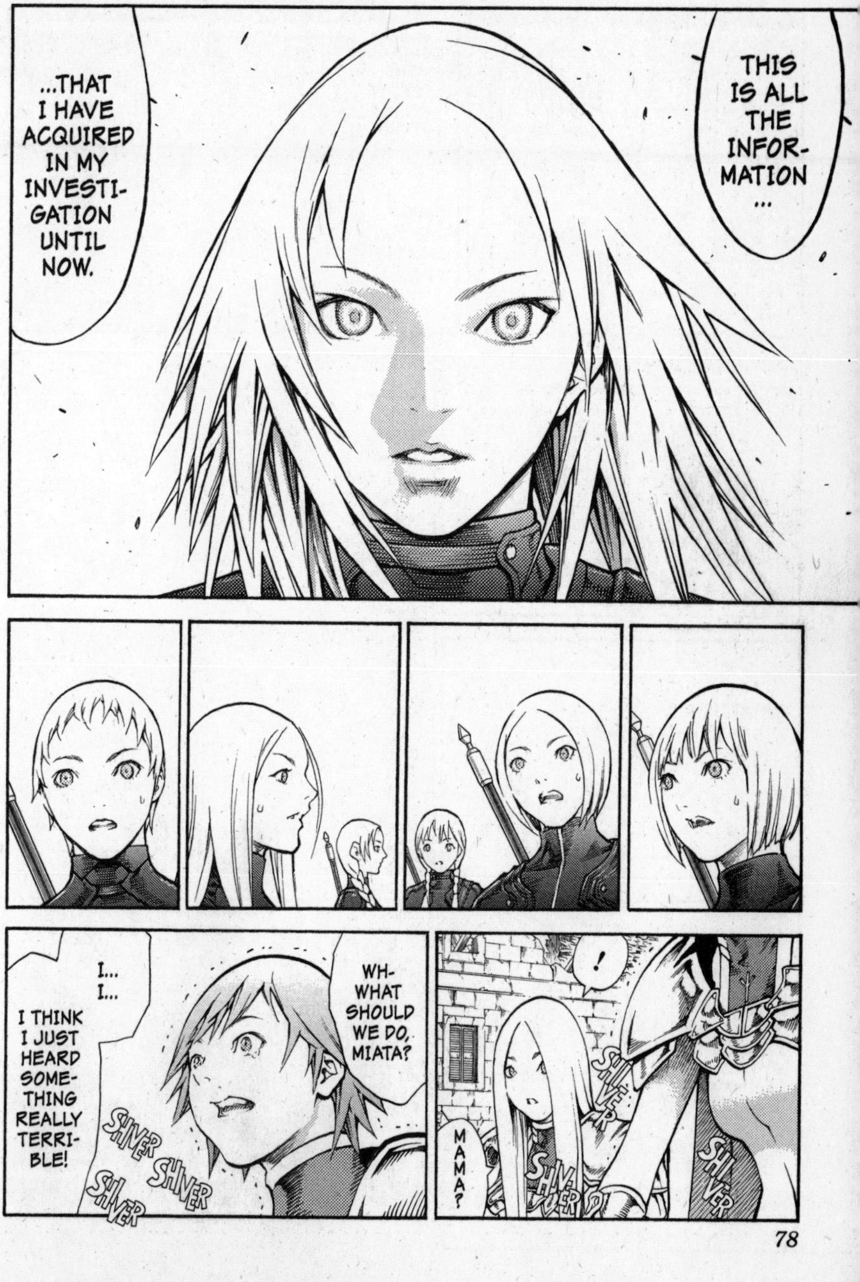

THIS IS ALL THE INFORMATION...
...THAT I HAVE ACQUIRED IN MY INVESTIGATION UNTIL NOW.
!
SHIVER
SHIVER
MAMA?
SHIVER
WH-WHAT SHOULD WE DO, MIATA?
I... I...
I THINK I JUST HEARD SOMETHING REALLY TERRIBLE!
SHIVER
SHIVER
SHIVER

READ THIS WAY

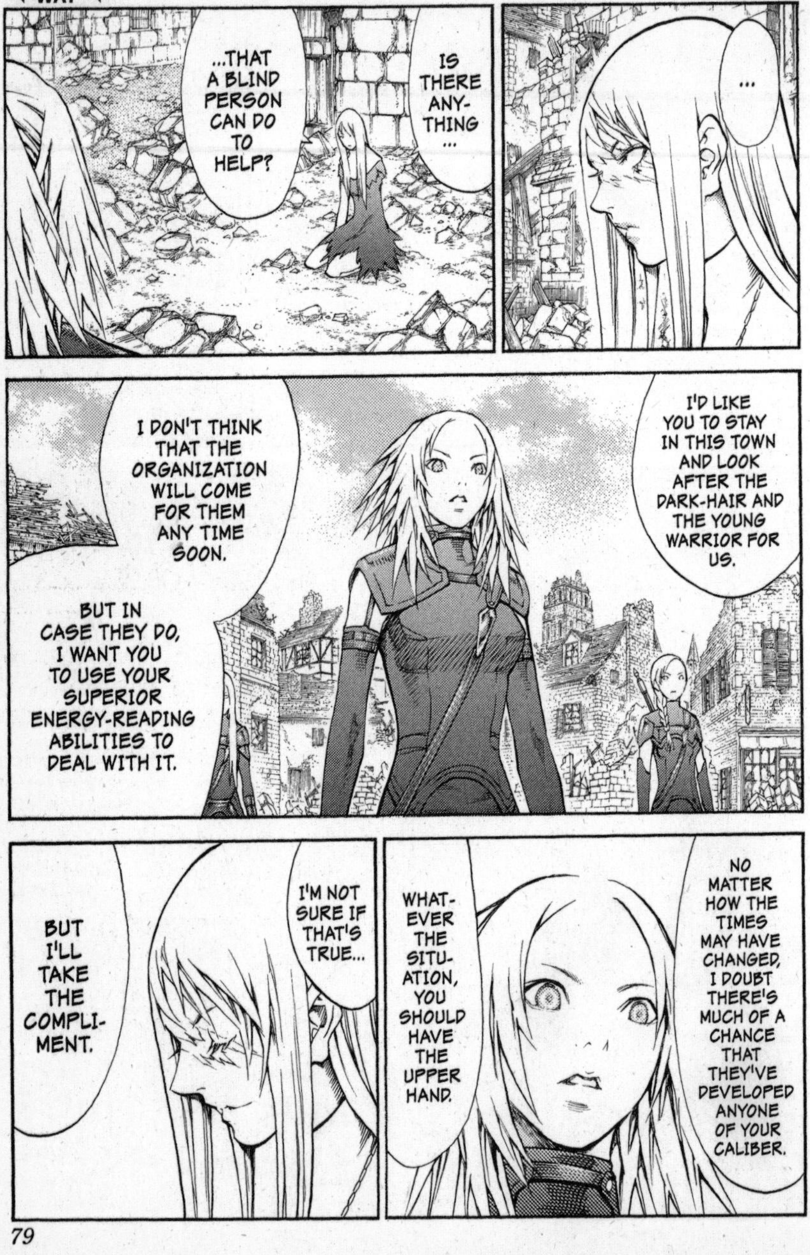
...
IS THERE ANYTHING...
...THAT A BLIND PERSON CAN DO TO HELP?
I'D LIKE YOU TO STAY IN THIS TOWN AND LOOK AFTER THE DARK-HAIR AND THE YOUNG WARRIOR FOR US.
I DON'T THINK THAT THE ORGANIZATION WILL COME FOR THEM ANY TIME SOON.
BUT IN CASE THEY DO, I WANT YOU TO USE YOUR SUPERIOR ENERGY-READING ABILITIES TO DEAL WITH IT.
NO MATTER HOW THE TIMES MAY HAVE CHANGED, I DOUBT THERE'S MUCH OF A CHANCE THAT THEY'VE DEVELOPED ANYONE OF YOUR CALIBER.
WHATEVER THE SITUATION, YOU SHOULD HAVE THE UPPER HAND.
I'M NOT SURE IF THAT'S TRUE...
BUT I'LL TAKE THE COMPLIMENT.

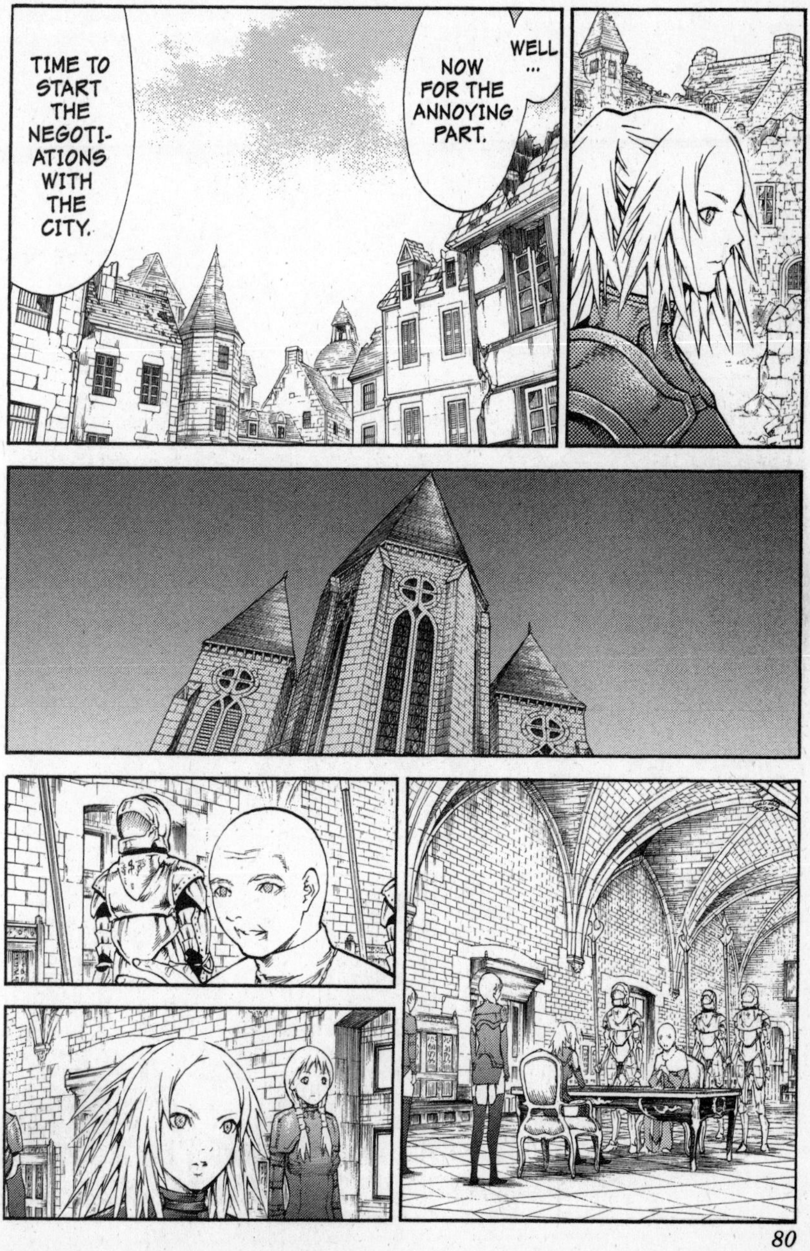
WELL ...
NOW FOR THE ANNOYING PART.
TIME TO START THE NEGOTI-ATIONS WITH THE CITY.

READ THIS WAY

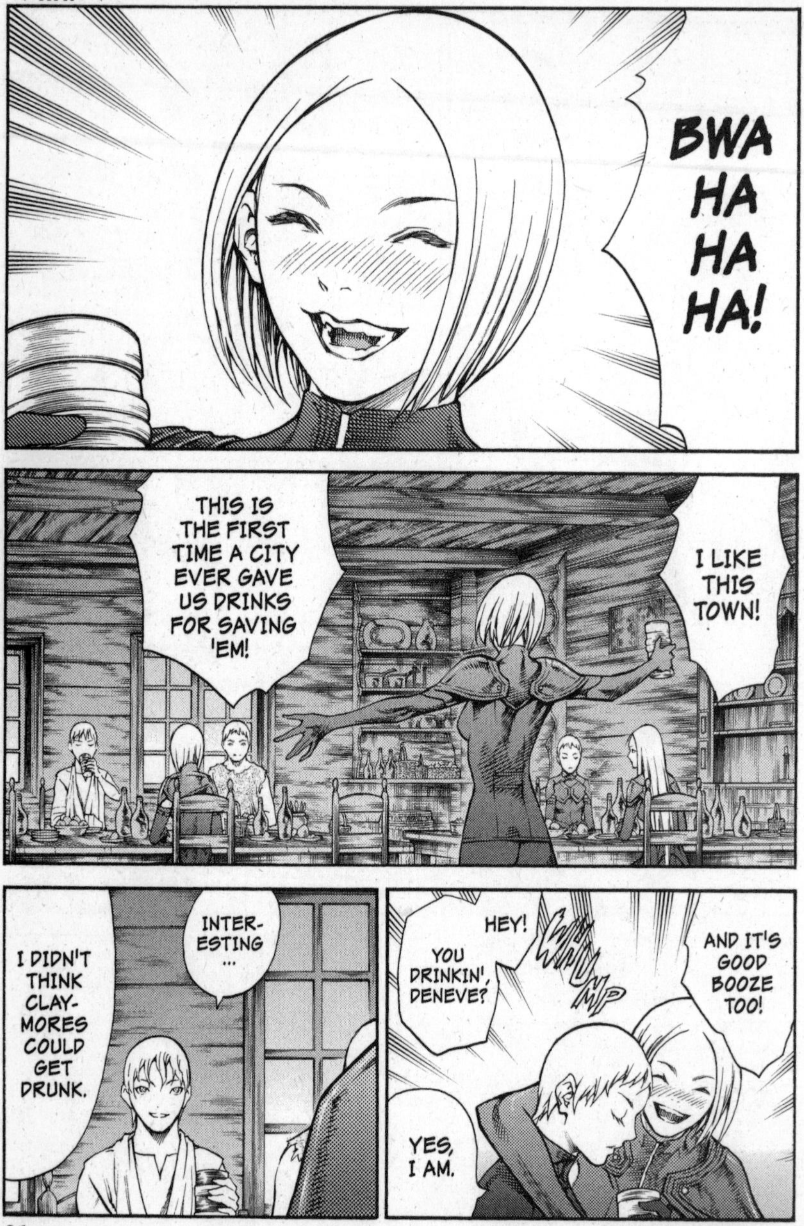
BWA HA HA HA!
THIS IS THE FIRST TIME A CITY EVER GAVE US DRINKS FOR SAVING 'EM!
I LIKE THIS TOWN!
AND IT'S GOOD BOOZE TOO!
HEY!
WHUMP
YOU DRINKIN', DENEVE?
YES, I AM.
INTER-ESTING ...
I DIDN'T THINK CLAY-MORES COULD GET DRUNK.

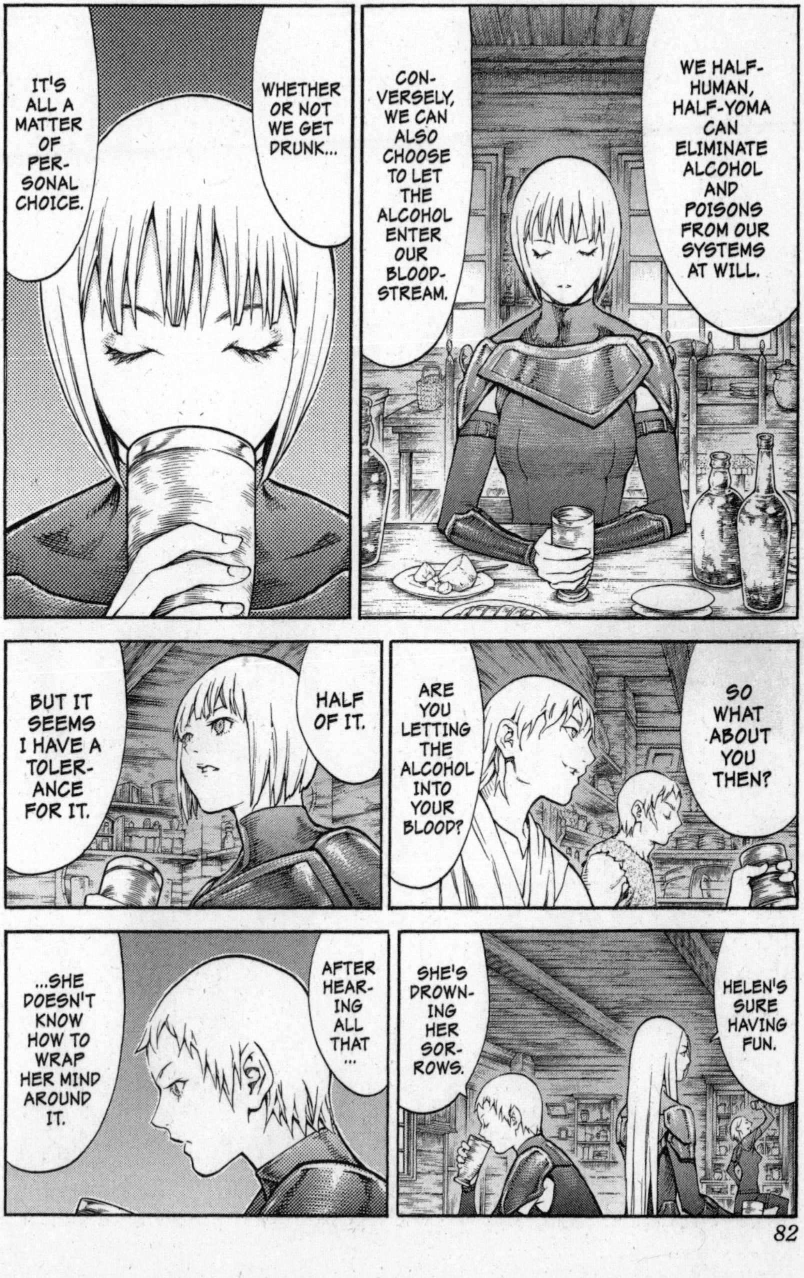
WE HALF-HUMAN, HALF-YOMA CAN ELIMINATE ALCOHOL AND POISONS FROM OUR SYSTEMS AT WILL.
CONVERSELY, WE CAN ALSO CHOOSE TO LET THE ALCOHOL ENTER OUR BLOODSTREAM.
WHETHER OR NOT WE GET DRUNK...
IT'S ALL A MATTER OF PERSONAL CHOICE.
SO WHAT ABOUT YOU THEN?
ARE YOU LETTING THE ALCOHOL INTO YOUR BLOOD?
HALF OF IT.
BUT IT SEEMS I HAVE A TOLERANCE FOR IT.
HELEN'S SURE HAVING FUN.
SHE'S DROWNING HER SORROWS.
AFTER HEARING ALL THAT ...
...SHE DOESN'T KNOW HOW TO WRAP HER MIND AROUND IT.

READ THIS WAY

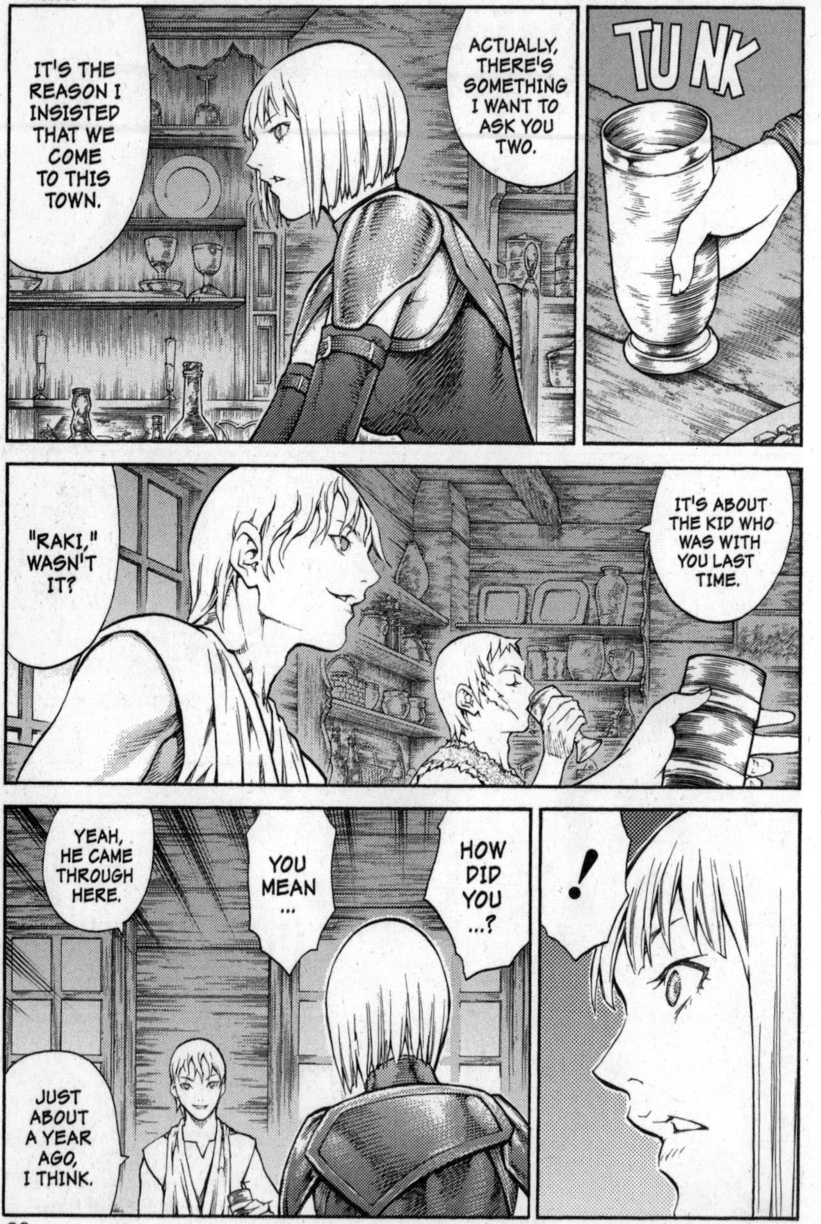
TUNK
ACTUALLY, THERE'S SOMETHING I WANT TO ASK YOU TWO.
IT'S THE REASON I INSISTED THAT WE COME TO THIS TOWN.
IT'S ABOUT THE KID WHO WAS WITH YOU LAST TIME.
"RAKI," WASN'T IT?
!
HOW DID YOU ...?
YOU MEAN ...
YEAH, HE CAME THROUGH HERE.
JUST ABOUT A YEAR AGO, I THINK.

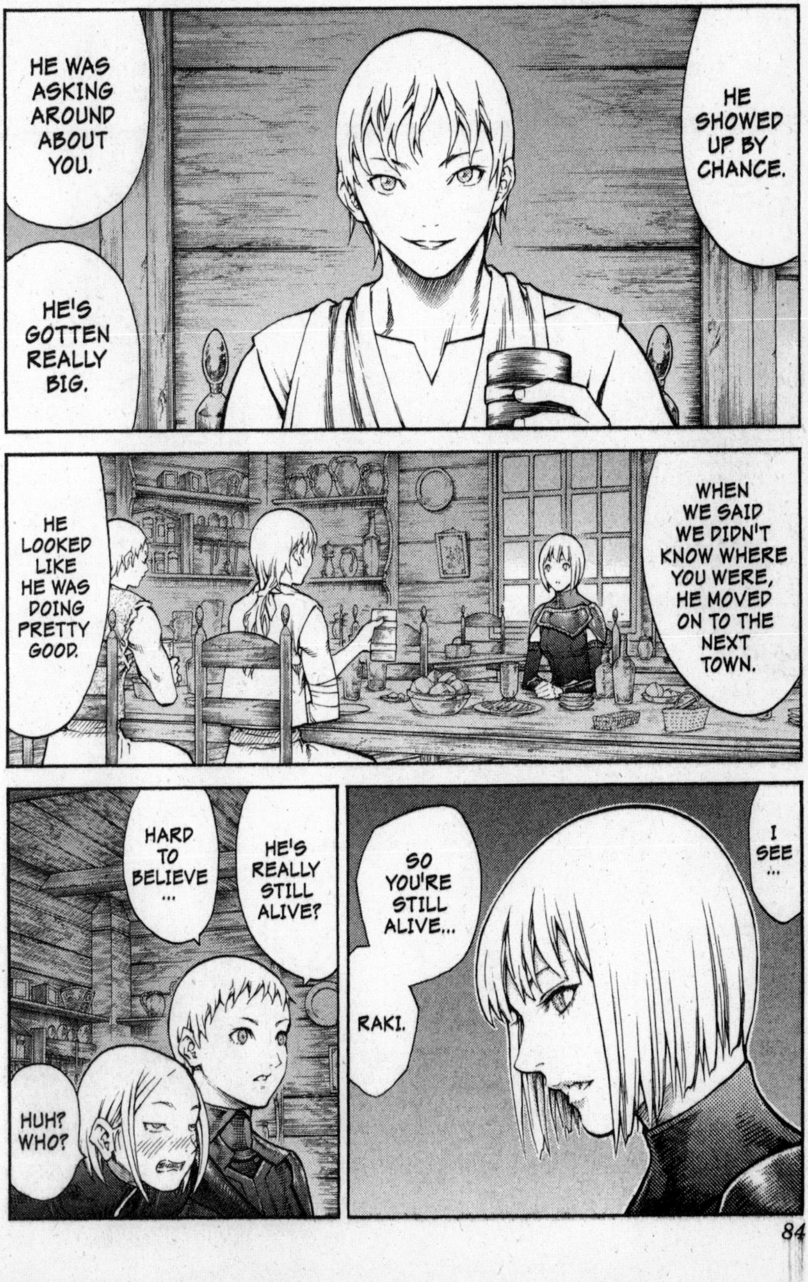
HE SHOWED UP BY CHANCE.
HE WAS ASKING AROUND ABOUT YOU.
HE'S GOTTEN REALLY BIG.
WHEN WE SAID WE DIDN'T KNOW WHERE YOU WERE, HE MOVED ON TO THE NEXT TOWN.
HE LOOKED LIKE HE WAS DOING PRETTY GOOD.
I SEE ...
SO YOU'RE STILL ALIVE...
RAKI.
HE'S REALLY STILL ALIVE?
HARD TO BELIEVE ...
HUH? WHO?

READ THIS WAY

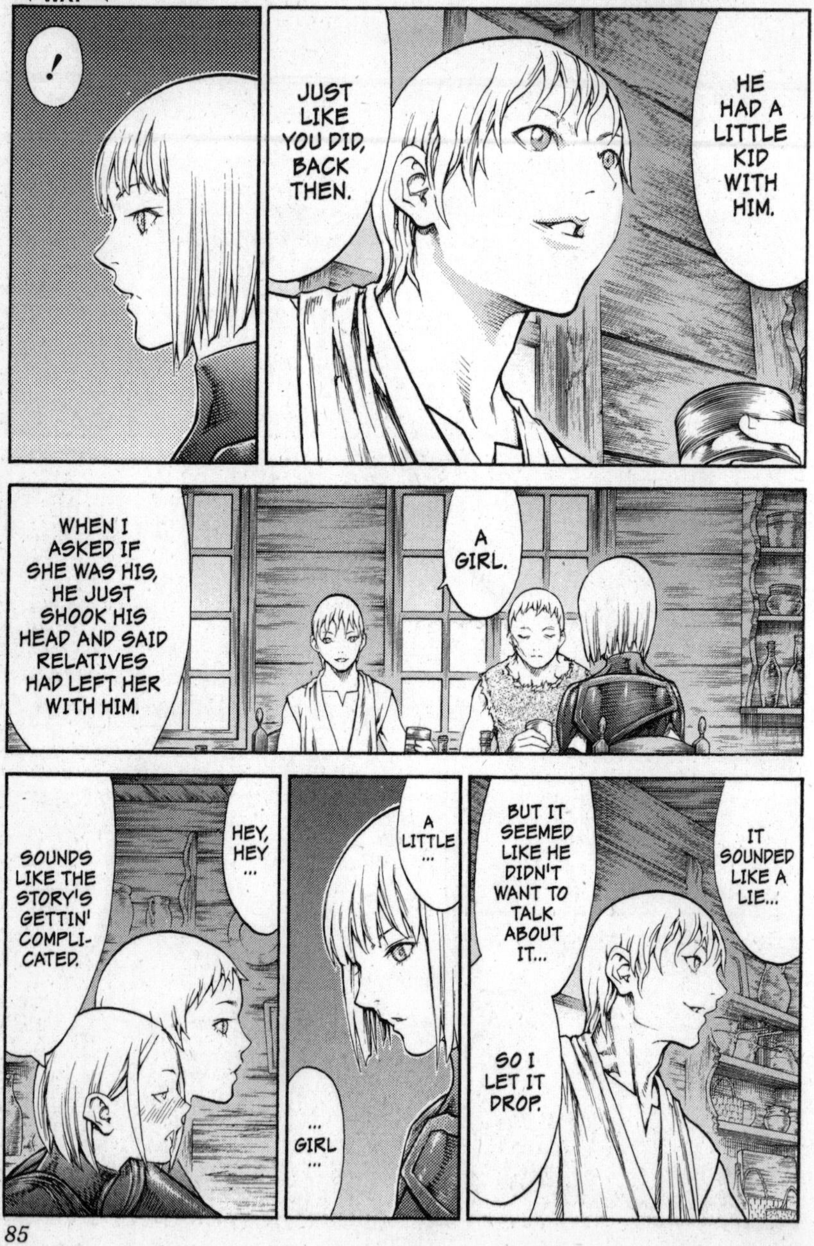
HE HAD A LITTLE KID WITH HIM.
JUST LIKE YOU DID, BACK THEN.
!
A GIRL.
WHEN I ASKED IF SHE WAS HIS, HE JUST SHOOK HIS HEAD AND SAID RELATIVES HAD LEFT HER WITH HIM.
IT SOUNDED LIKE A LIE...
BUT IT SEEMED LIKE HE DIDN'T WANT TO TALK ABOUT IT...
SO I LET IT DROP.
A LITTLE ...
... GIRL ...
HEY, HEY ...
SOUNDS LIKE THE STORY'S GETTIN' COMPLICATED.

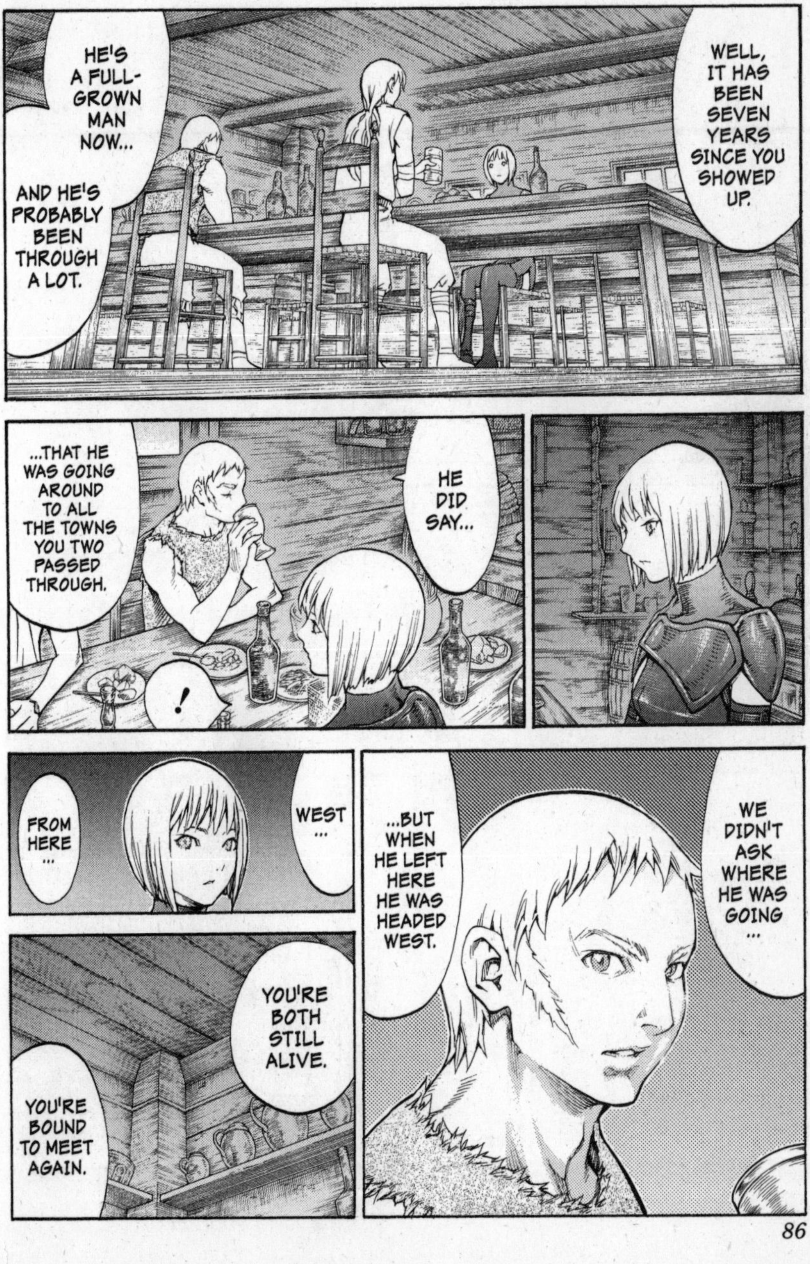
WELL, IT HAS BEEN SEVEN YEARS SINCE YOU SHOWED UP.
HE'S A FULL-GROWN MAN NOW...
AND HE'S PROBABLY BEEN THROUGH A LOT.
HE DID SAY...
...THAT HE WAS GOING AROUND TO ALL THE TOWNS YOU TWO PASSED THROUGH.
!
WE DIDN'T ASK WHERE HE WAS GOING...
...BUT WHEN HE LEFT HERE HE WAS HEADED WEST.
WEST...
FROM HERE...
YOU'RE BOTH STILL ALIVE.
YOU'RE BOUND TO MEET AGAIN.

READ THIS WAY

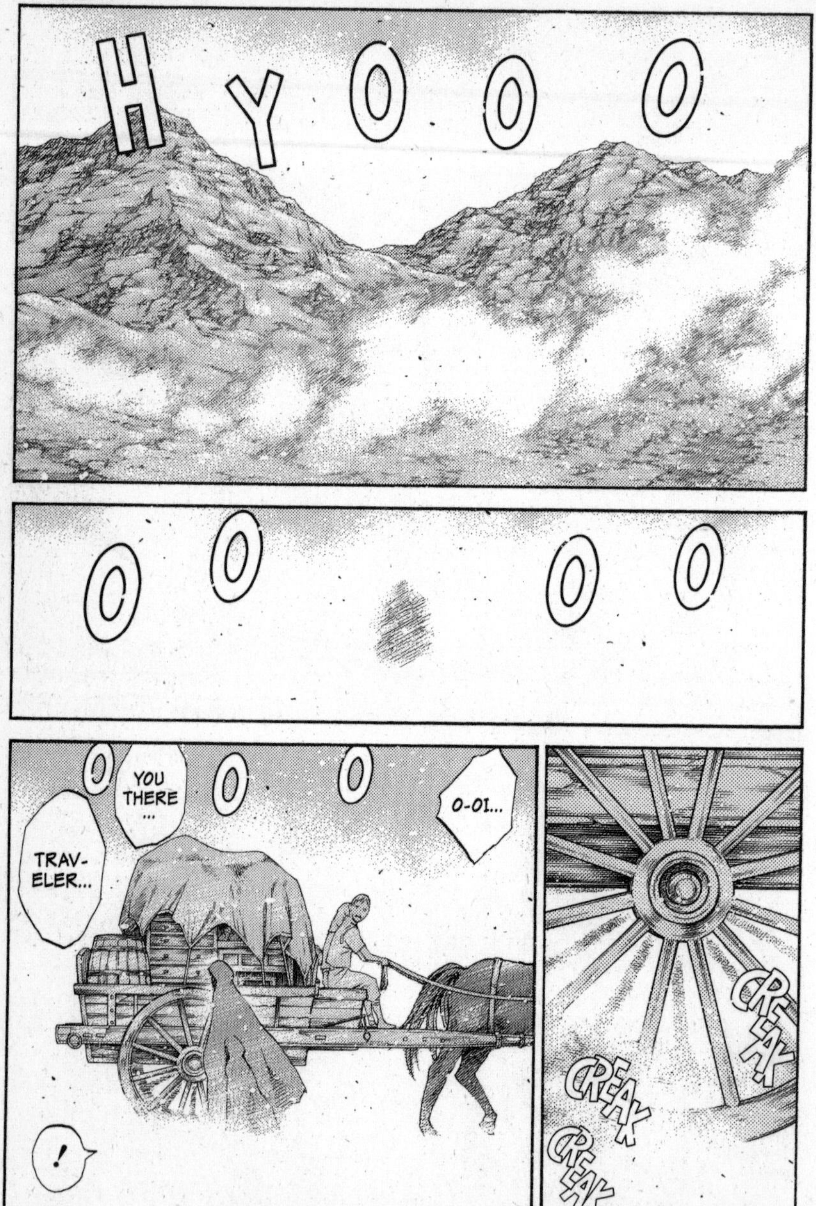
HYOOOO
OOOO
CREAK
CREAK
CREAK
O O O
O-OI...
YOU THERE...
TRAV-ELER...
!

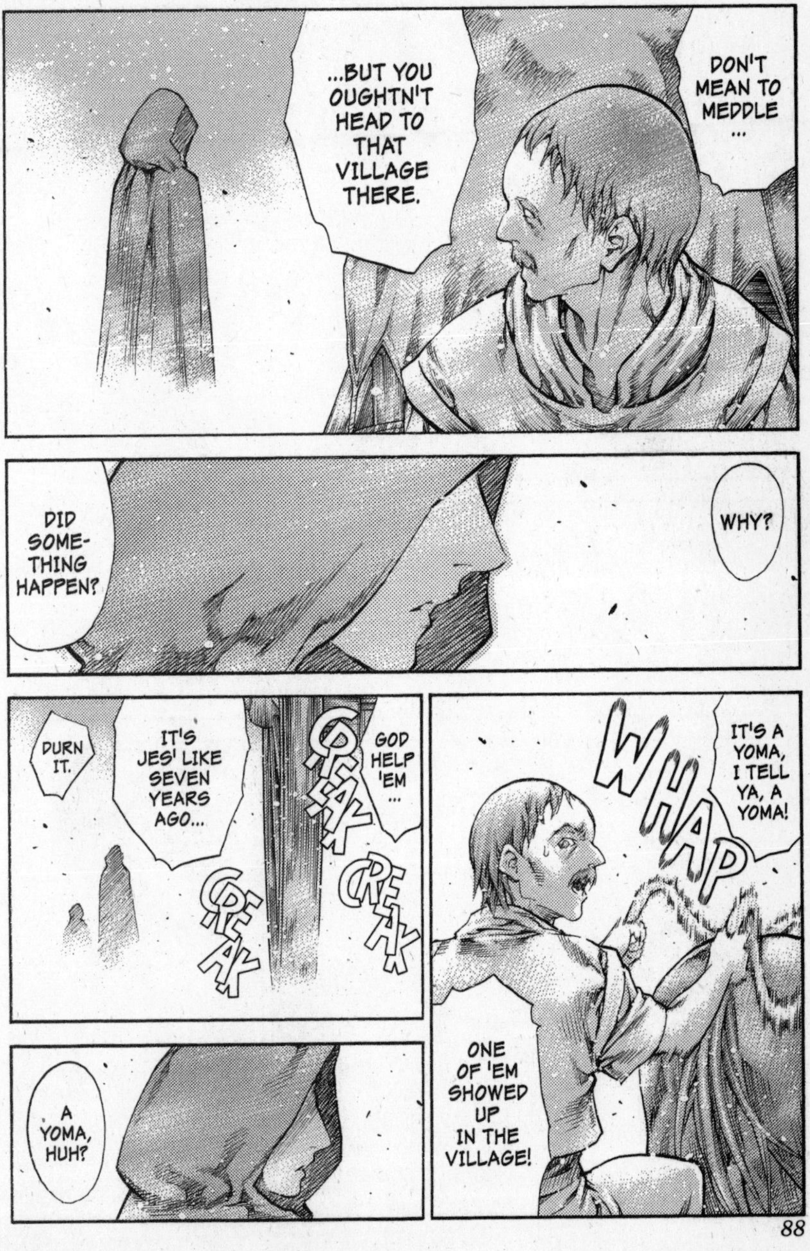
DON'T MEAN TO MEDDLE...
...BUT YOU OUGHTN'T HEAD TO THAT VILLAGE THERE.
WHY?
DID SOME-THING HAPPEN?
WHAP
IT'S A YOMA, I TELL YA, A YOMA!
ONE OF 'EM SHOWED UP IN THE VILLAGE!
GOD HELP 'EM...
CREAK
CREAK
CREAK
IT'S JES' LIKE SEVEN YEARS AGO...
DURN IT.
A YOMA, HUH?

READ THIS WAY

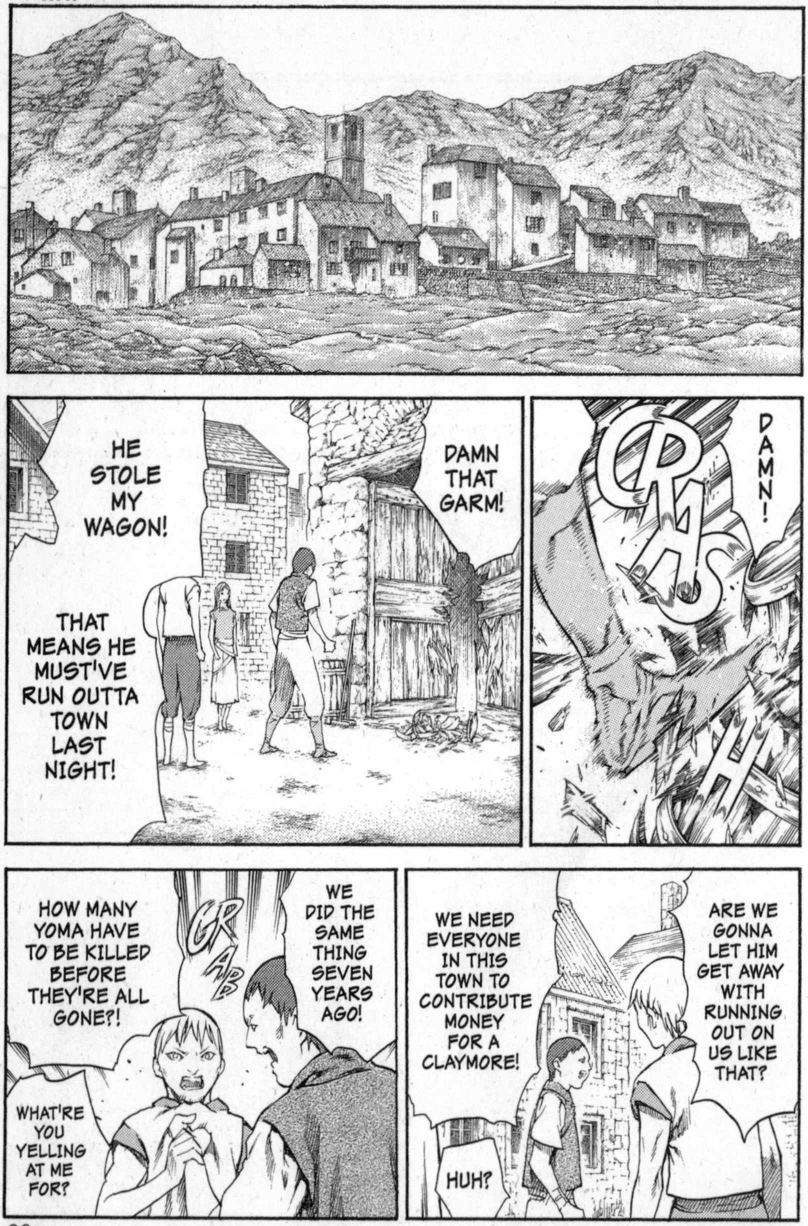

CRASH
DAMN!
DAMN THAT GARM!
HE STOLE MY WAGON!
THAT MEANS HE MUST'VE RUN OUTTA TOWN LAST NIGHT!
ARE WE GONNA LET HIM GET AWAY WITH RUNNING OUT ON US LIKE THAT?
WE NEED EVERYONE IN THIS TOWN TO CONTRIBUTE MONEY FOR A CLAYMORE!
HUH?
WE DID THE SAME THING SEVEN YEARS AGO!
GRAB
HOW MANY YOMA HAVE TO BE KILLED BEFORE THEY'RE ALL GONE?!
WHAT'RE YOU YELLING AT ME FOR?

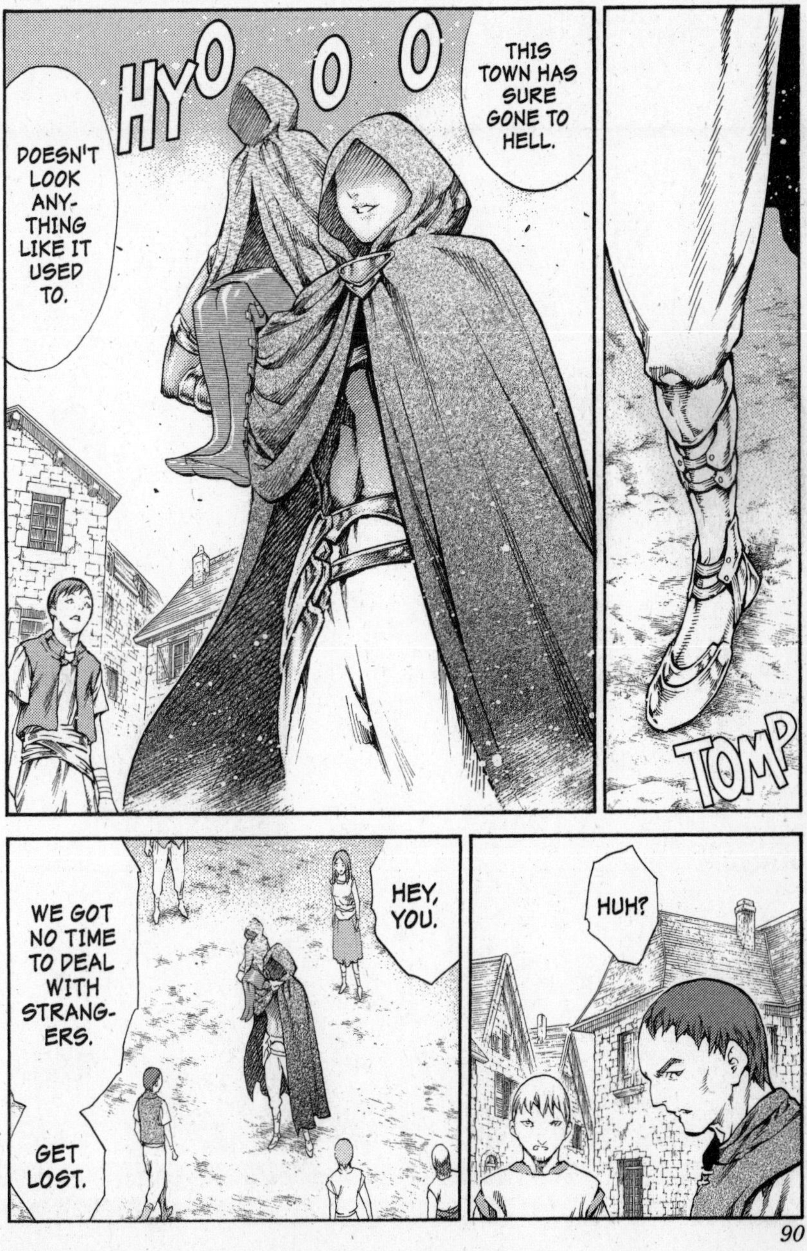
TOMP
THIS TOWN HAS SURE GONE TO HELL.
HYOOO
DOESN'T LOOK ANY-THING LIKE IT USED TO.
HUH?
HEY, YOU.
WE GOT NO TIME TO DEAL WITH STRANG-ERS.
GET LOST.

READ THIS WAY

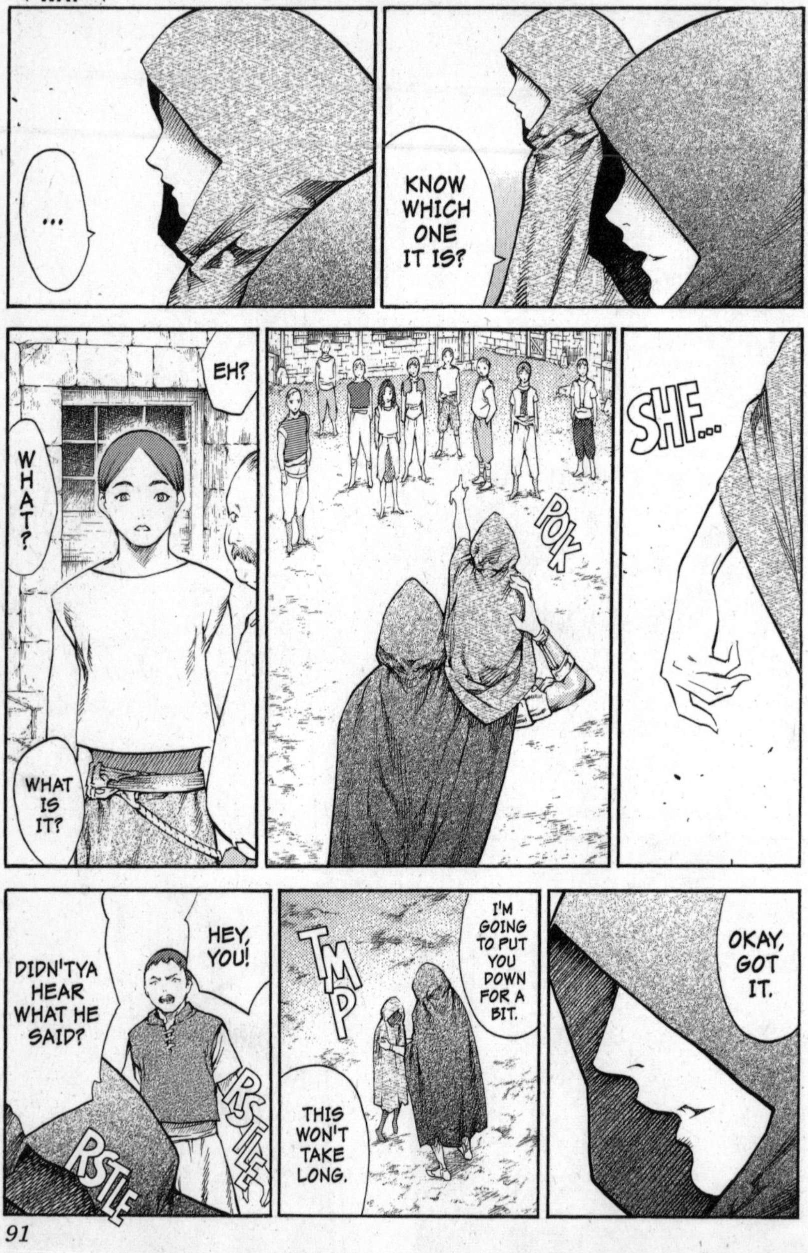

KNOW WHICH ONE IT IS?
...
SHF...
POK
EH?
WHAT?
WHAT IS IT?
OKAY, GOT IT.
I'M GOING TO PUT YOU DOWN FOR A BIT.
TMP
THIS WON'T TAKE LONG.
HEY, YOU!
DIDN'TYA HEAR WHAT HE SAID?
RSTLE
RSTLE

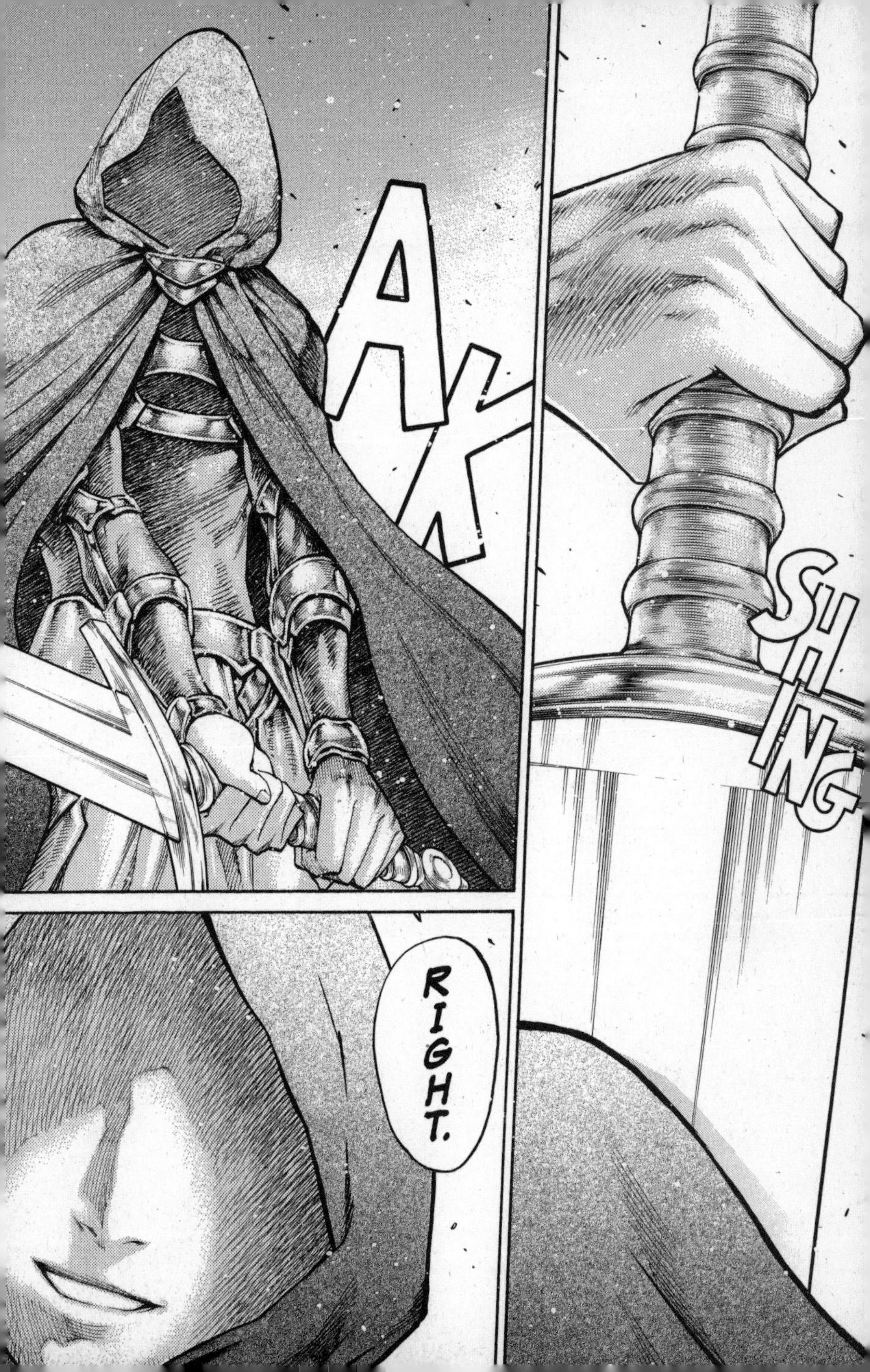
SHING
AK
RIGHT.

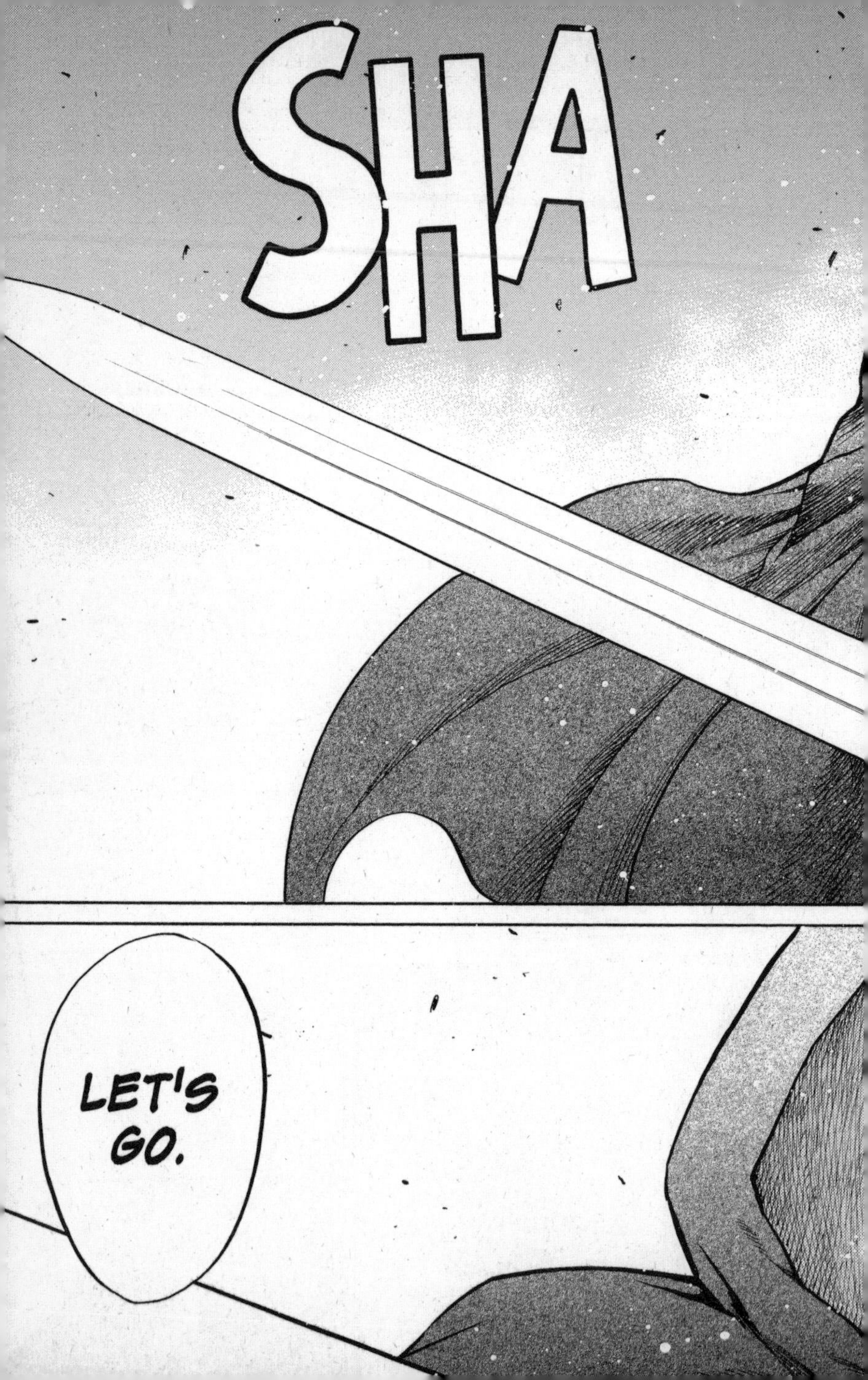
SHA
LET'S GO.

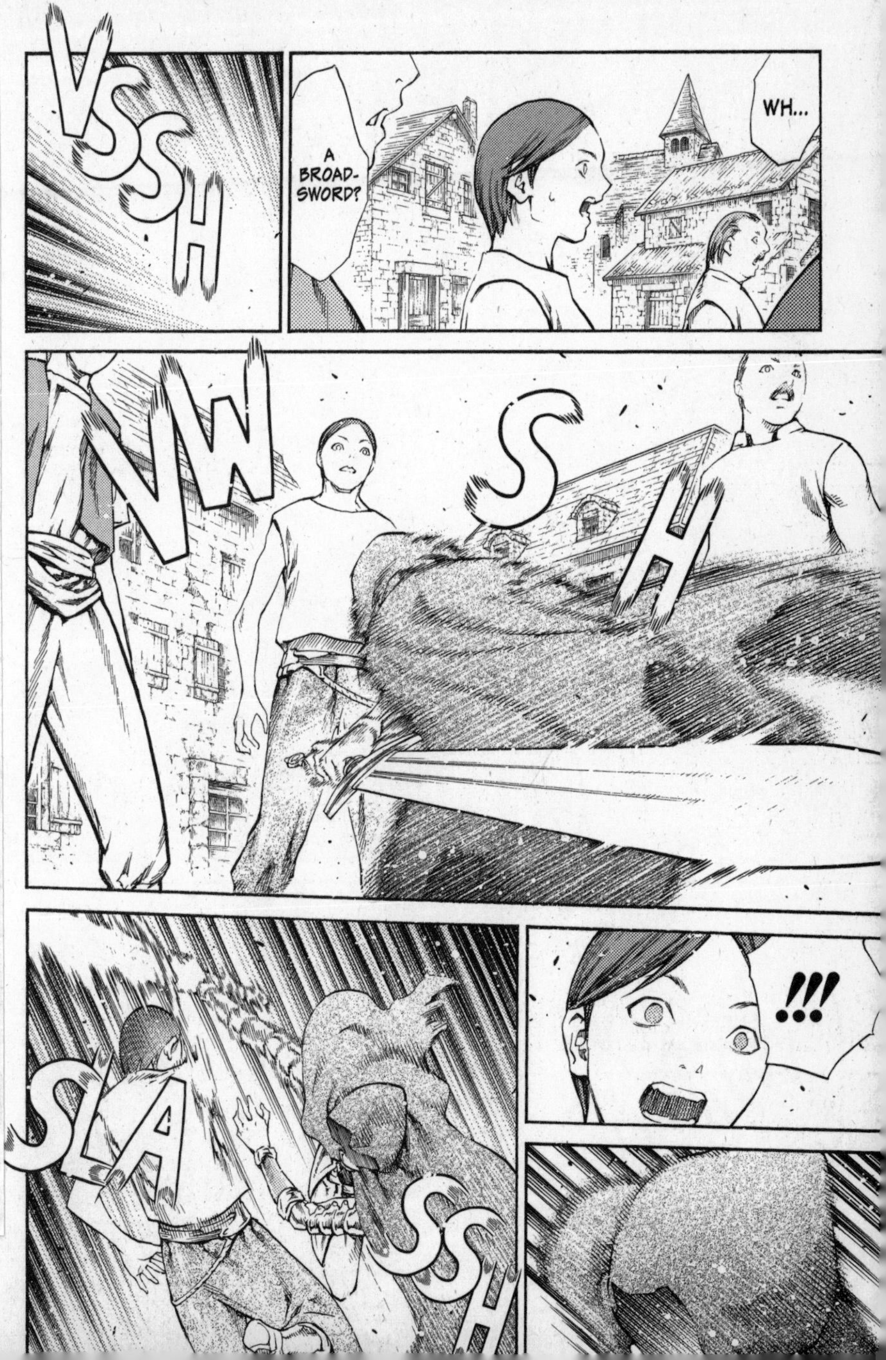
WH...
A BROAD-SWORD?
VSSH
VWSH
!!!
SLASSH

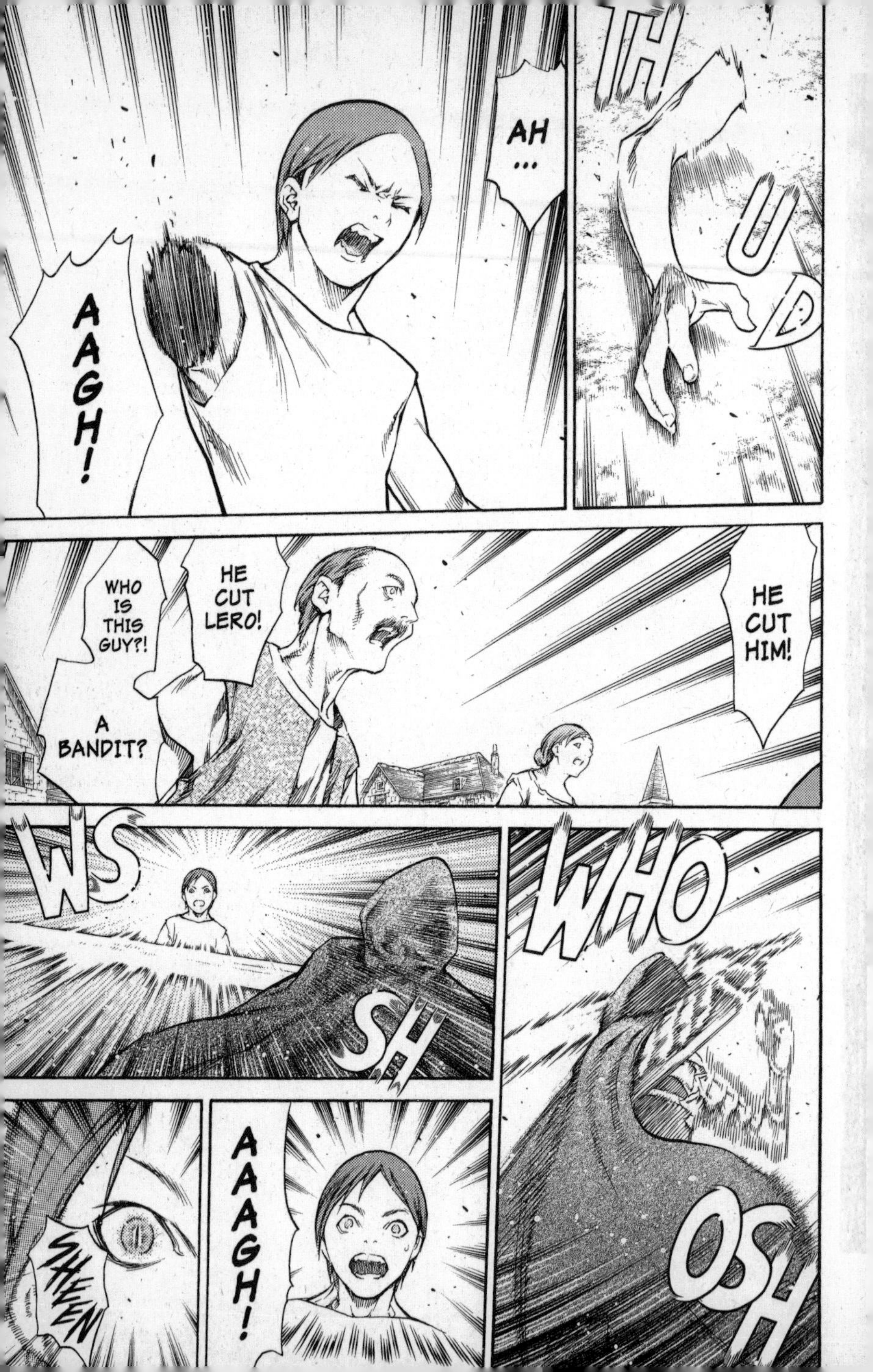
THUD
AH ...
AAGH!
HE CUT HIM!
HE CUT LERO!
WHO IS THIS GUY?!
A BANDIT?
WHOOSH
WSSH
AAAGH!
SHEEN

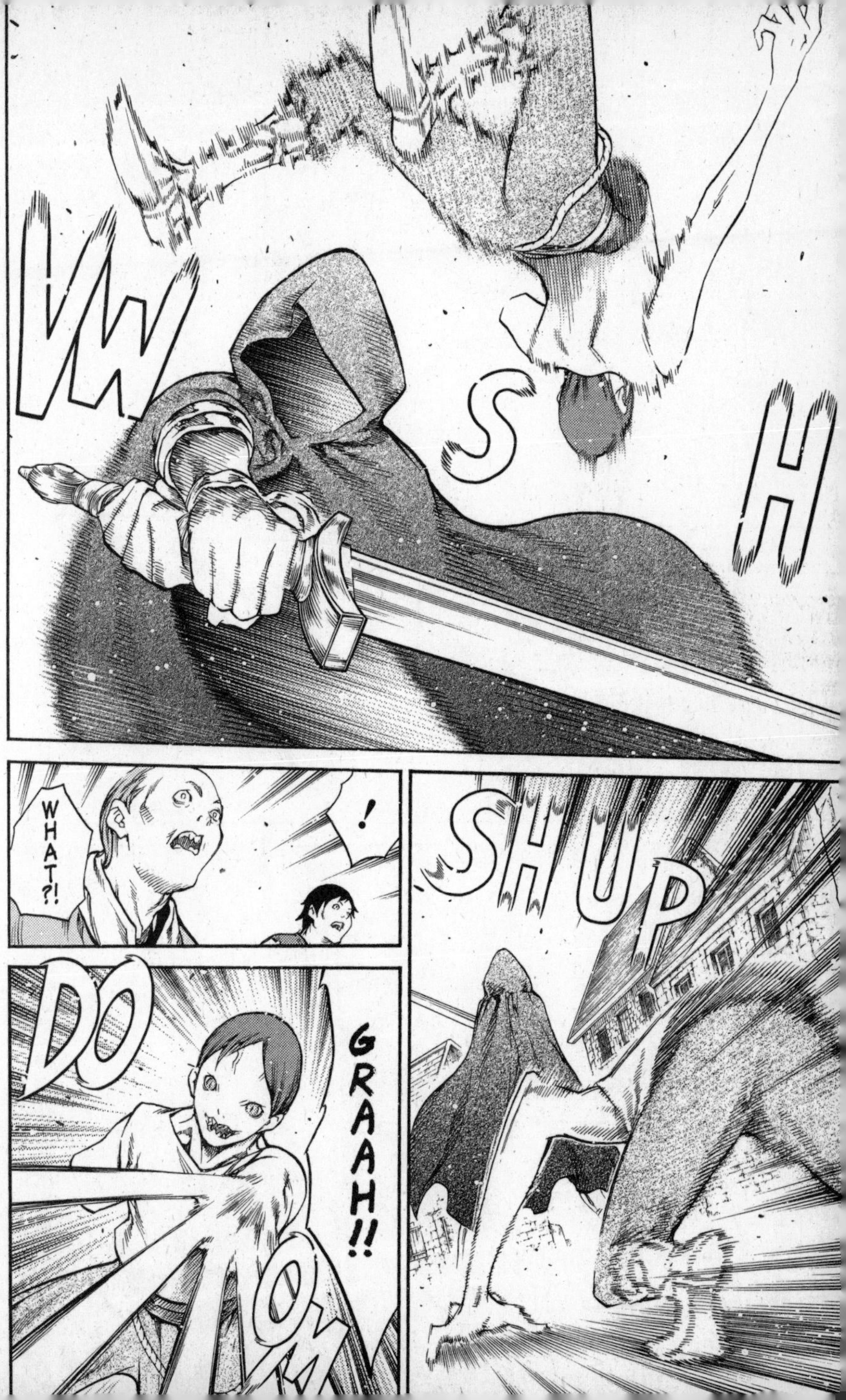
WSH
SHUP
!
WHAT?!
GRAAAH!!
DOOM

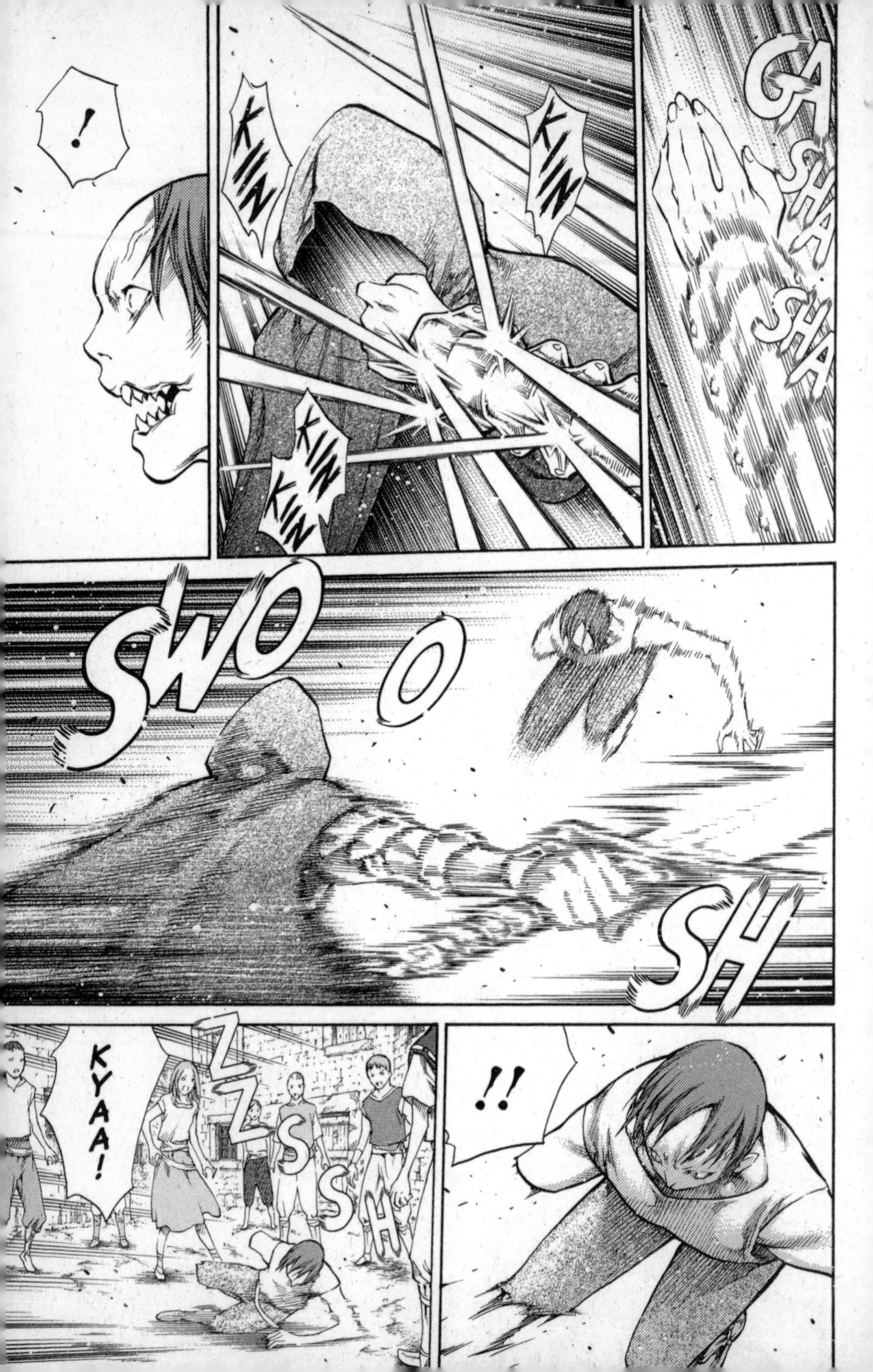
GASHA
SHA
SHA
KIIN
KIIN
KIIN KIIN KIIN
!
SWO O SH
!!
ZZSSSH
KYAA!

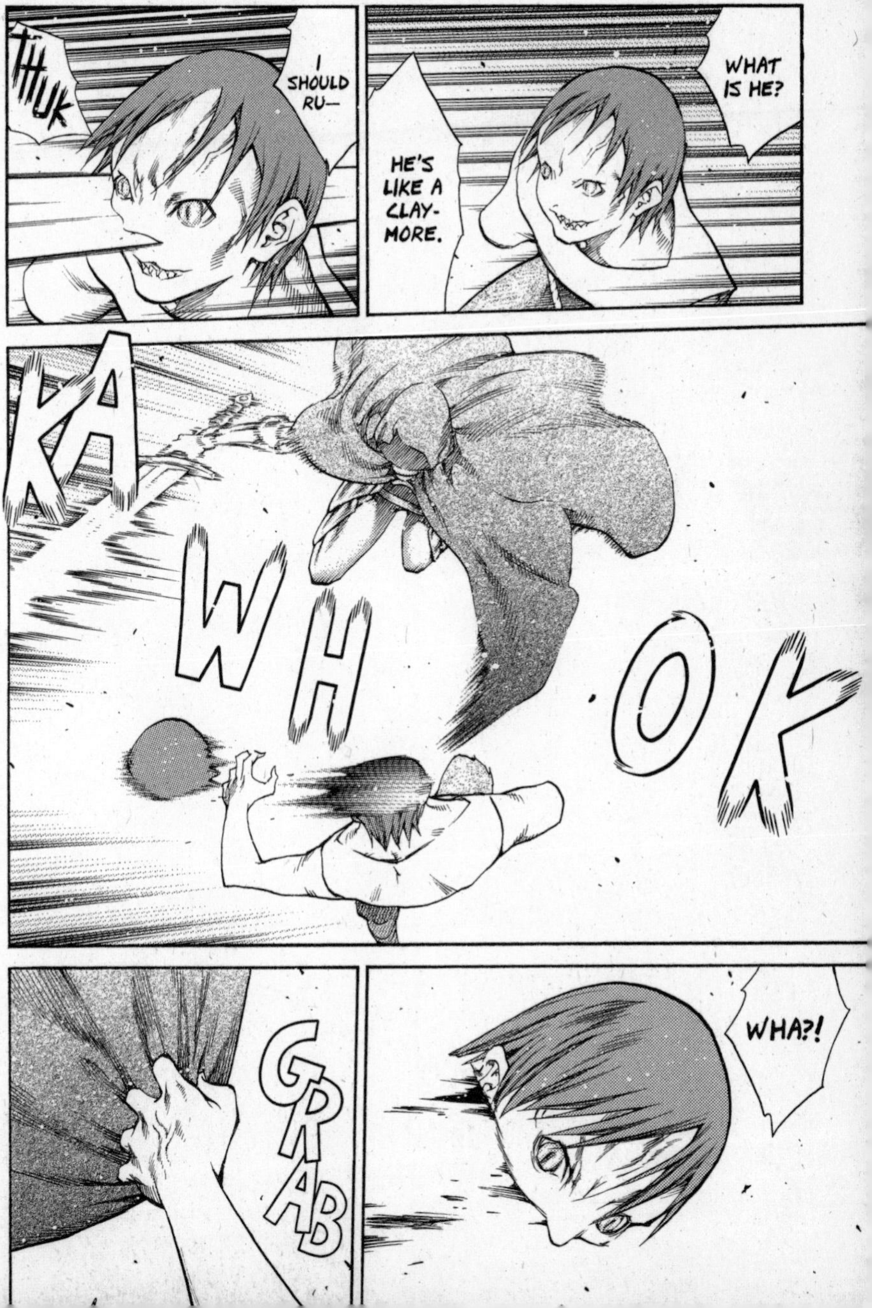
WHAT IS HE?
HE'S LIKE A CLAYMORE.
THUK
I SHOULD RU—
KA
WHOOK
WHA?!
GRAB

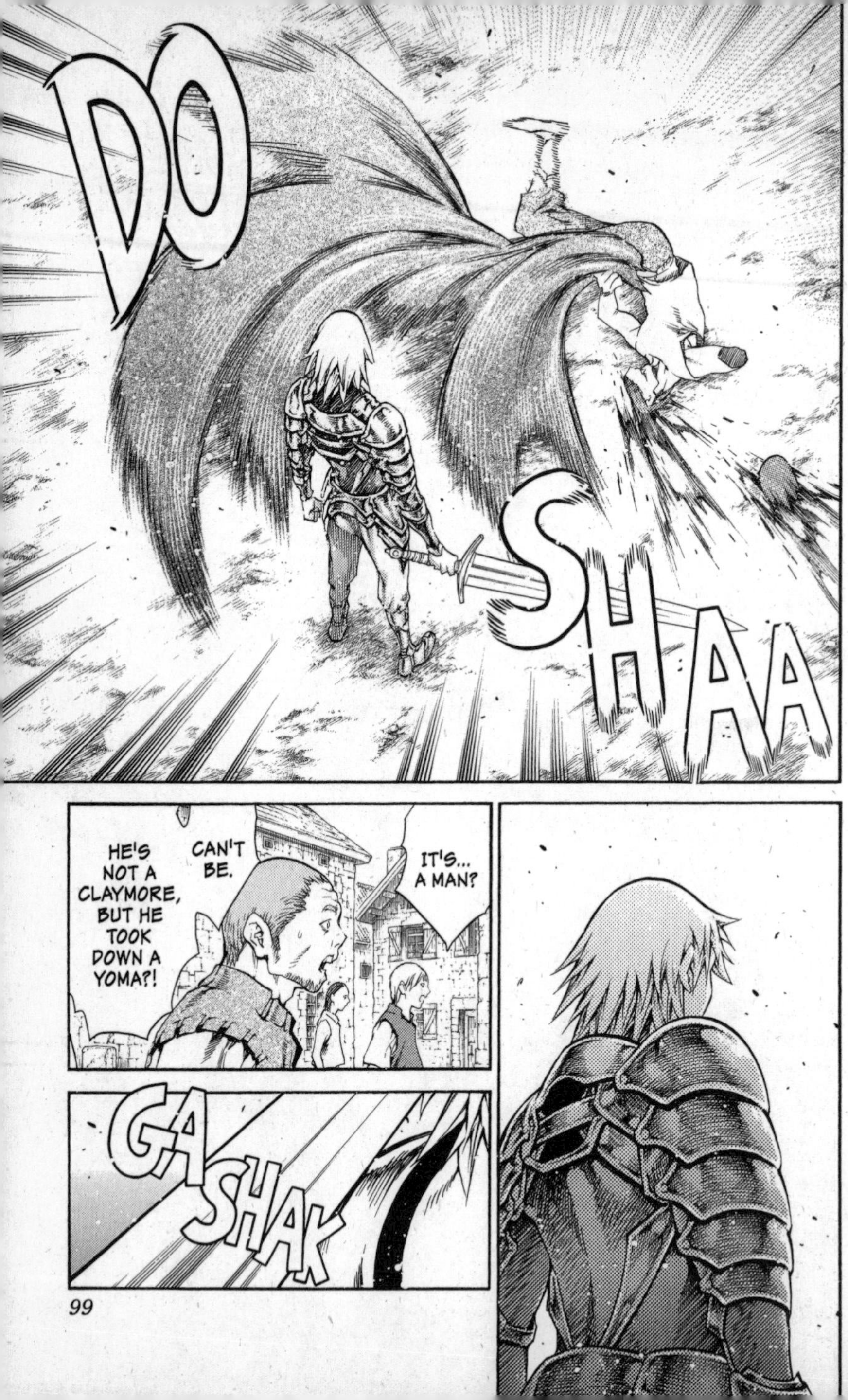
DO
SHAA
IT'S... A MAN?
CAN'T BE.
HE'S NOT A CLAYMORE, BUT HE TOOK DOWN A YOMA?!
GASHAK

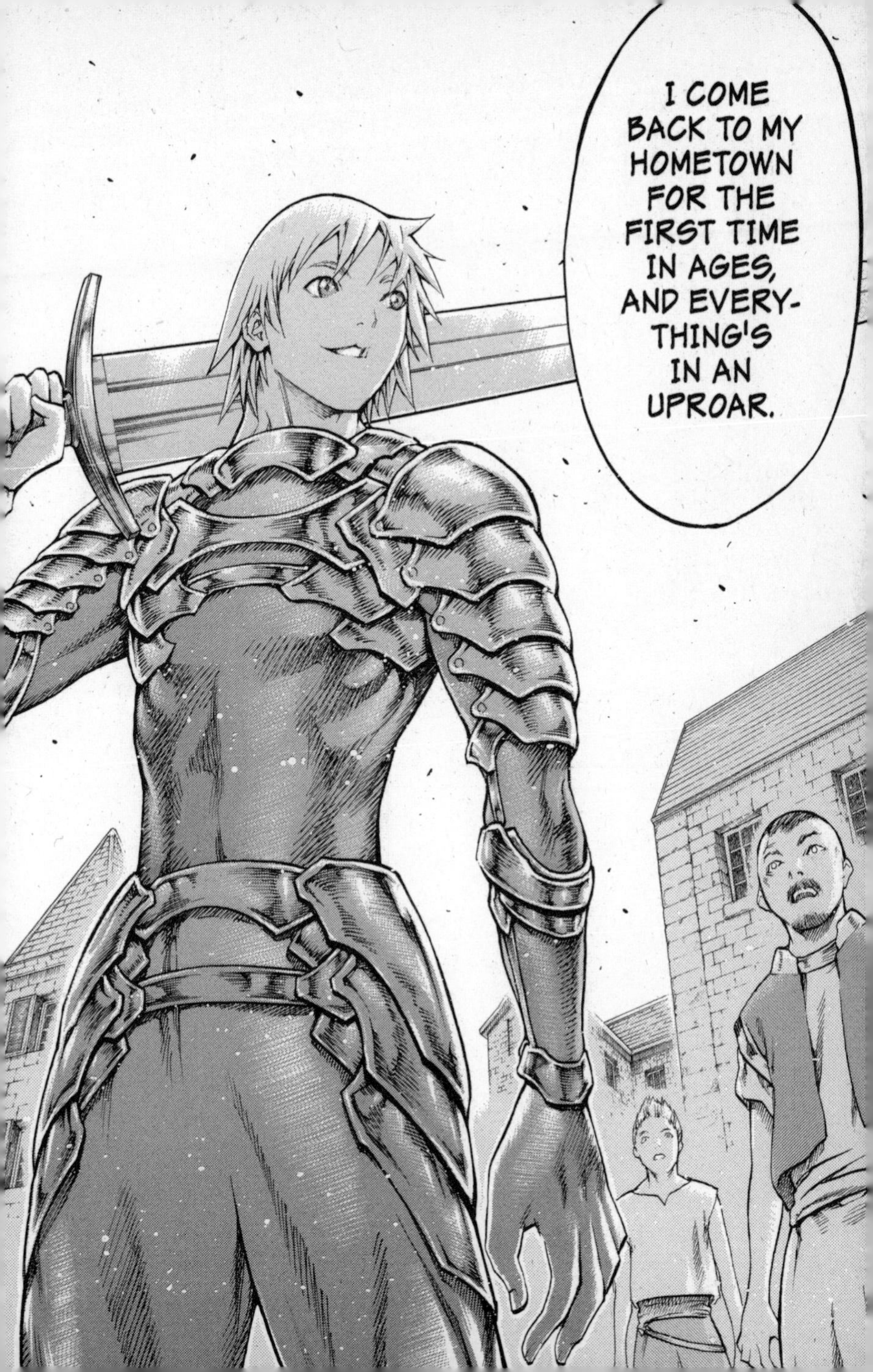
I COME BACK TO MY HOMETOWN FOR THE FIRST TIME IN AGES, AND EVERY-THING'S IN AN UPROAR.

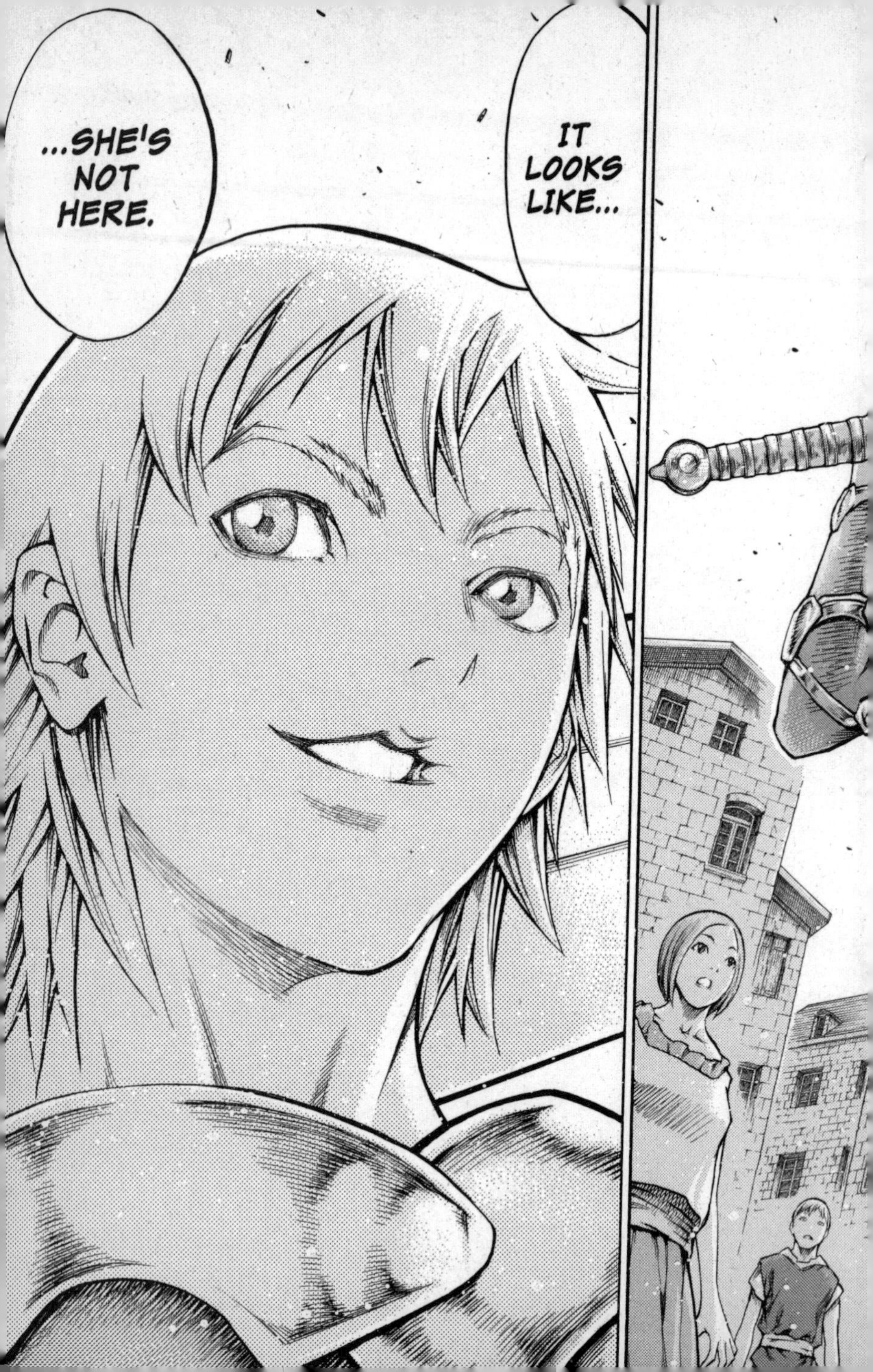
IT LOOKS LIKE...
...SHE'S NOT HERE.

クレイモア
Claymore

Scene 81: Genesis of War, Part 4

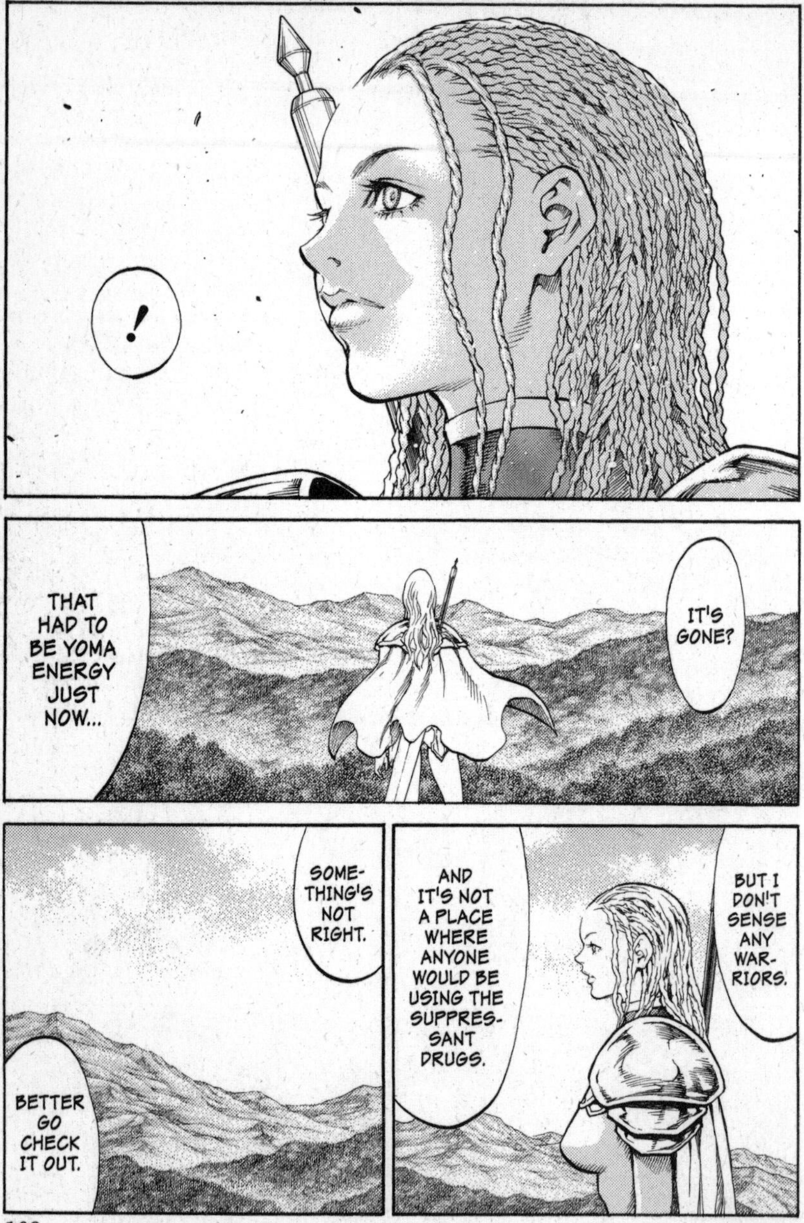
!
IT'S GONE?
THAT HAD TO BE YOMA ENERGY JUST NOW...
BUT I DON'T SENSE ANY WARRIORS.
AND IT'S NOT A PLACE WHERE ANYONE WOULD BE USING THE SUPPRESSANT DRUGS.
SOMETHING'S NOT RIGHT.
BETTER GO CHECK IT OUT.

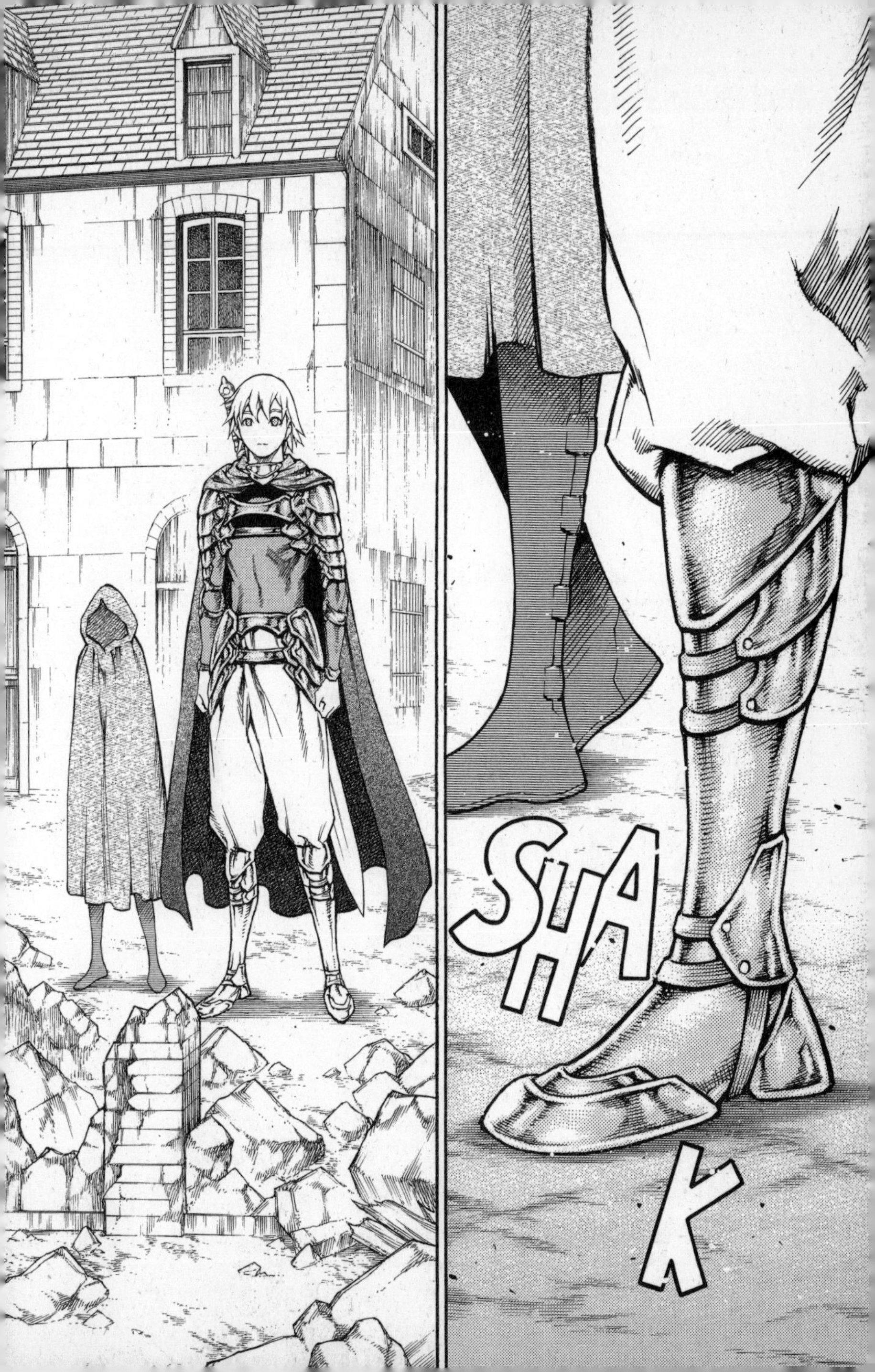
SHHAK

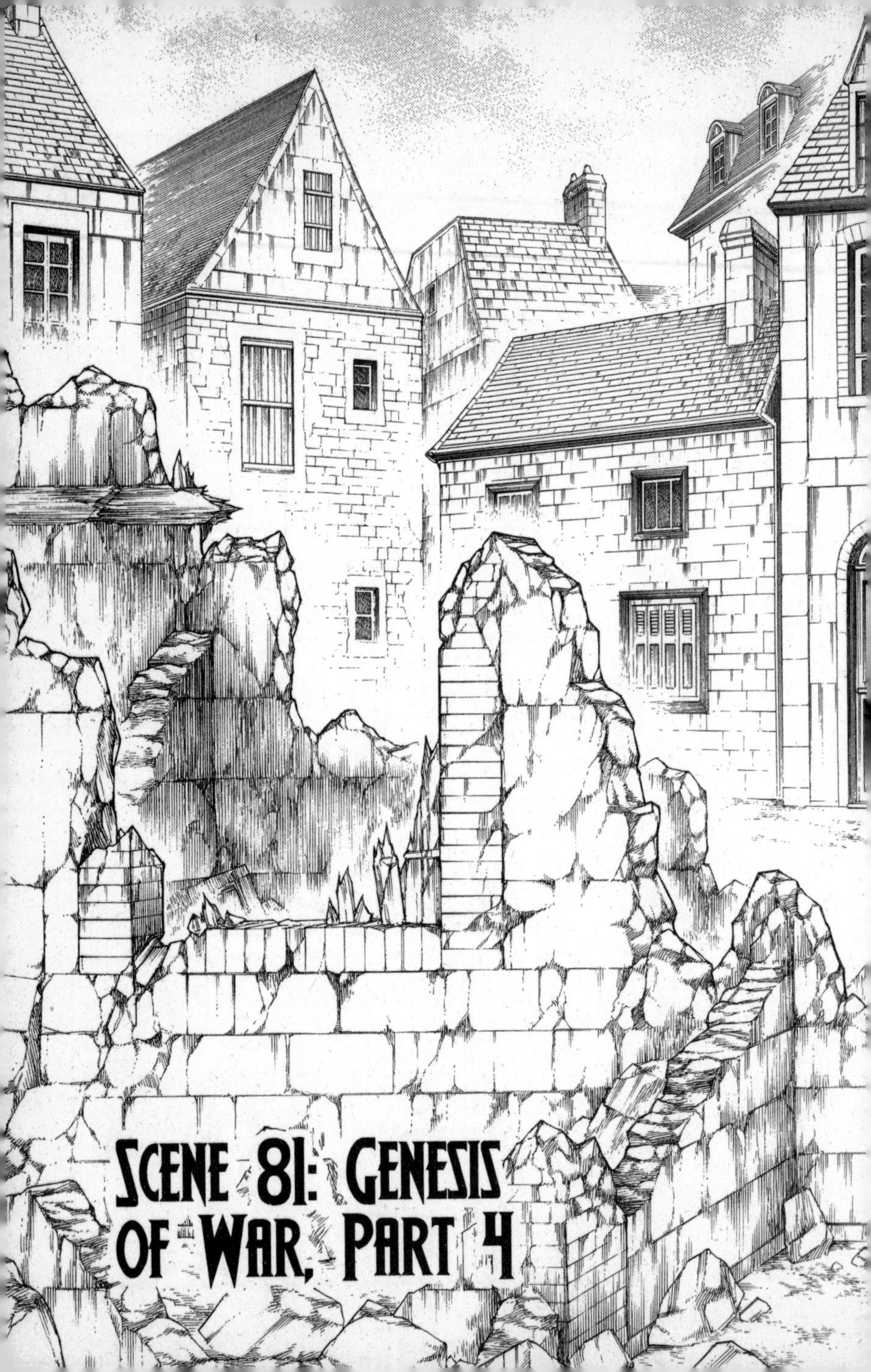
SCENE 81: GENESIS
OF WAR, PART 4

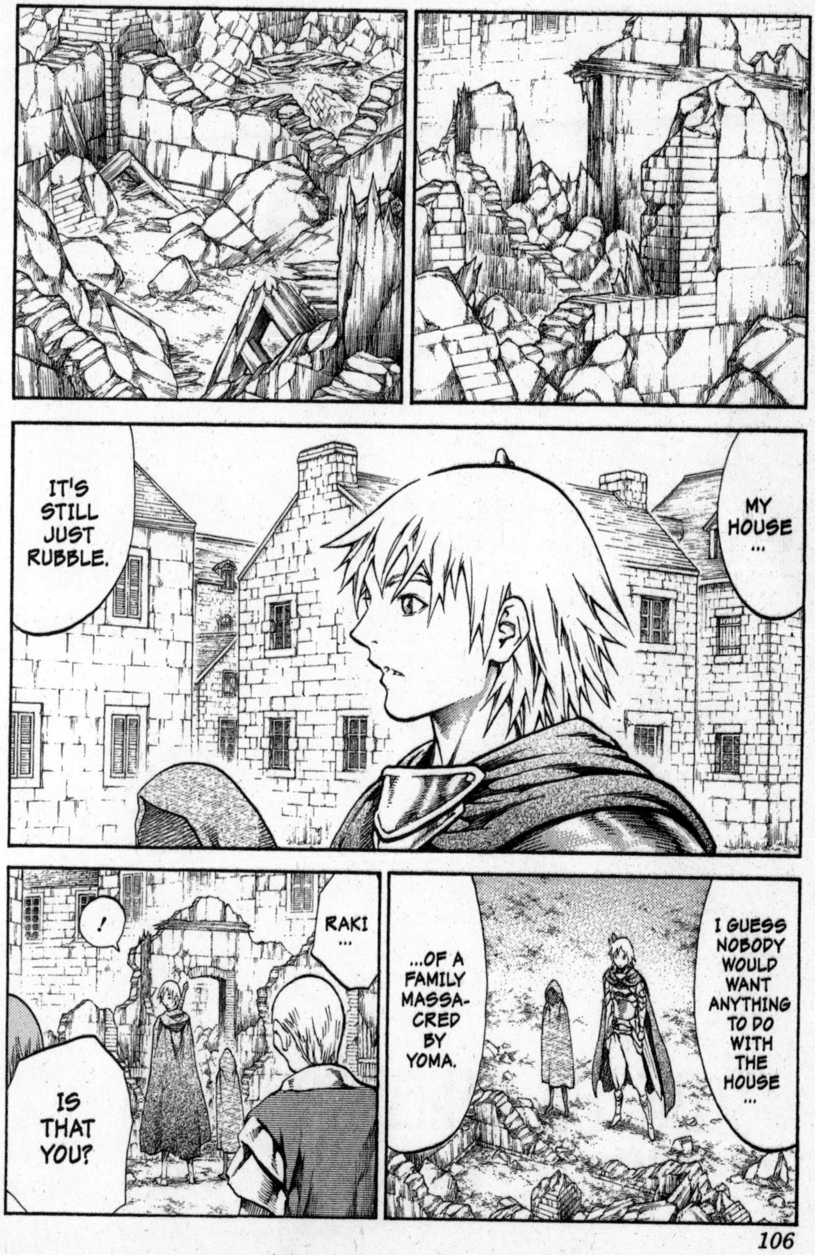
MY HOUSE ...
IT'S STILL JUST RUBBLE.
I GUESS NOBODY WOULD WANT ANYTHING TO DO WITH THE HOUSE ...
...OF A FAMILY MASSACRED BY YOMA.
RAKI ...
!
IS THAT YOU?

READ THIS WAY

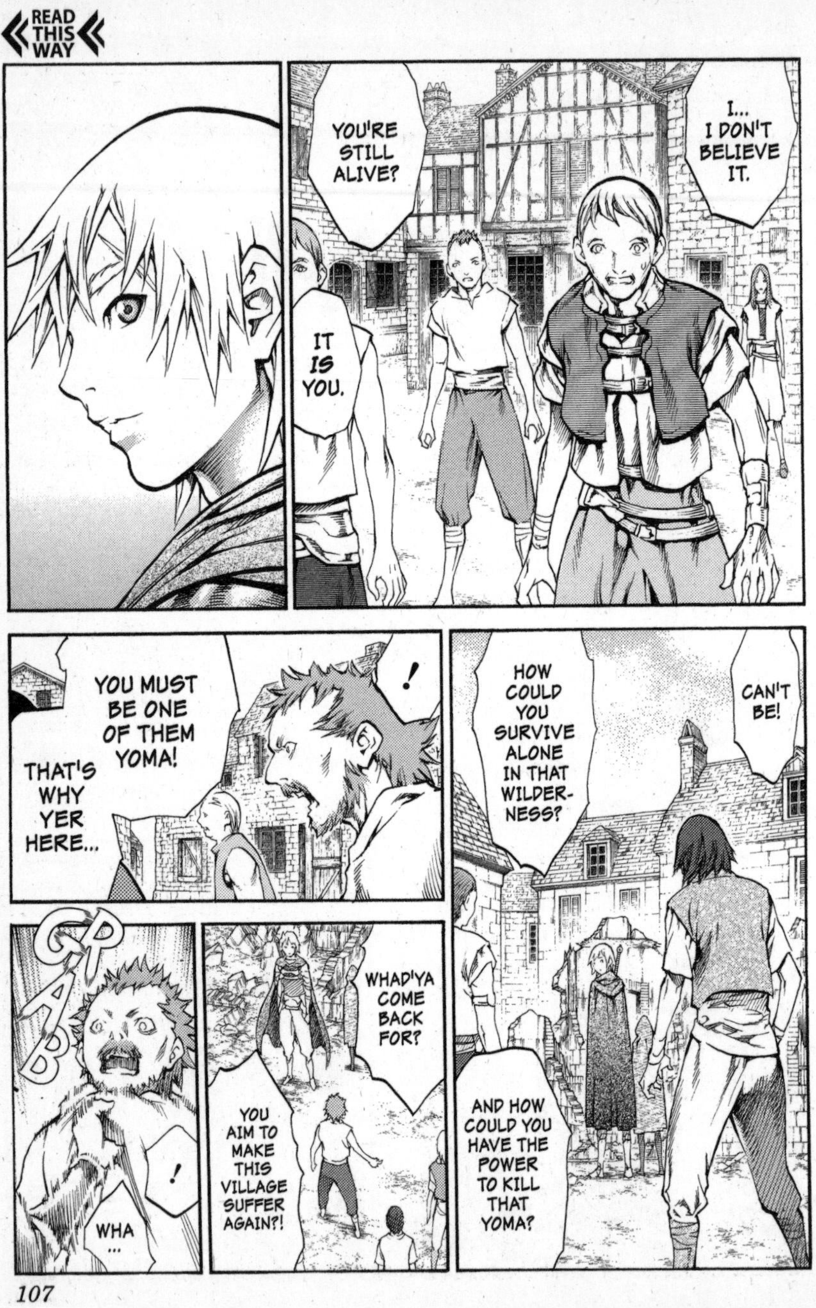

I... I DON'T BELIEVE IT.
YOU'RE STILL ALIVE?
IT IS YOU.
CAN'T BE!
HOW COULD YOU SURVIVE ALONE IN THAT WILDER-NESS?
AND HOW COULD YOU HAVE THE POWER TO KILL THAT YOMA?
!
YOU MUST BE ONE OF THEM YOMA!
THAT'S WHY YER HERE...
WHAD'YA COME BACK FOR?
YOU AIM TO MAKE THIS VILLAGE SUFFER AGAIN?!
GRAB
!
WHA...

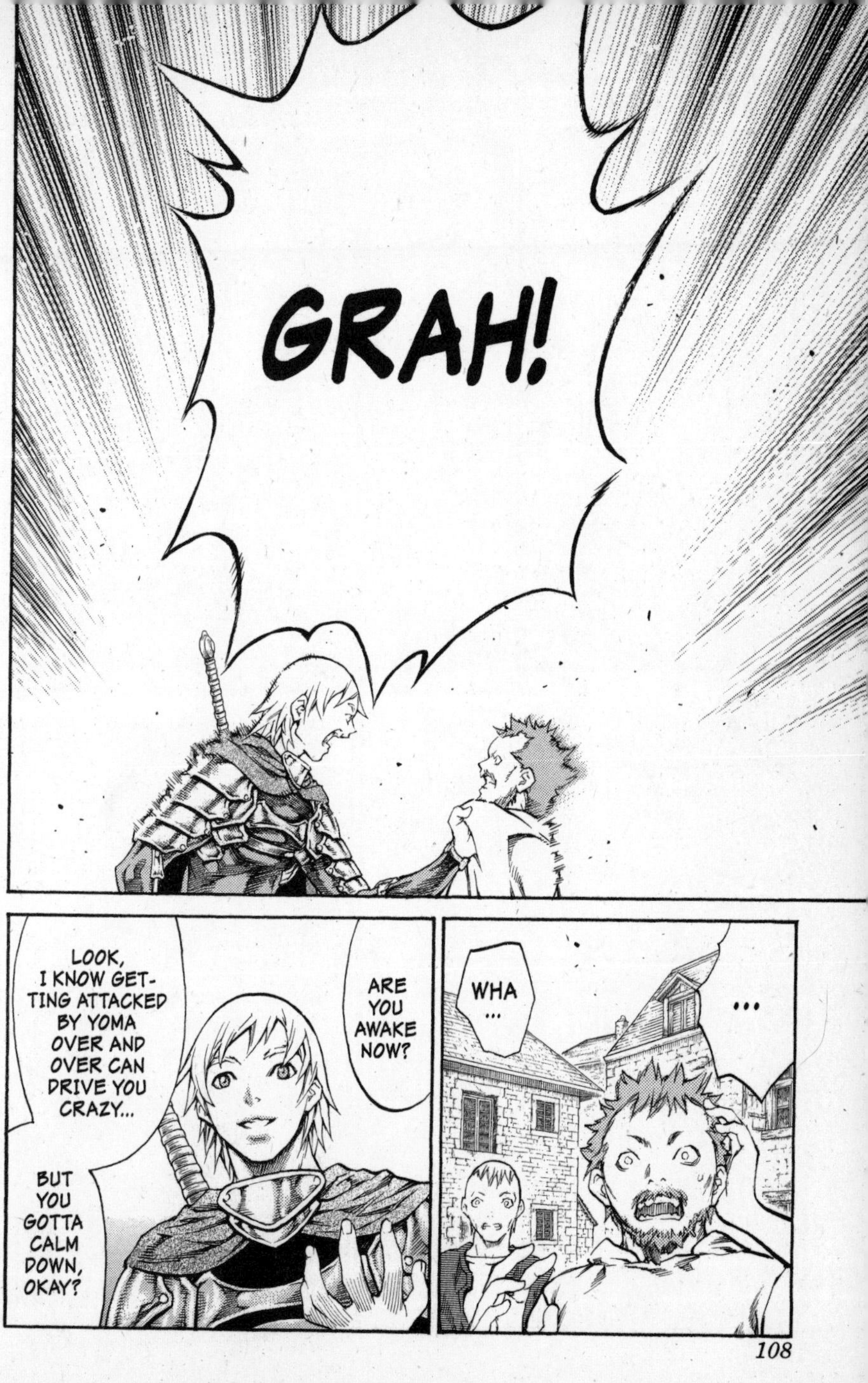
GRAH!
...
WHA ...
ARE YOU AWAKE NOW?
LOOK, I KNOW GETTING ATTACKED BY YOMA OVER AND OVER CAN DRIVE YOU CRAZY...
BUT YOU GOTTA CALM DOWN, OKAY?

READ THIS WAY

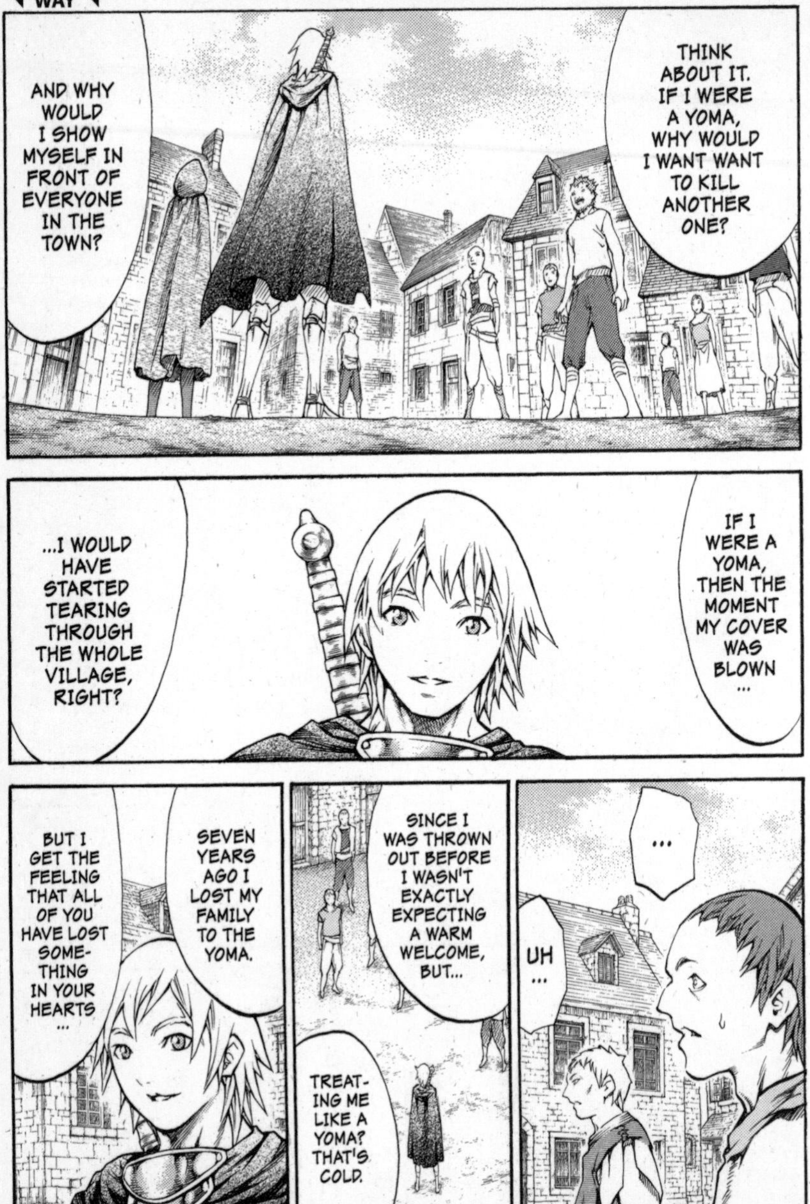
THINK ABOUT IT. IF I WERE A YOMA, WHY WOULD I WANT WANT TO KILL ANOTHER ONE?
AND WHY WOULD I SHOW MYSELF IN FRONT OF EVERYONE IN THE TOWN?
IF I WERE A YOMA, THEN THE MOMENT MY COVER WAS BLOWN ...
...I WOULD HAVE STARTED TEARING THROUGH THE WHOLE VILLAGE, RIGHT?
...
UH ...
SINCE I WAS THROWN OUT BEFORE I WASN'T EXACTLY EXPECTING A WARM WELCOME, BUT...
TREAT-ING ME LIKE A YOMA? THAT'S COLD.
SEVEN YEARS AGO I LOST MY FAMILY TO THE YOMA.
BUT I GET THE FEELING THAT ALL OF YOU HAVE LOST SOME-THING IN YOUR HEARTS ...

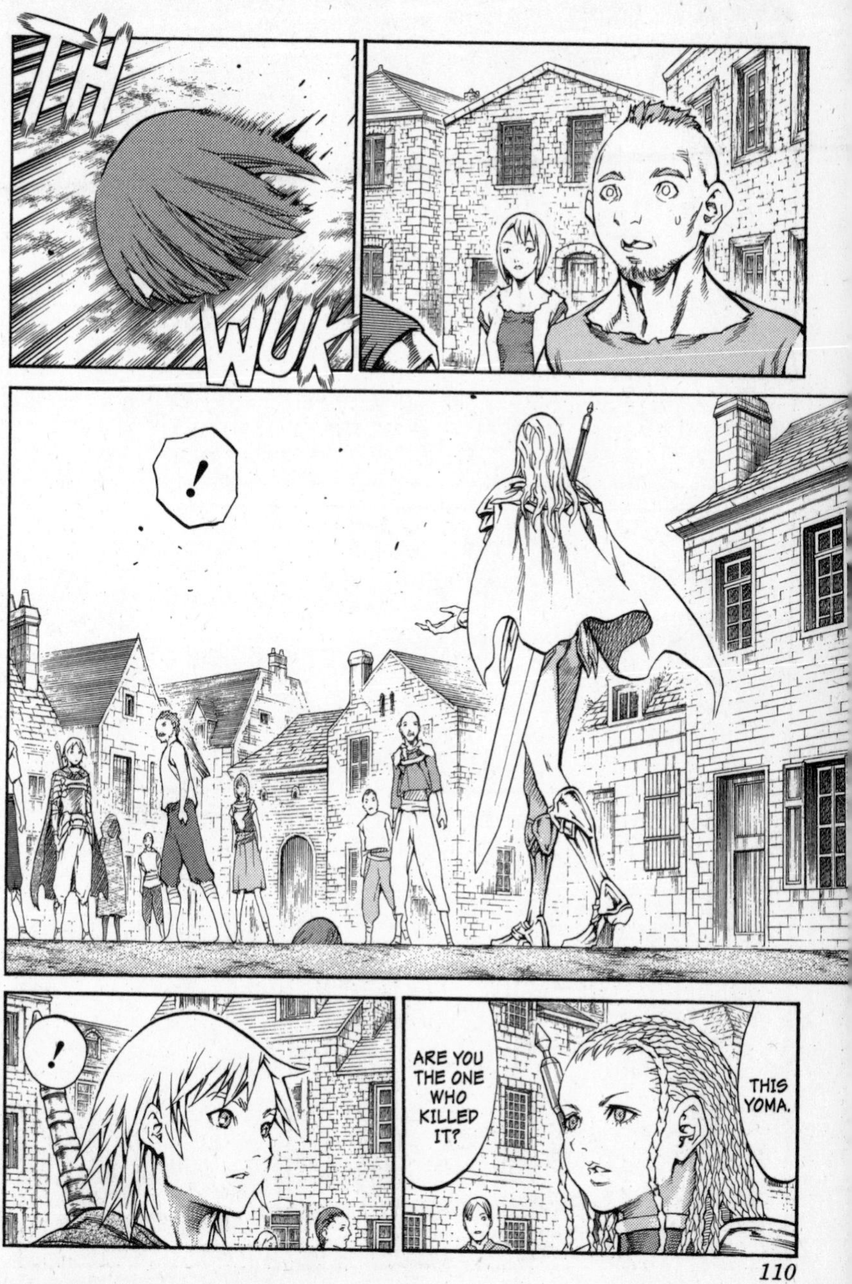
THWUK
!
THIS YOMA.
ARE YOU THE ONE WHO KILLED IT?
!

READ THIS WAY

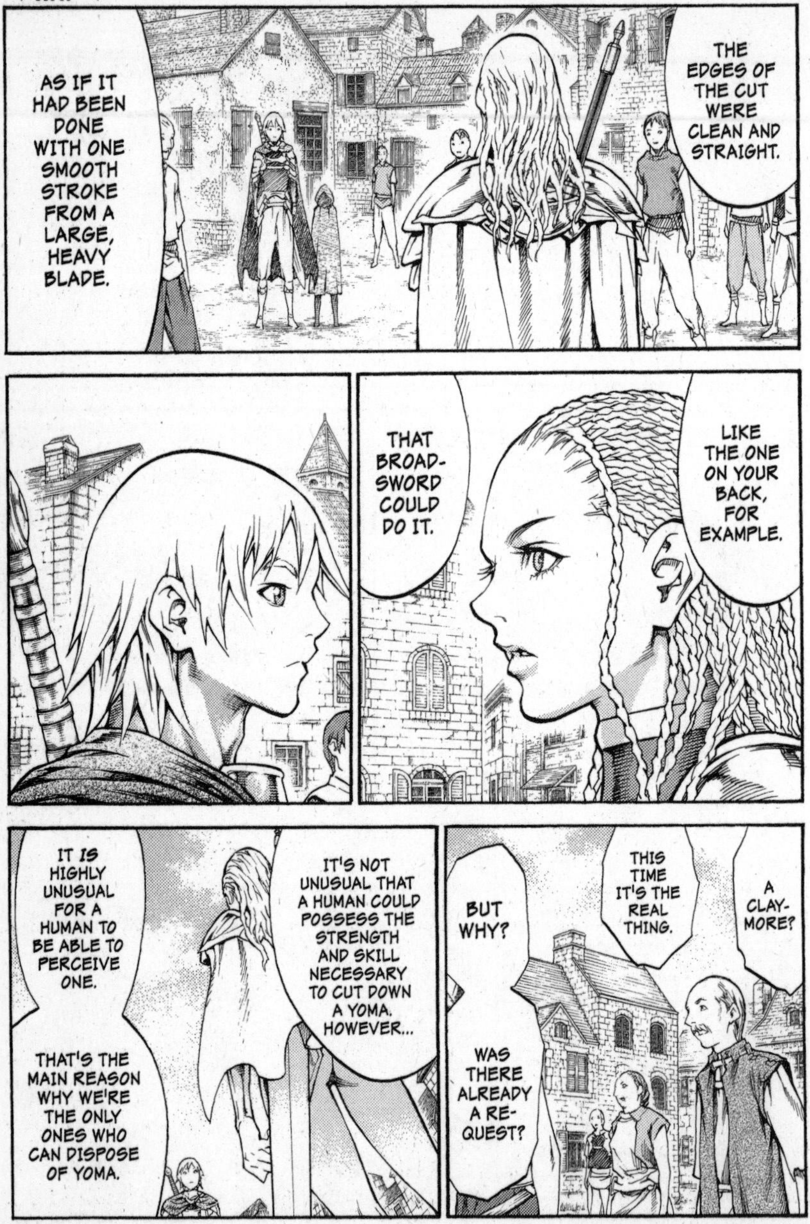

THE EDGES OF THE CUT WERE CLEAN AND STRAIGHT.
AS IF IT HAD BEEN DONE WITH ONE SMOOTH STROKE FROM A LARGE, HEAVY BLADE.
LIKE THE ONE ON YOUR BACK, FOR EXAMPLE.
THAT BROAD-SWORD COULD DO IT.
A CLAY-MORE?
THIS TIME IT'S THE REAL THING.
BUT WHY?
WAS THERE ALREADY A RE-QUEST?
IT'S NOT UNUSUAL THAT A HUMAN COULD POSSESS THE STRENGTH AND SKILL NECESSARY TO CUT DOWN A YOMA. HOWEVER...
IT IS HIGHLY UNUSUAL FOR A HUMAN TO BE ABLE TO PERCEIVE ONE.
THAT'S THE MAIN REASON WHY WE'RE THE ONLY ONES WHO CAN DISPOSE OF YOMA.

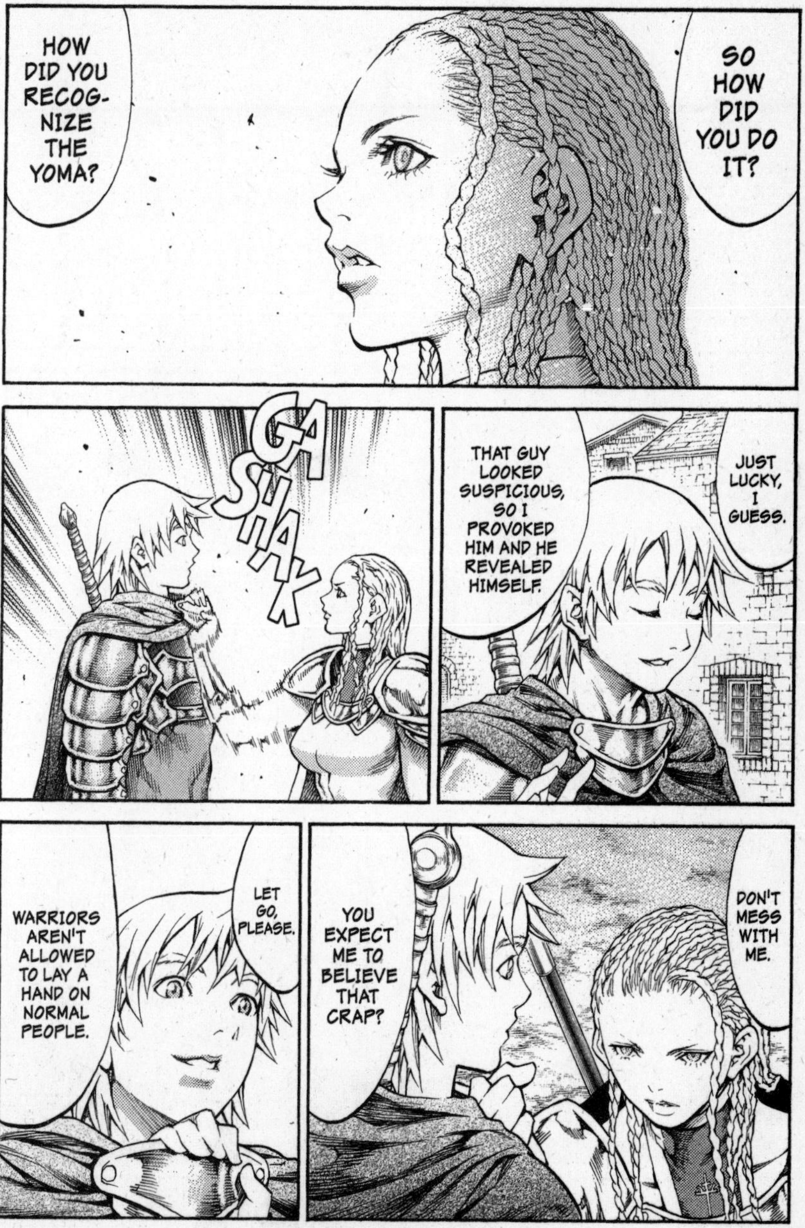
SO HOW DID YOU DO IT?
HOW DID YOU RECOGNIZE THE YOMA?
JUST LUCKY, I GUESS.
THAT GUY LOOKED SUSPICIOUS, SO I PROVOKED HIM AND HE REVEALED HIMSELF.
GASHAK
DON'T MESS WITH ME.
YOU EXPECT ME TO BELIEVE THAT CRAP?
LET GO, PLEASE.
WARRIORS AREN'T ALLOWED TO LAY A HAND ON NORMAL PEOPLE.

READ THIS WAY

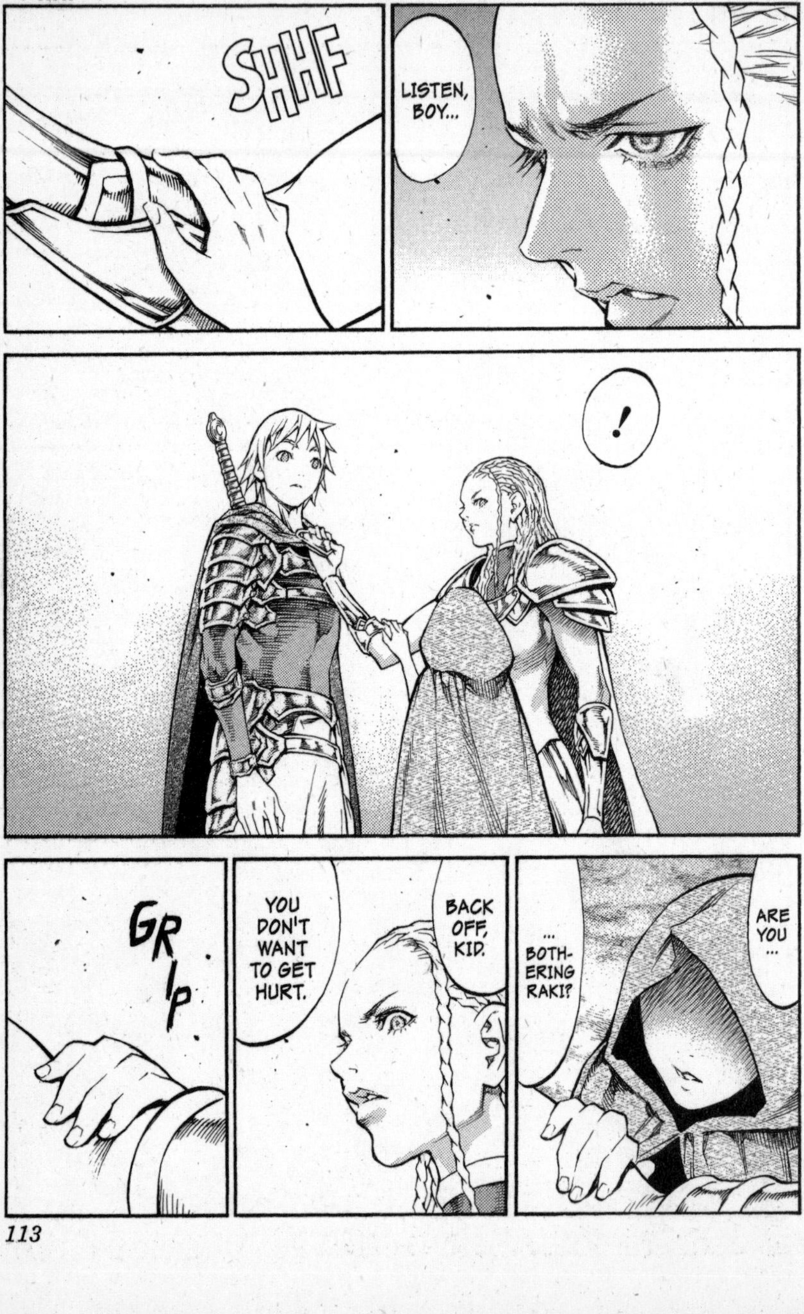
LISTEN, BOY...
SHHF
!
ARE YOU ...
... BOTH-ERING RAKI?
BACK OFF, KID.
YOU DON'T WANT TO GET HURT.
GRIP

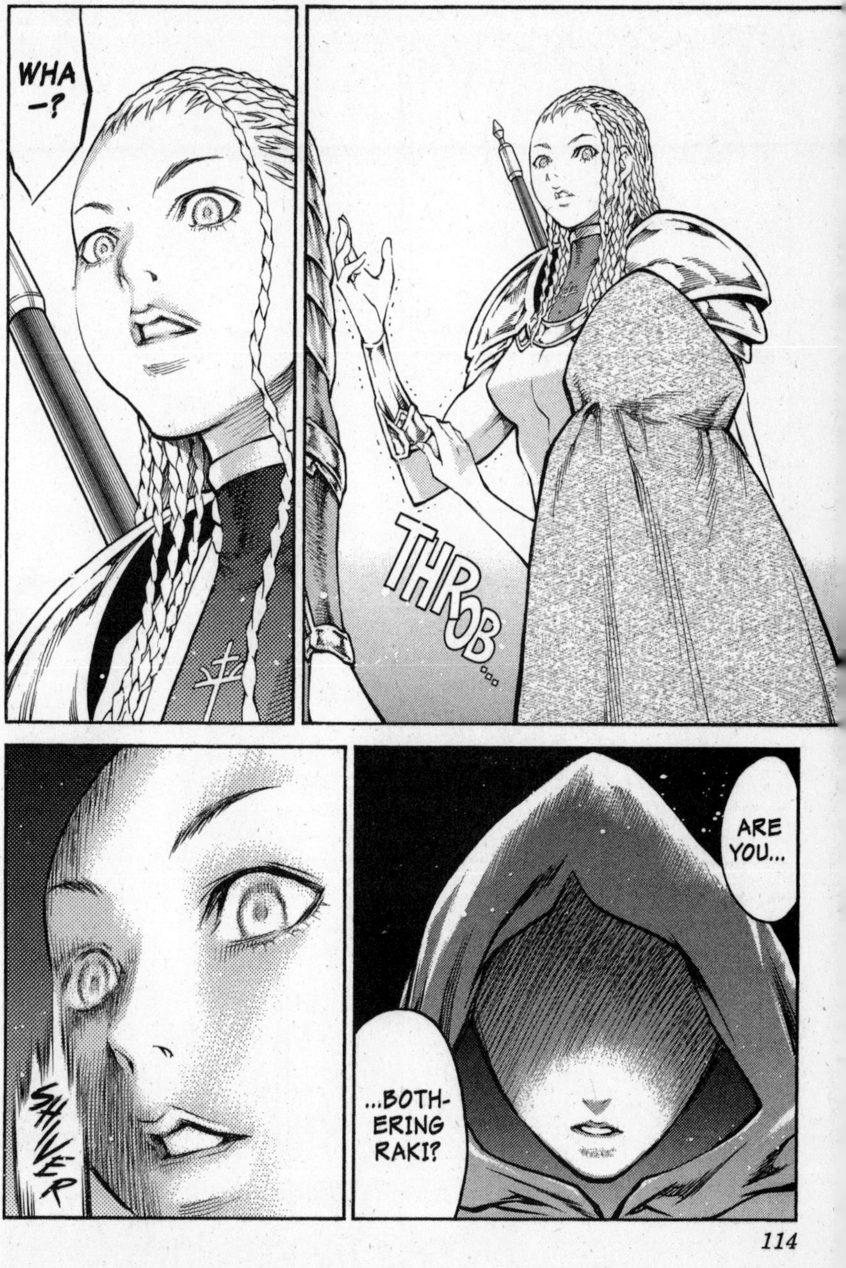
THROB...
WHA —?
ARE YOU...
...BOTH- ERING RAKI?
SHIVER

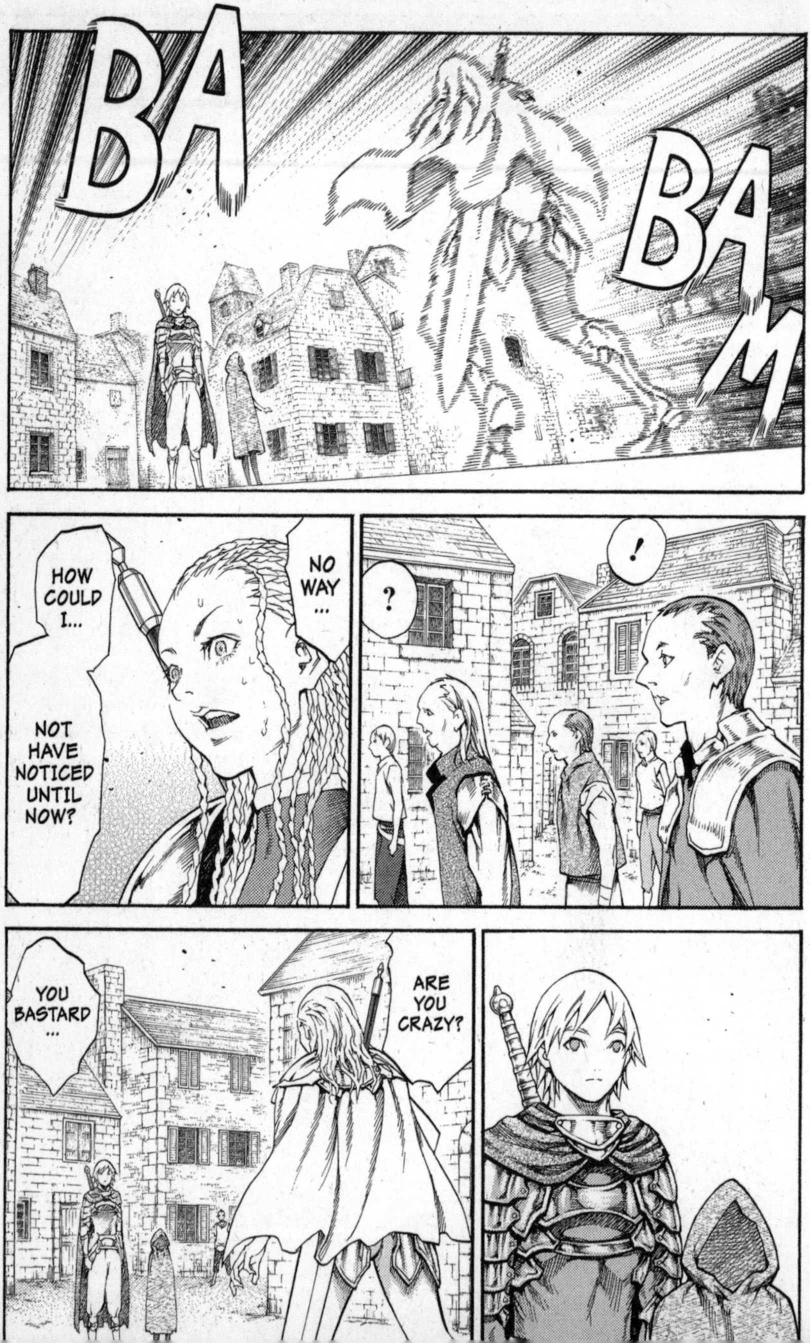
BABAM
BA
!
?
NO WAY ...
HOW COULD I...
NOT HAVE NOTICED UNTIL NOW?
ARE YOU CRAZY?
YOU BASTARD ...

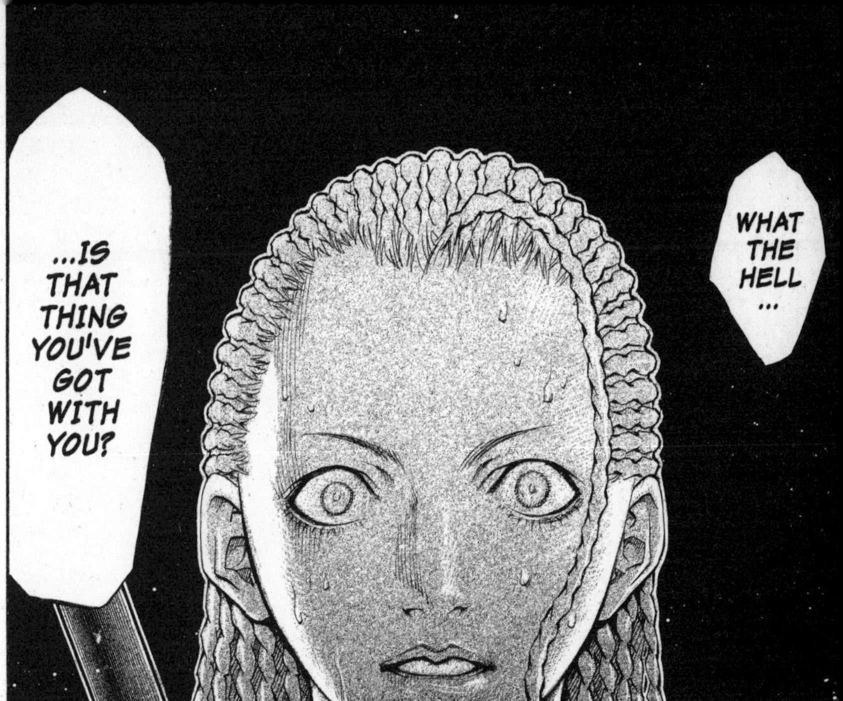
WHAT THE HELL ...
...IS THAT THING YOU'VE GOT WITH YOU?

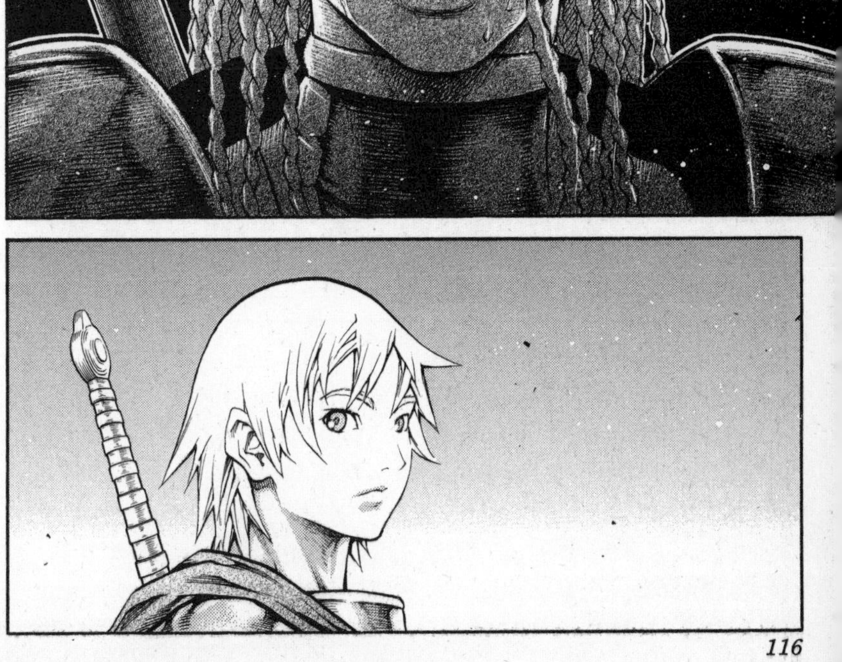

READ THIS WAY

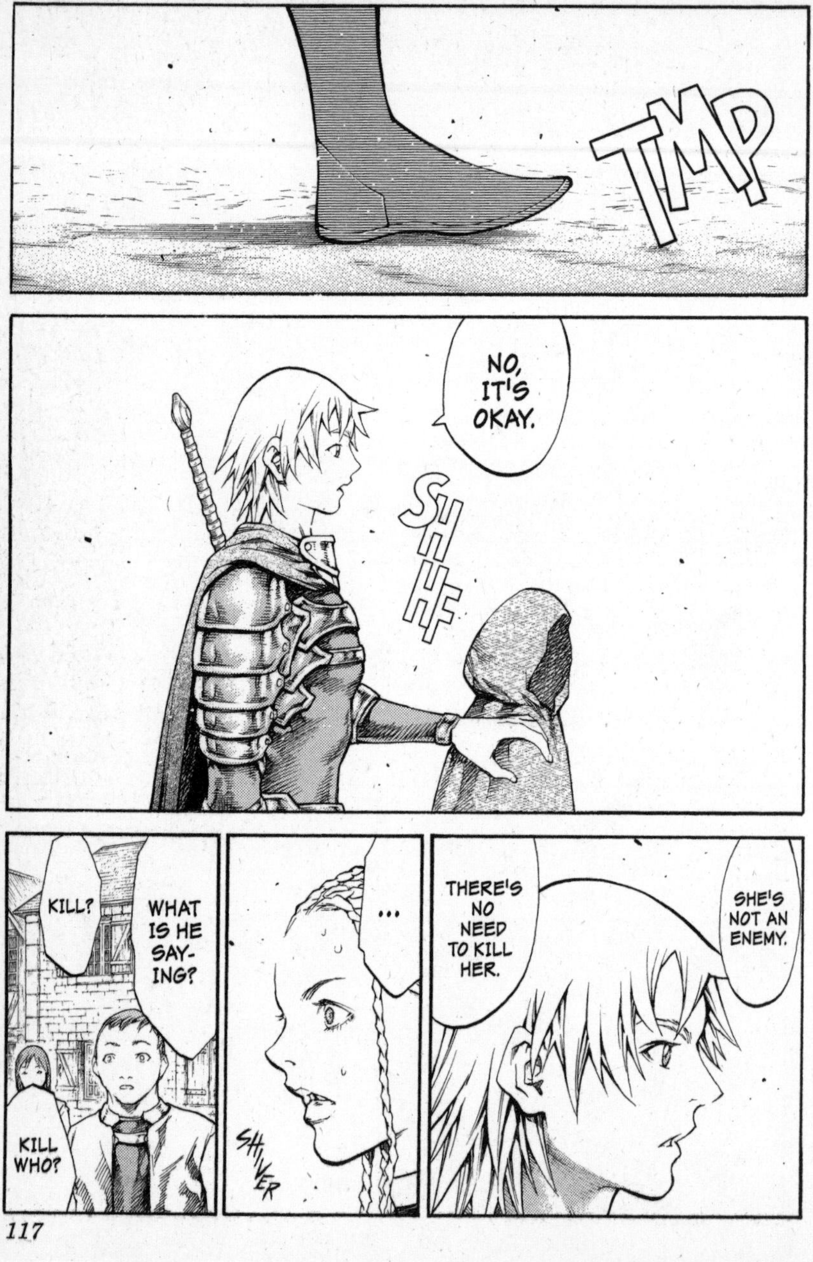

TMP
NO, IT'S OKAY.
SHHF
SHE'S NOT AN ENEMY.
THERE'S NO NEED TO KILL HER.
...
SHIVER
WHAT IS HE SAYING?
KILL?
KILL WHO?

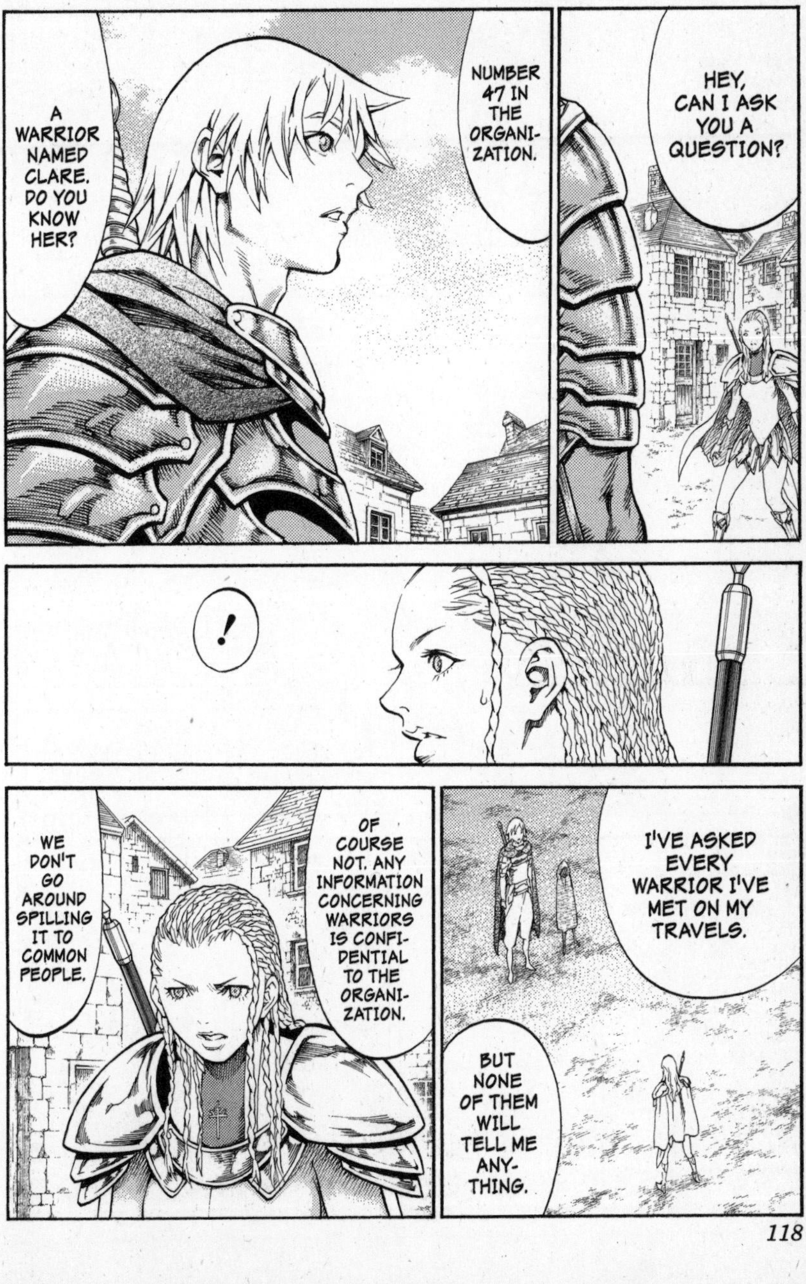
HEY, CAN I ASK YOU A QUESTION?
NUMBER 47 IN THE ORGANIZATION.
A WARRIOR NAMED CLARE. DO YOU KNOW HER?
!
I'VE ASKED EVERY WARRIOR I'VE MET ON MY TRAVELS.
BUT NONE OF THEM WILL TELL ME ANYTHING.
OF COURSE NOT. ANY INFORMATION CONCERNING WARRIORS IS CONFIDENTIAL TO THE ORGANIZATION.
WE DON'T GO AROUND SPILLING IT TO COMMON PEOPLE.

READ THIS WAY

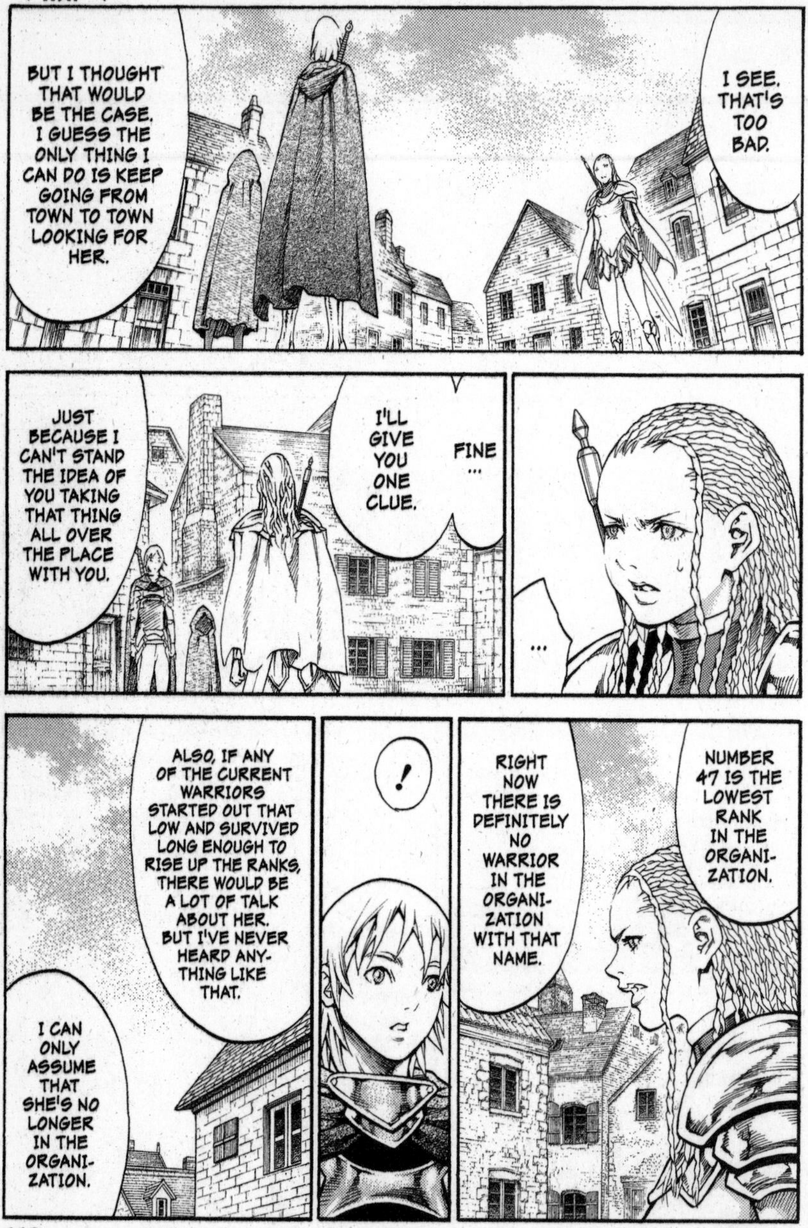

I SEE. THAT'S TOO BAD.
BUT I THOUGHT THAT WOULD BE THE CASE. I GUESS THE ONLY THING I CAN DO IS KEEP GOING FROM TOWN TO TOWN LOOKING FOR HER.
...
FINE ...
I'LL GIVE YOU ONE CLUE.
JUST BECAUSE I CAN'T STAND THE IDEA OF YOU TAKING THAT THING ALL OVER THE PLACE WITH YOU.
NUMBER 47 IS THE LOWEST RANK IN THE ORGANI-ZATION.
RIGHT NOW THERE IS DEFINITELY NO WARRIOR IN THE ORGANI-ZATION WITH THAT NAME.
!
ALSO, IF ANY OF THE CURRENT WARRIORS STARTED OUT THAT LOW AND SURVIVED LONG ENOUGH TO RISE UP THE RANKS, THERE WOULD BE A LOT OF TALK ABOUT HER. BUT I'VE NEVER HEARD ANY-THING LIKE THAT.
I CAN ONLY ASSUME THAT SHE'S NO LONGER IN THE ORGANI-ZATION.

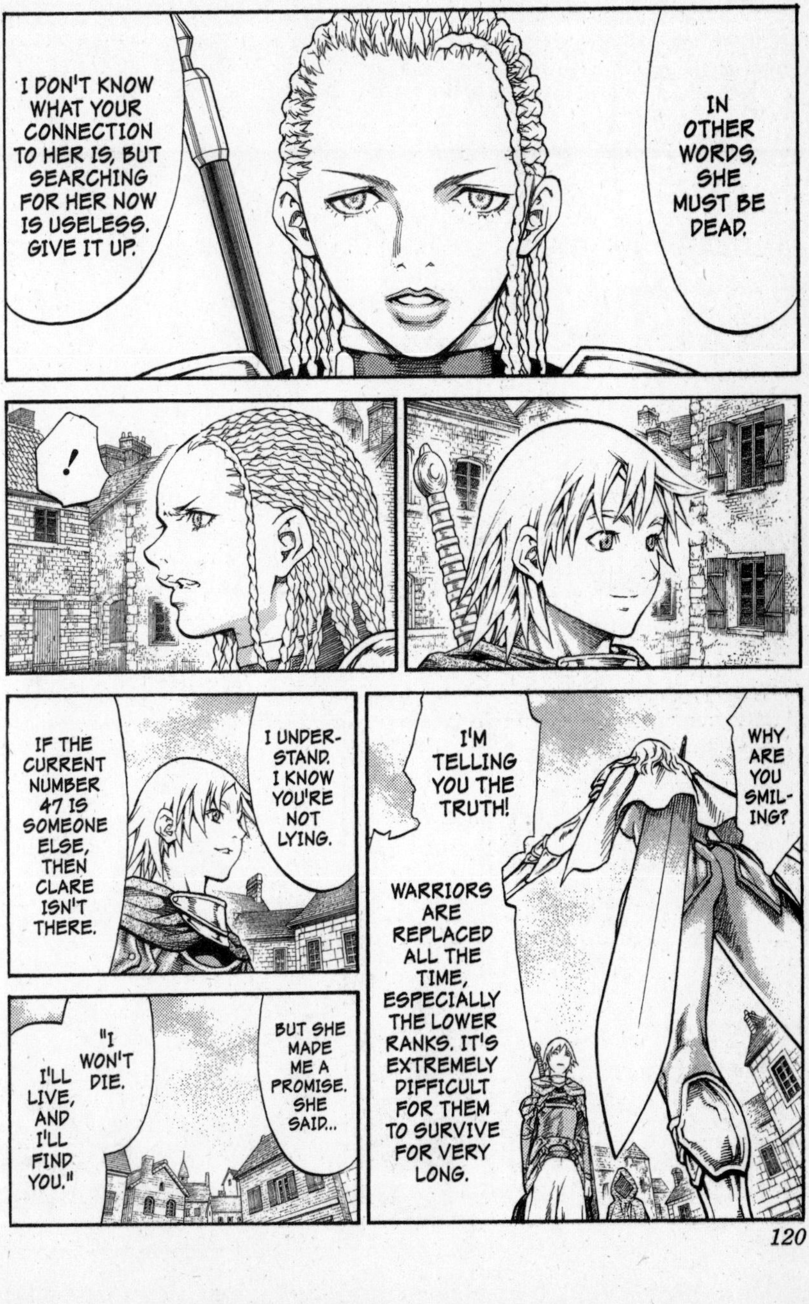
IN OTHER WORDS, SHE MUST BE DEAD.
I DON'T KNOW WHAT YOUR CONNECTION TO HER IS, BUT SEARCHING FOR HER NOW IS USELESS. GIVE IT UP.
!
WHY ARE YOU SMIL-ING?
I'M TELLING YOU THE TRUTH!
WARRIORS ARE REPLACED ALL THE TIME, ESPECIALLY THE LOWER RANKS. IT'S EXTREMELY DIFFICULT FOR THEM TO SURVIVE FOR VERY LONG.
I UNDER-STAND. I KNOW YOU'RE NOT LYING.
IF THE CURRENT NUMBER 47 IS SOMEONE ELSE, THEN CLARE ISN'T THERE.
BUT SHE MADE ME A PROMISE. SHE SAID...
"I WON'T DIE.
I'LL LIVE, AND I'LL FIND YOU."

READ THIS WAY

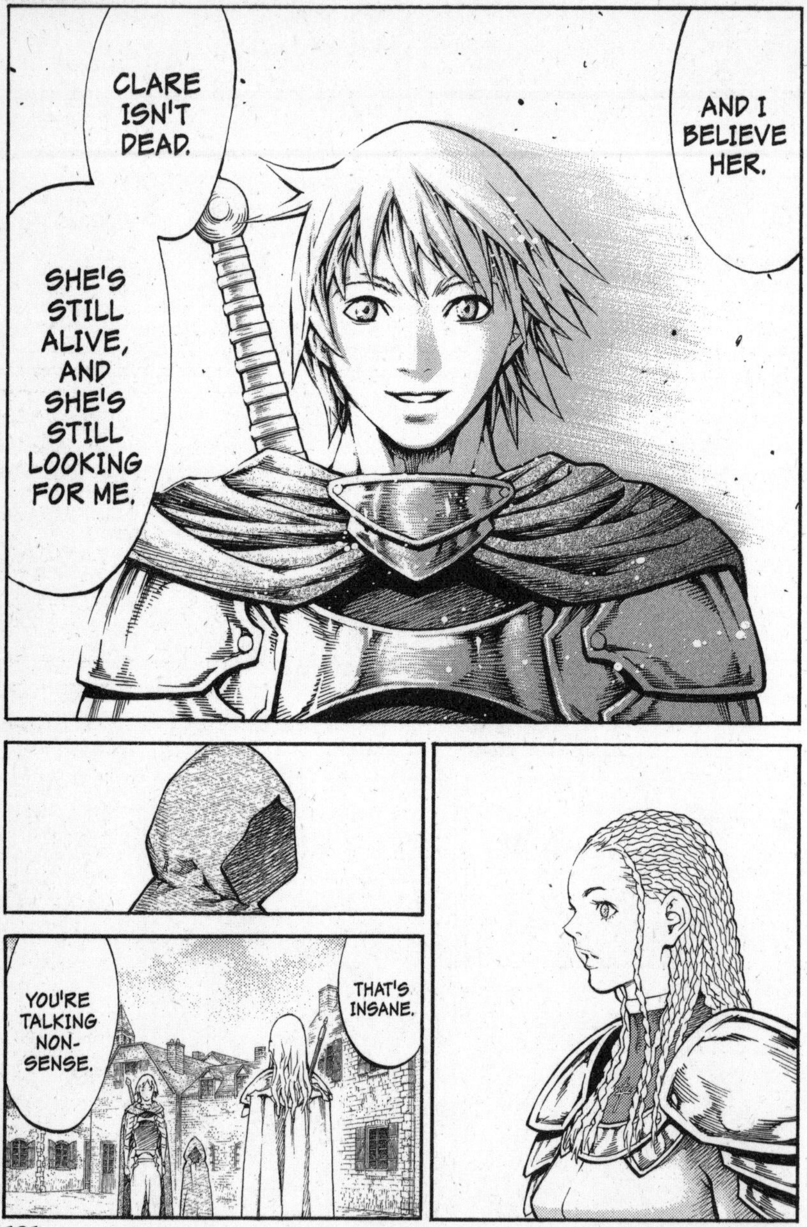
AND I BELIEVE HER.
CLARE ISN'T DEAD.
SHE'S STILL ALIVE, AND SHE'S STILL LOOKING FOR ME.
THAT'S INSANE.
YOU'RE TALKING NON-SENSE.

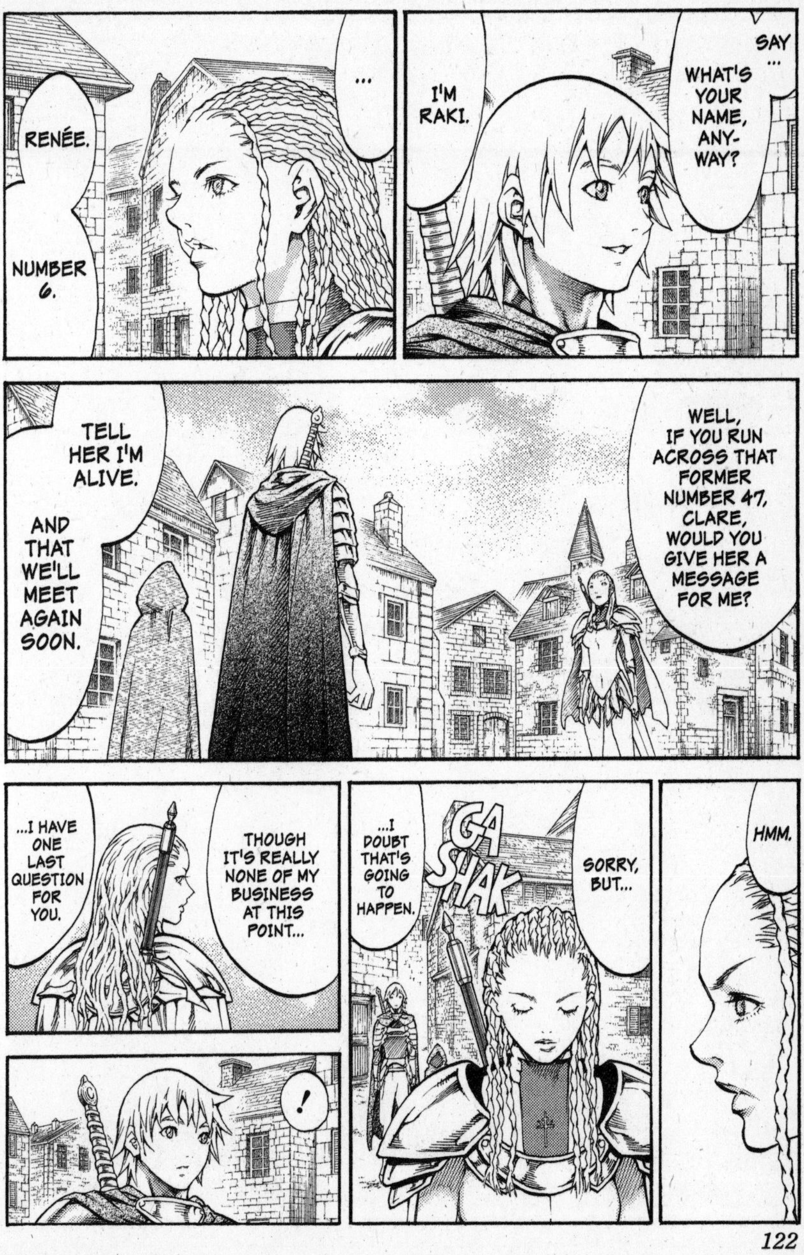
SAY ...
WHAT'S YOUR NAME, ANY-WAY?
I'M RAKI.
...
RENÉE.
NUMBER 6.
WELL, IF YOU RUN ACROSS THAT FORMER NUMBER 47, CLARE, WOULD YOU GIVE HER A MESSAGE FOR ME?
TELL HER I'M ALIVE.
AND THAT WE'LL MEET AGAIN SOON.
HMM.
SORRY, BUT...
GA SHAK
...I DOUBT THAT'S GOING TO HAPPEN.
THOUGH IT'S REALLY NONE OF MY BUSINESS AT THIS POINT...
...I HAVE ONE LAST QUESTION FOR YOU.
!

READ THIS WAY

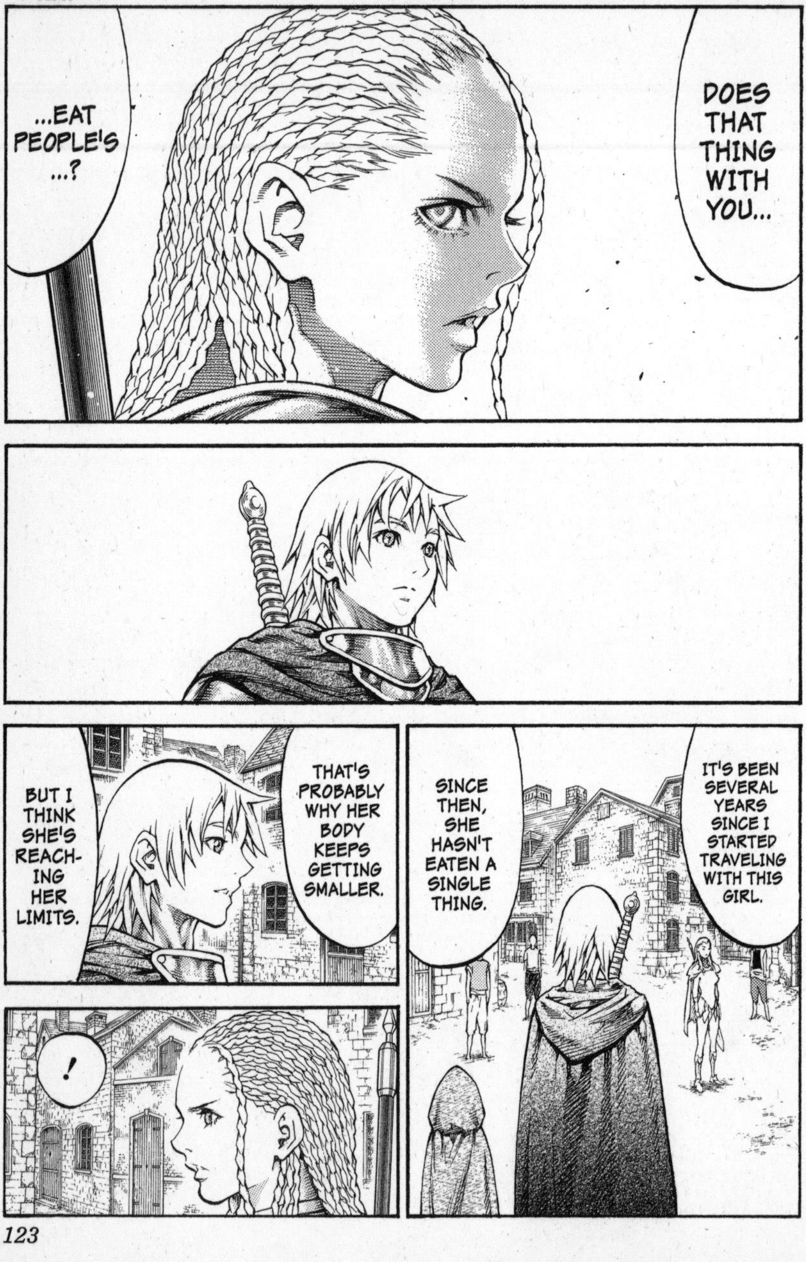
DOES THAT THING WITH YOU...
...EAT PEOPLE'S ...?
IT'S BEEN SEVERAL YEARS SINCE I STARTED TRAVELING WITH THIS GIRL.
SINCE THEN, SHE HASN'T EATEN A SINGLE THING.
THAT'S PROBABLY WHY HER BODY KEEPS GETTING SMALLER.
BUT I THINK SHE'S REACHING HER LIMITS.
!

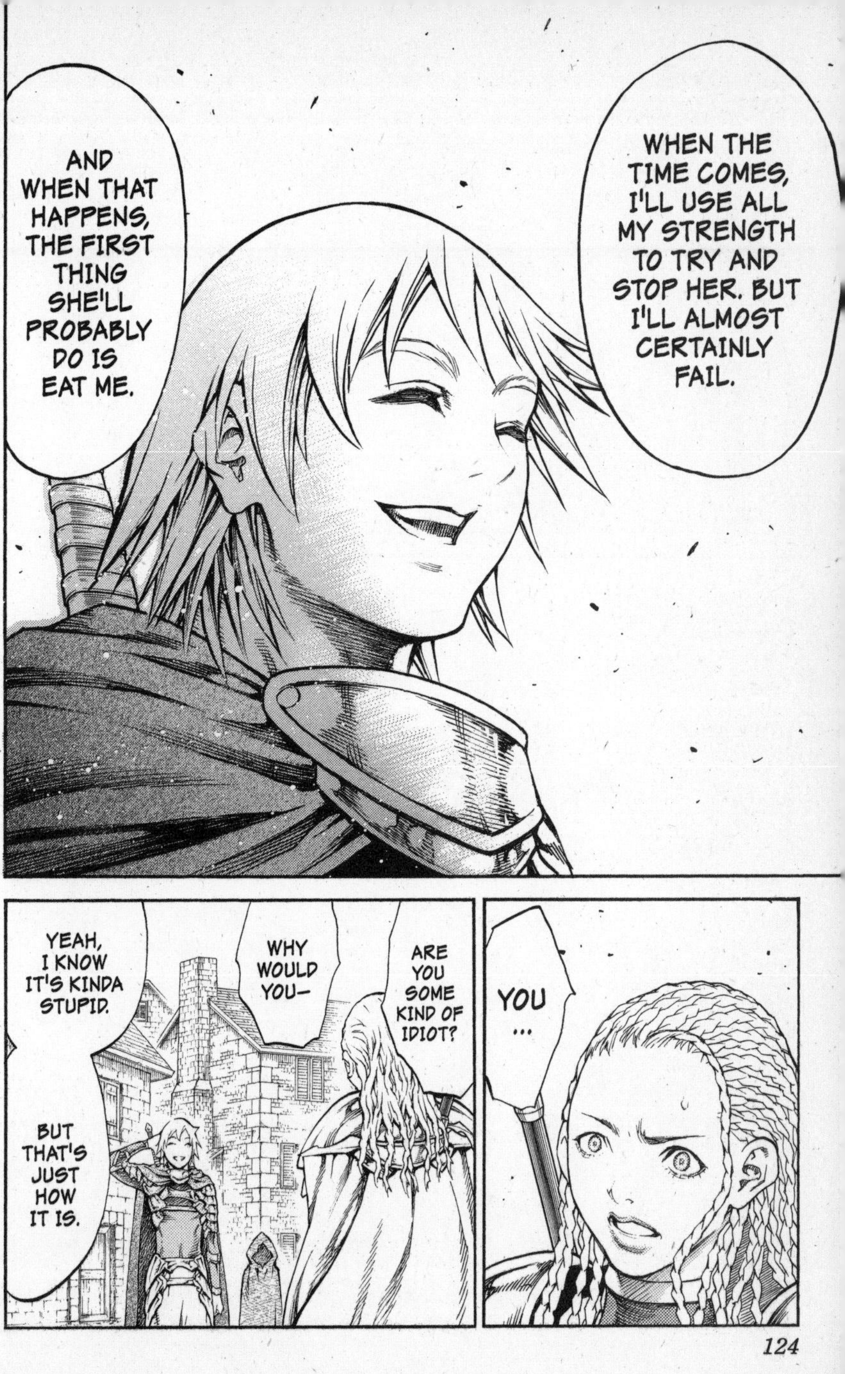
WHEN THE TIME COMES, I'LL USE ALL MY STRENGTH TO TRY AND STOP HER. BUT I'LL ALMOST CERTAINLY FAIL.
AND WHEN THAT HAPPENS, THE FIRST THING SHE'LL PROBABLY DO IS EAT ME.
YOU ...
ARE YOU SOME KIND OF IDIOT?
WHY WOULD YOU—
YEAH, I KNOW IT'S KINDA STUPID.
BUT THAT'S JUST HOW IT IS.

READ THIS WAY

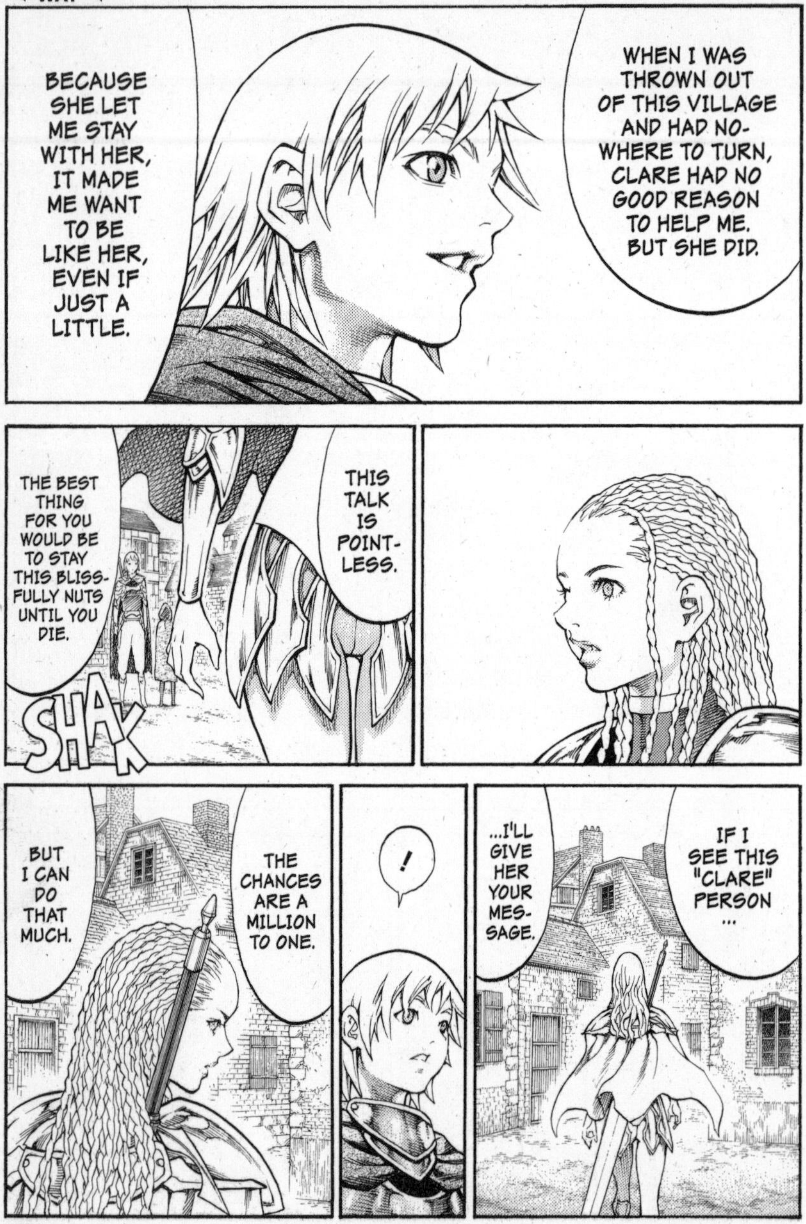
WHEN I WAS THROWN OUT OF THIS VILLAGE AND HAD NOWHERE TO TURN, CLARE HAD NO GOOD REASON TO HELP ME. BUT SHE DID.
BECAUSE SHE LET ME STAY WITH HER, IT MADE ME WANT TO BE LIKE HER, EVEN IF JUST A LITTLE.
THIS TALK IS POINTLESS.
THE BEST THING FOR YOU WOULD BE TO STAY THIS BLISSFULLY NUTS UNTIL YOU DIE.
SHAK
IF I SEE THIS "CLARE" PERSON ...
...I'LL GIVE HER YOUR MESSAGE.
!
THE CHANCES ARE A MILLION TO ONE.
BUT I CAN DO THAT MUCH.

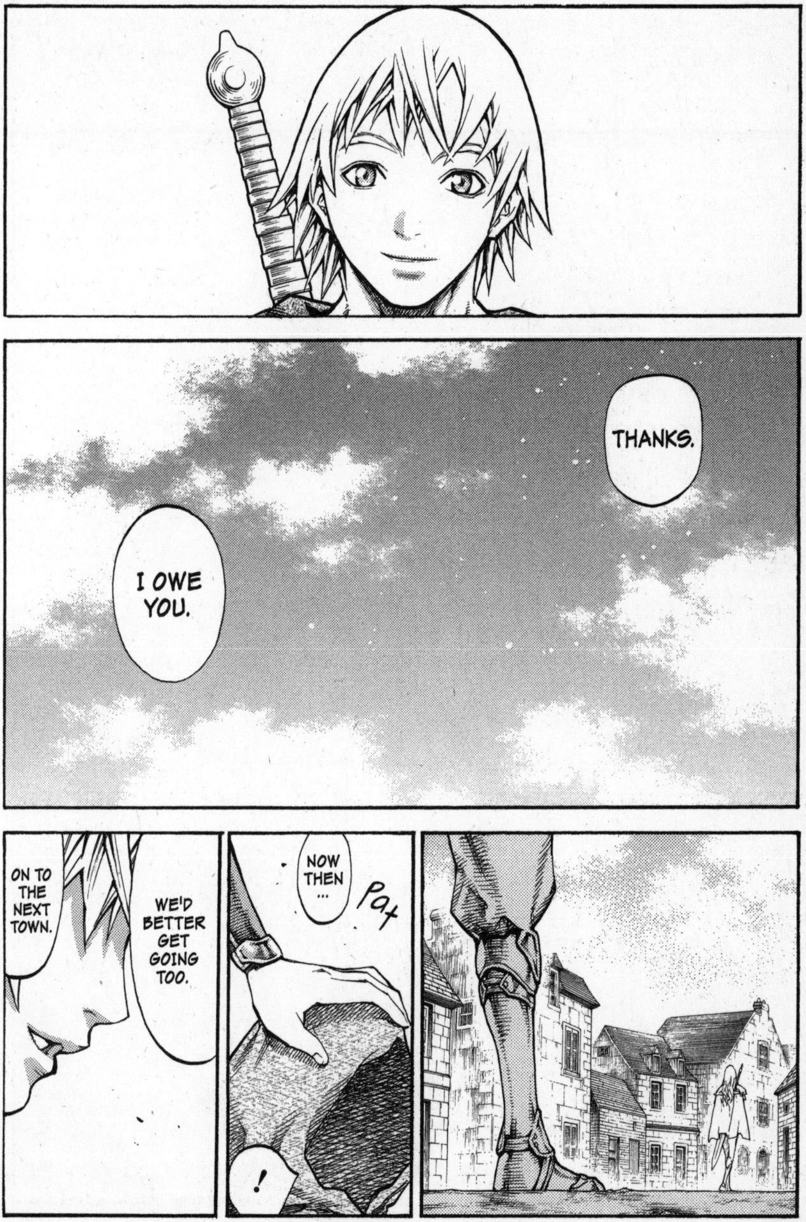
THANKS.
I OWE YOU.
NOW THEN ...
Pat
!
WE'D BETTER GET GOING TOO.
ON TO THE NEXT TOWN.

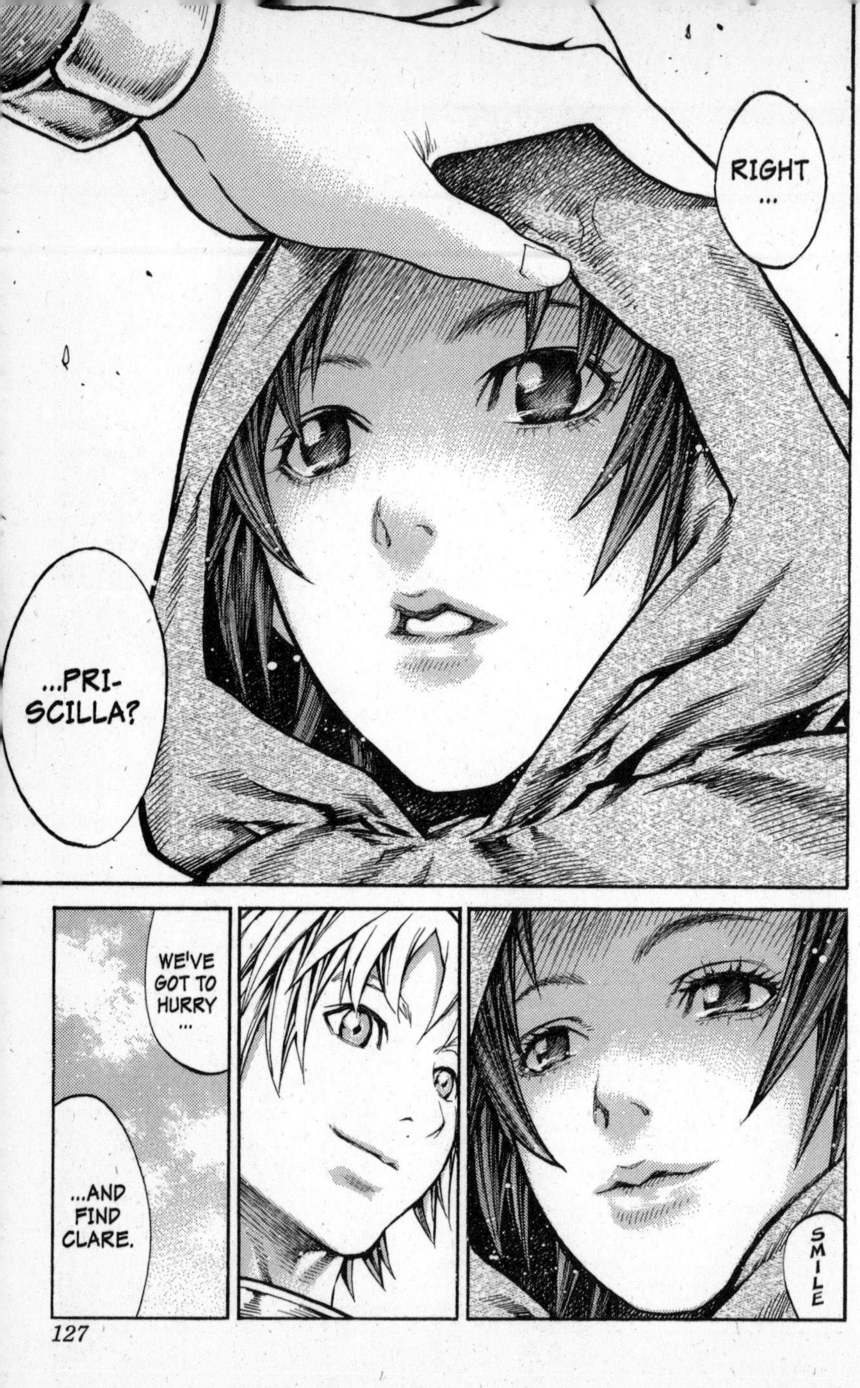
RIGHT...
...PRI-SCILLA?
SMILE
WE'VE GOT TO HURRY...
...AND FIND CLARE.

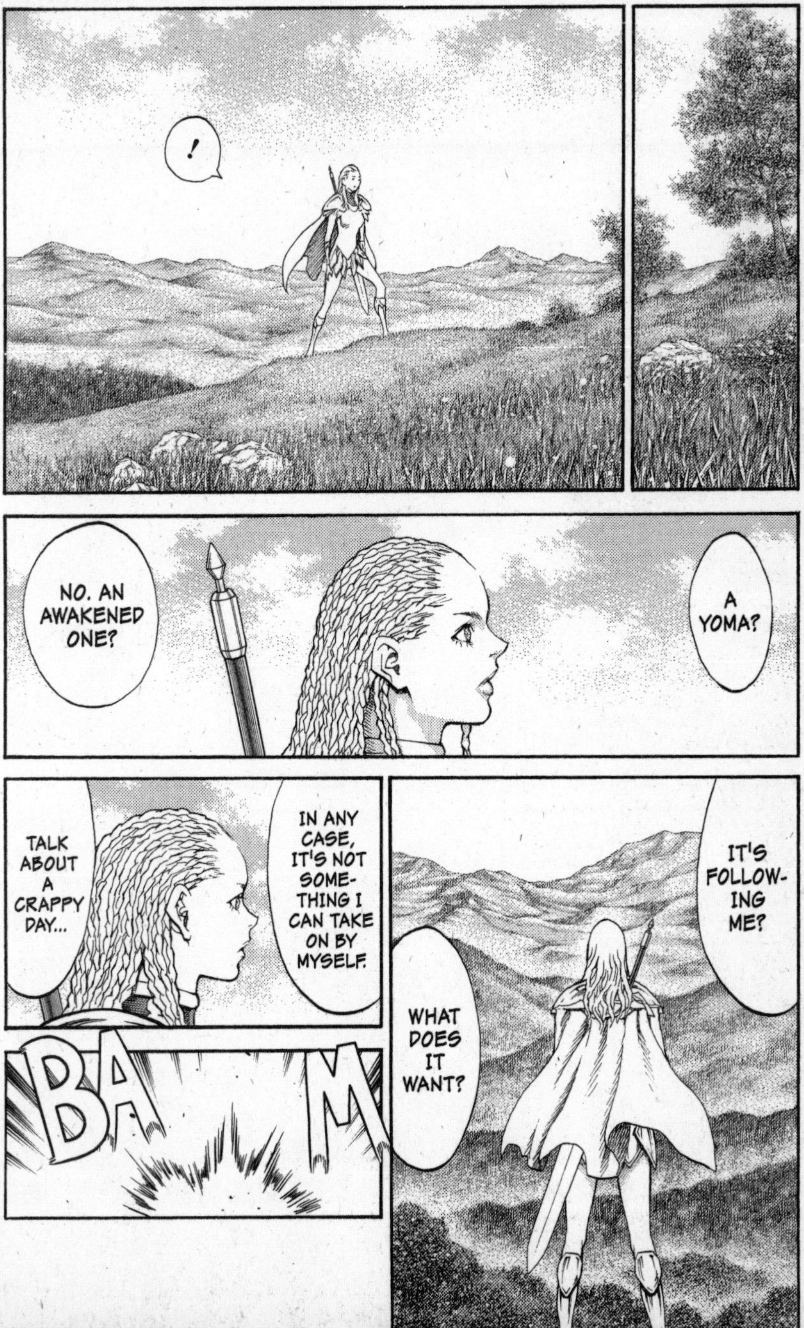
!
A YOMA?
NO. AN AWAKENED ONE?
IT'S FOLLOW-ING ME?
WHAT DOES IT WANT?
IN ANY CASE, IT'S NOT SOME-THING I CAN TAKE ON BY MYSELF.
TALK ABOUT A CRAPPY DAY...
BAM

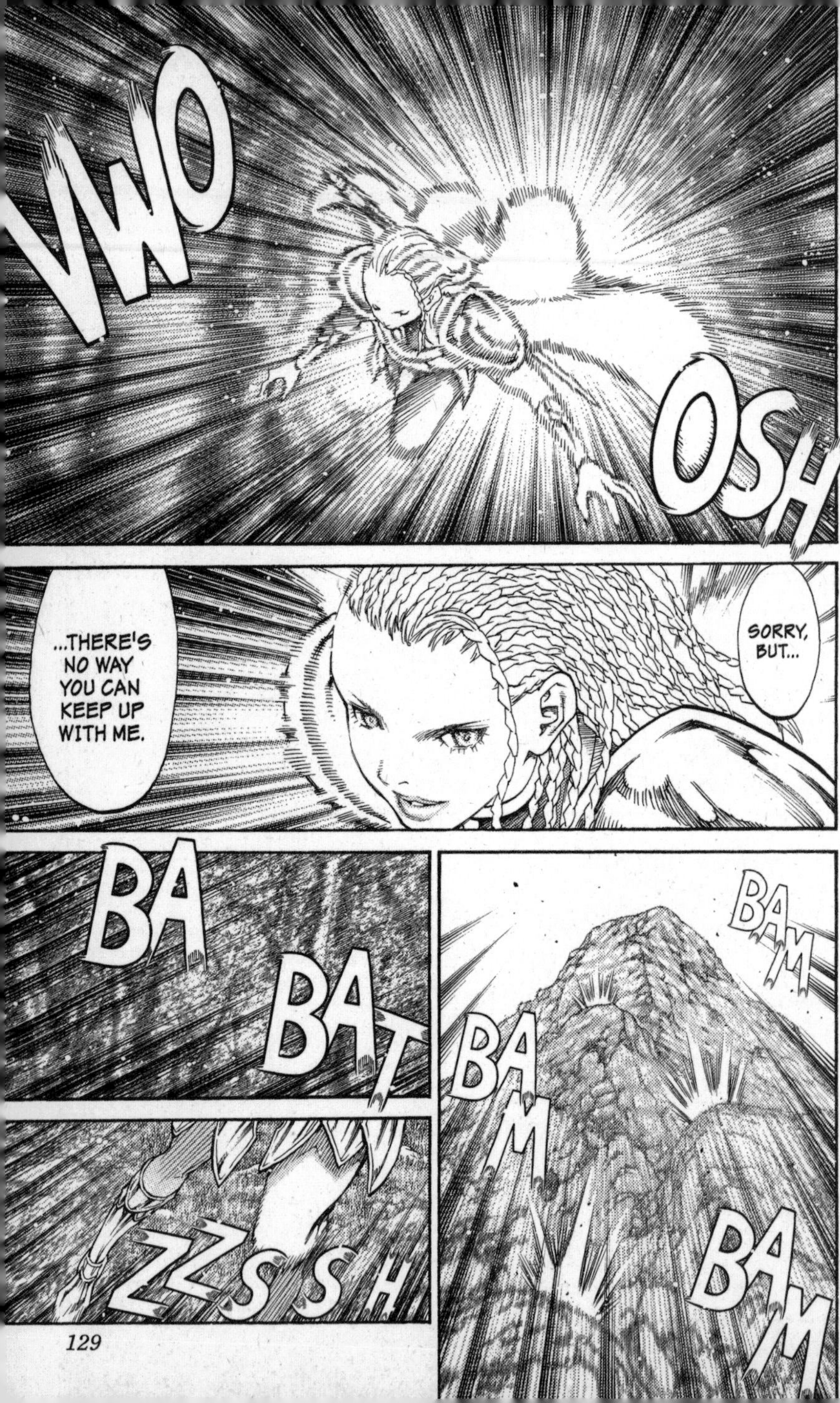
VWO
OSH
SORRY, BUT...
...THERE'S NO WAY YOU CAN KEEP UP WITH ME.
BAM
BAM
BAM
BA
BAT
ZZSSH

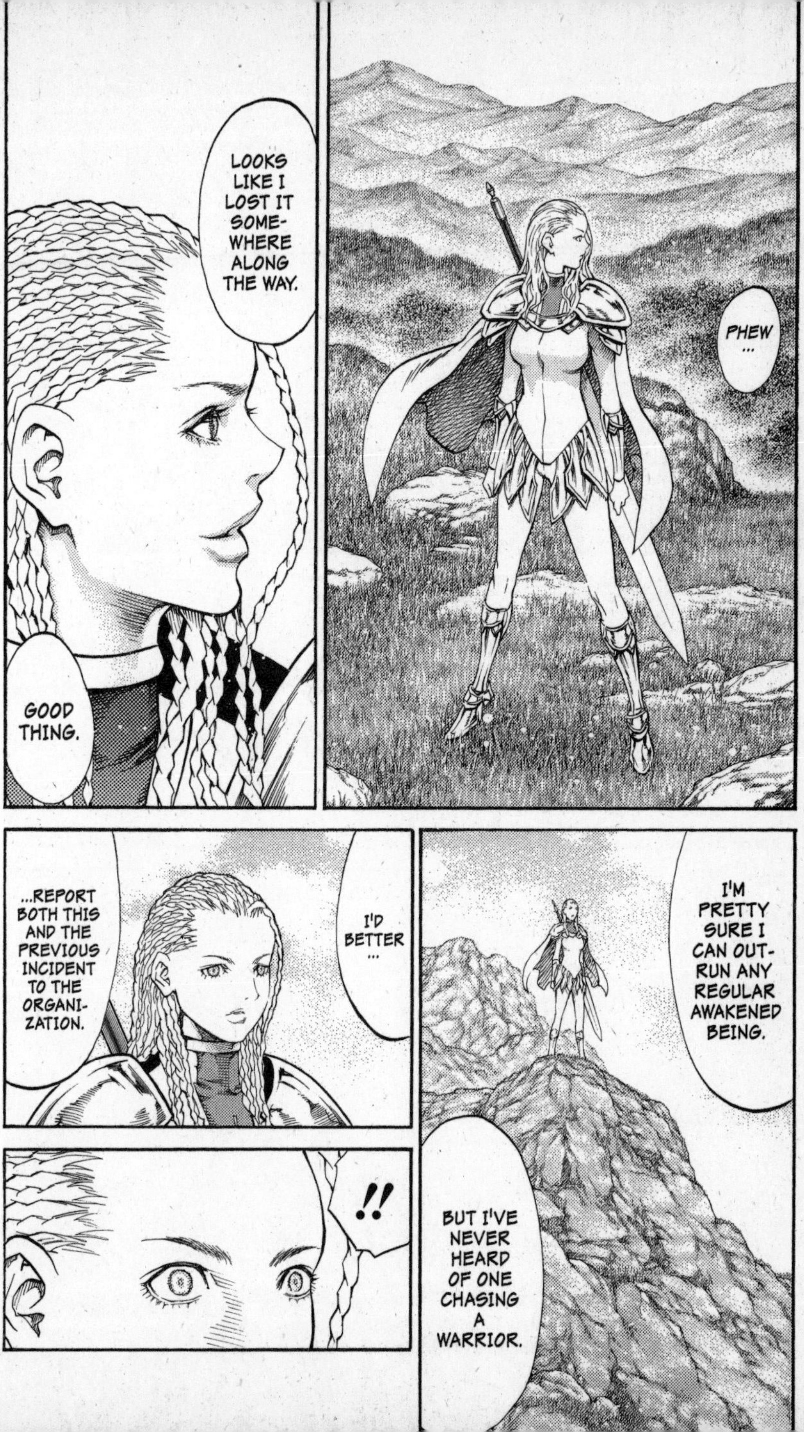
PHEW ...
LOOKS LIKE I LOST IT SOME-WHERE ALONG THE WAY.
GOOD THING.
I'M PRETTY SURE I CAN OUT-RUN ANY REGULAR AWAKENED BEING.
BUT I'VE NEVER HEARD OF ONE CHASING A WARRIOR.
I'D BETTER ...
...REPORT BOTH THIS AND THE PREVIOUS INCIDENT TO THE ORGANI-ZATION.
!!

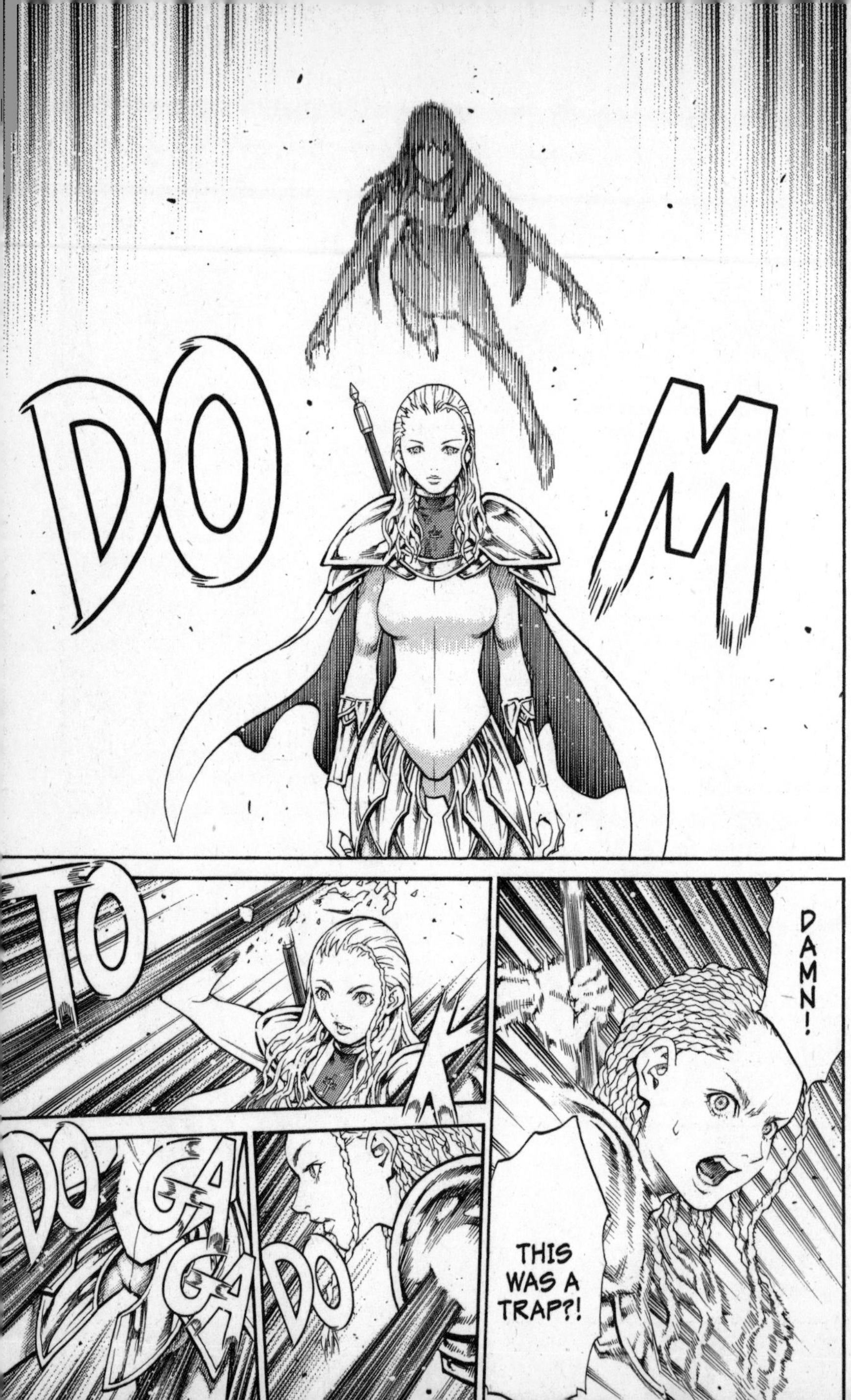
DOM
DAMN!
THIS WAS A TRAP?!
TO
DO GA
GA DO

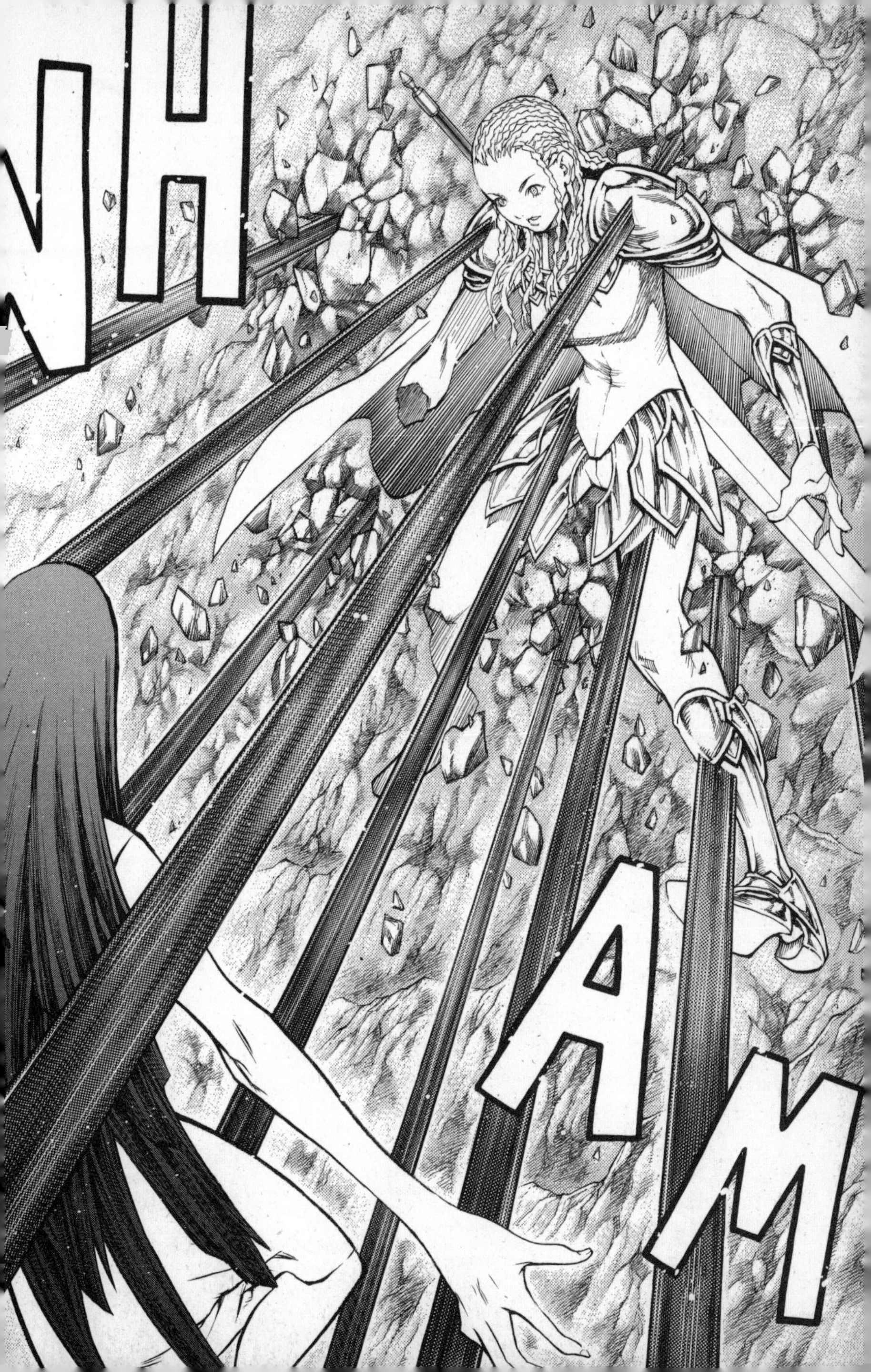
H
AM

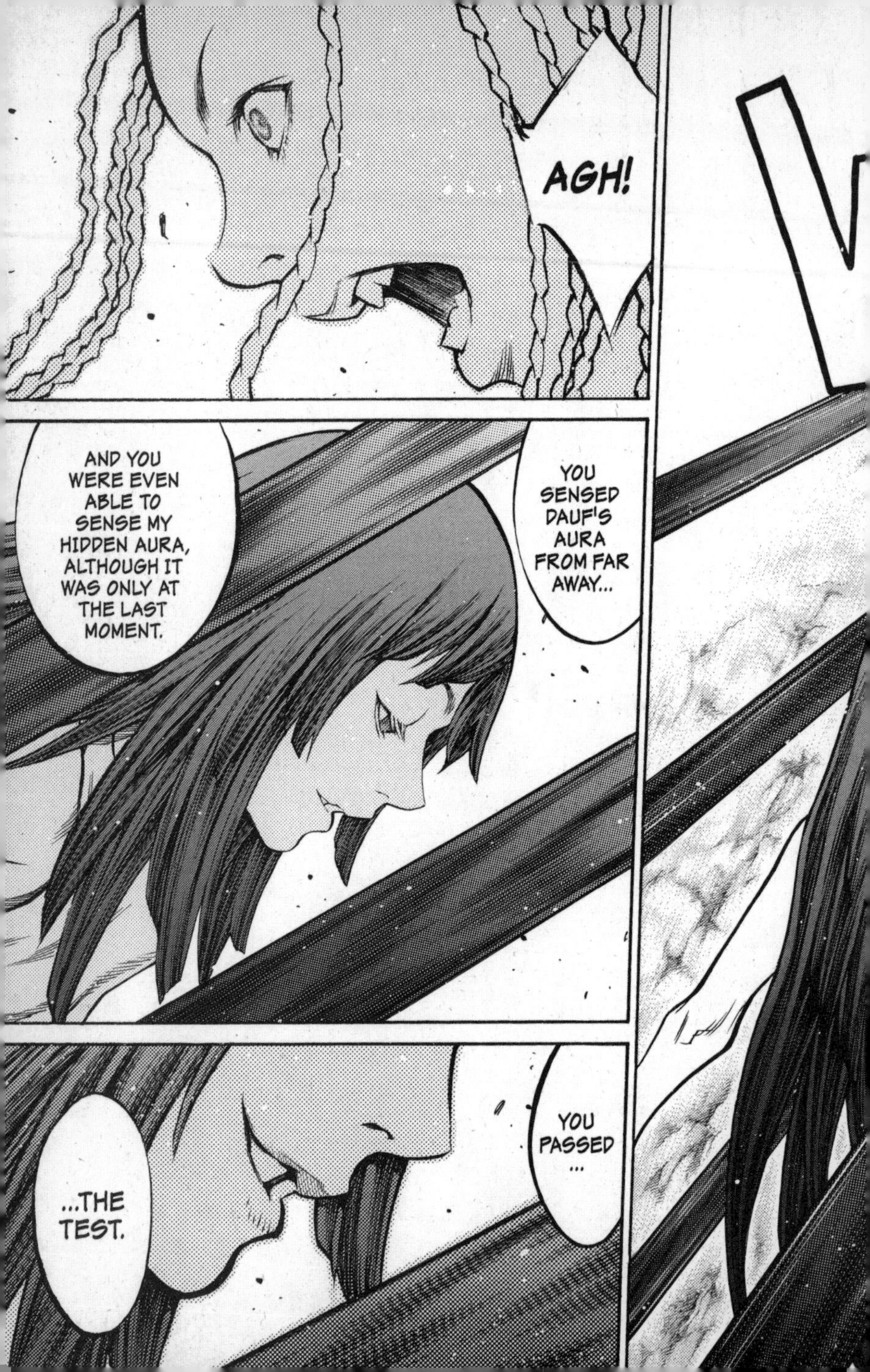
AGH!
YOU SENSED DAUF'S AURA FROM FAR AWAY...
AND YOU WERE EVEN ABLE TO SENSE MY HIDDEN AURA, ALTHOUGH IT WAS ONLY AT THE LAST MOMENT.
YOU PASSED ...
...THE TEST.

クレイモア
Claymore

SCENE 82: GENESIS OF WAR, PART 5

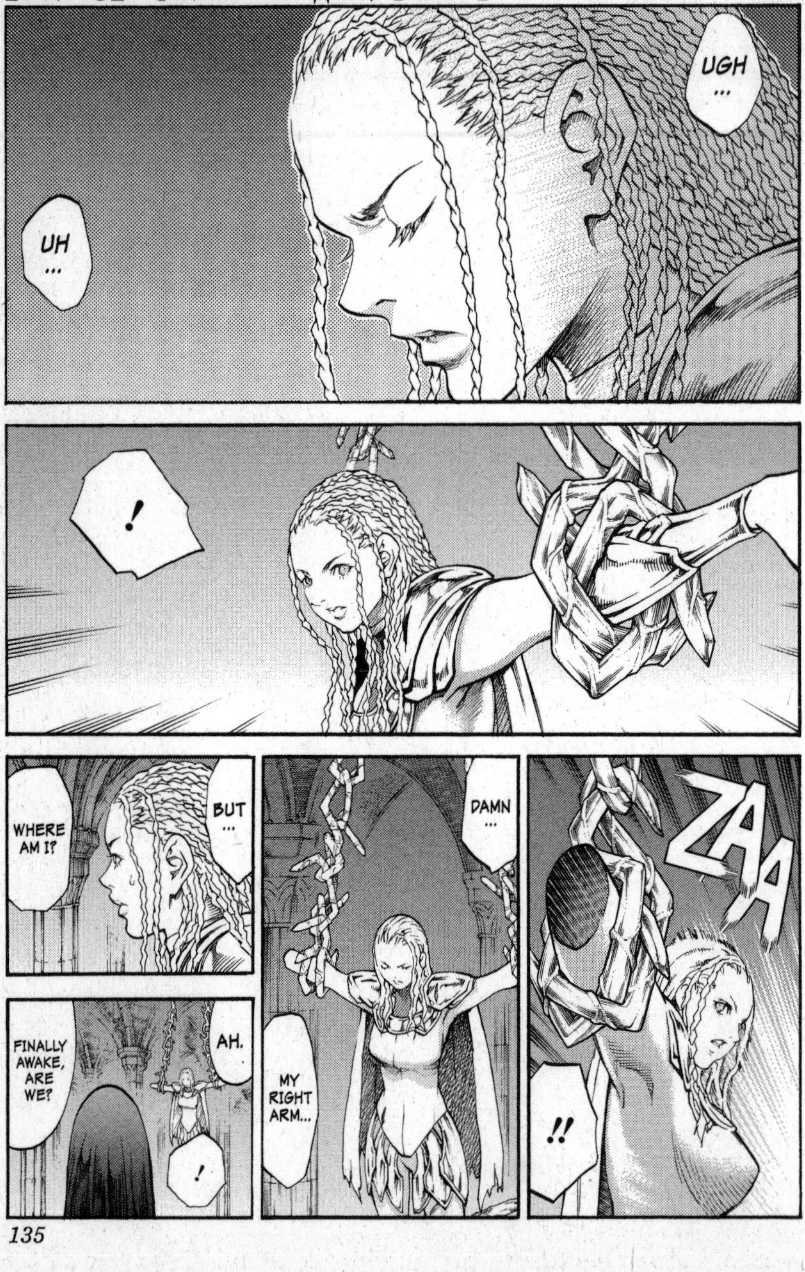
UGH...
UH...
!
ZAA
!!
DAMN...
MY RIGHT ARM...
BUT...
WHERE AM I?
AH.
FINALLY AWAKE, ARE WE?
!

Scene 82: Genesis of War, Part 5

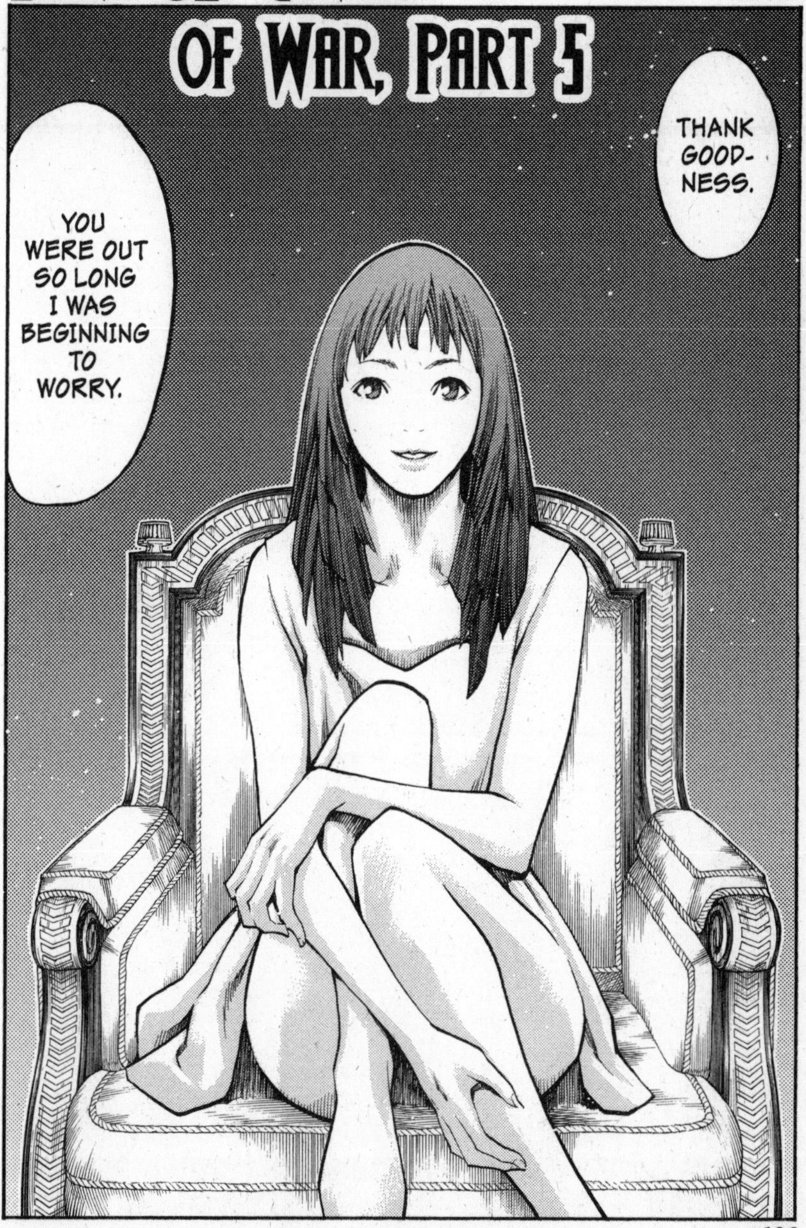
THANK GOOD-NESS.
YOU WERE OUT SO LONG I WAS BEGINNING TO WORRY.

READ THIS WAY

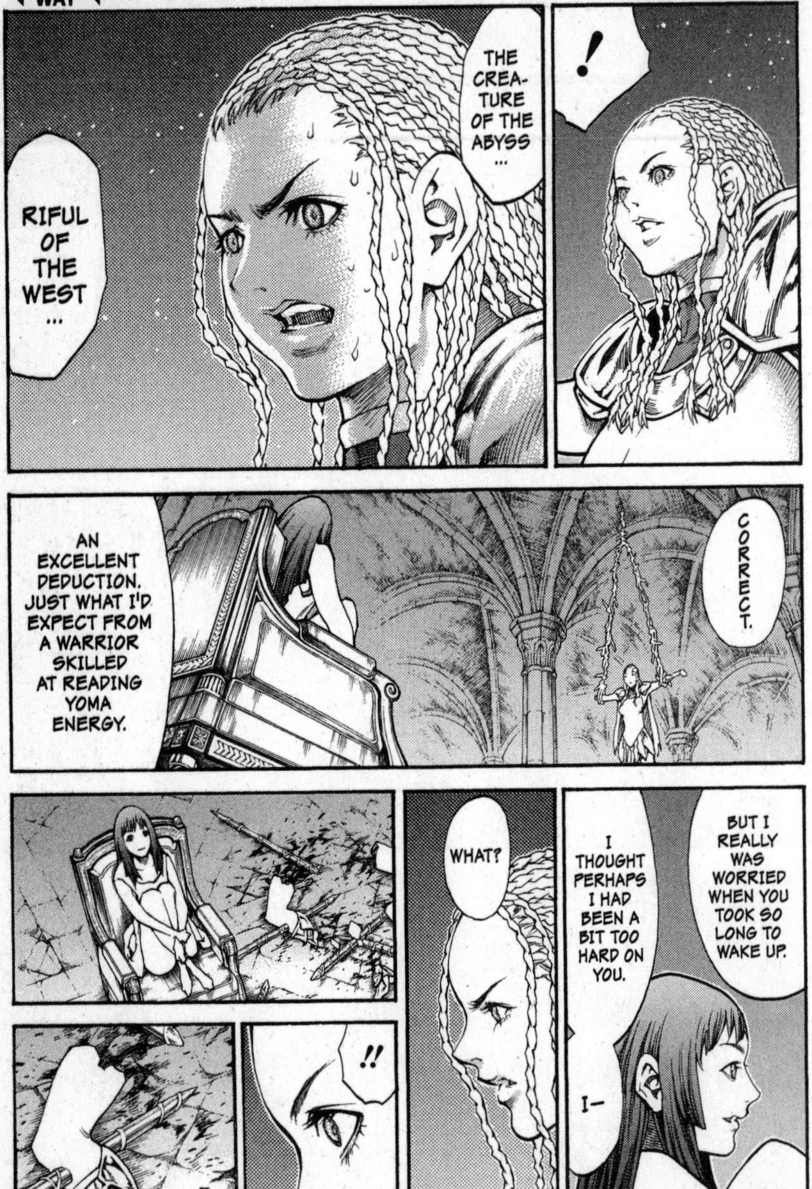
!
THE CREATURE OF THE ABYSS ...
RIFUL OF THE WEST ...
CORRECT.
AN EXCELLENT DEDUCTION. JUST WHAT I'D EXPECT FROM A WARRIOR SKILLED AT READING YOMA ENERGY.
BUT I REALLY WAS WORRIED WHEN YOU TOOK SO LONG TO WAKE UP.
I THOUGHT PERHAPS I HAD BEEN A BIT TOO HARD ON YOU.
I—
WHAT?
!!

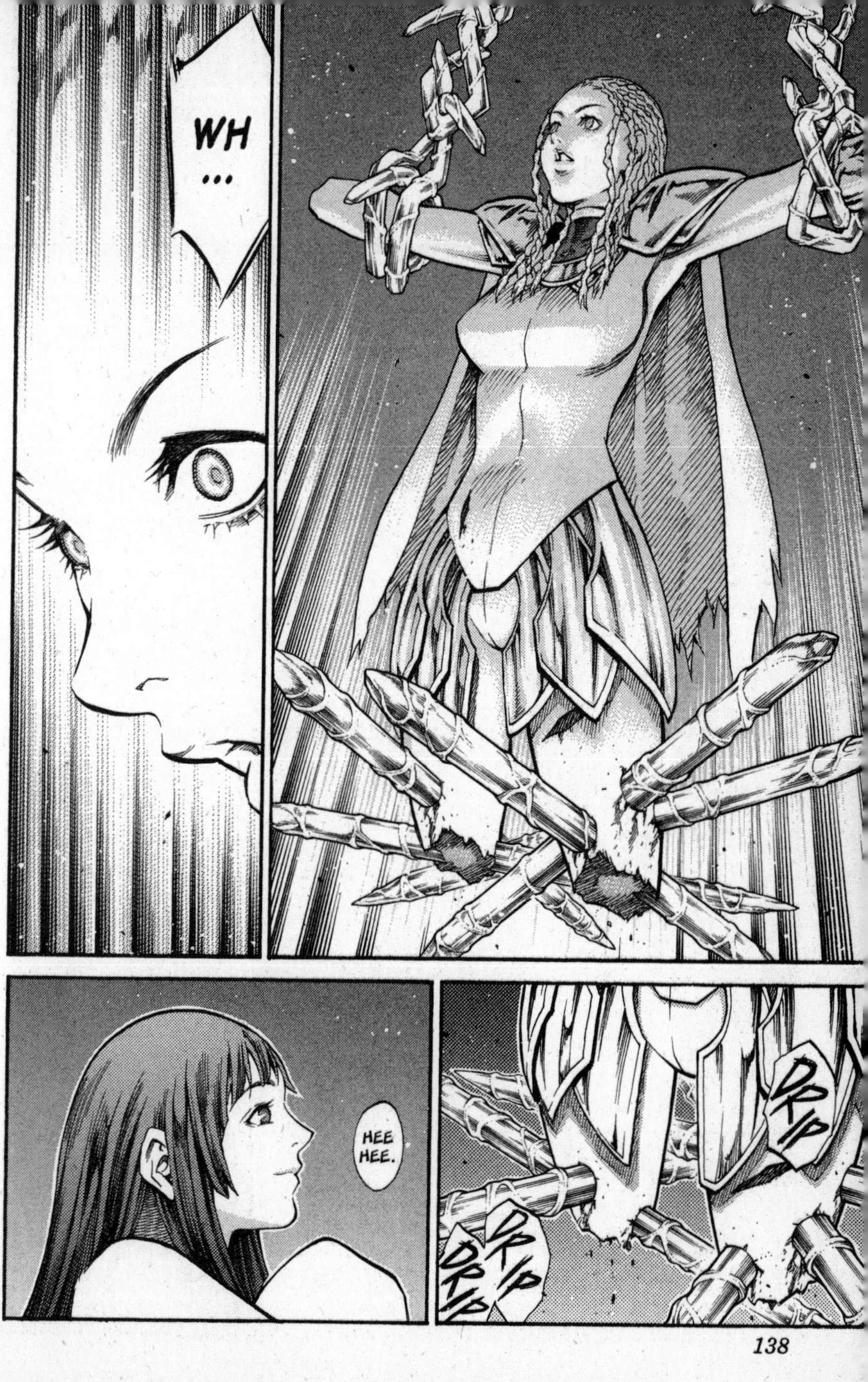
WH ...
DRIP
DRIP DRIP
HEE HEE.

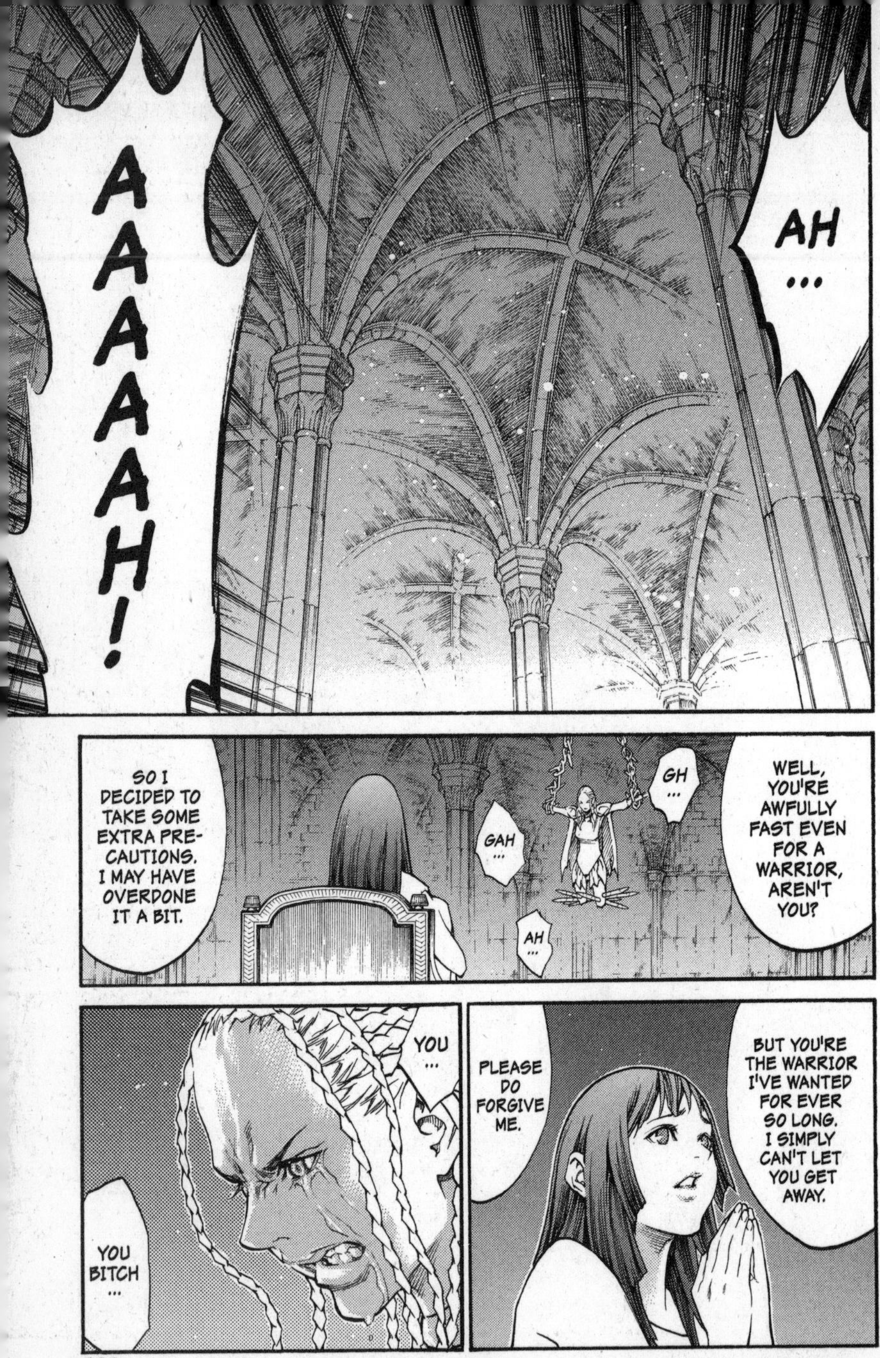
AH ...
AAAAAH!
WELL, YOU'RE AWFULLY FAST EVEN FOR A WARRIOR, AREN'T YOU?
GH ...
GAH ...
AH ...
SO I DECIDED TO TAKE SOME EXTRA PRE-CAUTIONS. I MAY HAVE OVERDONE IT A BIT.
BUT YOU'RE THE WARRIOR I'VE WANTED FOR EVER SO LONG. I SIMPLY CAN'T LET YOU GET AWAY.
PLEASE DO FORGIVE ME.
YOU ...
YOU BITCH ...

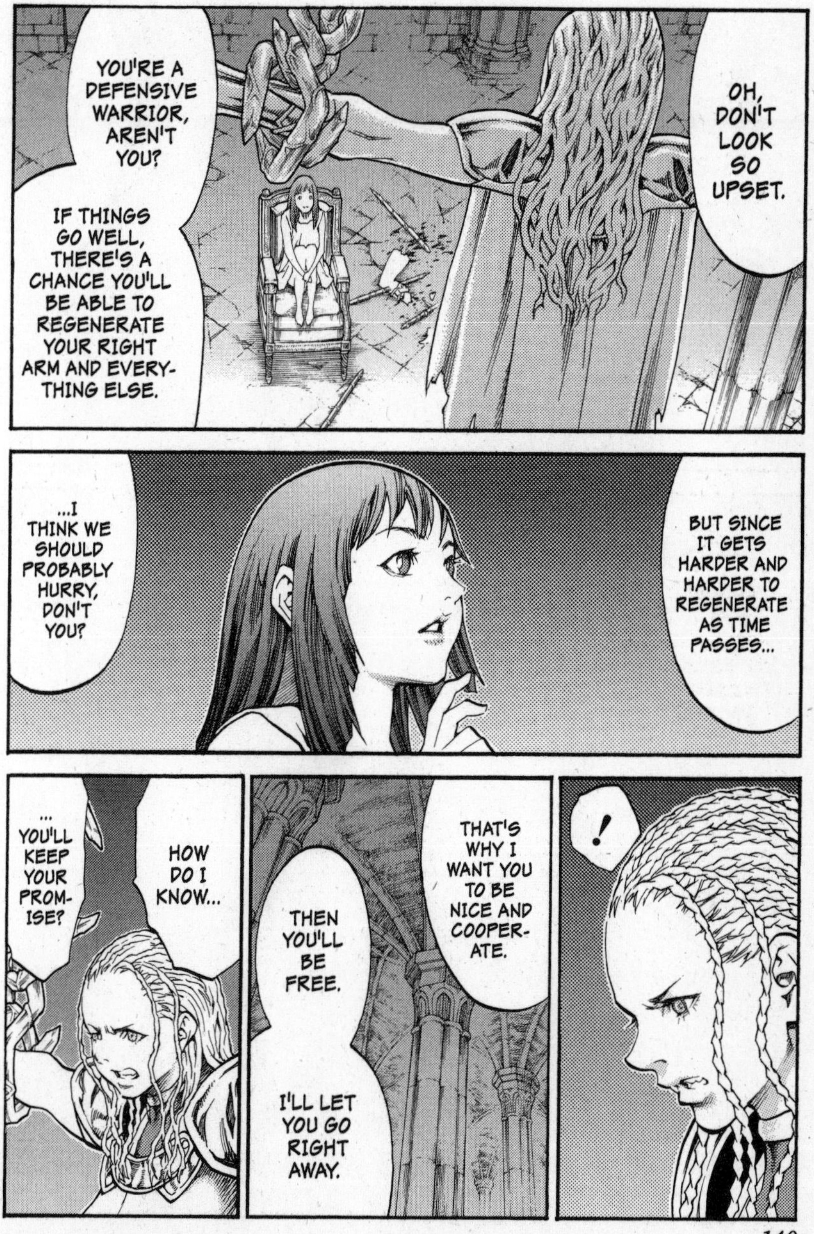
OH, DON'T LOOK SO UPSET.
YOU'RE A DEFENSIVE WARRIOR, AREN'T YOU?
IF THINGS GO WELL, THERE'S A CHANCE YOU'LL BE ABLE TO REGENERATE YOUR RIGHT ARM AND EVERY-THING ELSE.
BUT SINCE IT GETS HARDER AND HARDER TO REGENERATE AS TIME PASSES...
...I THINK WE SHOULD PROBABLY HURRY, DON'T YOU?
!
THAT'S WHY I WANT YOU TO BE NICE AND COOPER-ATE.
THEN YOU'LL BE FREE.
I'LL LET YOU GO RIGHT AWAY.
HOW DO I KNOW...
...YOU'LL KEEP YOUR PROM-ISE?

READ THIS WAY

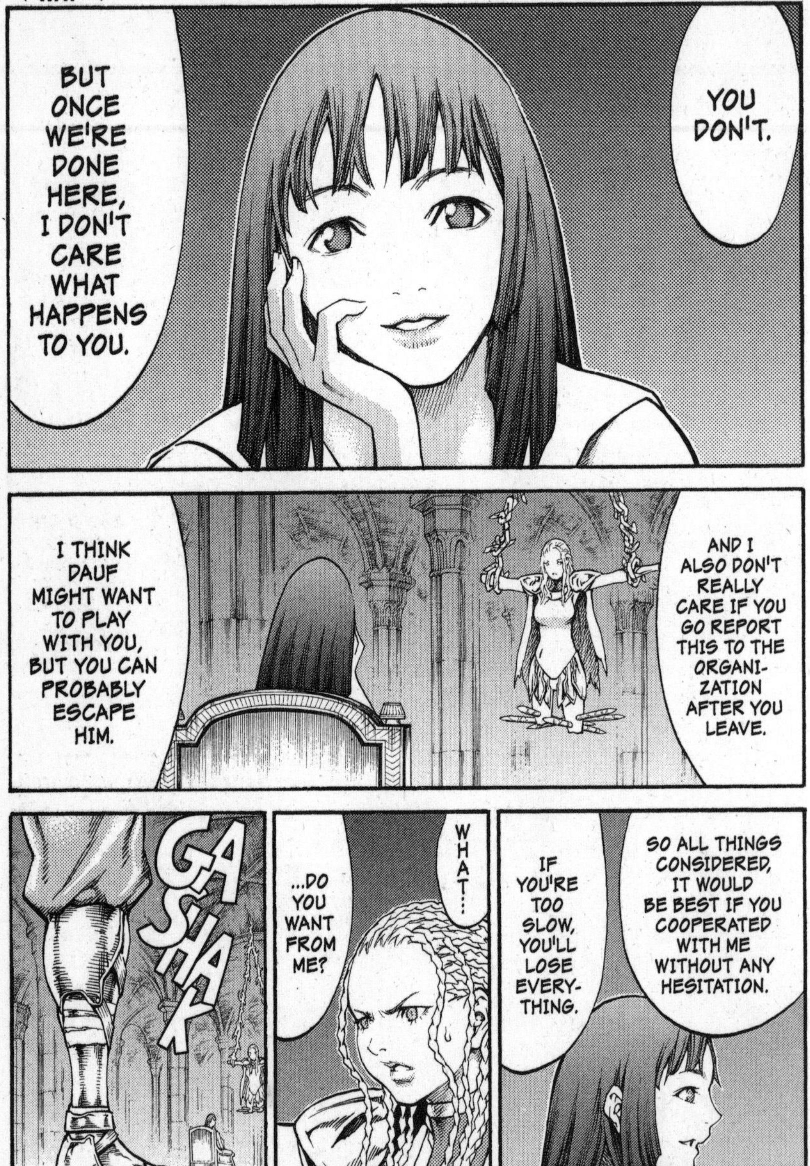
YOU DON'T.
BUT ONCE WE'RE DONE HERE, I DON'T CARE WHAT HAPPENS TO YOU.
AND I ALSO DON'T REALLY CARE IF YOU GO REPORT THIS TO THE ORGANI-ZATION AFTER YOU LEAVE.
I THINK DAUF MIGHT WANT TO PLAY WITH YOU, BUT YOU CAN PROBABLY ESCAPE HIM.
SO ALL THINGS CONSIDERED, IT WOULD BE BEST IF YOU COOPERATED WITH ME WITHOUT ANY HESITATION.
IF YOU'RE TOO SLOW, YOU'LL LOSE EVERY-THING.
WHAT...
...DO YOU WANT FROM ME?
GASHAK

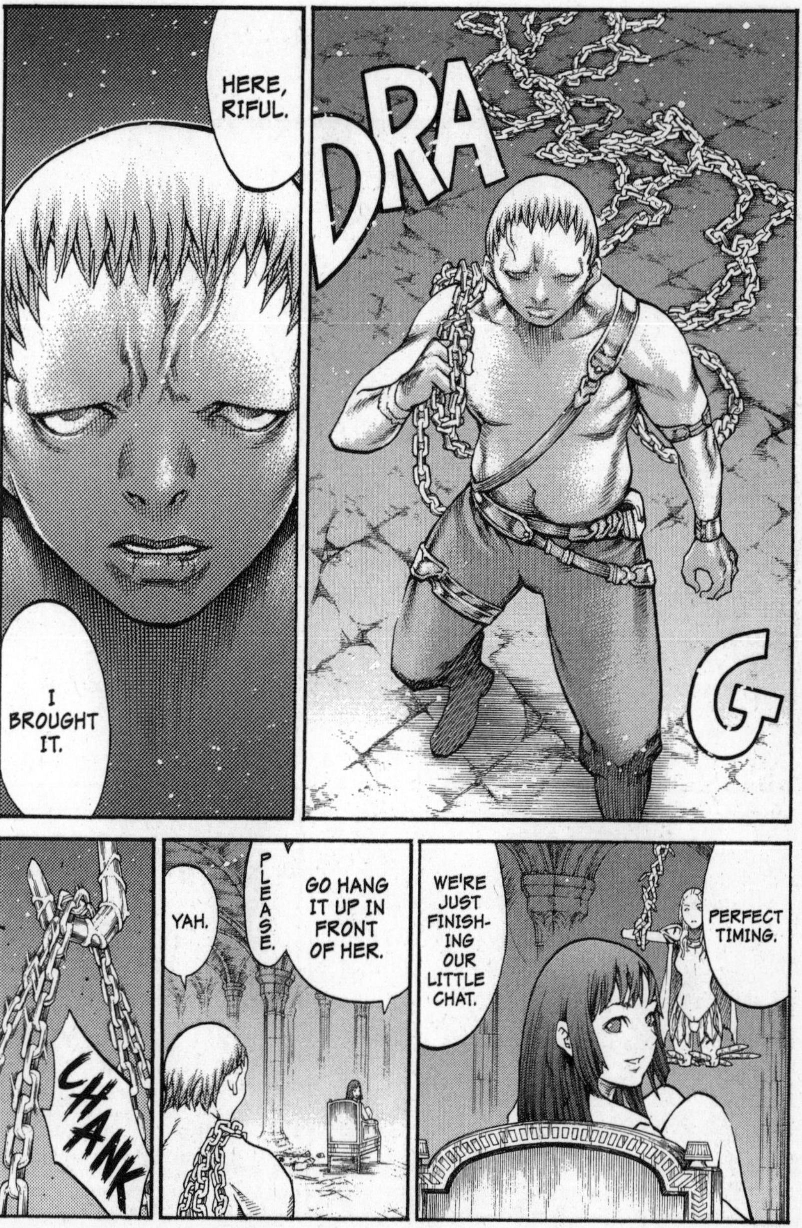
DRA
G
HERE, RIFUL.
I BROUGHT IT.
PERFECT TIMING.
WE'RE JUST FINISHING OUR LITTLE CHAT.
GO HANG IT UP IN FRONT OF HER.
PLEASE.
YAH.
CHANK

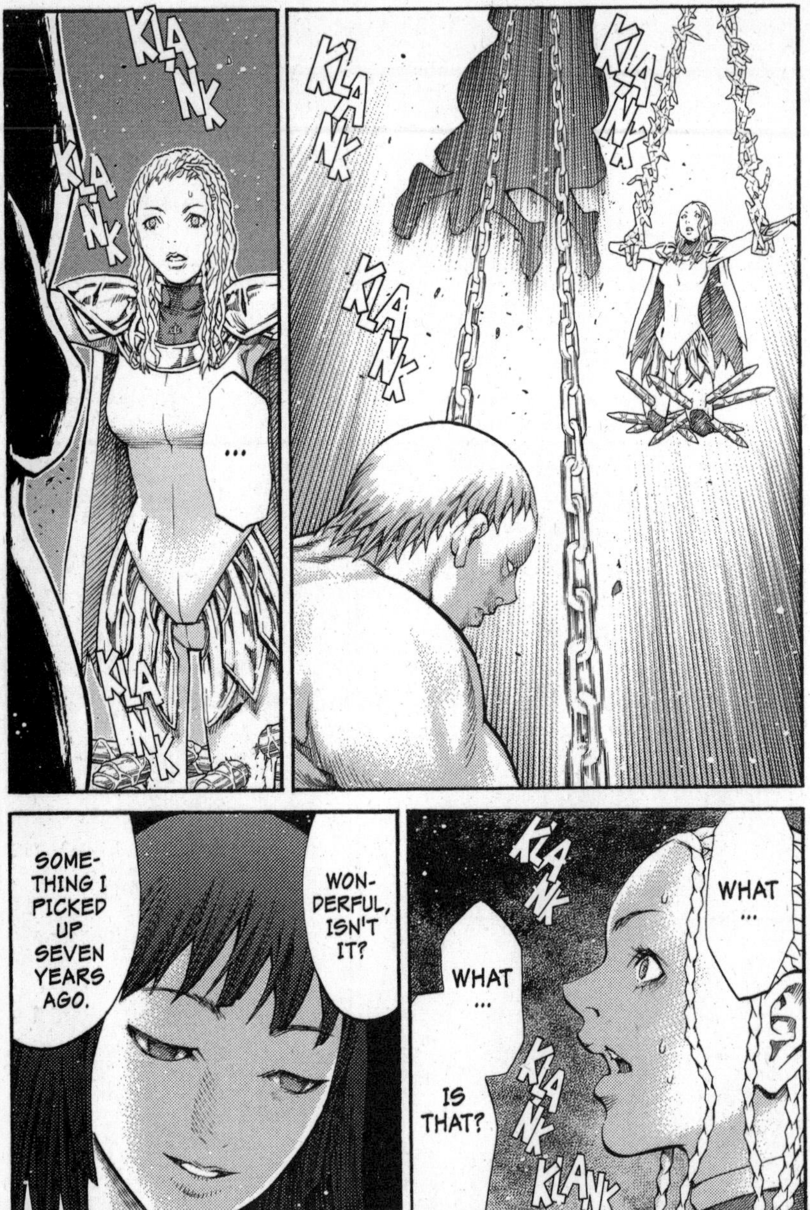
KLANK
KLANK
KLANK
KLANK
KLANK
...
KLANK
KLANK
WHAT ...
WHAT ... IS THAT?
KLANK
KLANK
WON-DERFUL, ISN'T IT?
SOME-THING I PICKED UP SEVEN YEARS AGO.

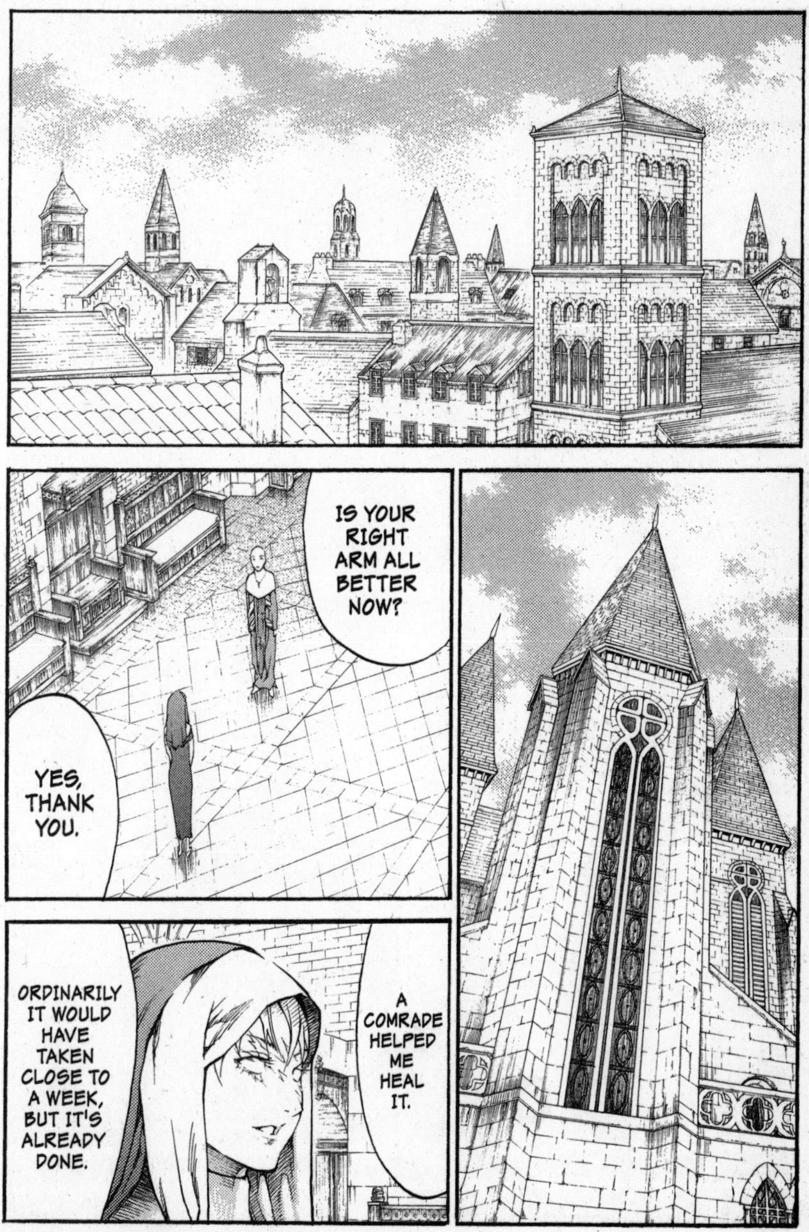
IS YOUR RIGHT ARM ALL BETTER NOW?
YES, THANK YOU.
A COMRADE HELPED ME HEAL IT.
ORDINARILY IT WOULD HAVE TAKEN CLOSE TO A WEEK, BUT IT'S ALREADY DONE.

READ THIS WAY

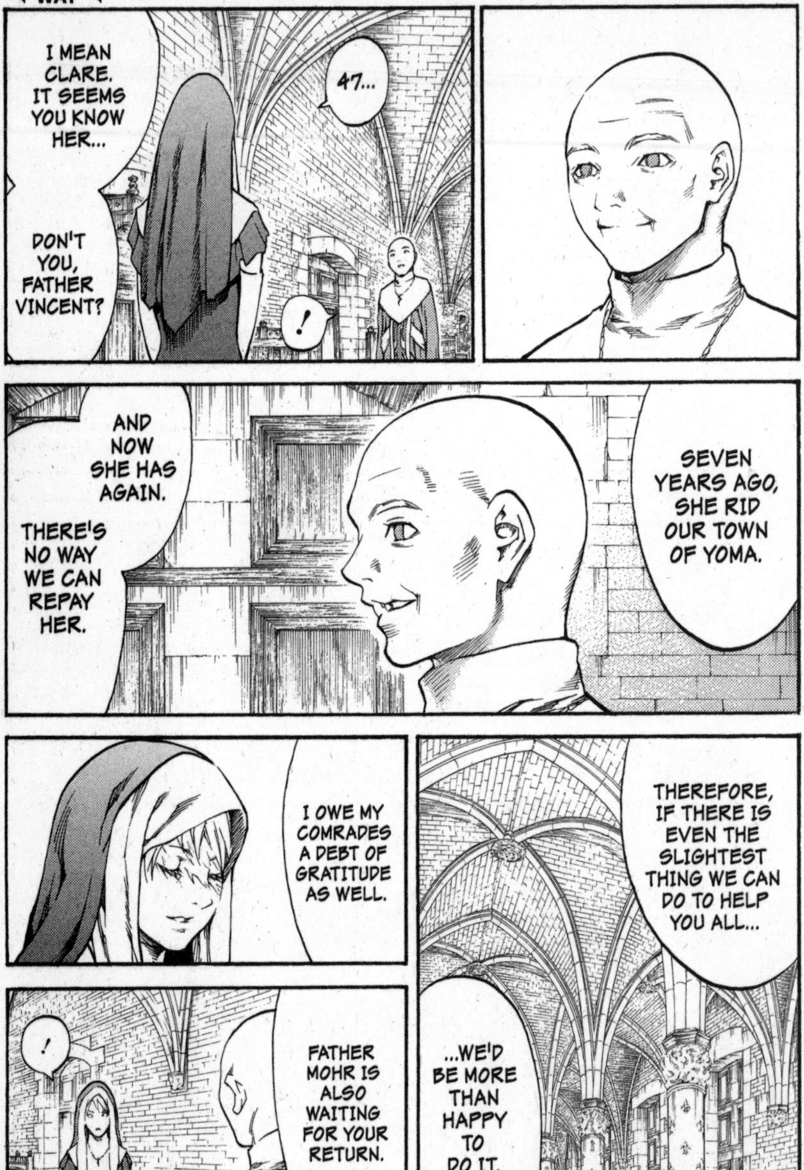
47...
I MEAN CLARE. IT SEEMS YOU KNOW HER...
DON'T YOU, FATHER VINCENT?
!
SEVEN YEARS AGO, SHE RID OUR TOWN OF YOMA.
AND NOW SHE HAS AGAIN.
THERE'S NO WAY WE CAN REPAY HER.
THEREFORE, IF THERE IS EVEN THE SLIGHTEST THING WE CAN DO TO HELP YOU ALL...
...WE'D BE MORE THAN HAPPY TO DO IT.
I OWE MY COMRADES A DEBT OF GRATITUDE AS WELL.
FATHER MOHR IS ALSO WAITING FOR YOUR RETURN.
!

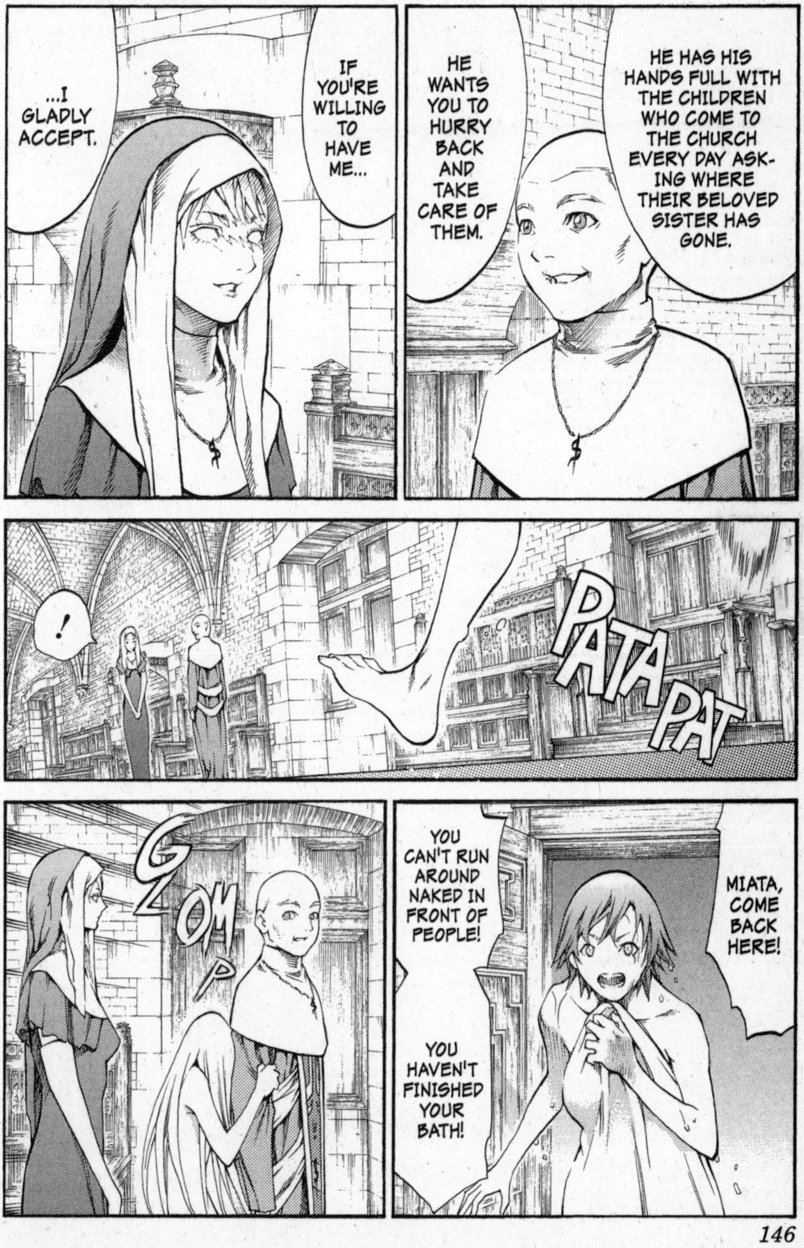
HE HAS HIS HANDS FULL WITH THE CHILDREN WHO COME TO THE CHURCH EVERY DAY ASK-ING WHERE THEIR BELOVED SISTER HAS GONE.
HE WANTS YOU TO HURRY BACK AND TAKE CARE OF THEM.
IF YOU'RE WILLING TO HAVE ME...
...I GLADLY ACCEPT.
!
PATA PAT
MIATA, COME BACK HERE!
YOU CAN'T RUN AROUND NAKED IN FRONT OF PEOPLE!
YOU HAVEN'T FINISHED YOUR BATH!
GLOMP

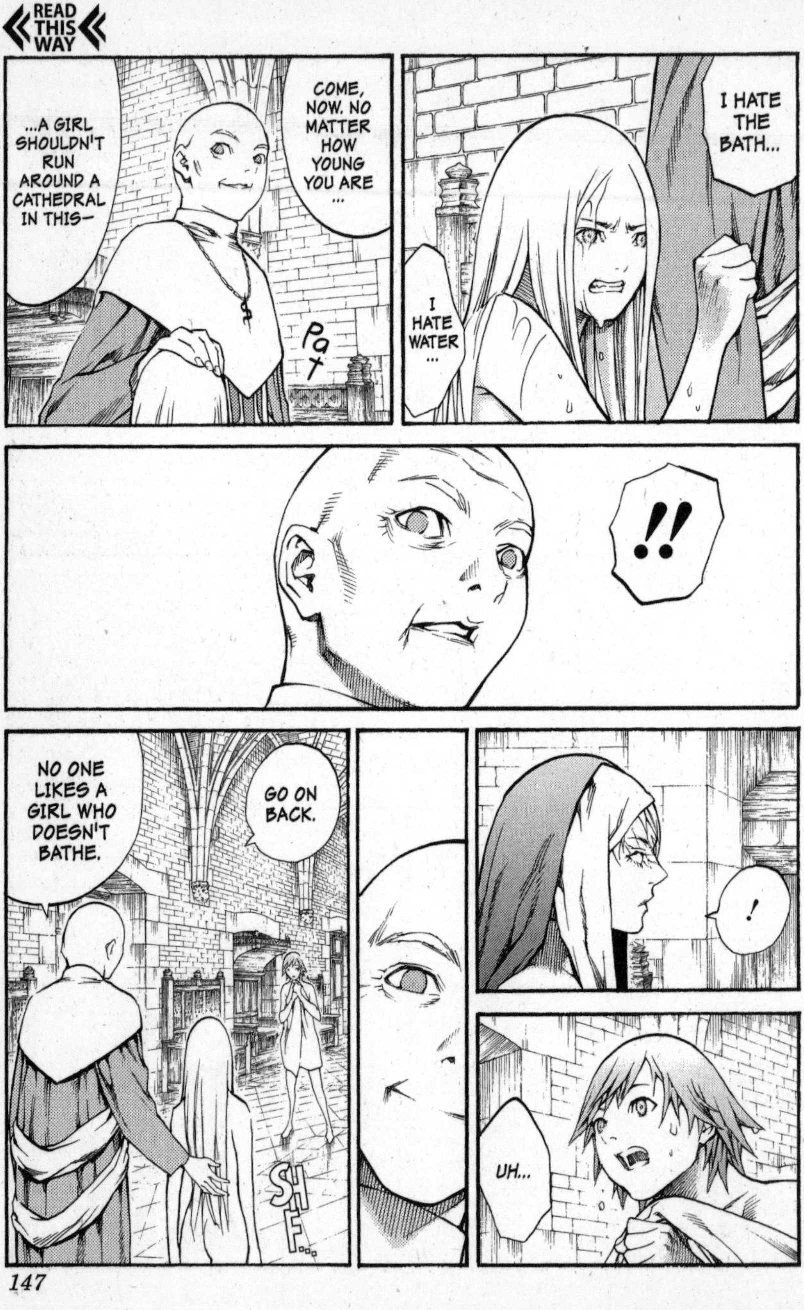
READ THIS WAY
I HATE THE BATH...
I HATE WATER ...
COME, NOW. NO MATTER HOW YOUNG YOU ARE ...
...A GIRL SHOULDN'T RUN AROUND A CATHEDRAL IN THIS—
Pat
!!
!
UH...
GO ON BACK.
NO ONE LIKES A GIRL WHO DOESN'T BATHE.
SHF...

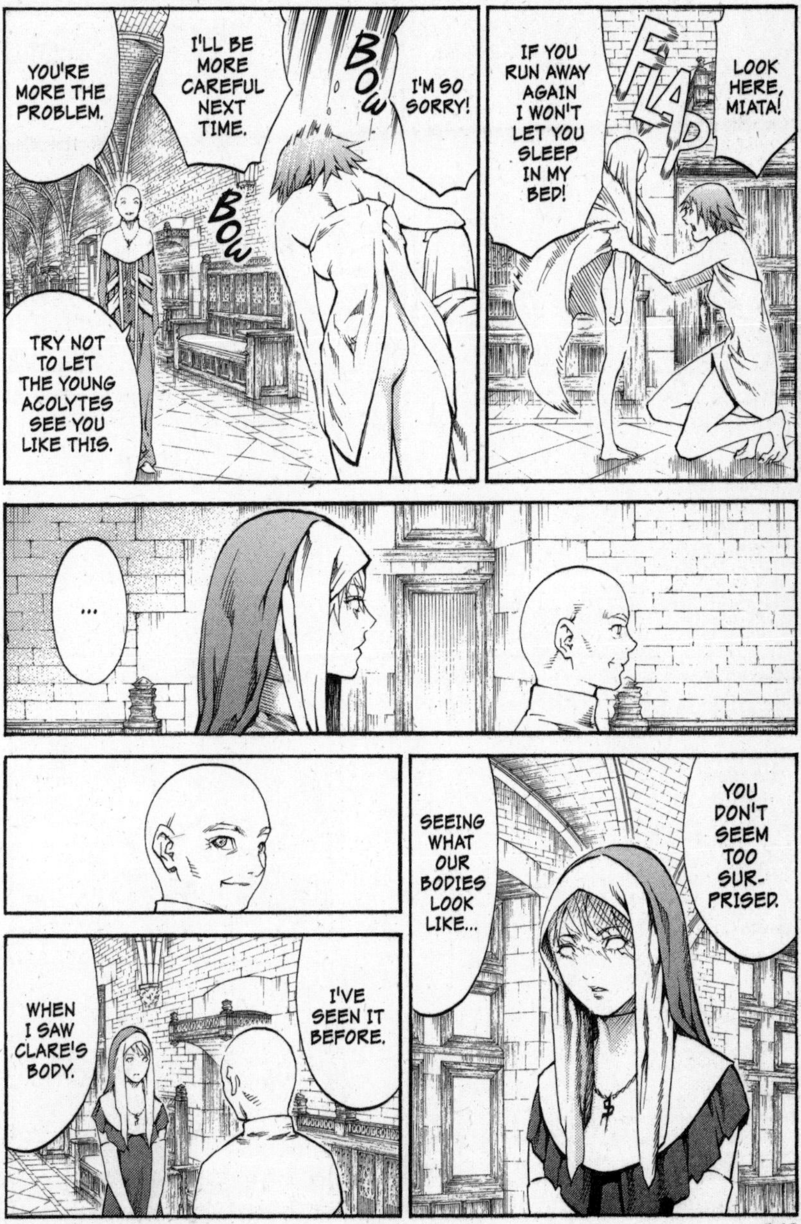
LOOK HERE, MIATA!
FLAP
IF YOU RUN AWAY AGAIN I WON'T LET YOU SLEEP IN MY BED!
I'M SO SORRY!
BOW
BOW
I'LL BE MORE CAREFUL NEXT TIME.
YOU'RE MORE THE PROBLEM.
TRY NOT TO LET THE YOUNG ACOLYTES SEE YOU LIKE THIS.
...
YOU DON'T SEEM TOO SUR-PRISED.
SEEING WHAT OUR BODIES LOOK LIKE...
I'VE SEEN IT BEFORE.
WHEN I SAW CLARE'S BODY.

READ THIS WAY

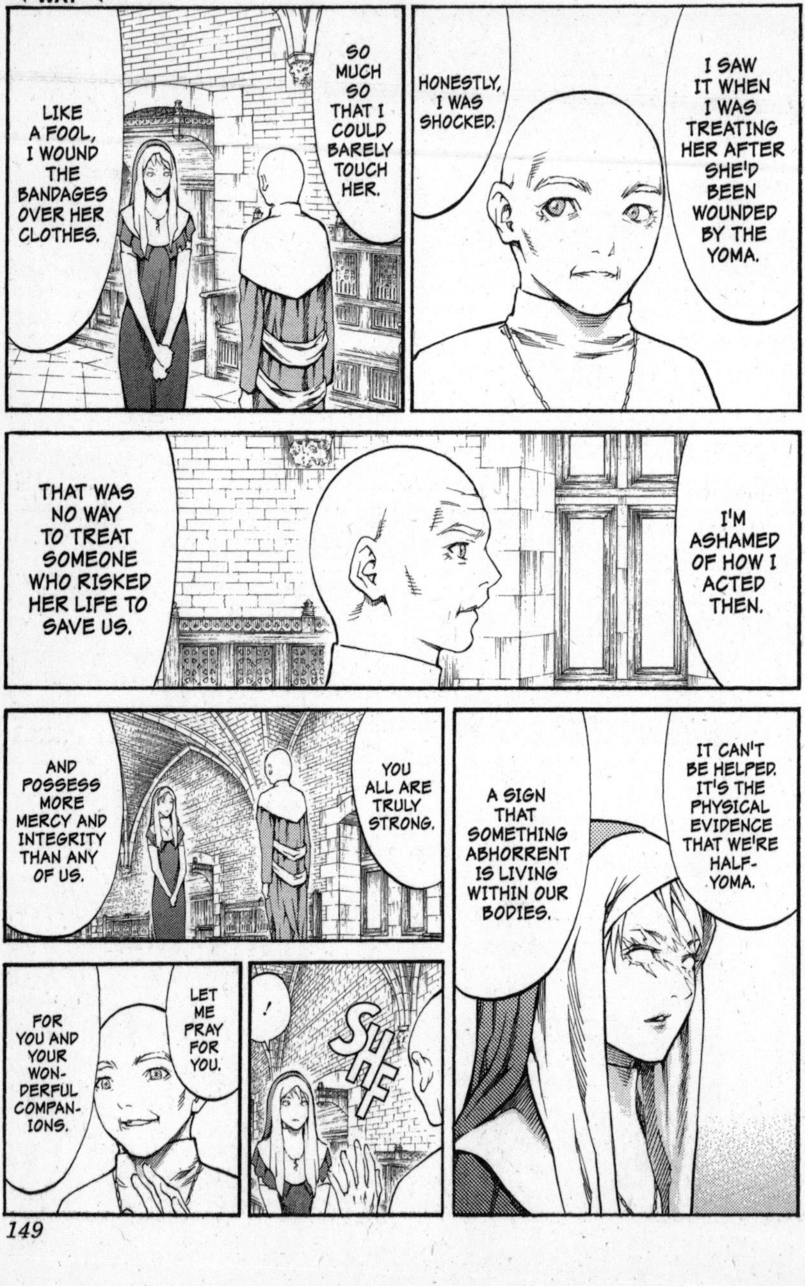

I SAW IT WHEN I WAS TREATING HER AFTER SHE'D BEEN WOUNDED BY THE YOMA.
HONESTLY, I WAS SHOCKED.
SO MUCH SO THAT I COULD BARELY TOUCH HER.
LIKE A FOOL, I WOUND THE BANDAGES OVER HER CLOTHES.
I'M ASHAMED OF HOW I ACTED THEN.
THAT WAS NO WAY TO TREAT SOMEONE WHO RISKED HER LIFE TO SAVE US.
IT CAN'T BE HELPED. IT'S THE PHYSICAL EVIDENCE THAT WE'RE HALF-YOMA.
A SIGN THAT SOMETHING ABHORRENT IS LIVING WITHIN OUR BODIES.
YOU ALL ARE TRULY STRONG.
AND POSSESS MORE MERCY AND INTEGRITY THAN ANY OF US.
!
SHF
LET ME PRAY FOR YOU.
FOR YOU AND YOUR WONDERFUL COMPANIONS.

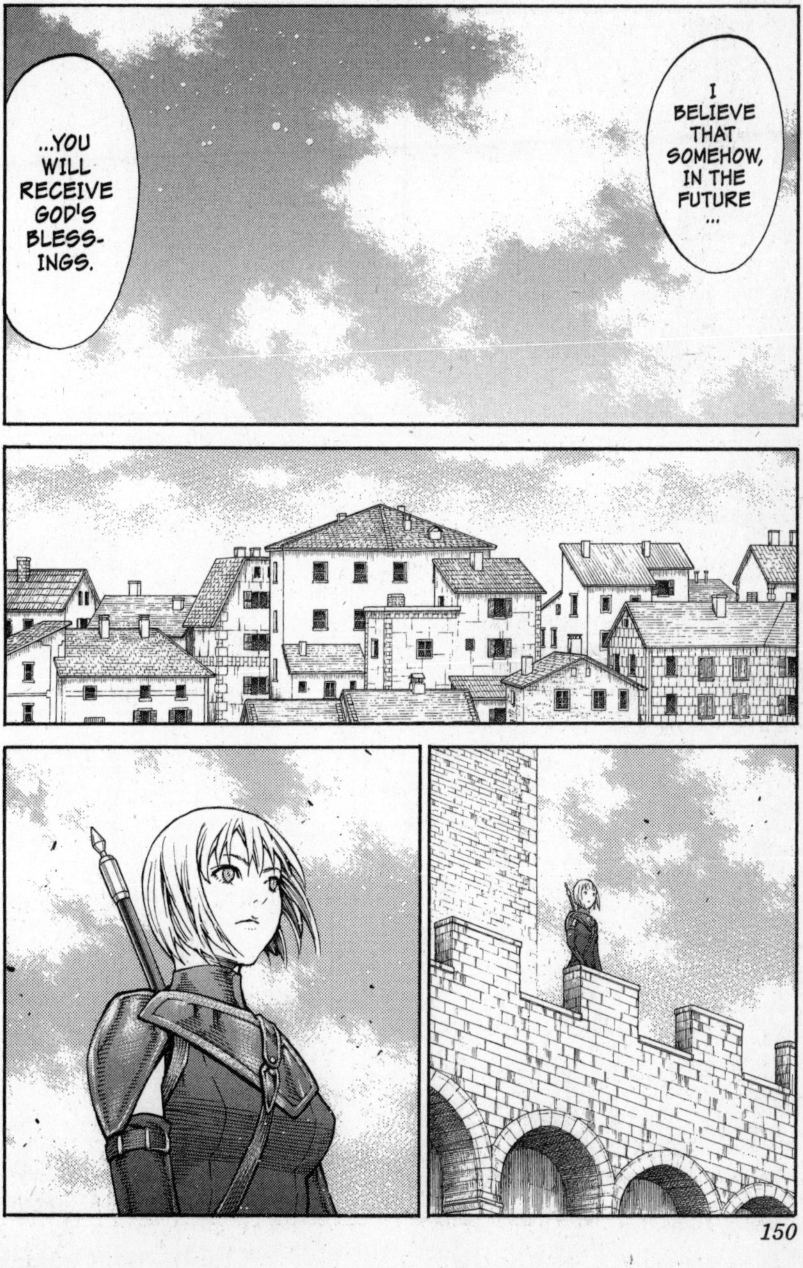
I BELIEVE THAT SOMEHOW, IN THE FUTURE ...
...YOU WILL RECEIVE GOD'S BLESS-INGS.

READ THIS WAY

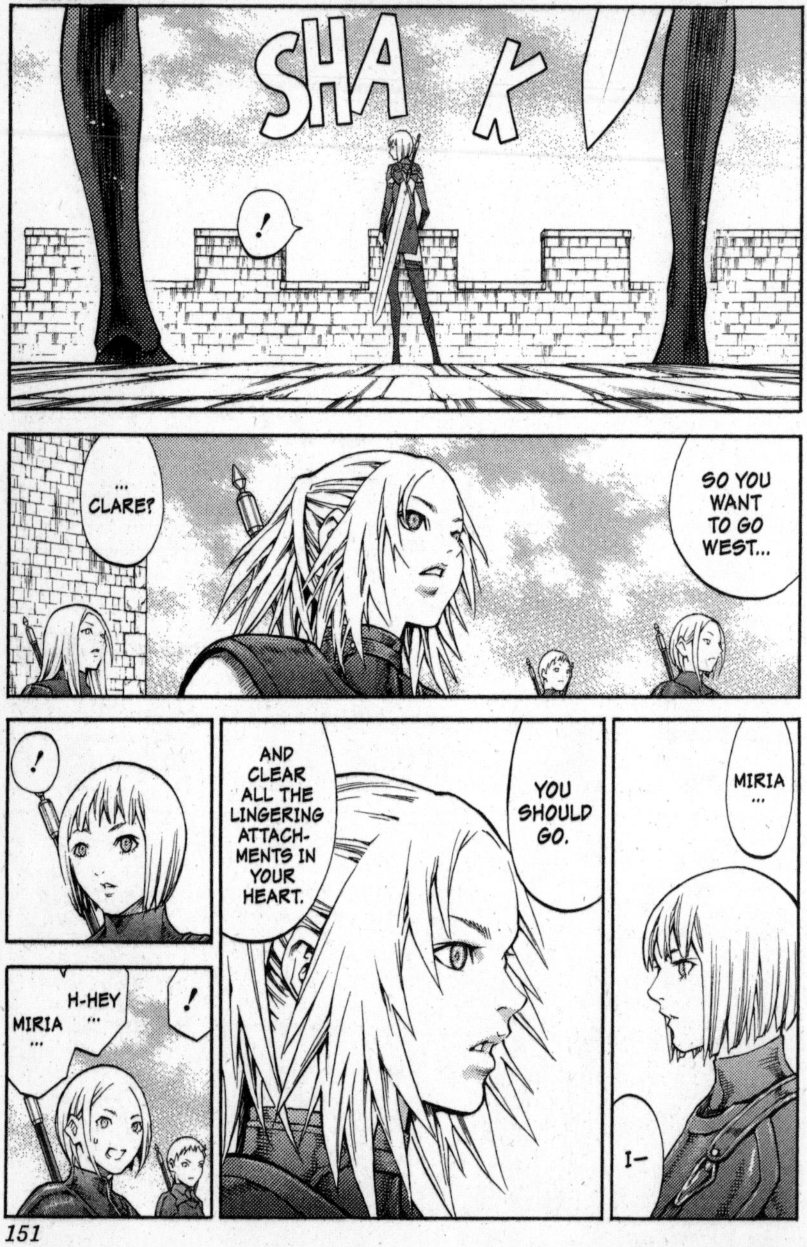
SHAK
!
SO YOU WANT TO GO WEST...
... CLARE?
MIRIA ...
I—
YOU SHOULD GO.
AND CLEAR ALL THE LINGERING ATTACHMENTS IN YOUR HEART.
!
!
H-HEY ...
MIRIA ...

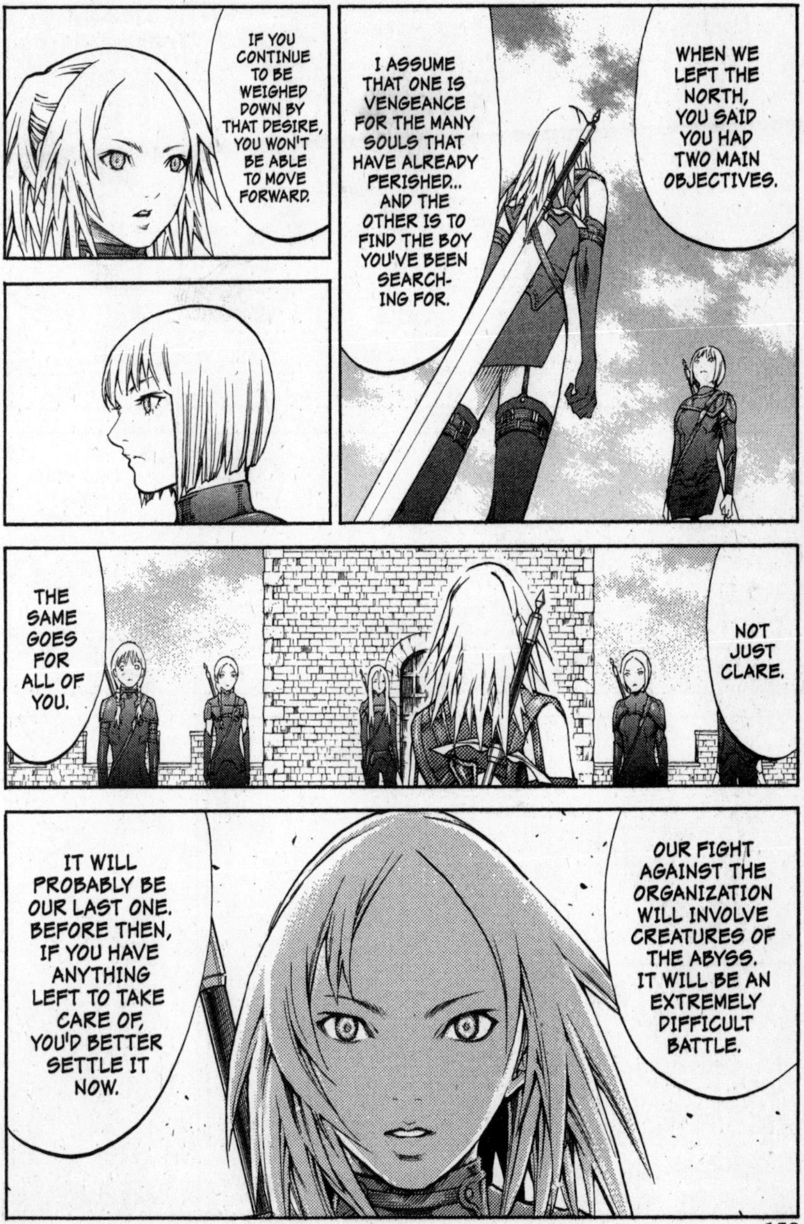
WHEN WE LEFT THE NORTH, YOU SAID YOU HAD TWO MAIN OBJECTIVES.
I ASSUME THAT ONE IS VENGEANCE FOR THE MANY SOULS THAT HAVE ALREADY PERISHED... AND THE OTHER IS TO FIND THE BOY YOU'VE BEEN SEARCH-ING FOR.
IF YOU CONTINUE TO BE WEIGHED DOWN BY THAT DESIRE, YOU WON'T BE ABLE TO MOVE FORWARD.
NOT JUST CLARE.
THE SAME GOES FOR ALL OF YOU.
OUR FIGHT AGAINST THE ORGANIZATION WILL INVOLVE CREATURES OF THE ABYSS. IT WILL BE AN EXTREMELY DIFFICULT BATTLE.
IT WILL PROBABLY BE OUR LAST ONE. BEFORE THEN, IF YOU HAVE ANYTHING LEFT TO TAKE CARE OF, YOU'D BETTER SETTLE IT NOW.

READ THIS WAY

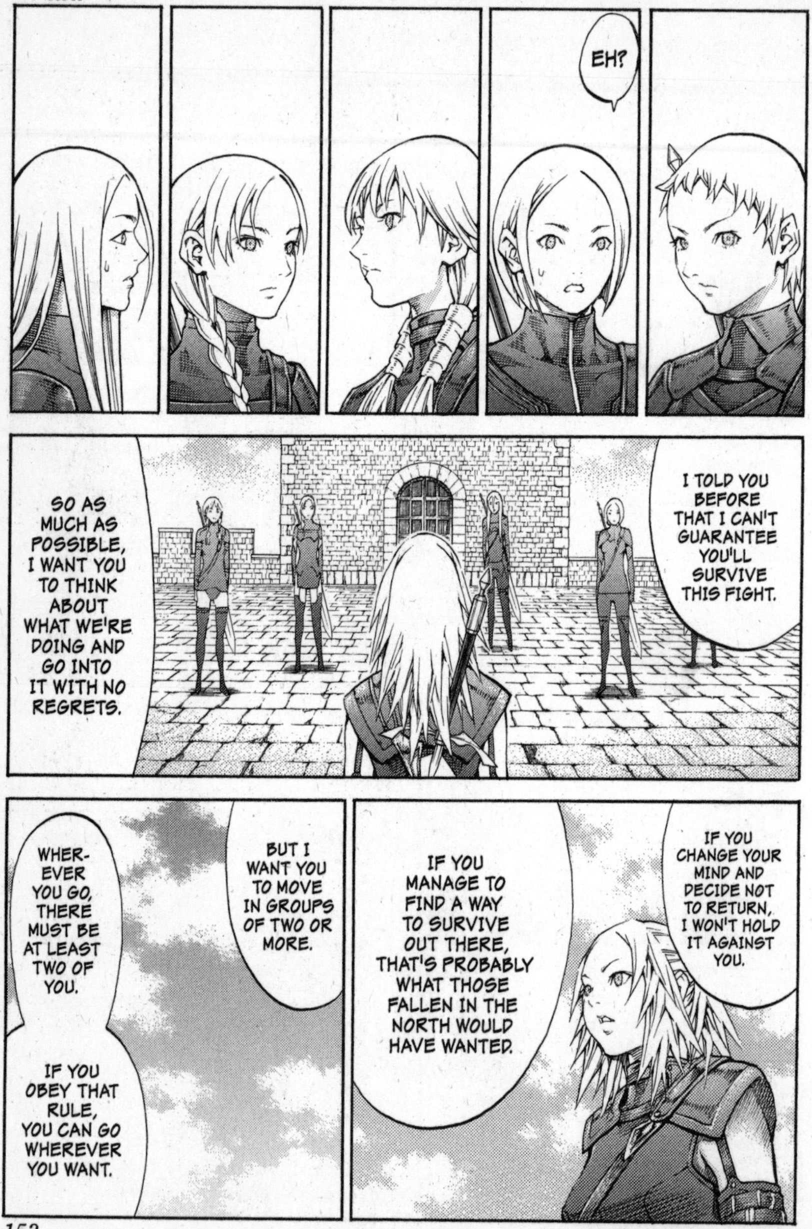
EH?
I TOLD YOU BEFORE THAT I CAN'T GUARANTEE YOU'LL SURVIVE THIS FIGHT.
SO AS MUCH AS POSSIBLE, I WANT YOU TO THINK ABOUT WHAT WE'RE DOING AND GO INTO IT WITH NO REGRETS.
IF YOU CHANGE YOUR MIND AND DECIDE NOT TO RETURN, I WON'T HOLD IT AGAINST YOU.
IF YOU MANAGE TO FIND A WAY TO SURVIVE OUT THERE, THAT'S PROBABLY WHAT THOSE FALLEN IN THE NORTH WOULD HAVE WANTED.
BUT I WANT YOU TO MOVE IN GROUPS OF TWO OR MORE.
WHER-EVER YOU GO, THERE MUST BE AT LEAST TWO OF YOU.
IF YOU OBEY THAT RULE, YOU CAN GO WHEREVER YOU WANT.

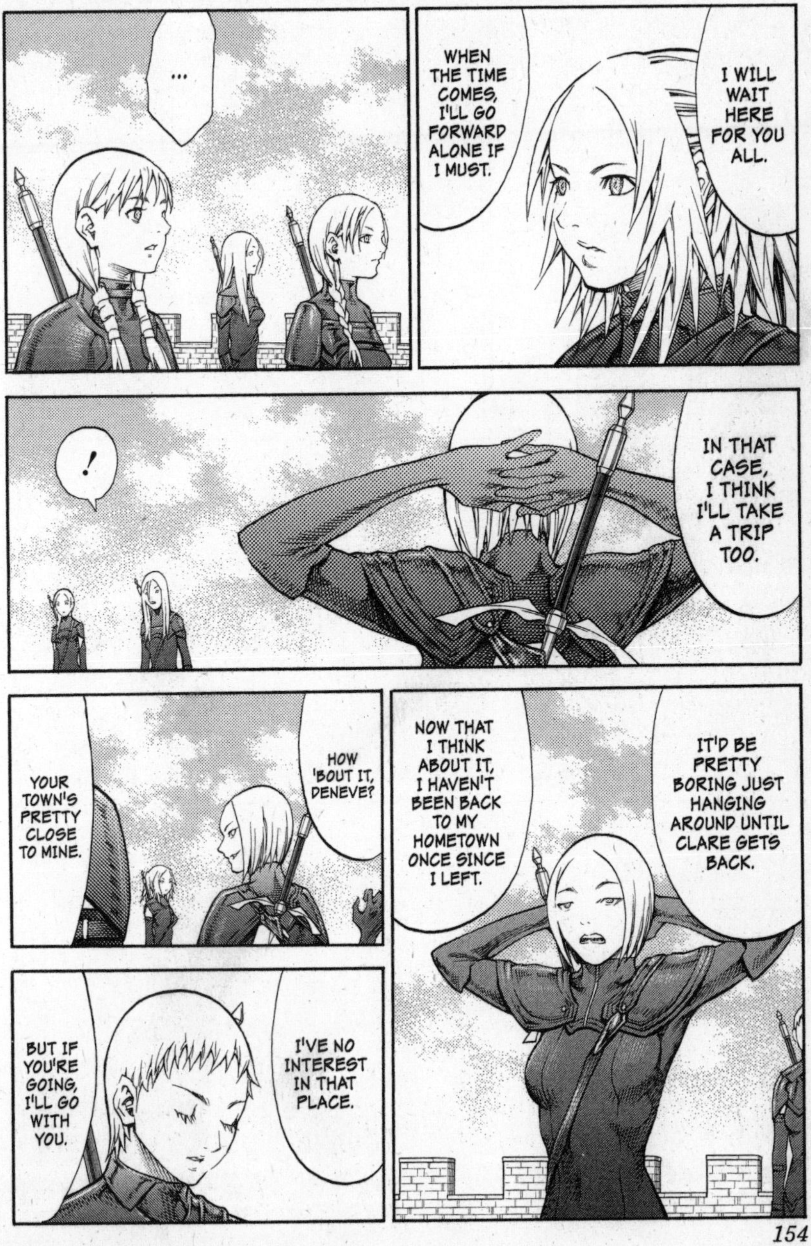
I WILL WAIT HERE FOR YOU ALL.
WHEN THE TIME COMES, I'LL GO FORWARD ALONE IF I MUST.
...
IN THAT CASE, I THINK I'LL TAKE A TRIP TOO.
!
IT'D BE PRETTY BORING JUST HANGING AROUND UNTIL CLARE GETS BACK.
NOW THAT I THINK ABOUT IT, I HAVEN'T BEEN BACK TO MY HOMETOWN ONCE SINCE I LEFT.
HOW 'BOUT IT, DENEVE?
YOUR TOWN'S PRETTY CLOSE TO MINE.
I'VE NO INTEREST IN THAT PLACE.
BUT IF YOU'RE GOING, I'LL GO WITH YOU.

READ THIS WAY

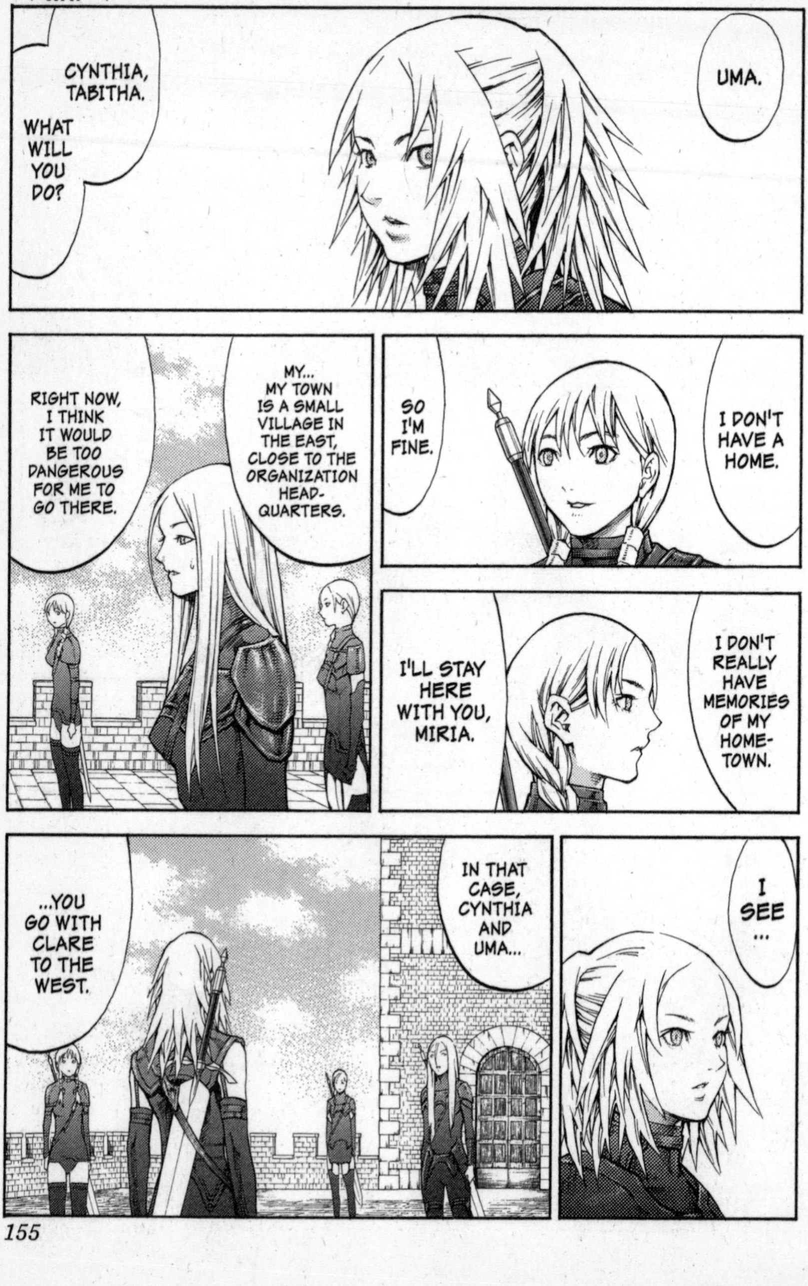
UMA.
CYNTHIA, TABITHA.
WHAT WILL YOU DO?
I DON'T HAVE A HOME.
SO I'M FINE.
I DON'T REALLY HAVE MEMORIES OF MY HOME-TOWN.
I'LL STAY HERE WITH YOU, MIRIA.
MY... MY TOWN IS A SMALL VILLAGE IN THE EAST, CLOSE TO THE ORGANIZATION HEAD-QUARTERS.
RIGHT NOW, I THINK IT WOULD BE TOO DANGEROUS FOR ME TO GO THERE.
I SEE...
IN THAT CASE, CYNTHIA AND UMA...
...YOU GO WITH CLARE TO THE WEST.

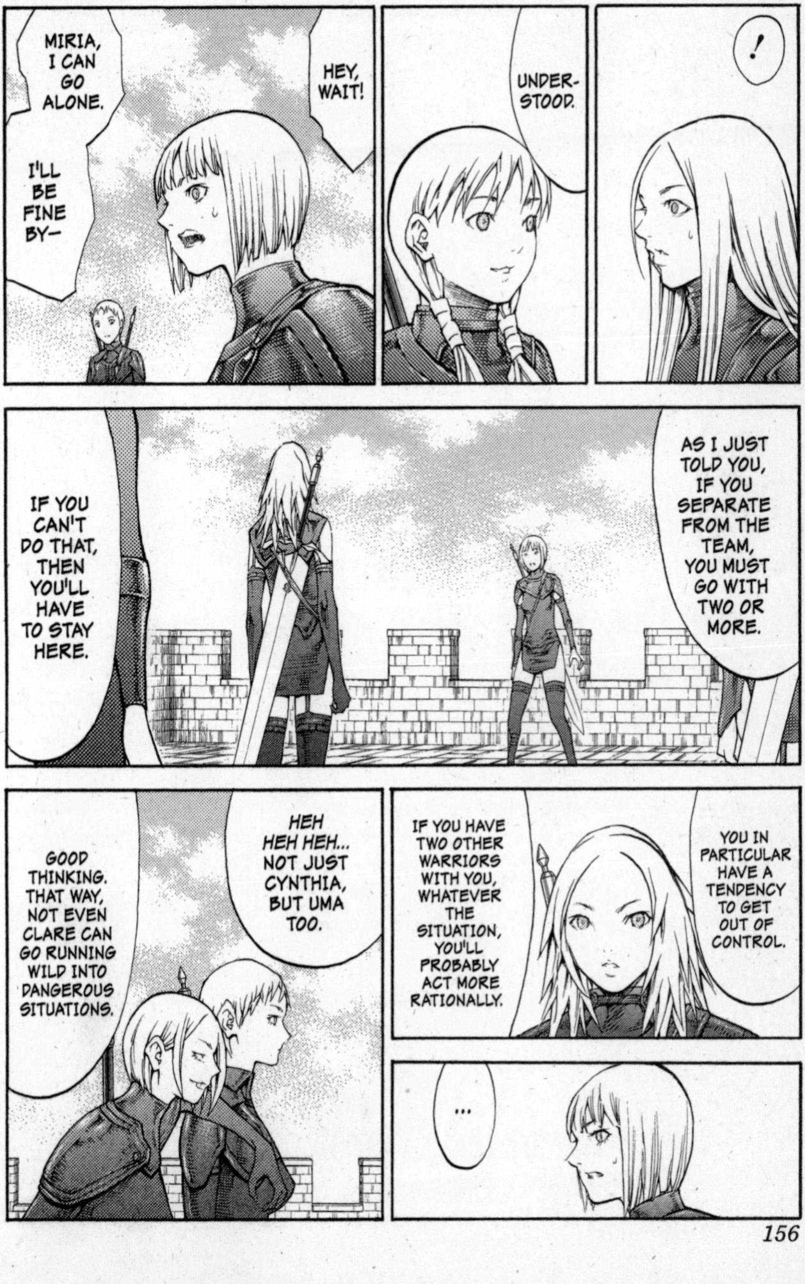
!
UNDER-STOOD.
HEY, WAIT!
MIRIA, I CAN GO ALONE.
I'LL BE FINE BY—
AS I JUST TOLD YOU, IF YOU SEPARATE FROM THE TEAM, YOU MUST GO WITH TWO OR MORE.
IF YOU CAN'T DO THAT, THEN YOU'LL HAVE TO STAY HERE.
YOU IN PARTICULAR HAVE A TENDENCY TO GET OUT OF CONTROL.
IF YOU HAVE TWO OTHER WARRIORS WITH YOU, WHATEVER THE SITUATION, YOU'LL PROBABLY ACT MORE RATIONALLY.
...
HEH HEH HEH... NOT JUST CYNTHIA, BUT UMA TOO.
GOOD THINKING. THAT WAY, NOT EVEN CLARE CAN GO RUNNING WILD INTO DANGEROUS SITUATIONS.

READ THIS WAY

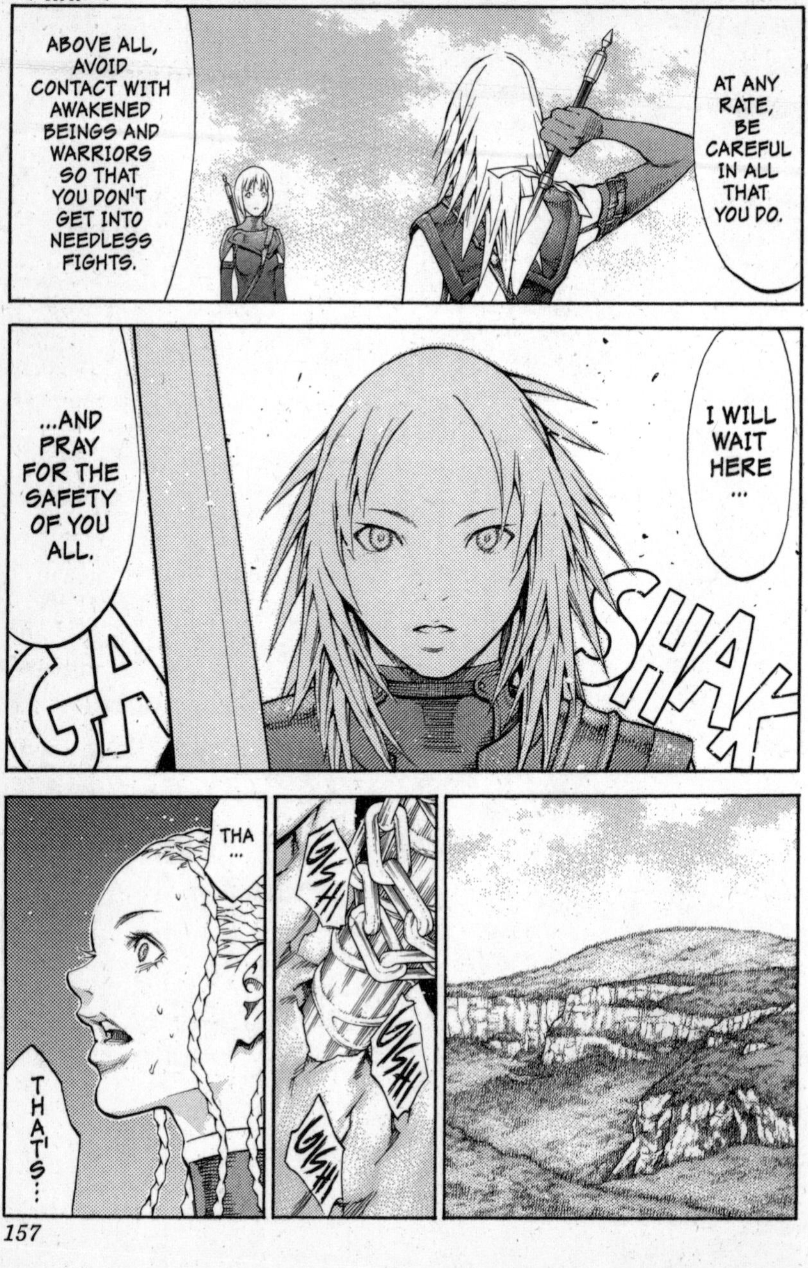
AT ANY RATE, BE CAREFUL IN ALL THAT YOU DO.
ABOVE ALL, AVOID CONTACT WITH AWAKENED BEINGS AND WARRIORS SO THAT YOU DON'T GET INTO NEEDLESS FIGHTS.
I WILL WAIT HERE...
SHAK
...AND PRAY FOR THE SAFETY OF YOU ALL.
GA
GISH
GISH
GISH
THA...
THAT'S...

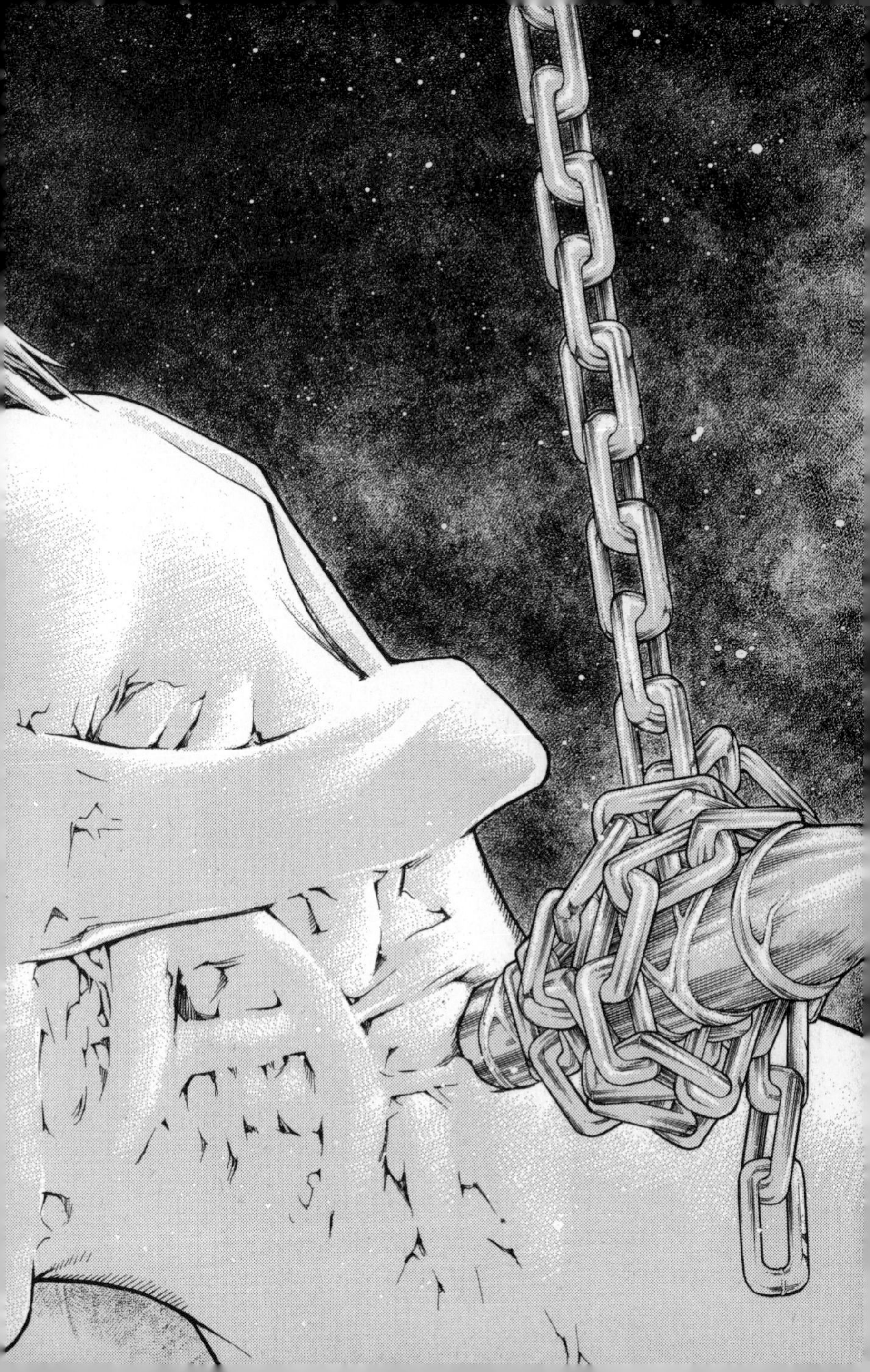

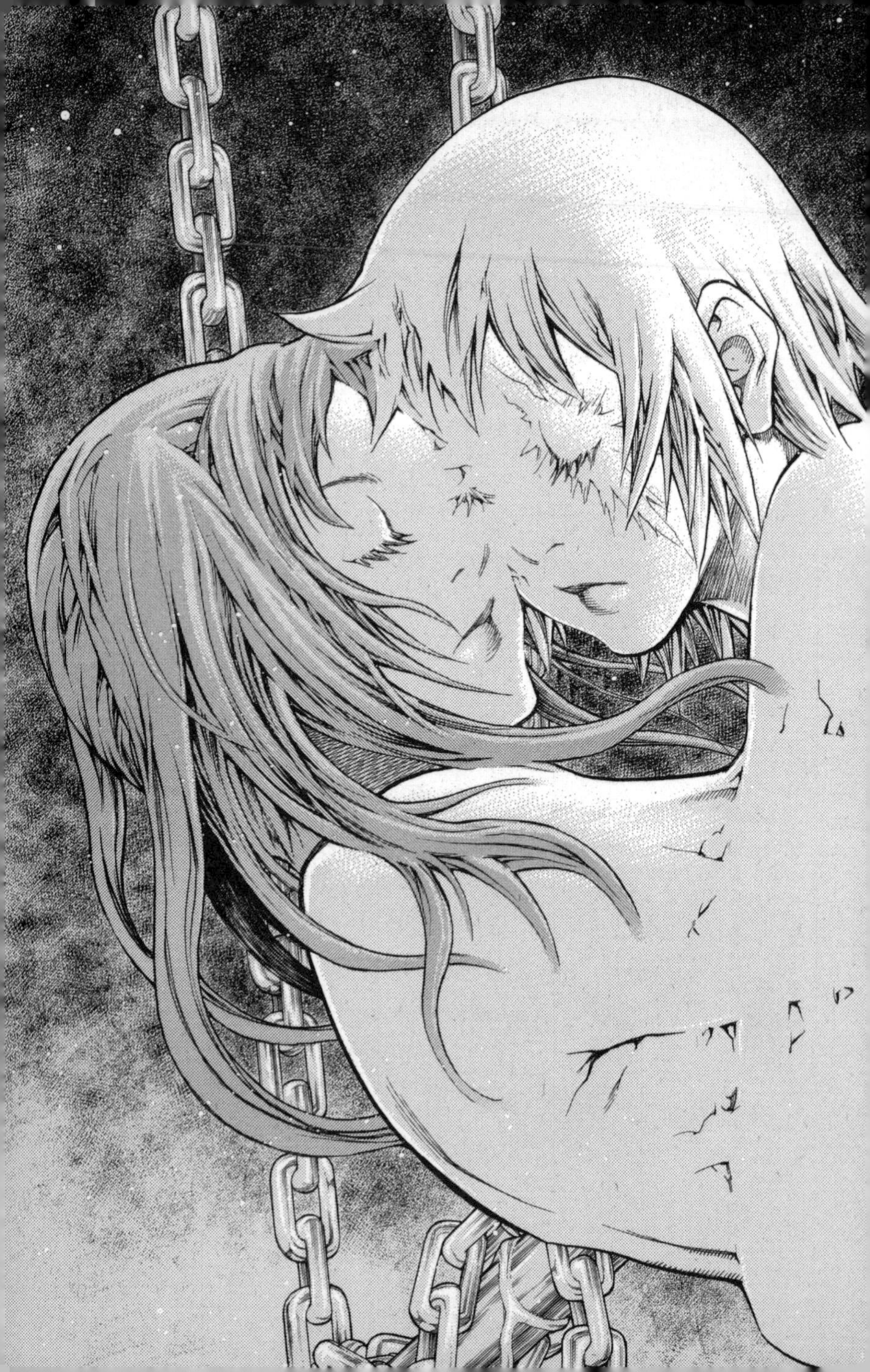

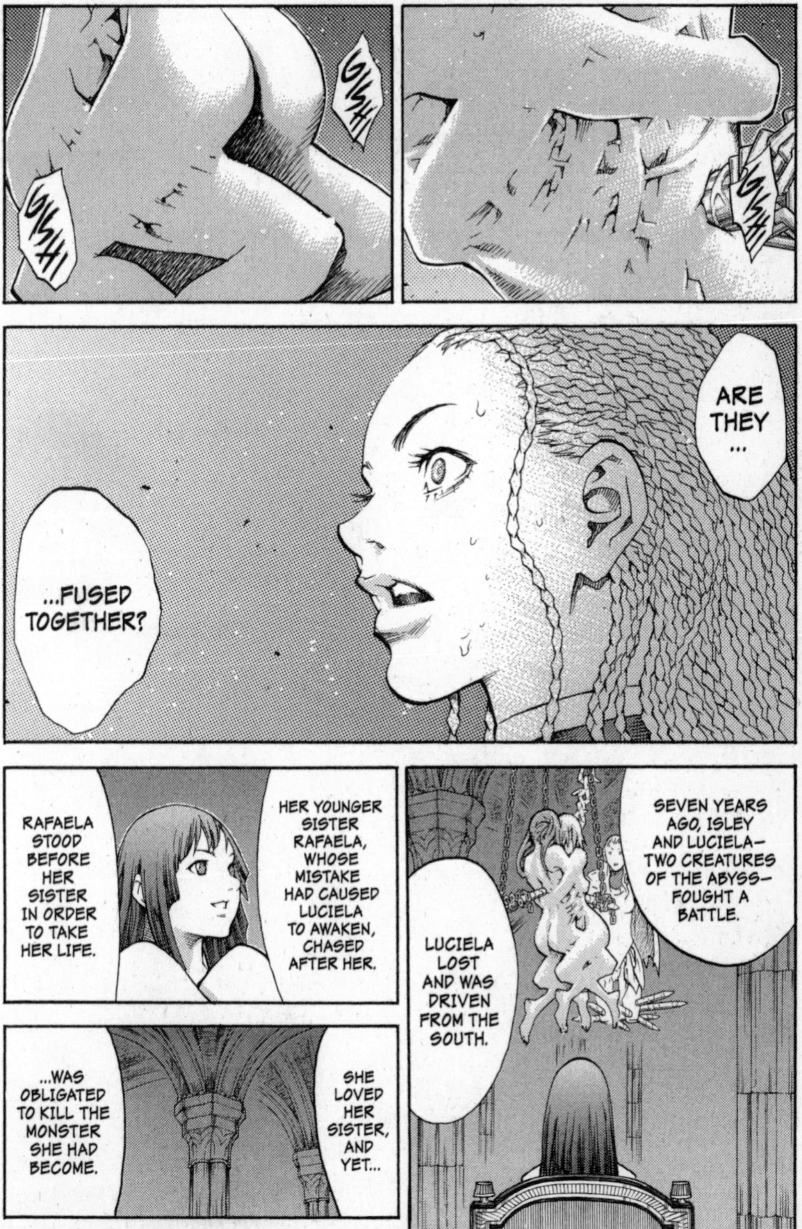
GISHI
GISHI
GISHI
ARE THEY ...
...FUSED TOGETHER?
SEVEN YEARS AGO, ISLEY AND LUCIELA—TWO CREATURES OF THE ABYSS—FOUGHT A BATTLE.
LUCIELA LOST AND WAS DRIVEN FROM THE SOUTH.
HER YOUNGER SISTER RAFAELA, WHOSE MISTAKE HAD CAUSED LUCIELA TO AWAKEN, CHASED AFTER HER.
RAFAELA STOOD BEFORE HER SISTER IN ORDER TO TAKE HER LIFE.
SHE LOVED HER SISTER, AND YET...
...WAS OBLIGATED TO KILL THE MONSTER SHE HAD BECOME.

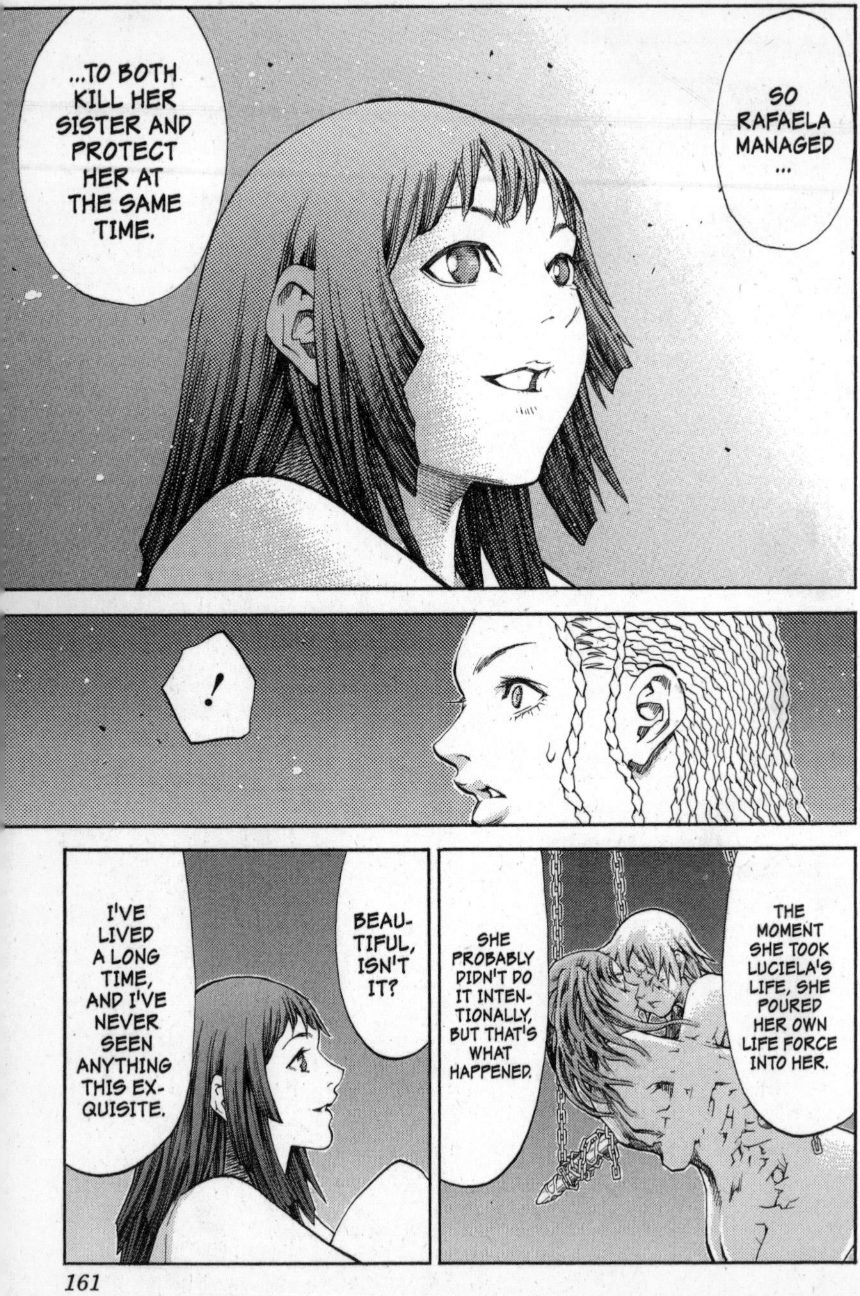
SO RAFAELA MANAGED ...
...TO BOTH KILL HER SISTER AND PROTECT HER AT THE SAME TIME.
!
THE MOMENT SHE TOOK LUCIELA'S LIFE, SHE POURED HER OWN LIFE FORCE INTO HER.
SHE PROBABLY DIDN'T DO IT INTENTIONALLY, BUT THAT'S WHAT HAPPENED.
BEAUTIFUL, ISN'T IT?
I'VE LIVED A LONG TIME, AND I'VE NEVER SEEN ANYTHING THIS EXQUISITE.

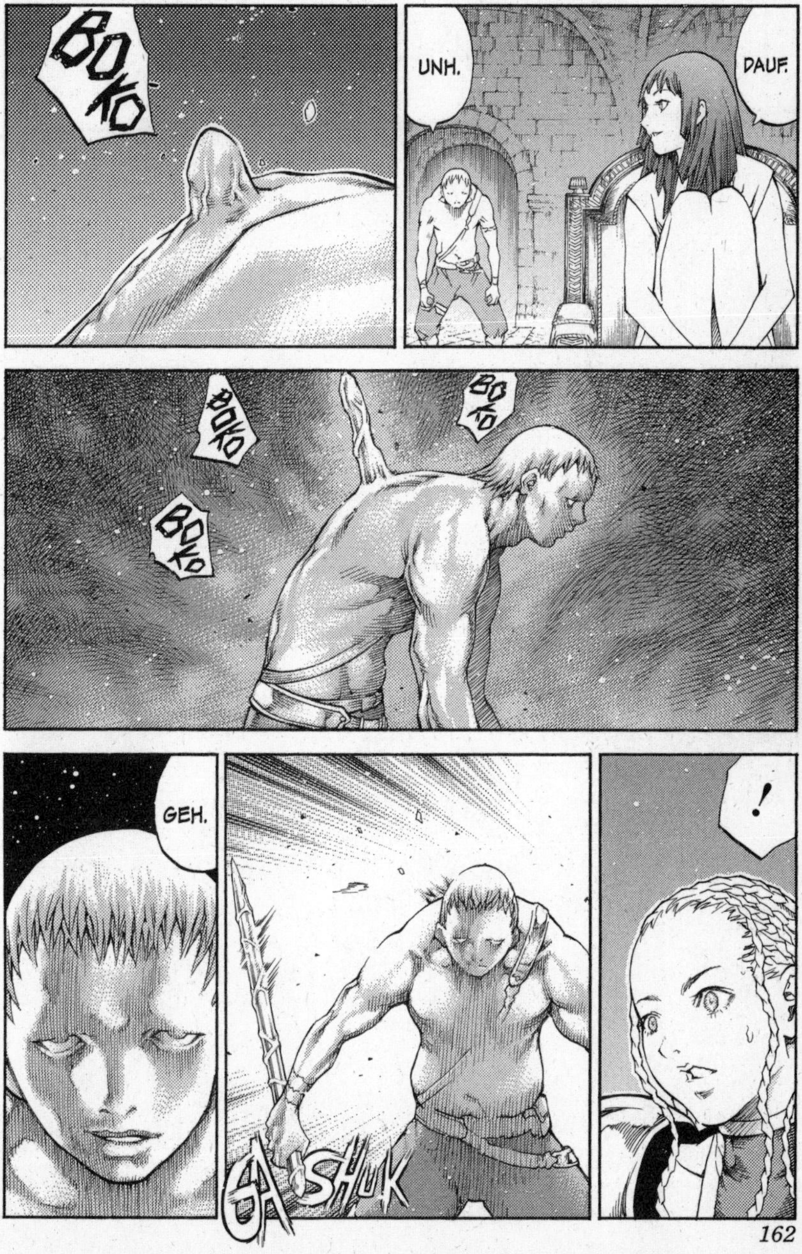
DAUF.
UNH.
BOKO
BOKO
BOKO
BOKO
!
GASHUK
GEH.

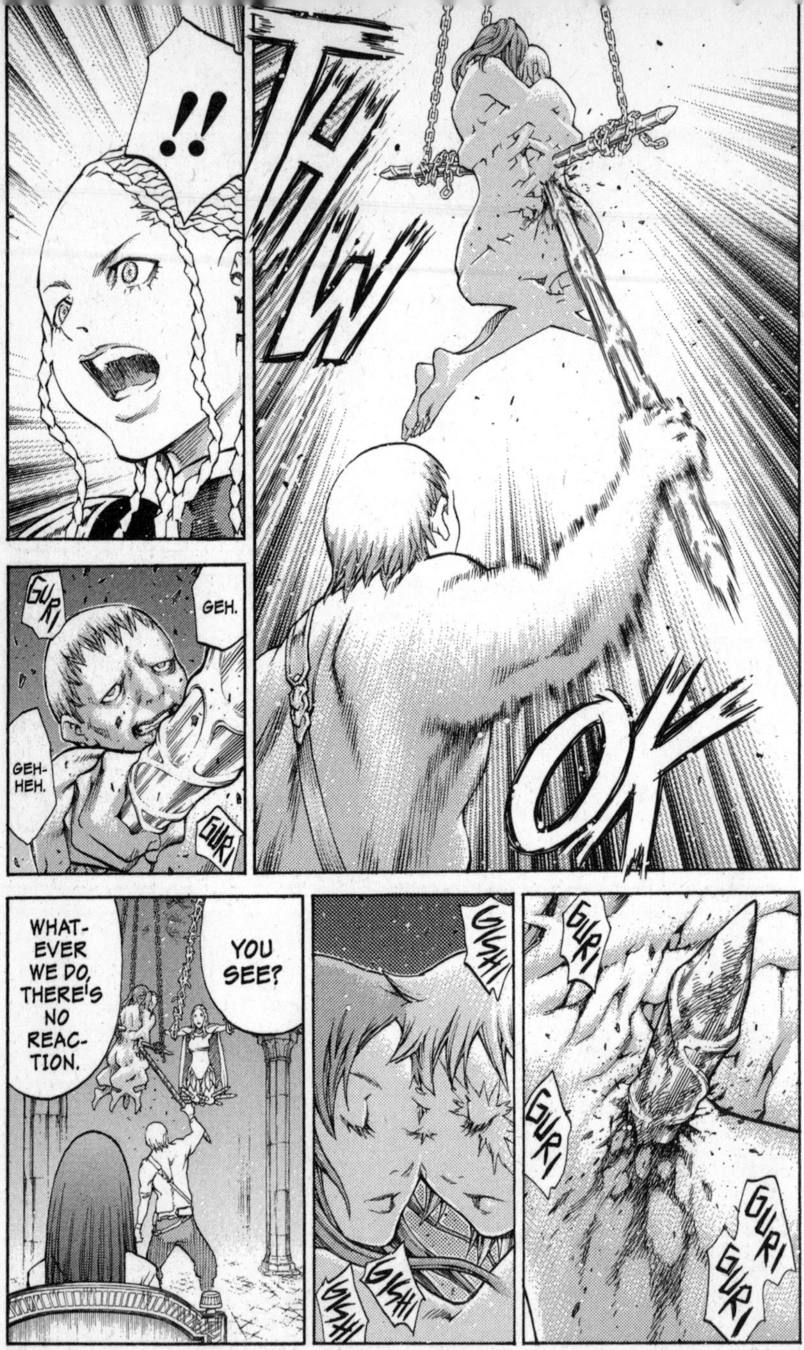
THWOK
!!
GURI
GEH.
GEH-HEH.
GURI
GURI
GURI
GURI GURI
GISHI
GISHI
GISHI
YOU SEE?
WHAT-EVER WE DO, THERE'S NO REAC-TION.

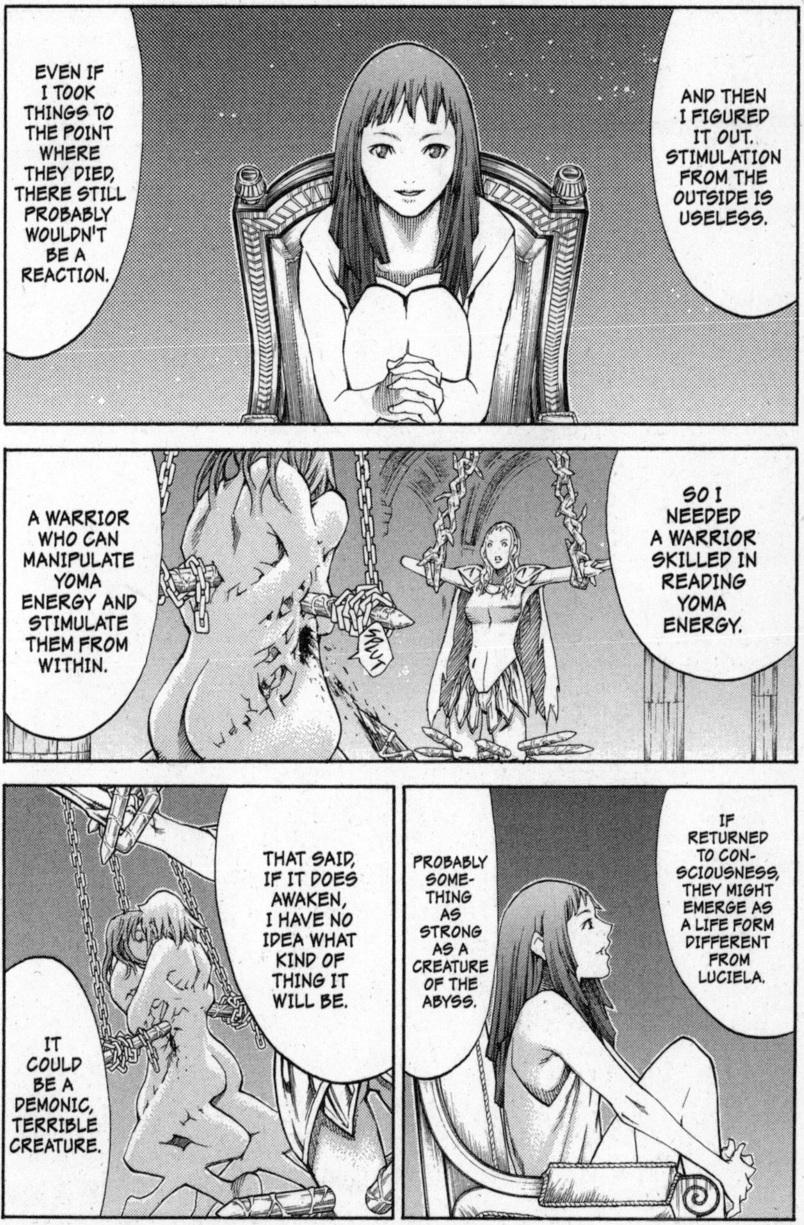
AND THEN I FIGURED IT OUT. STIMULATION FROM THE OUTSIDE IS USELESS.
EVEN IF I TOOK THINGS TO THE POINT WHERE THEY DIED, THERE STILL PROBABLY WOULDN'T BE A REACTION.
SO I NEEDED A WARRIOR SKILLED IN READING YOMA ENERGY.
A WARRIOR WHO CAN MANIPULATE YOMA ENERGY AND STIMULATE THEM FROM WITHIN.
IF RETURNED TO CON-SCIOUSNESS, THEY MIGHT EMERGE AS A LIFE FORM DIFFERENT FROM LUCIELA.
PROBABLY SOME-THING AS STRONG AS A CREATURE OF THE ABYSS.
THAT SAID, IF IT DOES AWAKEN, I HAVE NO IDEA WHAT KIND OF THING IT WILL BE.
IT COULD BE A DEMONIC, TERRIBLE CREATURE.

READ THIS WAY

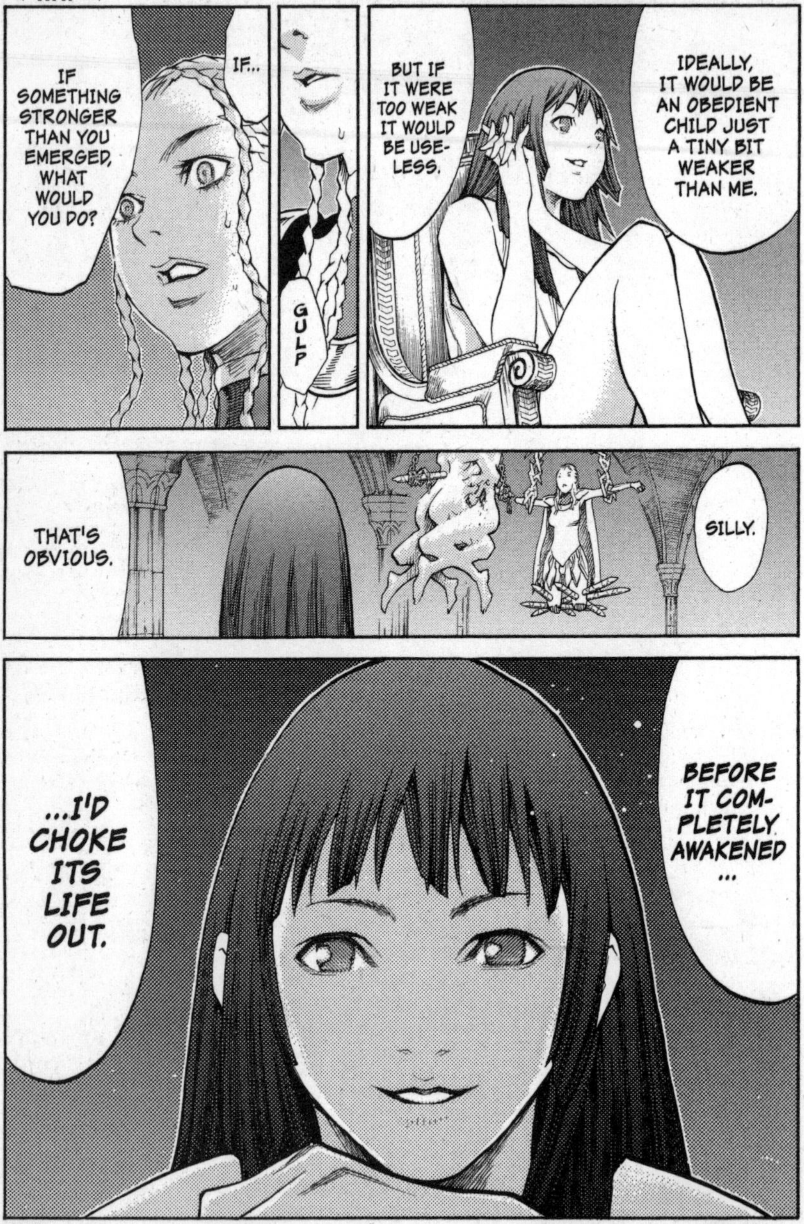
IDEALLY, IT WOULD BE AN OBEDIENT CHILD JUST A TINY BIT WEAKER THAN ME.
BUT IF IT WERE TOO WEAK IT WOULD BE USE-LESS.
IF...
GULP
IF SOMETHING STRONGER THAN YOU EMERGED, WHAT WOULD YOU DO?
SILLY.
THAT'S OBVIOUS.
BEFORE IT COM-PLETELY AWAKENED...
...I'D CHOKE ITS LIFE OUT.

クレイモア
Claymore

Scene 83: The Lamentation of the Earth, Part 1

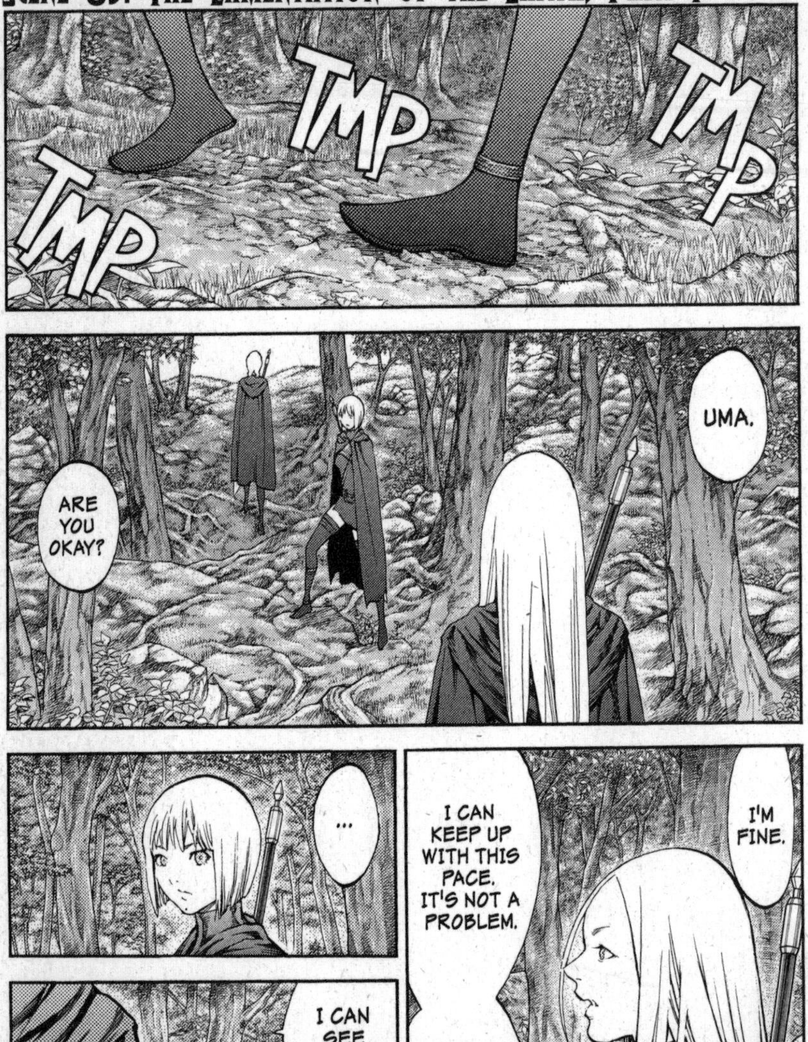
TMP
TMP
TMP
UMA.
ARE YOU OKAY?
I'M FINE.
I CAN KEEP UP WITH THIS PACE. IT'S NOT A PROBLEM.
NO NEED TO WORRY.
...
I CAN SEE IT.
!

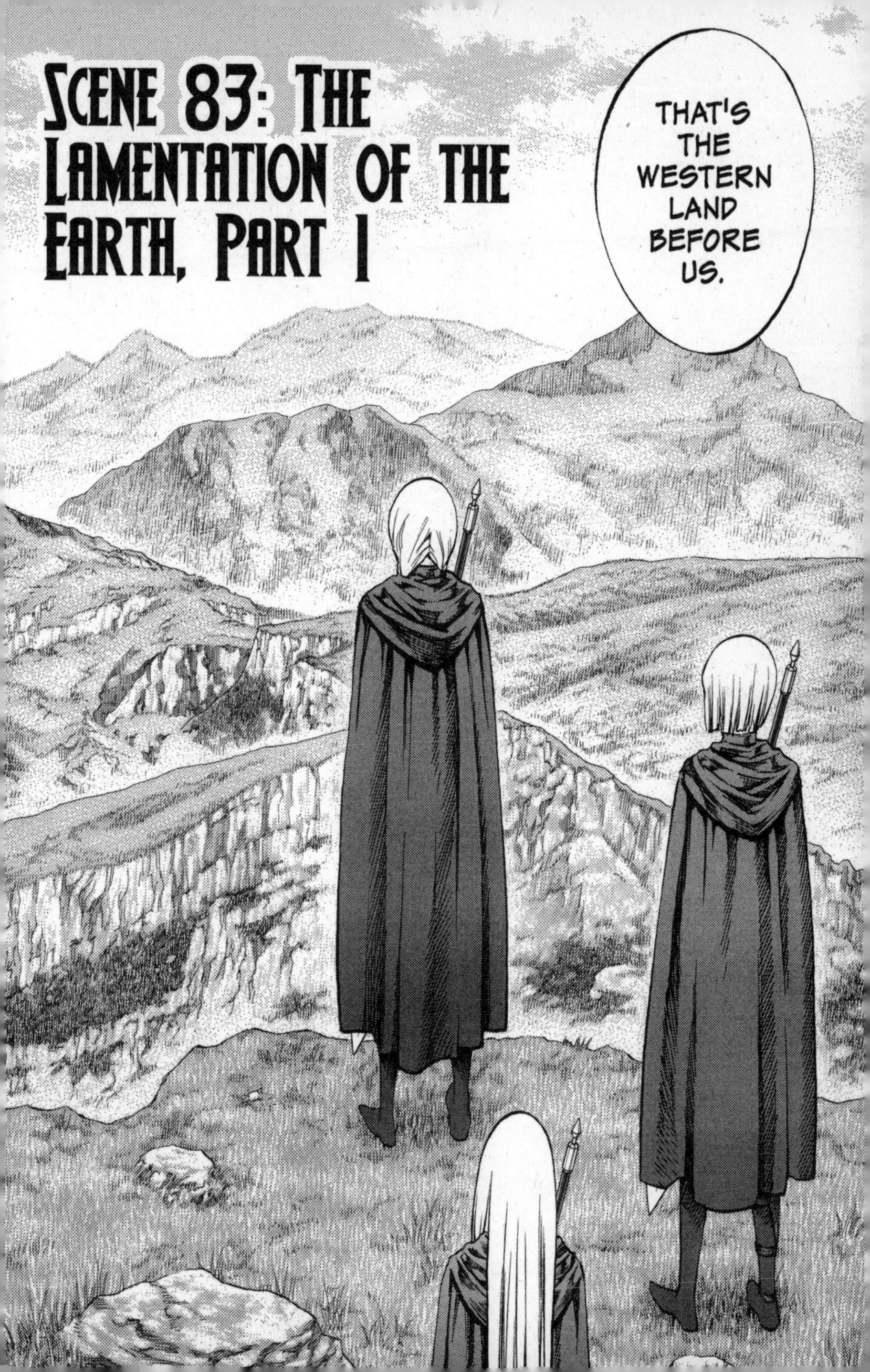
SCENE 83: THE LAMENTATION OF THE EARTH, PART 1
THAT'S THE WESTERN LAND BEFORE US.

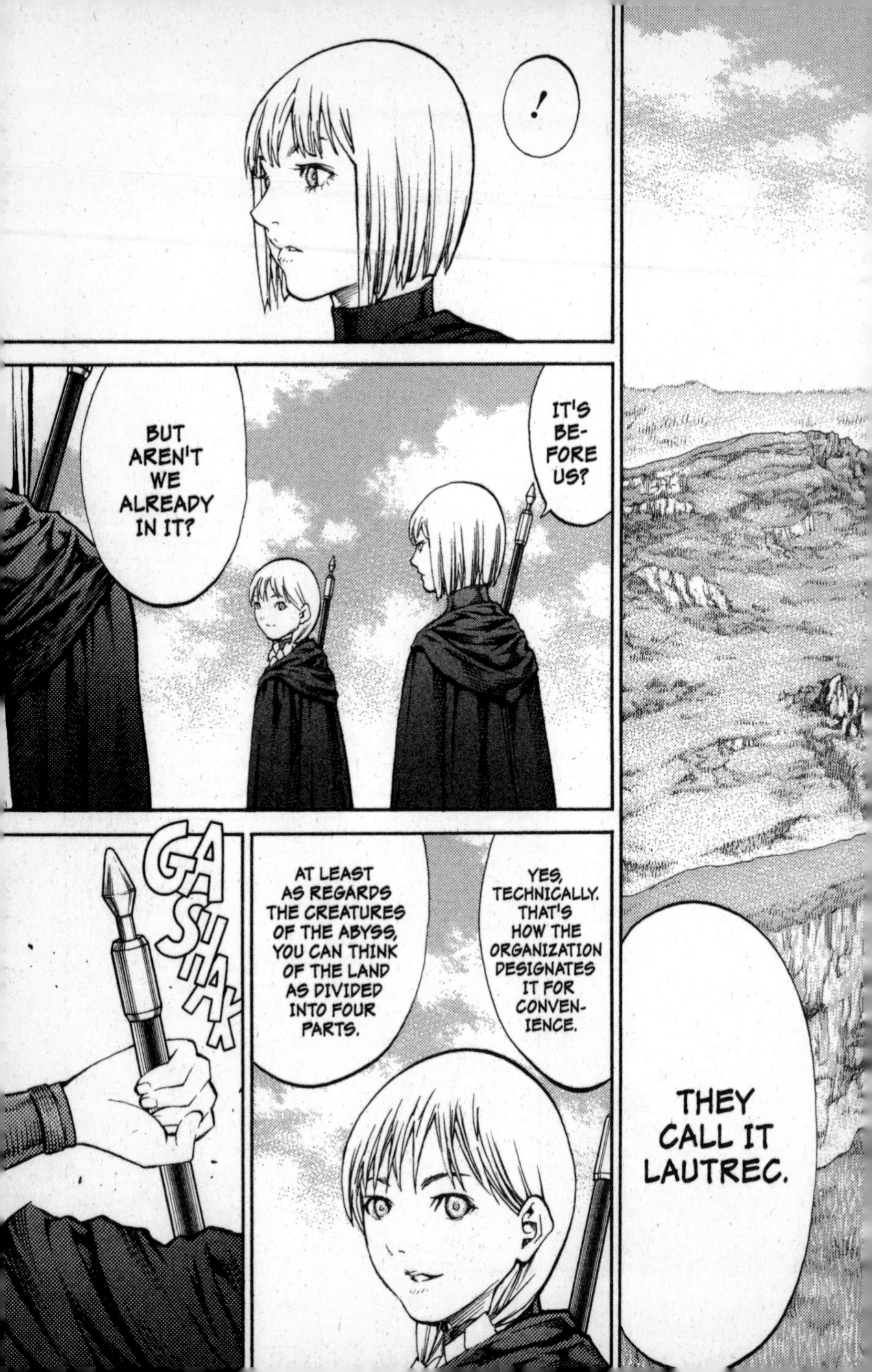
THEY CALL IT LAUTREC.
!
IT'S BE-FORE US?
BUT AREN'T WE ALREADY IN IT?
YES, TECHNICALLY. THAT'S HOW THE ORGANIZATION DESIGNATES IT FOR CONVEN-IENCE.
AT LEAST AS REGARDS THE CREATURES OF THE ABYSS, YOU CAN THINK OF THE LAND AS DIVIDED INTO FOUR PARTS.
GASHAK

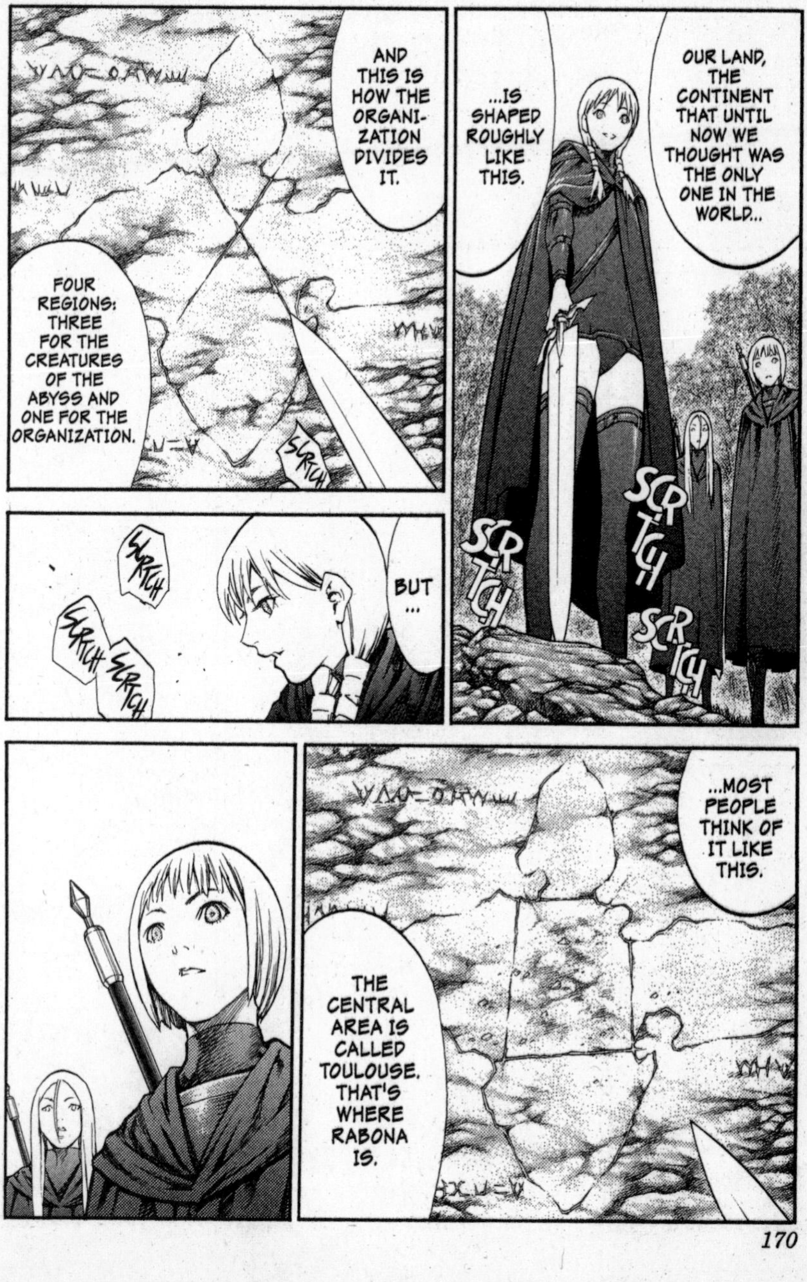
OUR LAND, THE CONTINENT THAT UNTIL NOW WE THOUGHT WAS THE ONLY ONE IN THE WORLD...
...IS SHAPED ROUGHLY LIKE THIS.
SCRTCH
SCRTCH
SCRTCH
AND THIS IS HOW THE ORGANIZATION DIVIDES IT.
FOUR REGIONS: THREE FOR THE CREATURES OF THE ABYSS AND ONE FOR THE ORGANIZATION.
SCRTCH
BUT ...
SCRTCH
SCRTCH
SCRTCH
...MOST PEOPLE THINK OF IT LIKE THIS.
THE CENTRAL AREA IS CALLED TOULOUSE. THAT'S WHERE RABONA IS.

READ THIS WAY

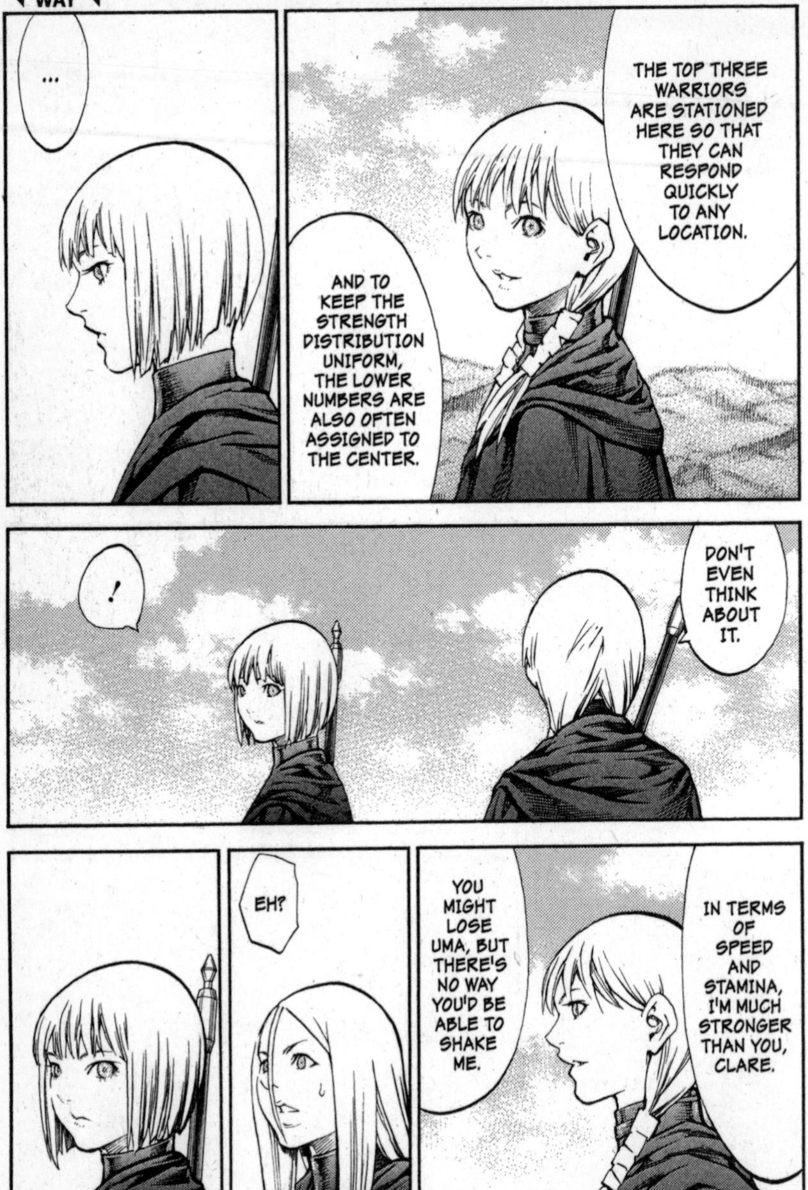
THE TOP THREE WARRIORS ARE STATIONED HERE SO THAT THEY CAN RESPOND QUICKLY TO ANY LOCATION.
AND TO KEEP THE STRENGTH DISTRIBUTION UNIFORM, THE LOWER NUMBERS ARE ALSO OFTEN ASSIGNED TO THE CENTER.
...
DON'T EVEN THINK ABOUT IT.
!
IN TERMS OF SPEED AND STAMINA, I'M MUCH STRONGER THAN YOU, CLARE.
YOU MIGHT LOSE UMA, BUT THERE'S NO WAY YOU'D BE ABLE TO SHAKE ME.
EH?

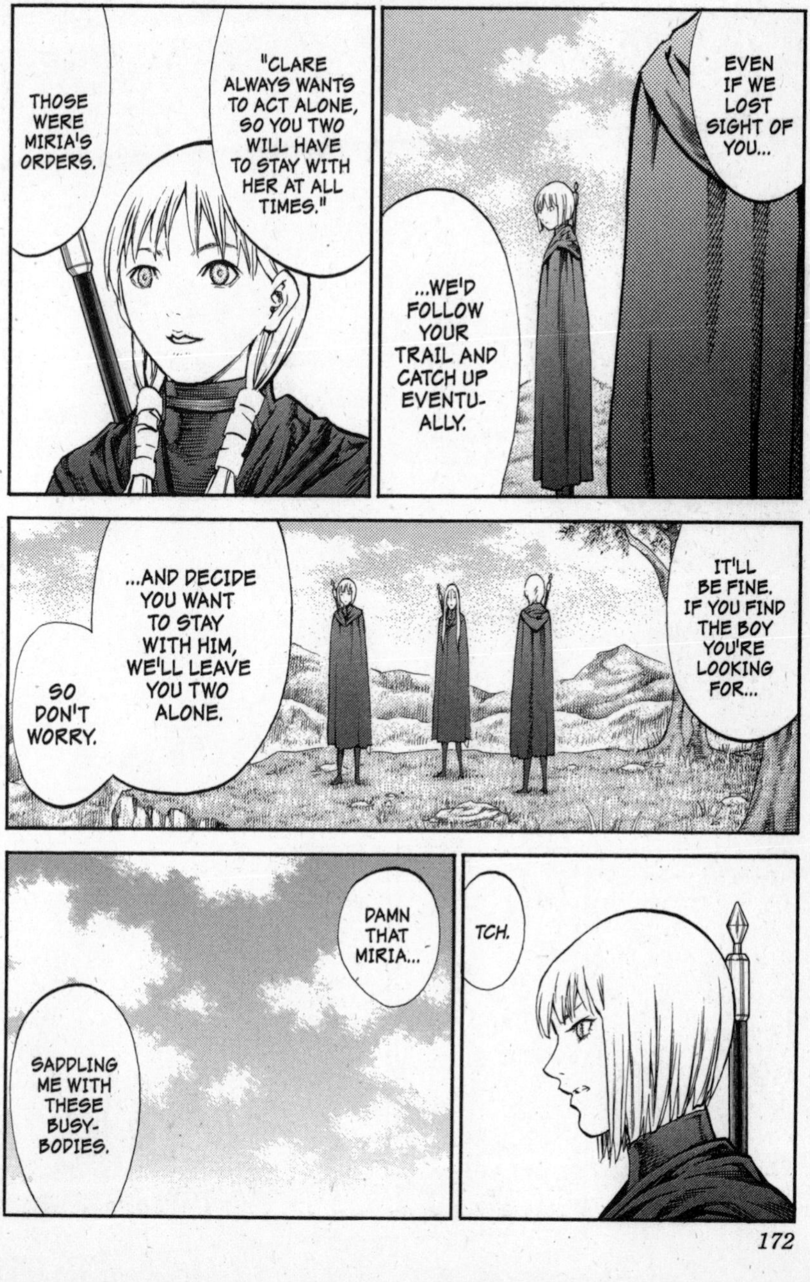
EVEN IF WE LOST SIGHT OF YOU...
...WE'D FOLLOW YOUR TRAIL AND CATCH UP EVENTU-ALLY.
"CLARE ALWAYS WANTS TO ACT ALONE, SO YOU TWO WILL HAVE TO STAY WITH HER AT ALL TIMES."
THOSE WERE MIRIA'S ORDERS.
IT'LL BE FINE. IF YOU FIND THE BOY YOU'RE LOOKING FOR...
...AND DECIDE YOU WANT TO STAY WITH HIM, WE'LL LEAVE YOU TWO ALONE.
SO DON'T WORRY.
TCH.
DAMN THAT MIRIA...
SADDLING ME WITH THESE BUSY-BODIES.

READ THIS WAY

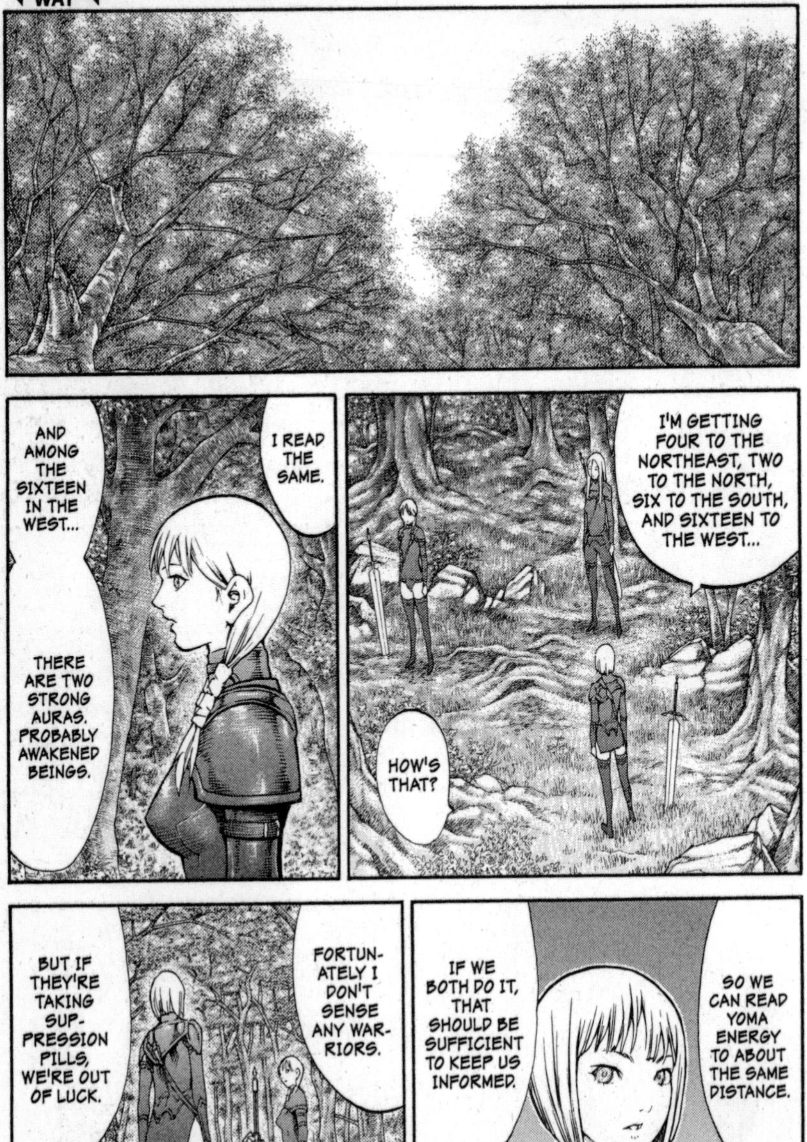
I'M GETTING FOUR TO THE NORTHEAST, TWO TO THE NORTH, SIX TO THE SOUTH, AND SIXTEEN TO THE WEST...
HOW'S THAT?
I READ THE SAME.
AND AMONG THE SIXTEEN IN THE WEST...
THERE ARE TWO STRONG AURAS. PROBABLY AWAKENED BEINGS.
SO WE CAN READ YOMA ENERGY TO ABOUT THE SAME DISTANCE.
IF WE BOTH DO IT, THAT SHOULD BE SUFFICIENT TO KEEP US INFORMED.
FORTUNATELY I DON'T SENSE ANY WARRIORS.
BUT IF THEY'RE TAKING SUPPRESSION PILLS, WE'RE OUT OF LUCK.

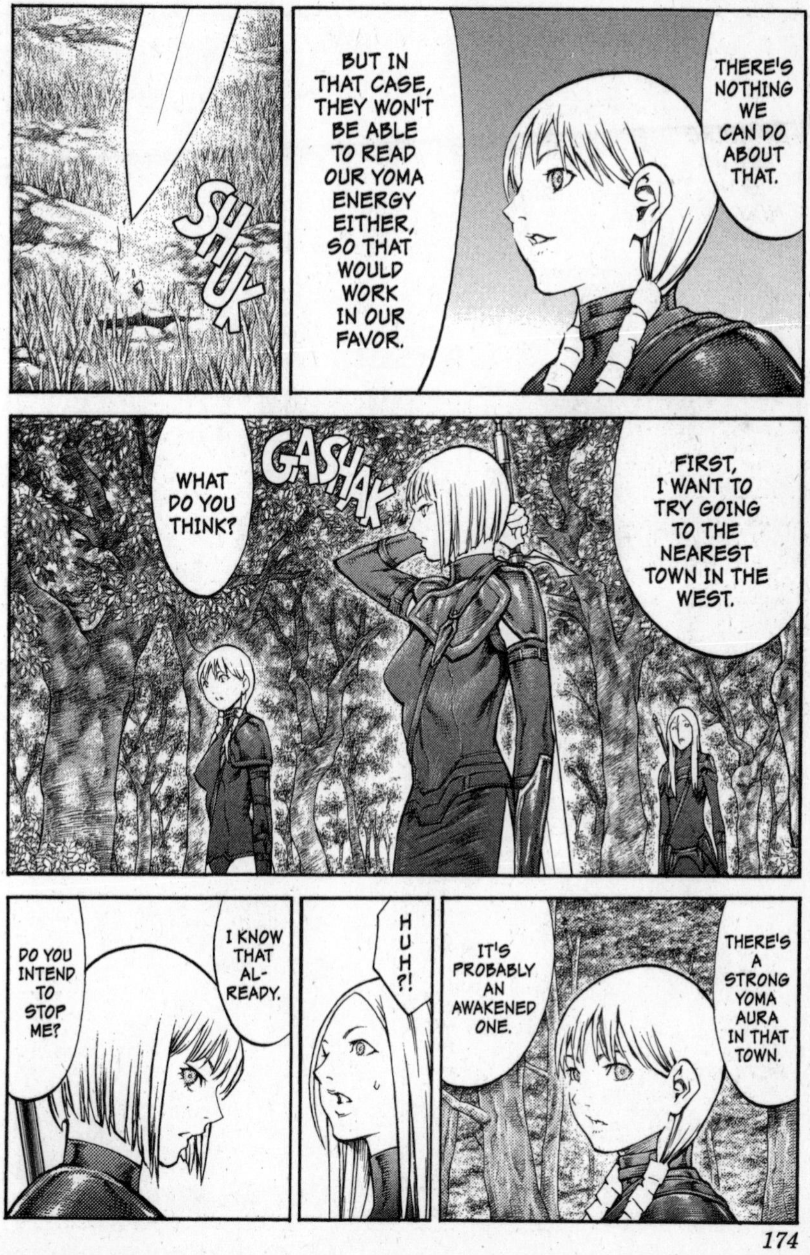
THERE'S NOTHING WE CAN DO ABOUT THAT.
BUT IN THAT CASE, THEY WON'T BE ABLE TO READ OUR YOMA ENERGY EITHER, SO THAT WOULD WORK IN OUR FAVOR.
SHUK
FIRST, I WANT TO TRY GOING TO THE NEAREST TOWN IN THE WEST.
GASHAK
WHAT DO YOU THINK?
THERE'S A STRONG YOMA AURA IN THAT TOWN.
IT'S PROBABLY AN AWAKENED ONE.
HUH?!
I KNOW THAT AL-READY.
DO YOU INTEND TO STOP ME?

READ THIS WAY

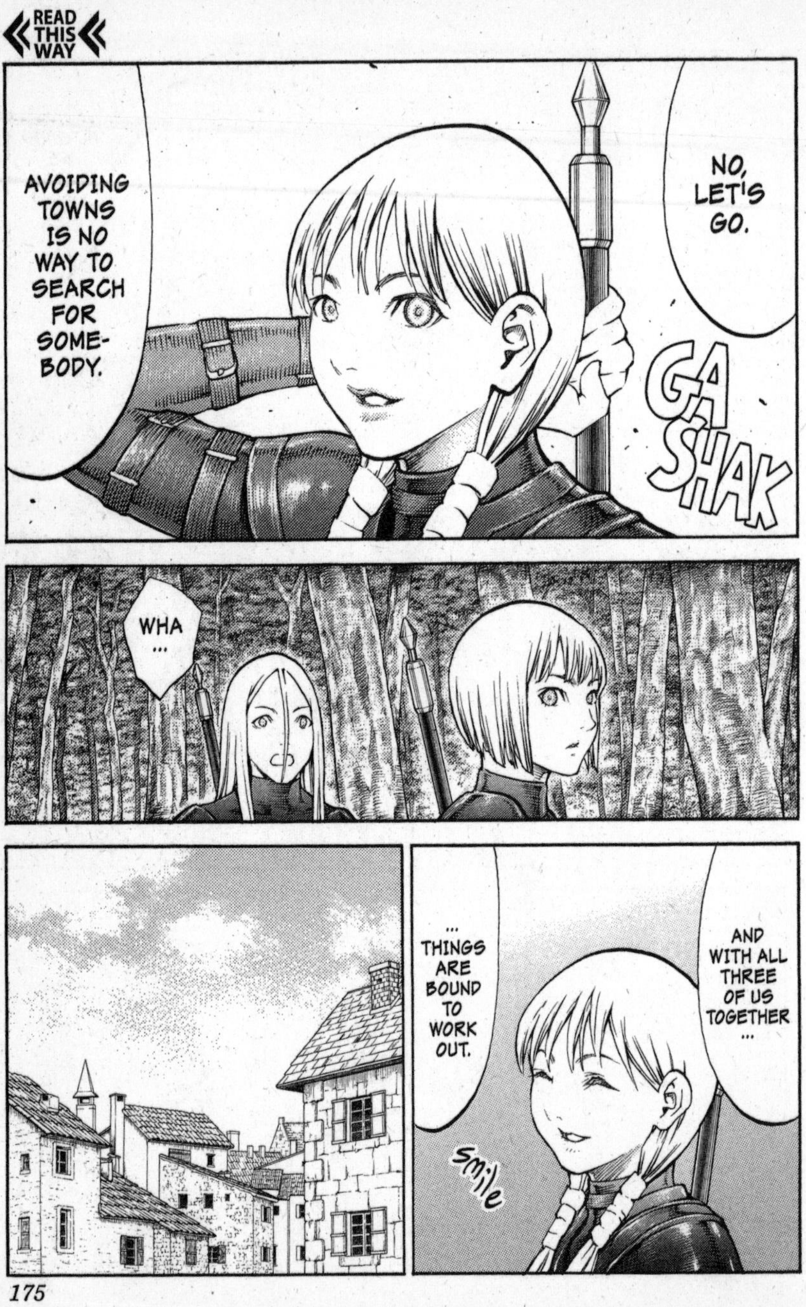
NO, LET'S GO.
AVOIDING TOWNS IS NO WAY TO SEARCH FOR SOME-BODY.
GA SHAK
WHA ...
AND WITH ALL THREE OF US TOGETHER ...
... THINGS ARE BOUND TO WORK OUT.
Smile

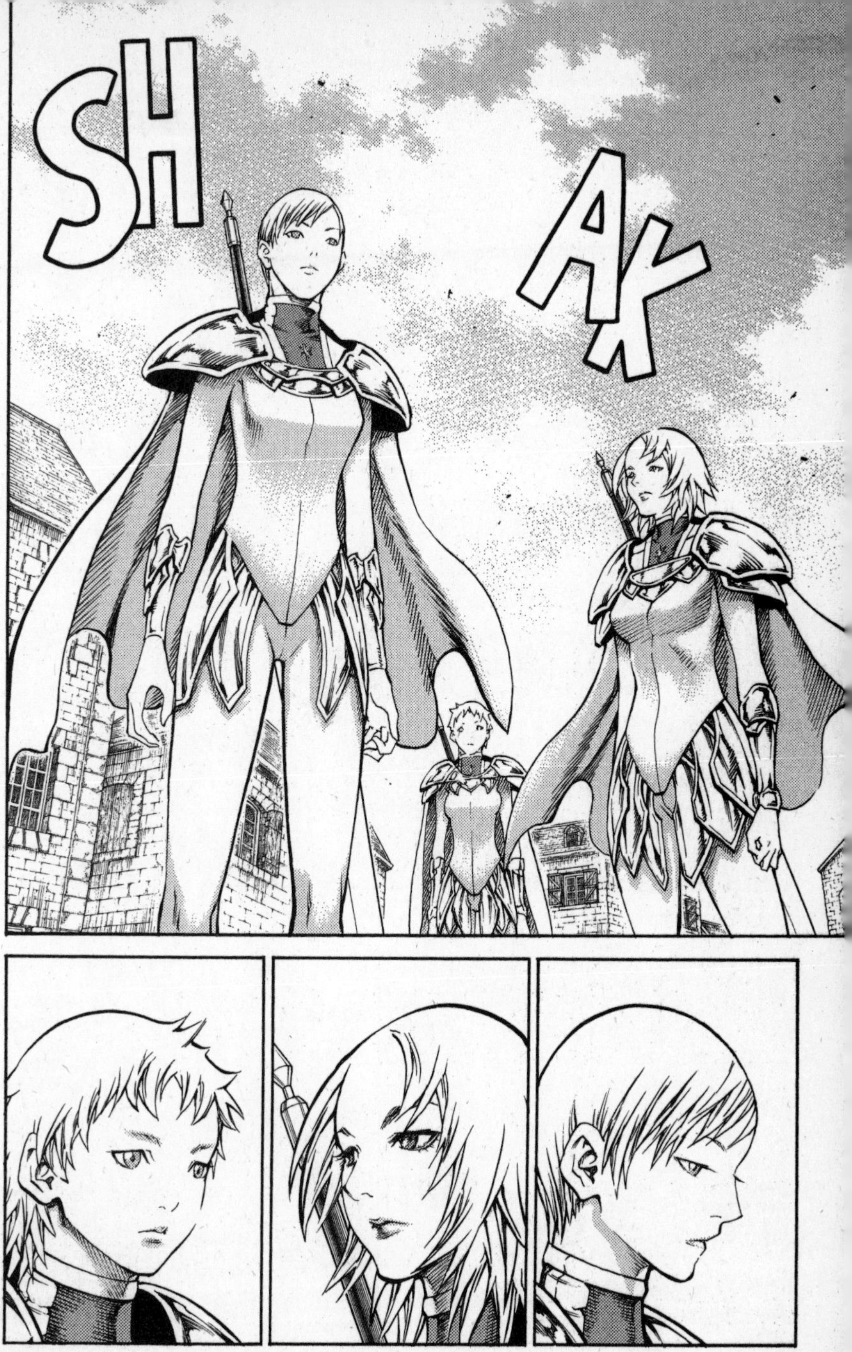
SHAK

READ THIS WAY

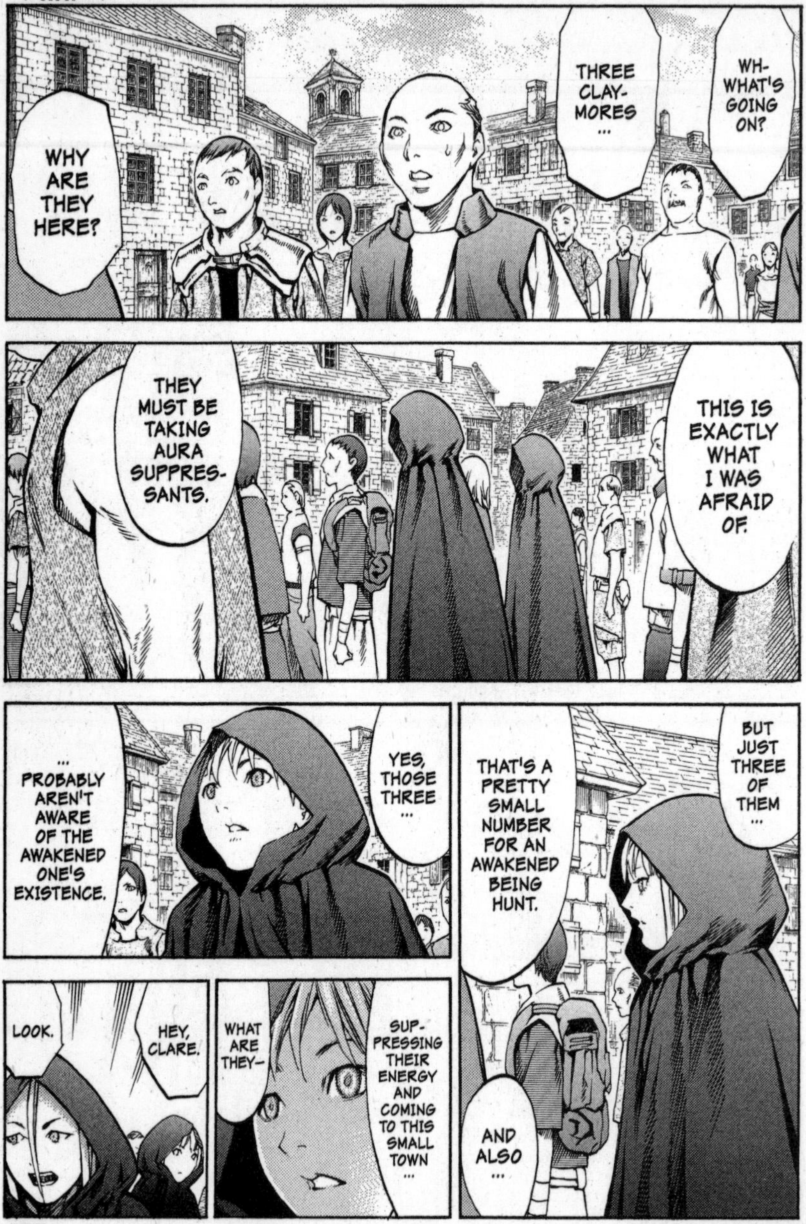
WH- WHAT'S GOING ON?
THREE CLAY- MORES ...
WHY ARE THEY HERE?
THIS IS EXACTLY WHAT I WAS AFRAID OF.
THEY MUST BE TAKING AURA SUPPRES- SANTS.
BUT JUST THREE OF THEM ...
THAT'S A PRETTY SMALL NUMBER FOR AN AWAKENED BEING HUNT.
AND ALSO ...
YES, THOSE THREE ...
... PROBABLY AREN'T AWARE OF THE AWAKENED ONE'S EXISTENCE.
SUP- PRESSING THEIR ENERGY AND COMING TO THIS SMALL TOWN ...
WHAT ARE THEY—
HEY, CLARE.
LOOK.

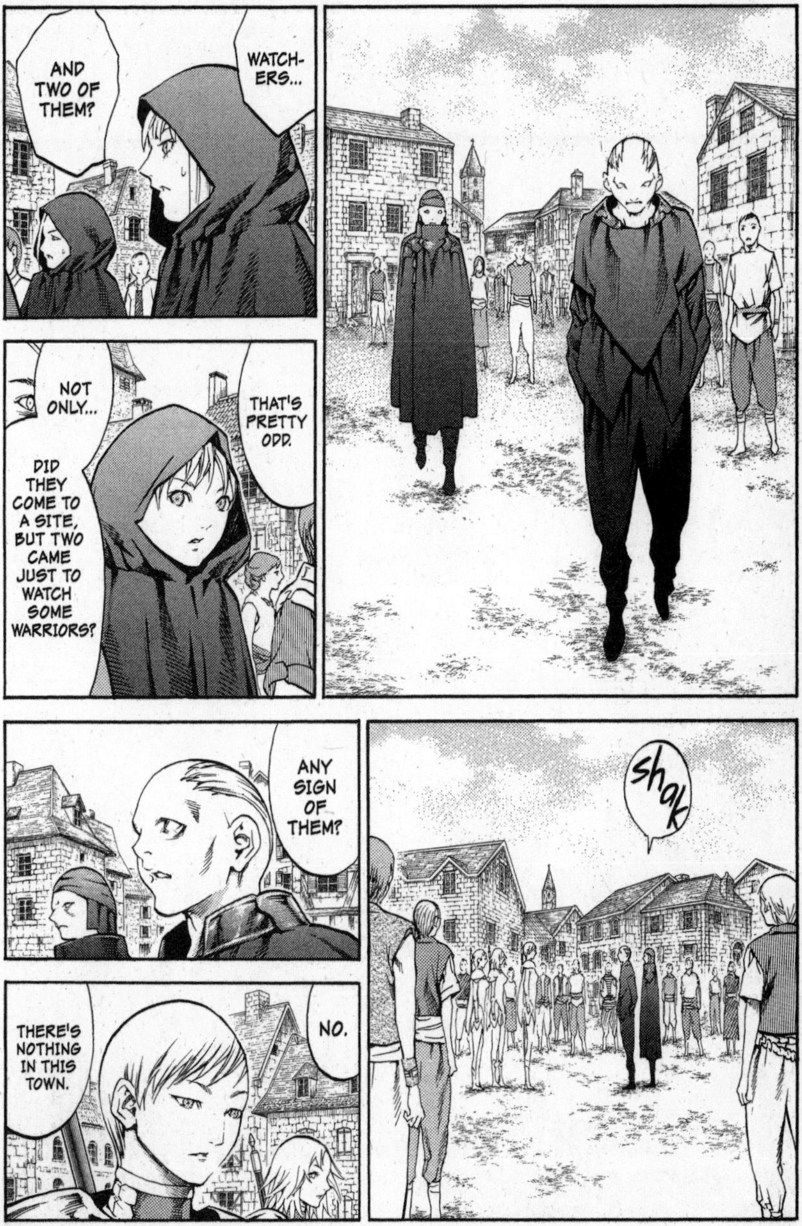
WATCHERS...
AND TWO OF THEM?
THAT'S PRETTY ODD.
NOT ONLY...
DID THEY COME TO A SITE, BUT TWO CAME JUST TO WATCH SOME WARRIORS?
shak
ANY SIGN OF THEM?
NO.
THERE'S NOTHING IN THIS TOWN.

READ THIS WAY

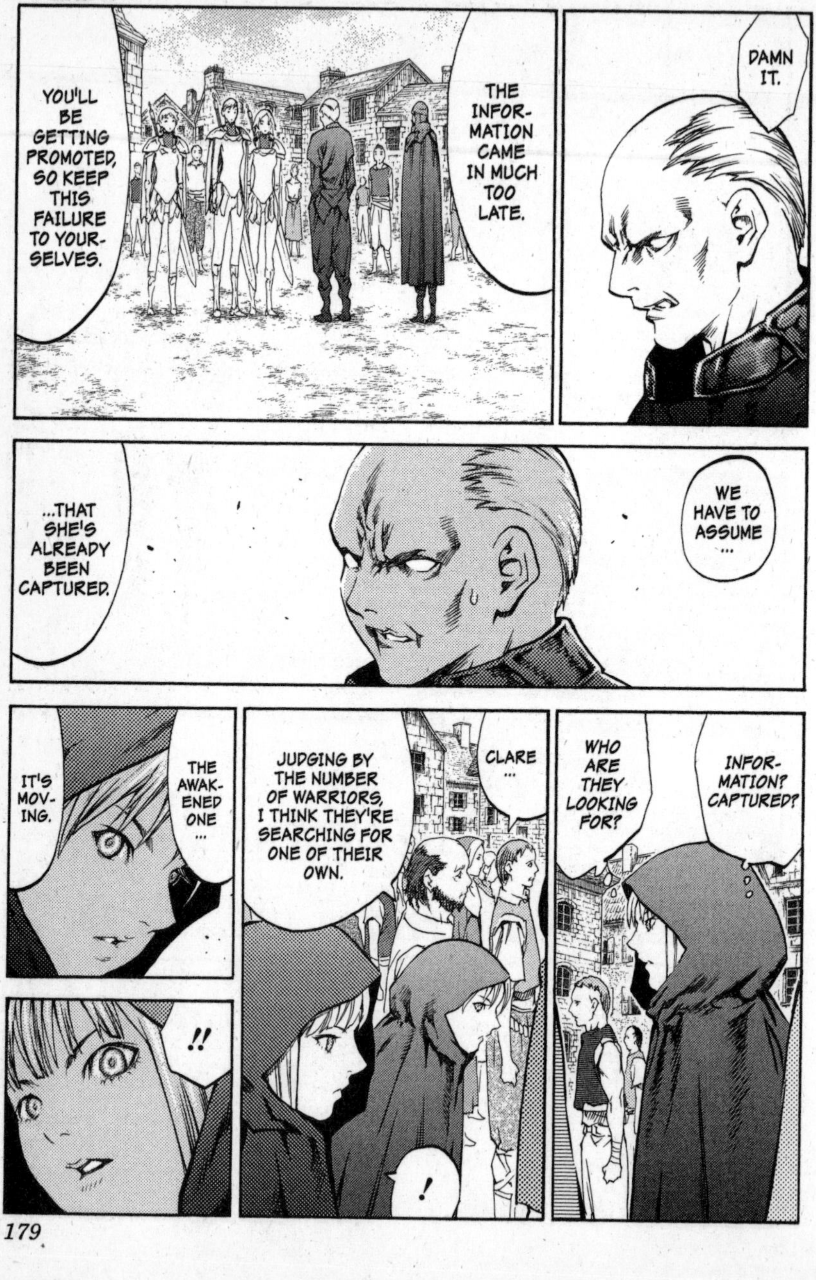
DAMN IT.
THE INFORMATION CAME IN MUCH TOO LATE.
YOU'LL BE GETTING PROMOTED, SO KEEP THIS FAILURE TO YOURSELVES.
WE HAVE TO ASSUME...
...THAT SHE'S ALREADY BEEN CAPTURED.
INFORMATION? CAPTURED?
WHO ARE THEY LOOKING FOR?
CLARE...
JUDGING BY THE NUMBER OF WARRIORS, I THINK THEY'RE SEARCHING FOR ONE OF THEIR OWN.
!
THE AWAKENED ONE...
IT'S MOVING.
!!

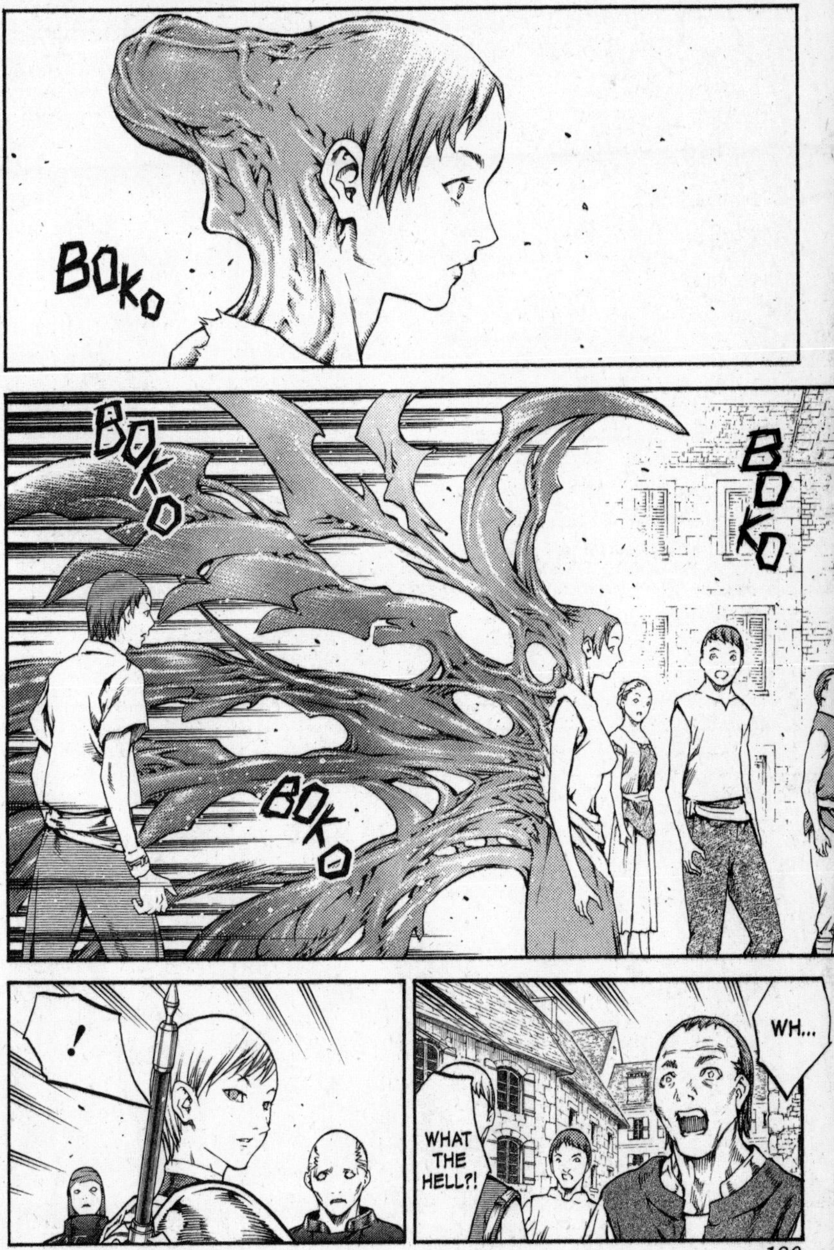
BOKO
BOKO
BOKO
BOKO
WH...
WHAT THE HELL?!
!

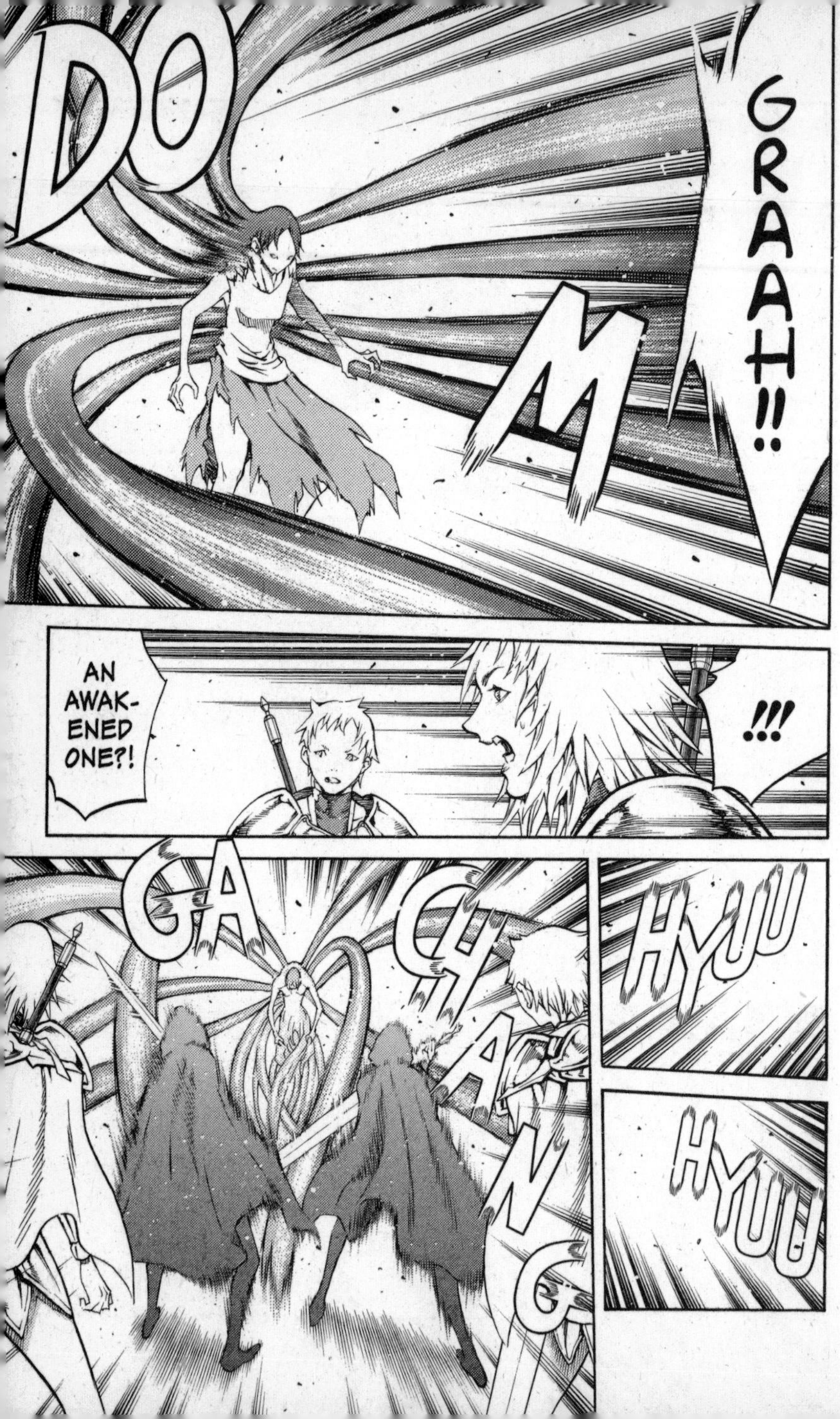
GRAAH!!
DO
M
!!!
AN AWAK-ENED ONE?!
HYUU
HYUU
GA
CHANG

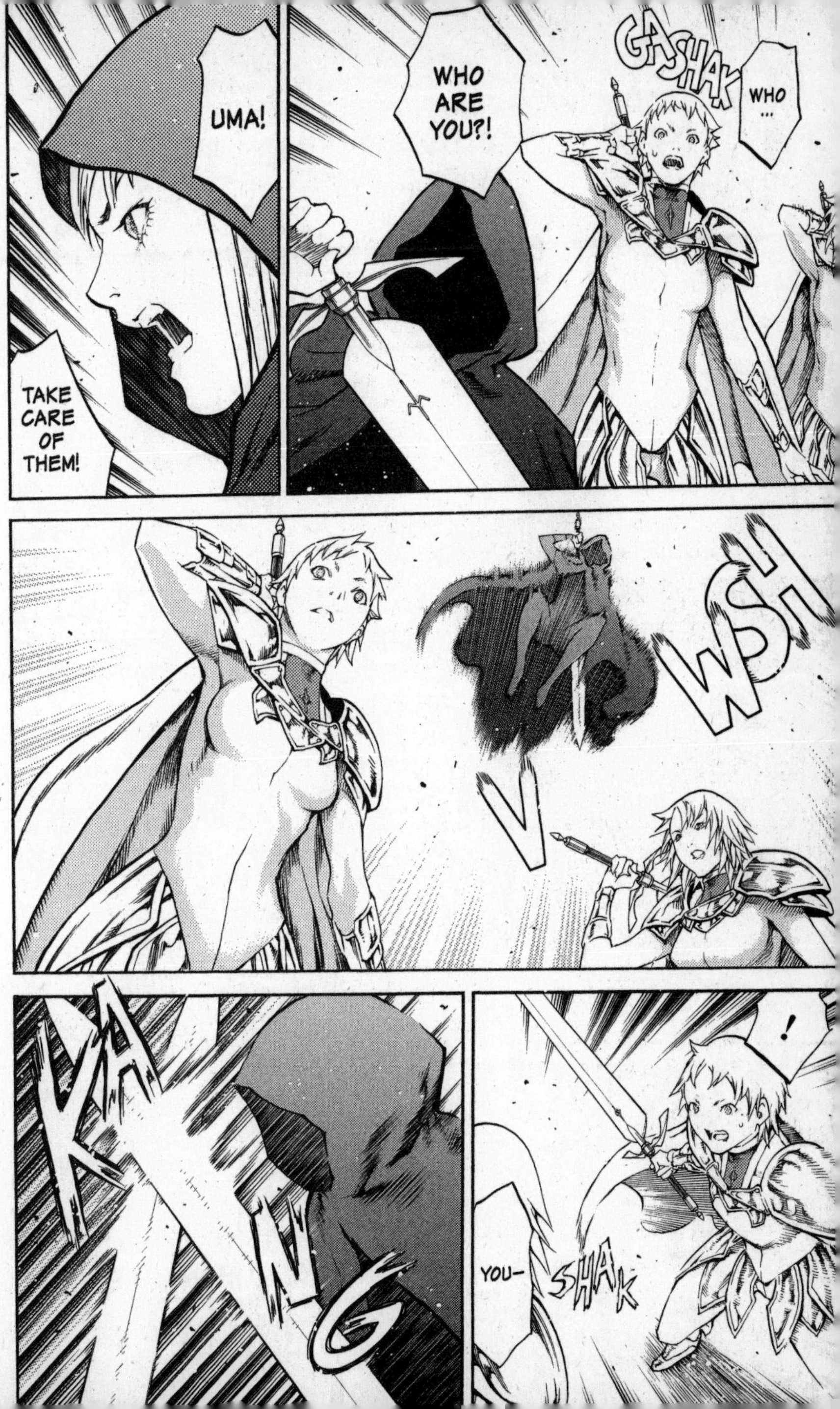
GASHAK
WHO ...
WHO ARE YOU?!
UMA!
TAKE CARE OF THEM!
WSH
V
!
YOU—
SHAK
KANG

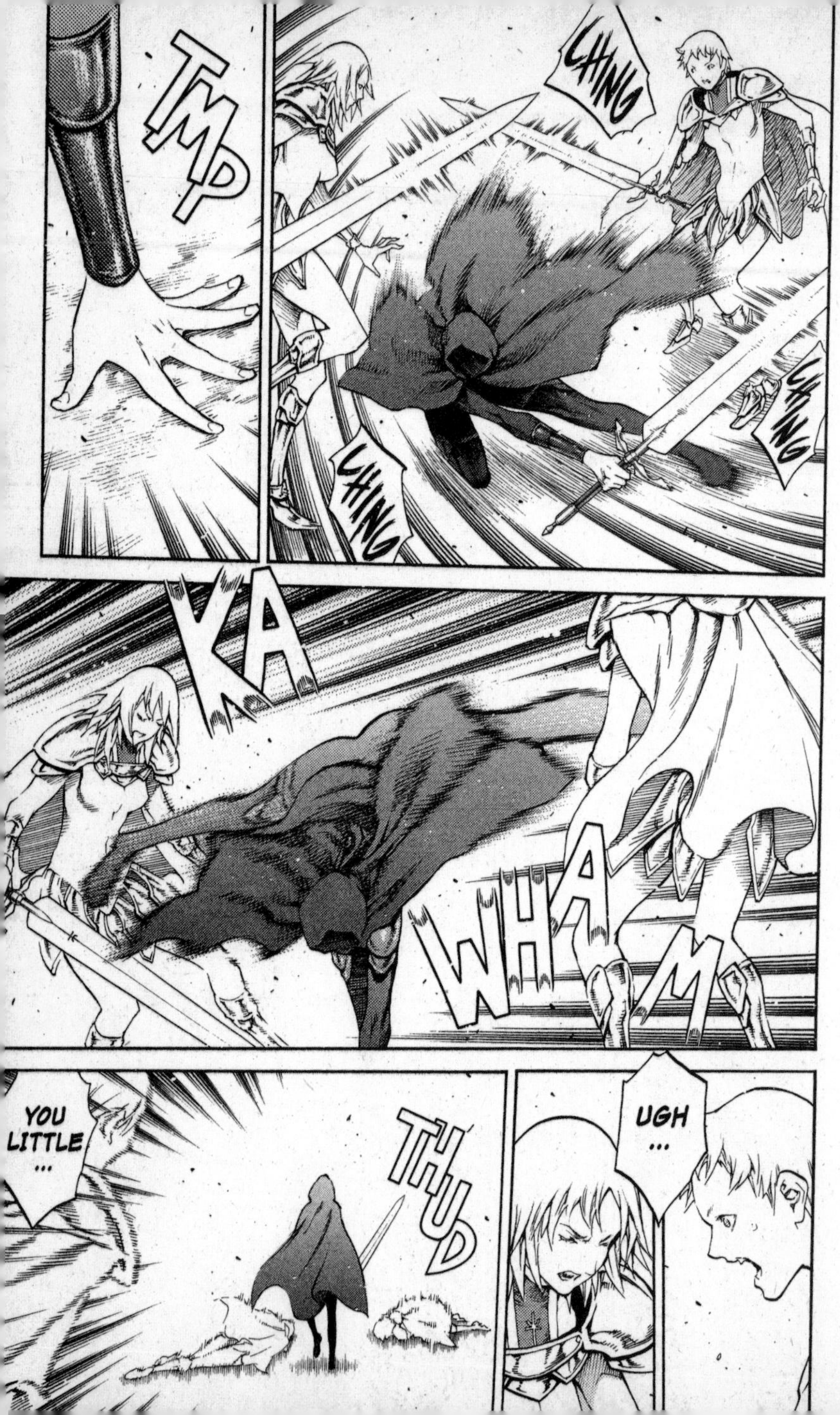
CHING
CHING
CHING
TMP
KA
WHAM
UGH ...
THUD
YOU LITTLE ...

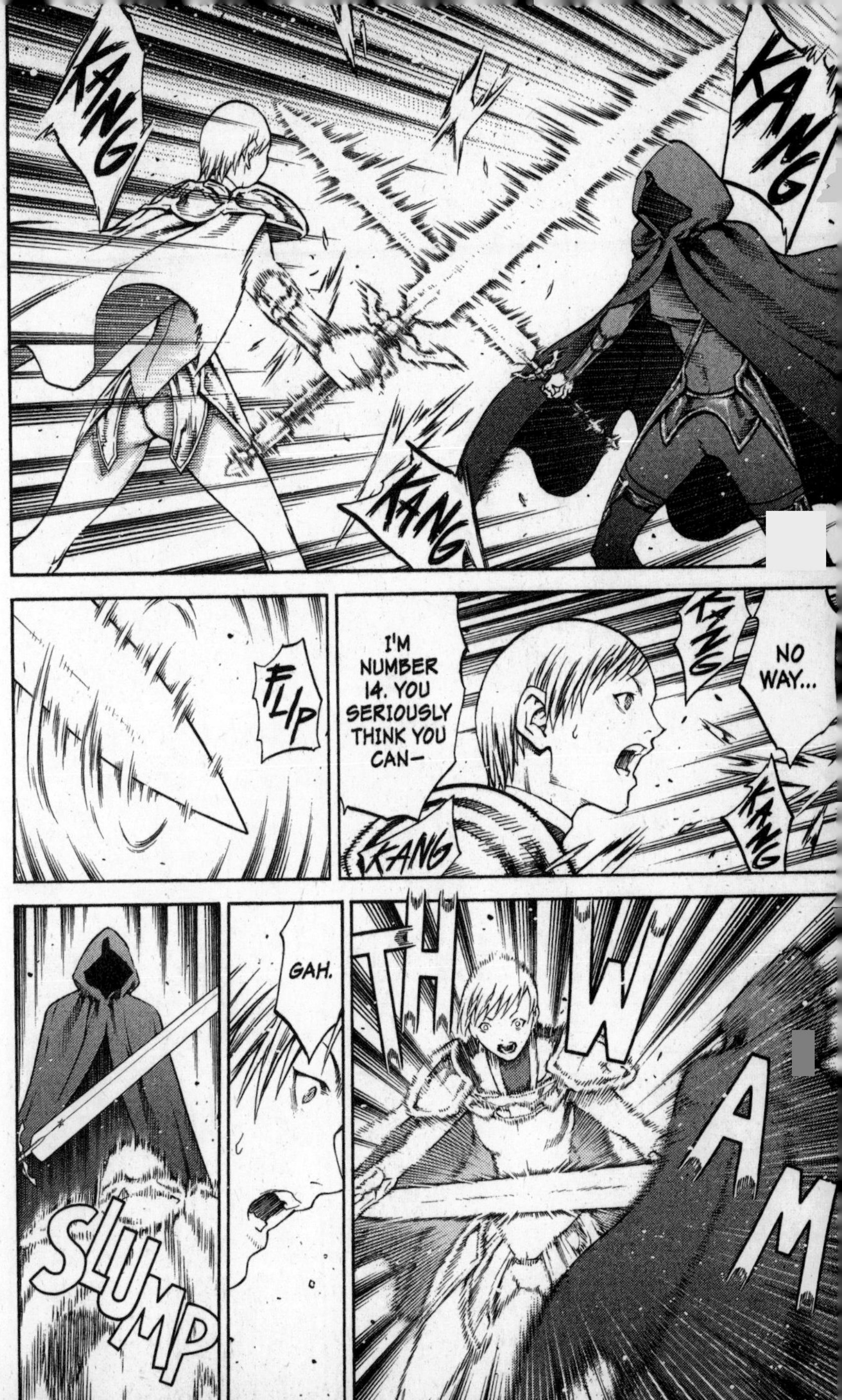
KANG
KANG
KANG
KANG
NO WAY...
I'M NUMBER 14. YOU SERIOUSLY THINK YOU CAN–
KANG
KANG
FLIP
THWAM
GAH.
SLUMP

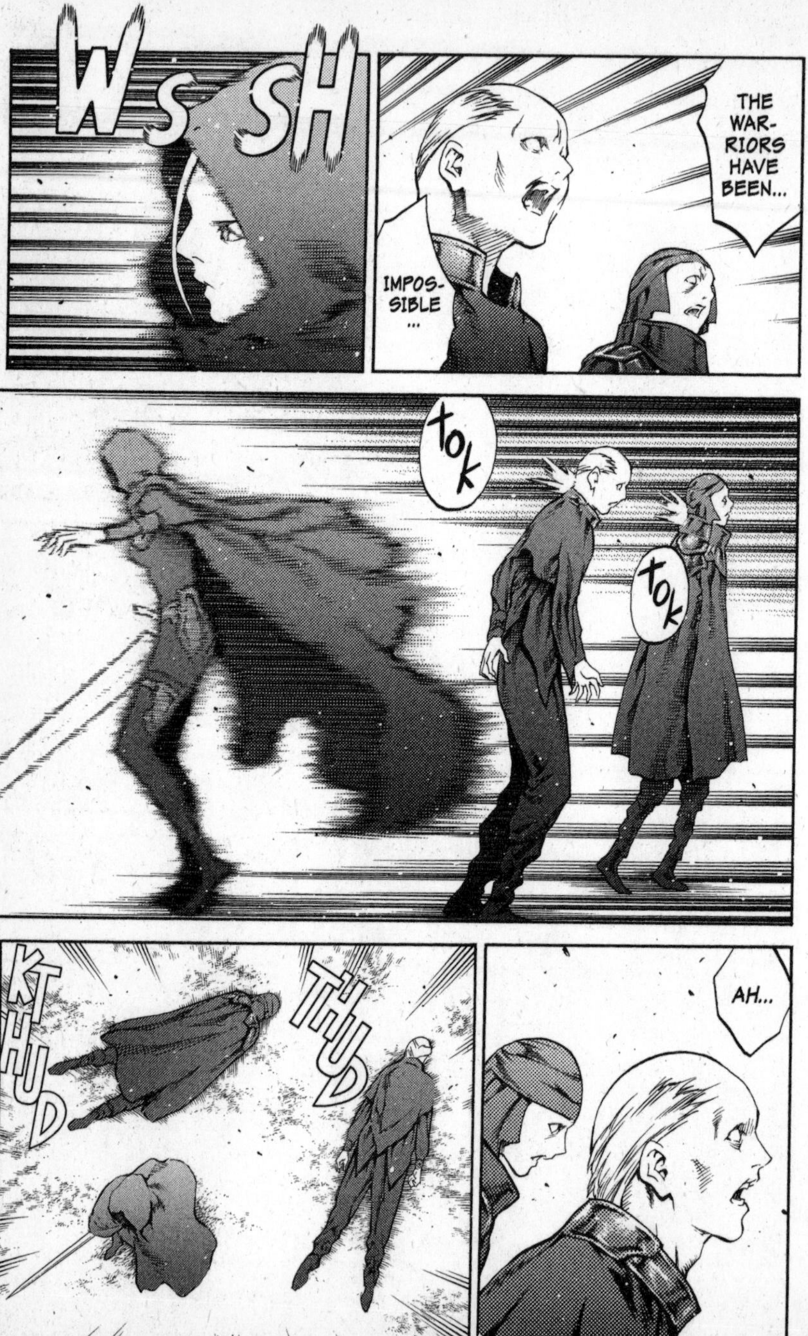
THE WAR-RIORS HAVE BEEN...
IMPOS-SIBLE ...
WsSH
TOK
TOK
AH...
THUD
KTHUD

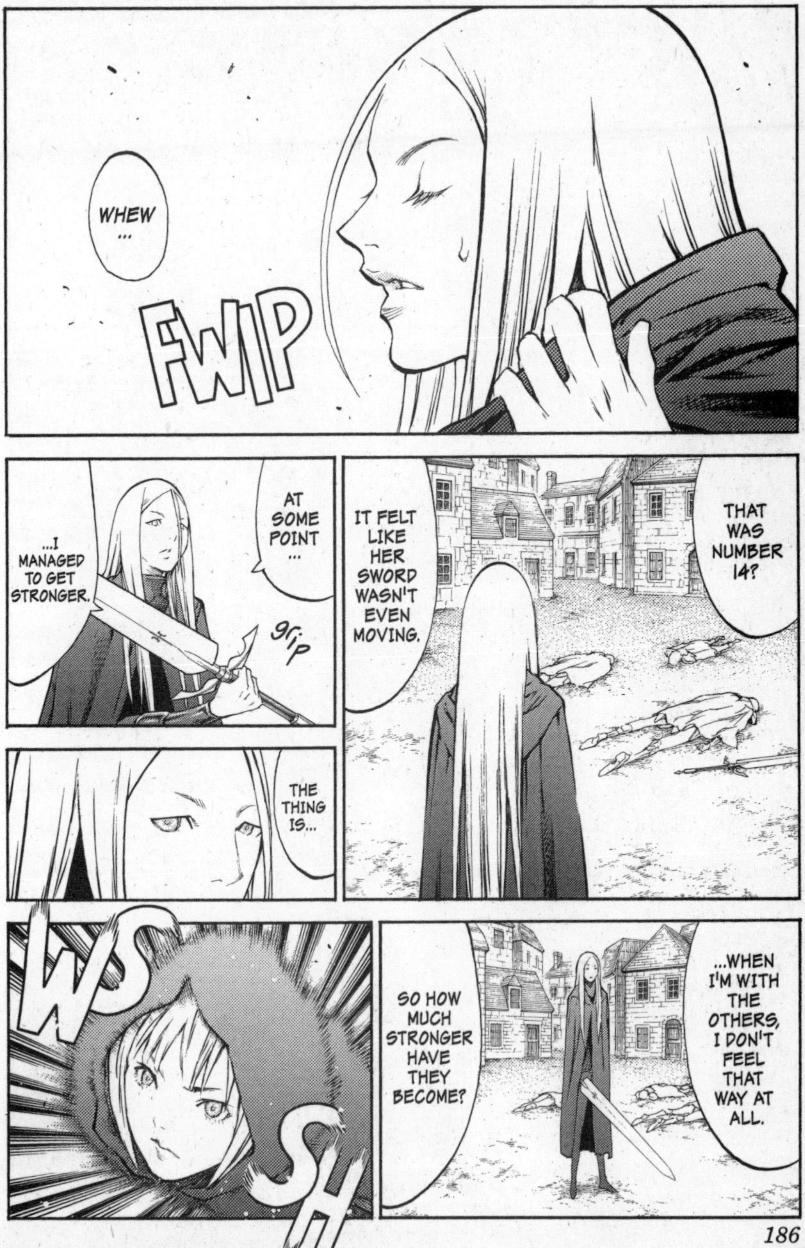
WHEW ...
FWIP
THAT WAS NUMBER 14?
IT FELT LIKE HER SWORD WASN'T EVEN MOVING.
AT SOME POINT ...
...I MANAGED TO GET STRONGER.
grip
THE THING IS...
...WHEN I'M WITH THE OTHERS, I DON'T FEEL THAT WAY AT ALL.
SO HOW MUCH STRONGER HAVE THEY BECOME?
WSSH

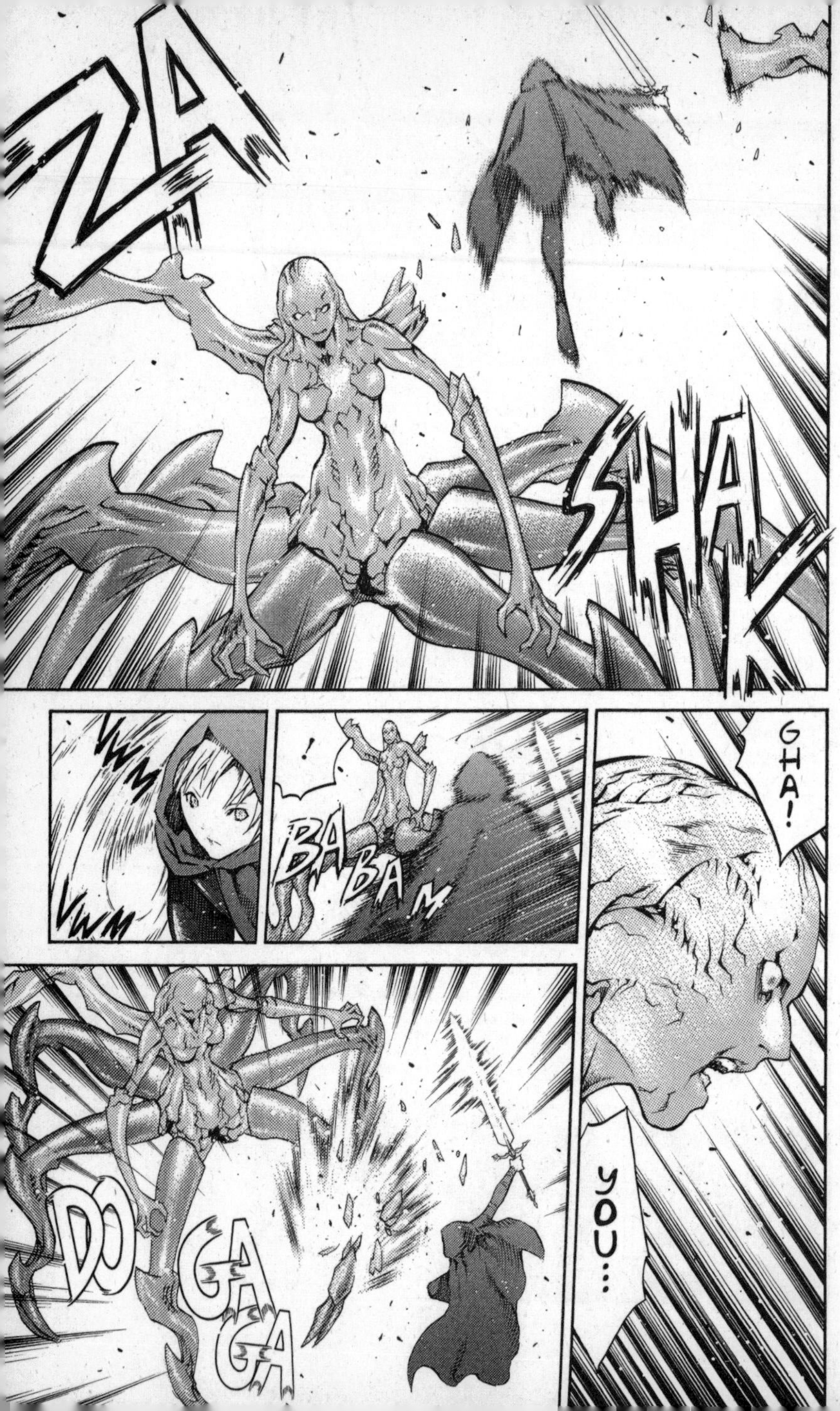
ZA
SHAK
GHA!
YOU...
!
BABAM
VWM
VWM
DO GA GA

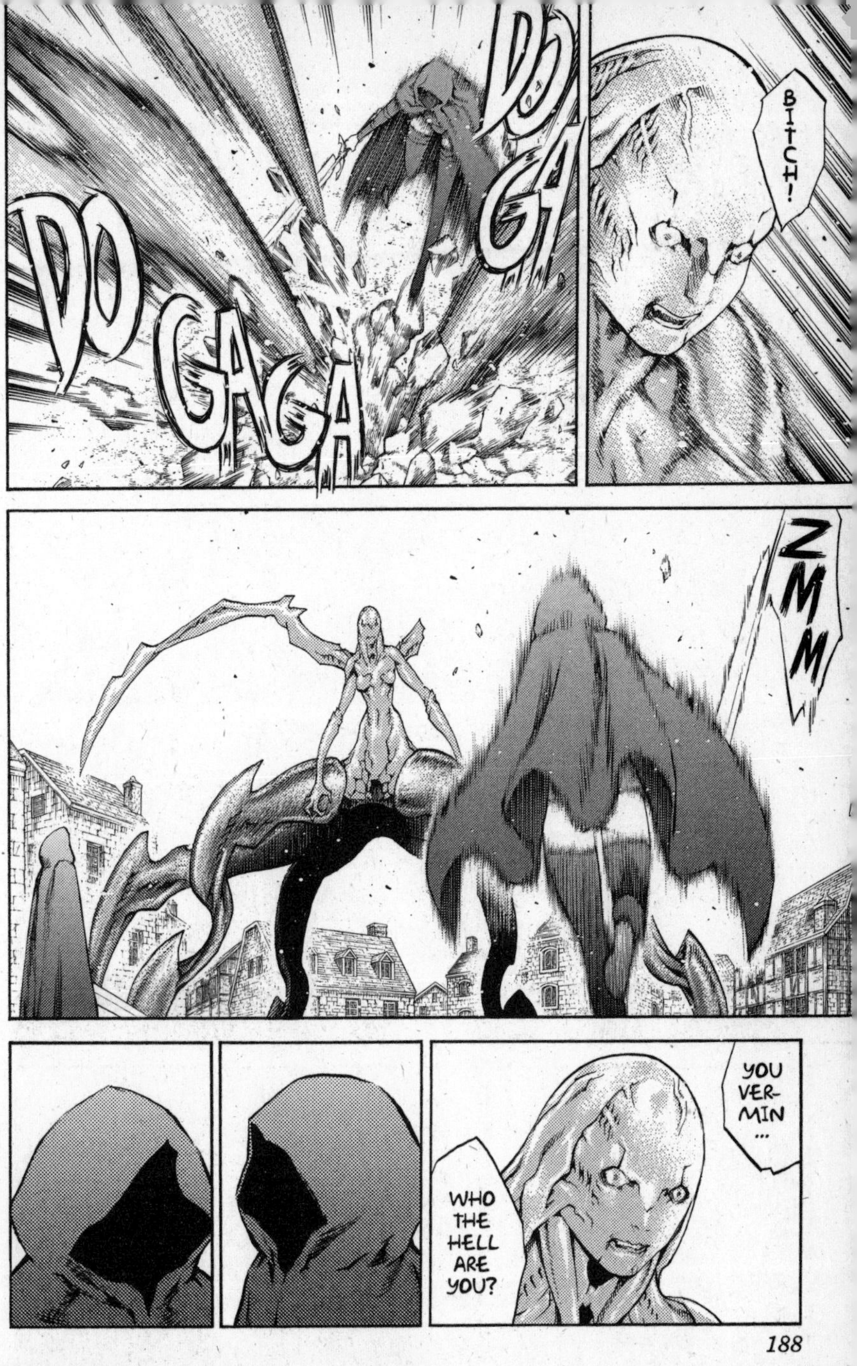
BITCH!
DO GA
DO GAGA
ZMM
YOU VER-MIN...
WHO THE HELL ARE YOU?

READ THIS WAY

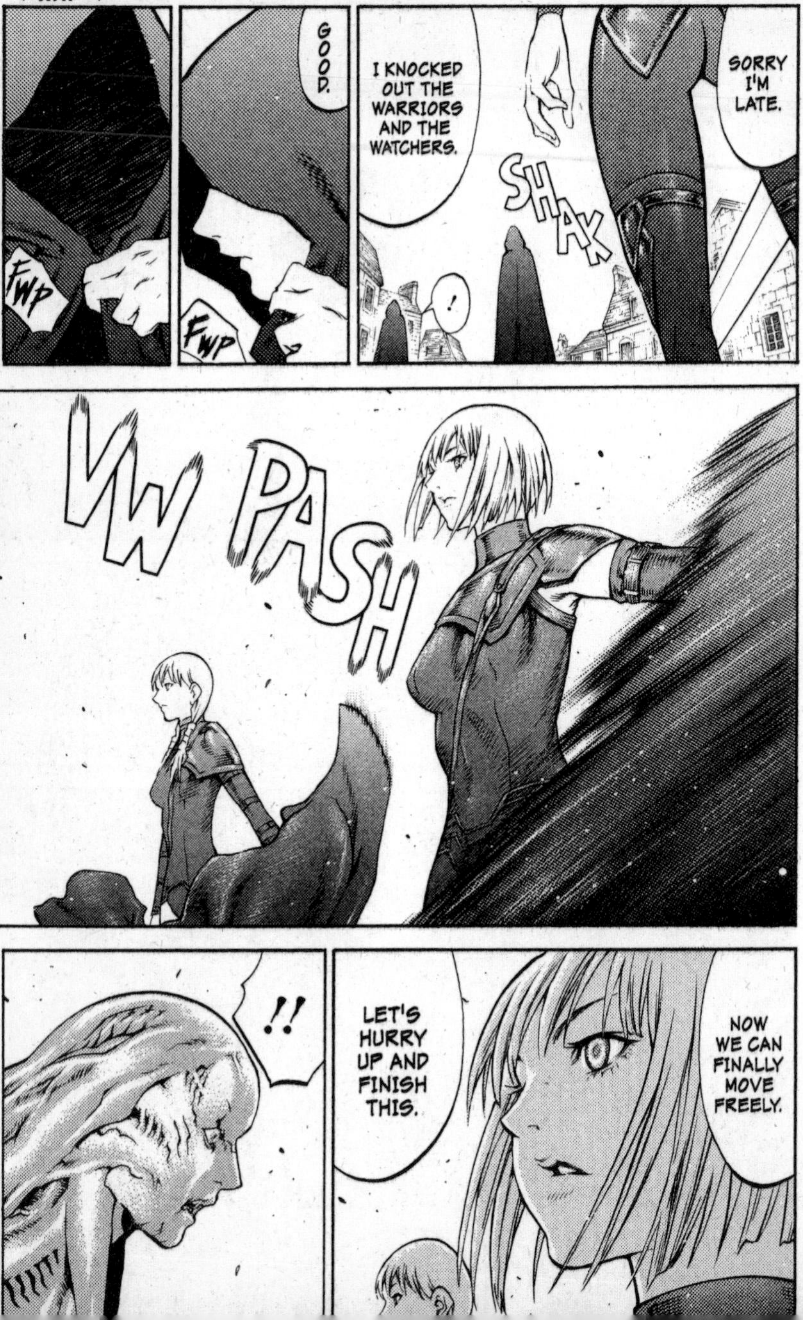
SORRY I'M LATE.
SHAK
!
I KNOCKED OUT THE WARRIORS AND THE WATCHERS.
GOOD.
FWP
FWP
VW PASH
NOW WE CAN FINALLY MOVE FREELY.
LET'S HURRY UP AND FINISH THIS.
!!

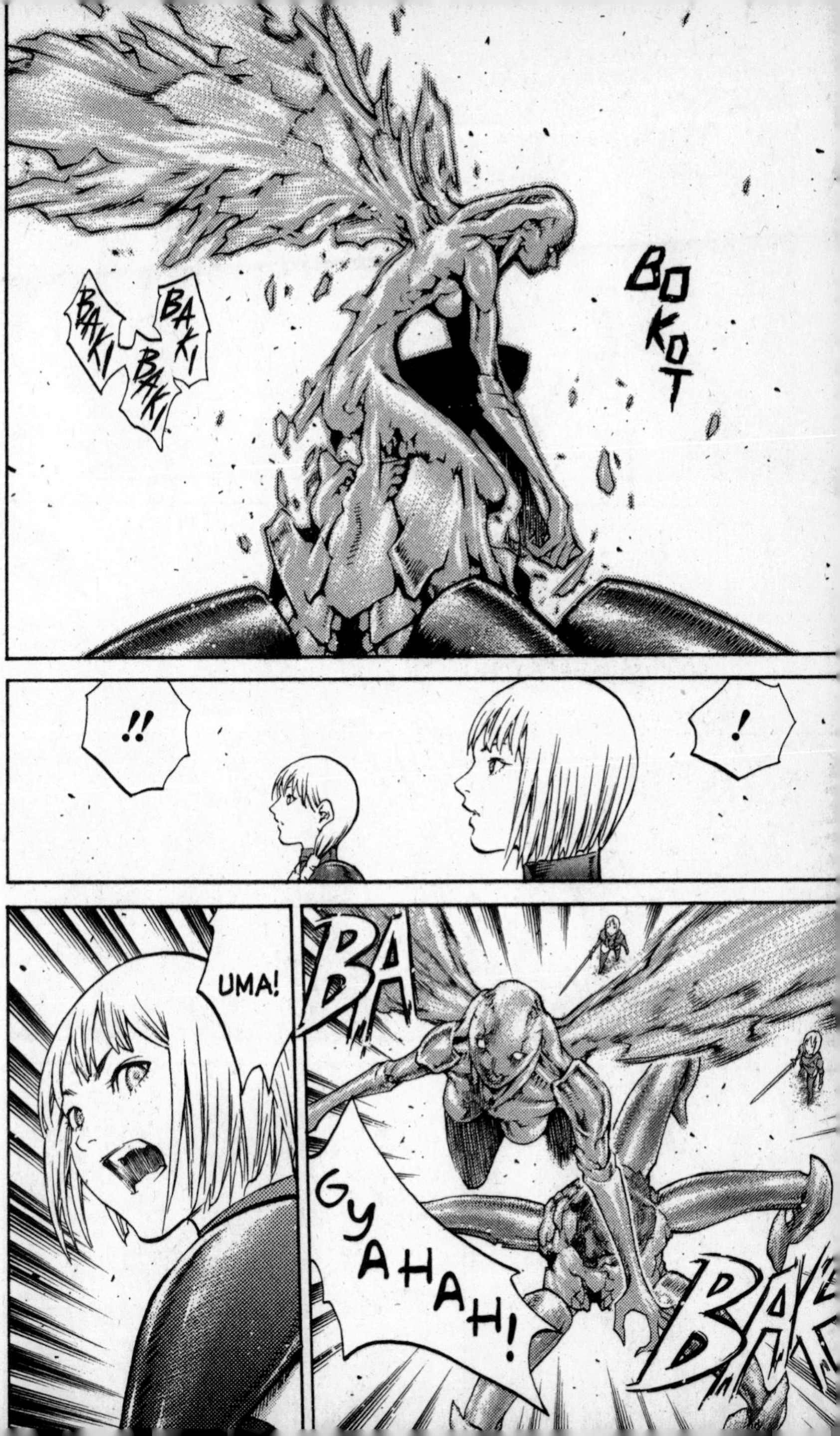
BOKOT
BAKI BAKI BAKI
!
!!
BA
GYAHAHAH!
BAK
UMA!

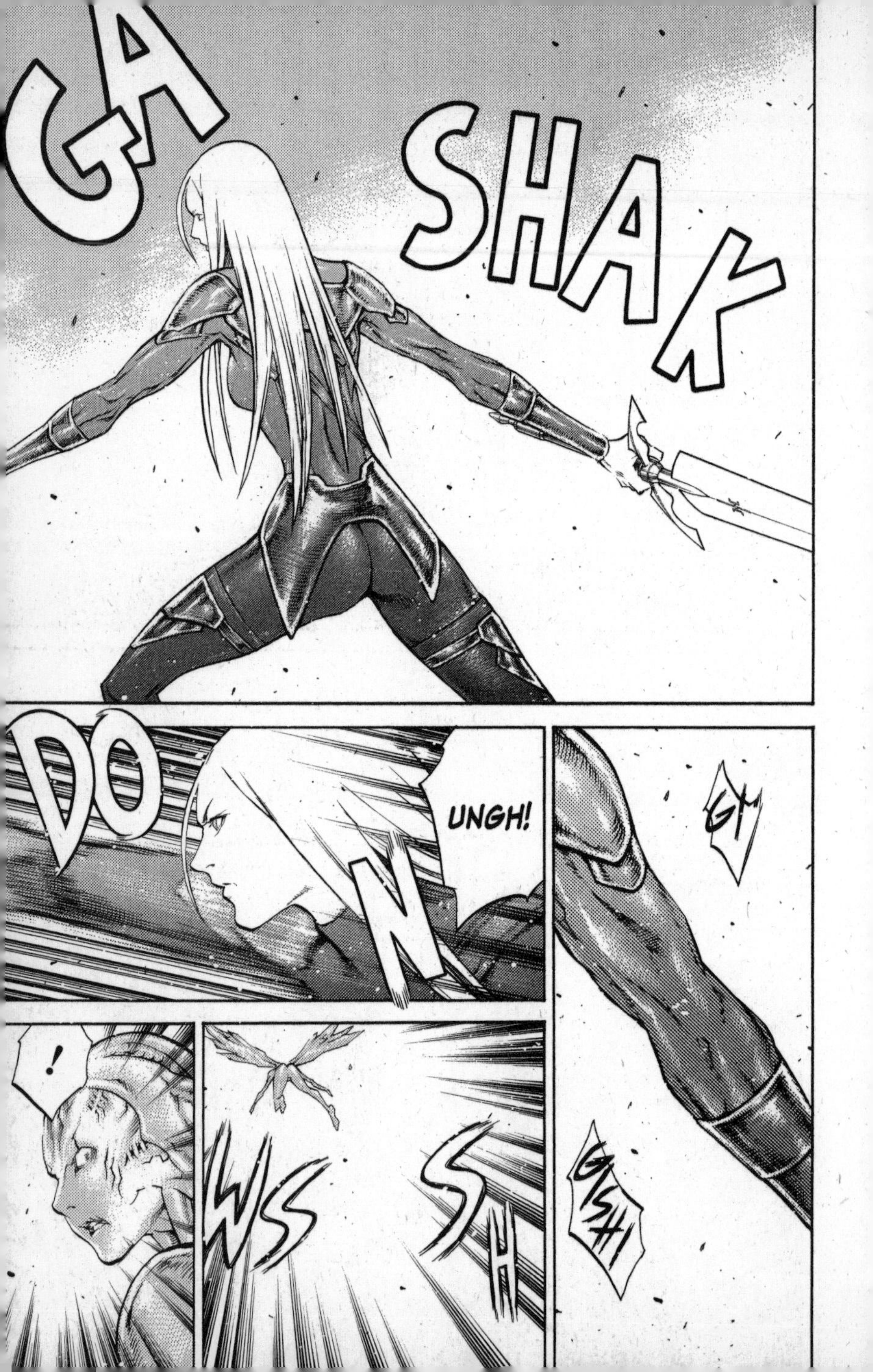
GASHAK
GI
GISHI
DON
UNGH!
WSSSH
!

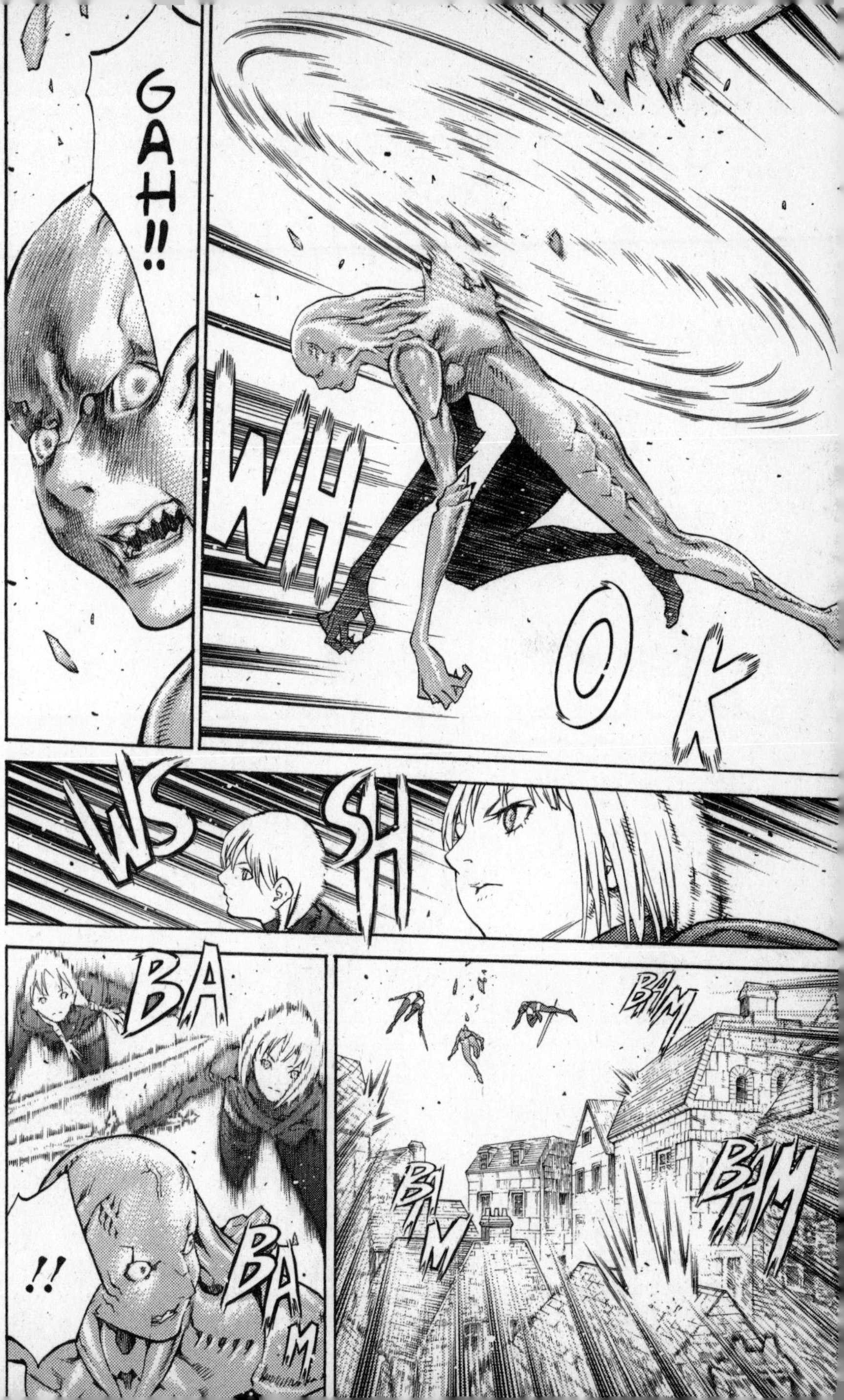

WHOOK
GAH!!
WSSH
BAM
BAM
BAM
BA
BAM
!!

READ THIS WAY

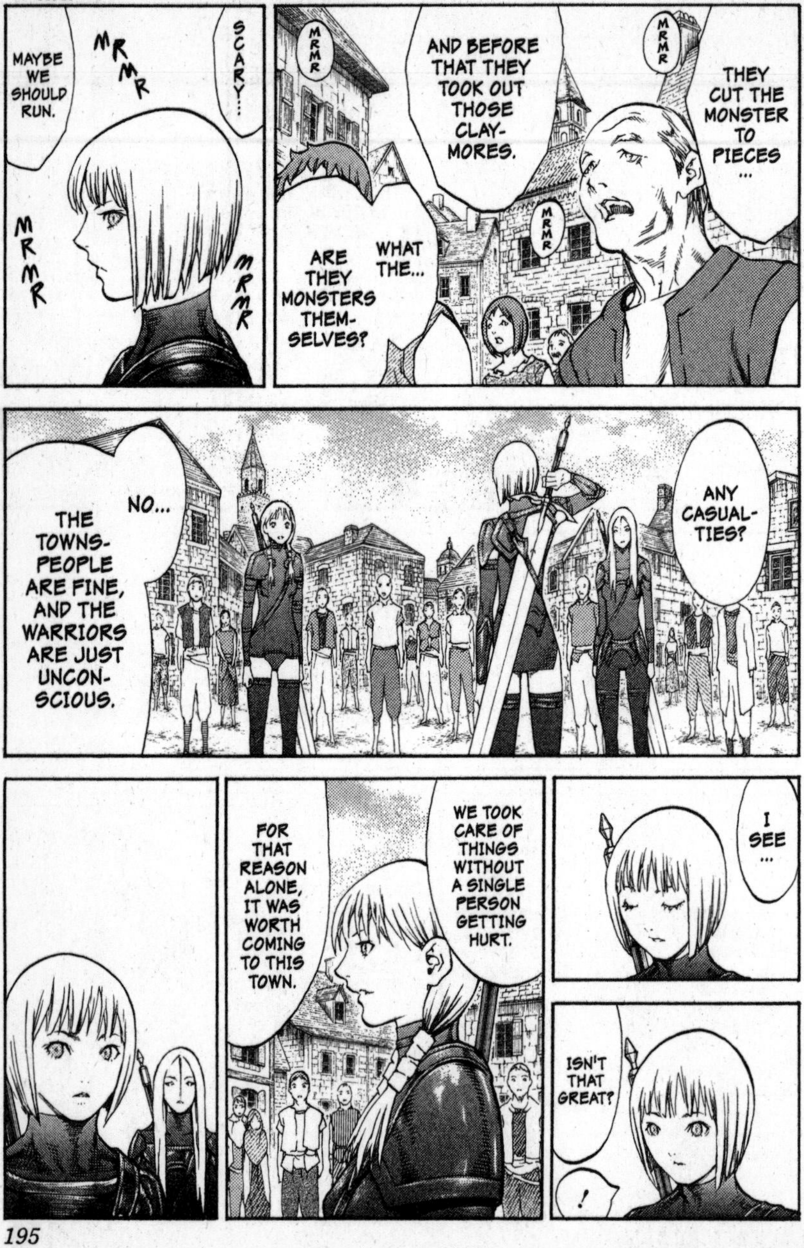
THEY CUT THE MONSTER TO PIECES ...
MRMR
AND BEFORE THAT THEY TOOK OUT THOSE CLAY-MORES.
MRMR
MRMR
WHAT THE...
ARE THEY MONSTERS THEM-SELVES?
SCARY...
MRMR
MAYBE WE SHOULD RUN.
MRMR
MRMR
ANY CASUAL-TIES?
NO...
THE TOWNS-PEOPLE ARE FINE, AND THE WARRIORS ARE JUST UNCON-SCIOUS.
I SEE ...
ISN'T THAT GREAT?
!
WE TOOK CARE OF THINGS WITHOUT A SINGLE PERSON GETTING HURT.
FOR THAT REASON ALONE, IT WAS WORTH COMING TO THIS TOWN.

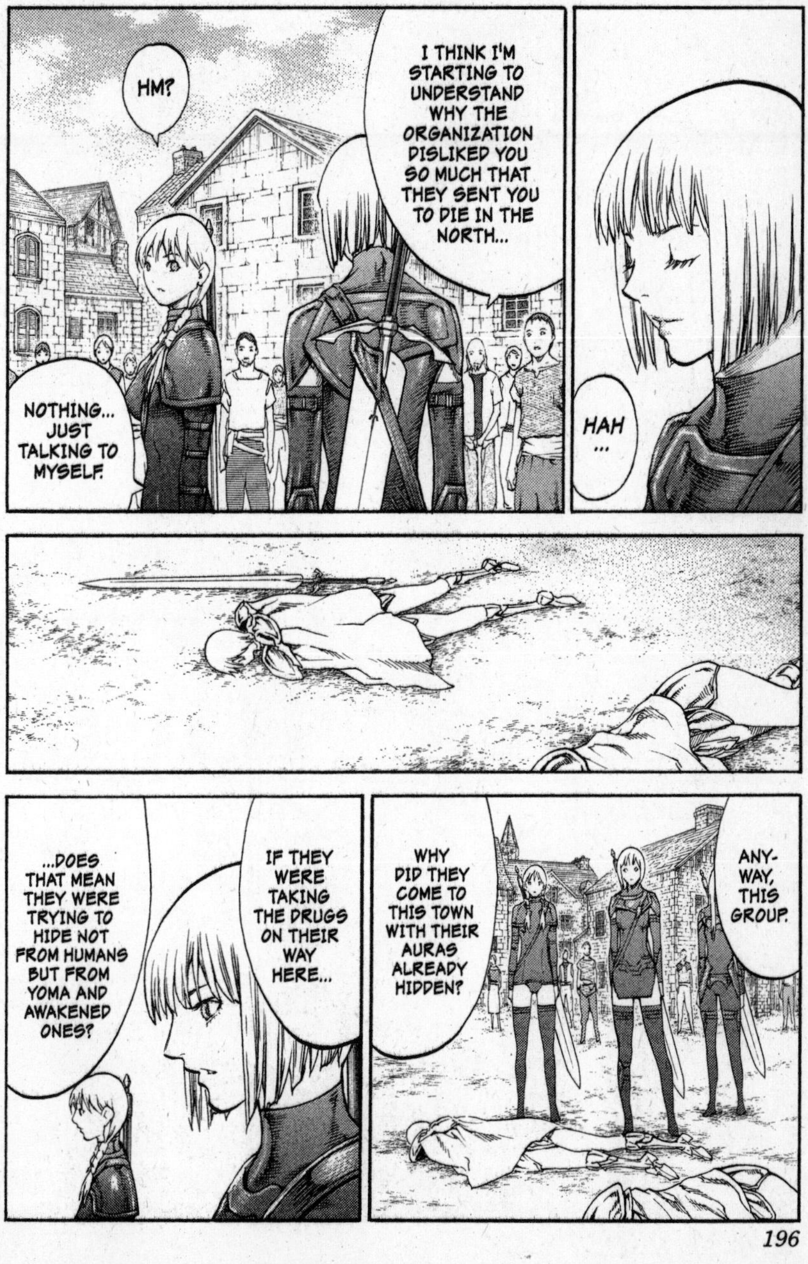
HAH ...
I THINK I'M STARTING TO UNDERSTAND WHY THE ORGANIZATION DISLIKED YOU SO MUCH THAT THEY SENT YOU TO DIE IN THE NORTH...
HM?
NOTHING... JUST TALKING TO MYSELF.
ANY-WAY, THIS GROUP.
WHY DID THEY COME TO THIS TOWN WITH THEIR AURAS ALREADY HIDDEN?
IF THEY WERE TAKING THE DRUGS ON THEIR WAY HERE...
...DOES THAT MEAN THEY WERE TRYING TO HIDE NOT FROM HUMANS BUT FROM YOMA AND AWAKENED ONES?

READ THIS WAY

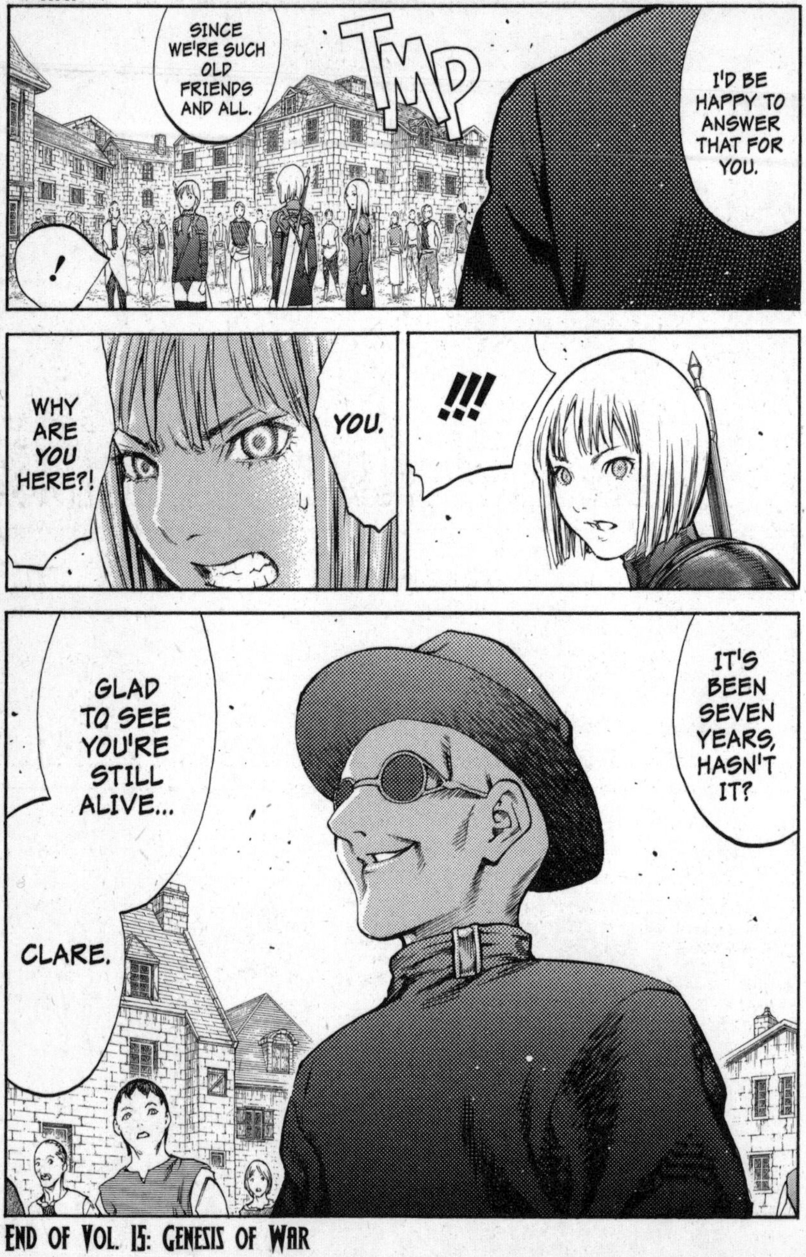
I'D BE HAPPY TO ANSWER THAT FOR YOU.
TMP
SINCE WE'RE SUCH OLD FRIENDS AND ALL.
!
!!!
YOU.
WHY ARE YOU HERE?!
IT'S BEEN SEVEN YEARS, HASN'T IT?
GLAD TO SEE YOU'RE STILL ALIVE...
CLARE.

END OF VOL. 15: GENESIS OF WAR

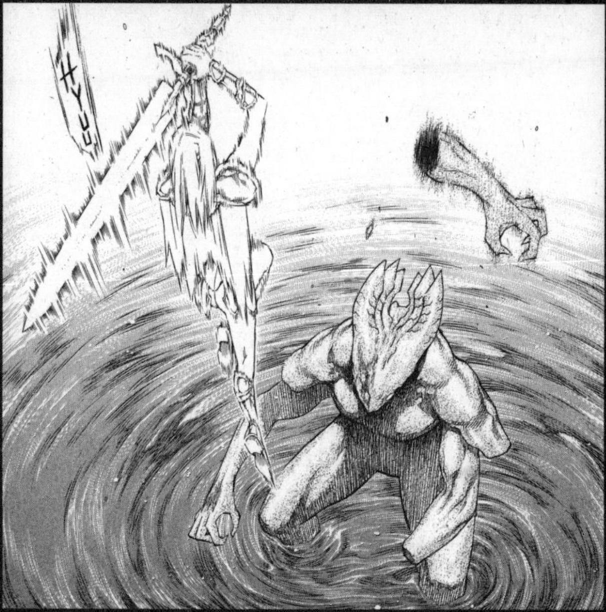
HYUU

IN THE NEXT VOLUME

Renée's situation becomes increasingly desperate as she struggles with the terrible task Riful has set before her. Meanwhile, Clare and her companions receive some startling information from Rubel, and one of the current generation of Claymores teaches Helen and Deneve about the Organization's newest weapon.

Available June 2010

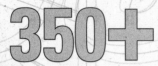
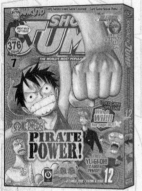
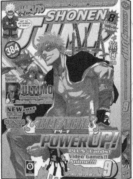
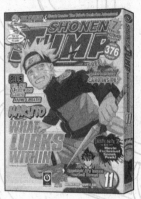

You're Reading in the Wrong Direction!!

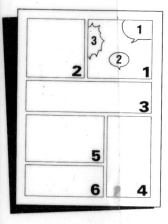

Whoops! Guess what? You're starting at the wrong end of the comic!

…It's true! In keeping with the original Japanese format, **Claymore** is meant to be read from right to left, starting in the upper-right corner.

Unlike English, which is read from left to right, Japanese is read from right to left, meaning that action, sound effects and word-balloon order are completely reversed… something which can make readers unfamiliar with Japanese feel pretty backwards themselves. For this reason, manga or Japanese comics published in the U.S. in English have sometimes been published "flopped"–that is, printed in exact reverse order, as though seen from the other side of a mirror.

By flopping pages, U.S. publishers can avoid confusing readers, but the compromise is not without its downside. For one thing, a character in a flopped manga series who once wore in the original Japanese version a T-shirt emblazoned with "M A Y" (as in "the merry month of") now wears one which reads "Y A M"! Additionally, many manga creators in Japan are themselves unhappy with the process, as some feel the mirror-imaging of their art skews their original intentions.

We are proud to bring you Norihiro Yagi's **Claymore** in the original unflopped format. For now, though, turn to the other side of the book and let the adventure begin…!

–Editor

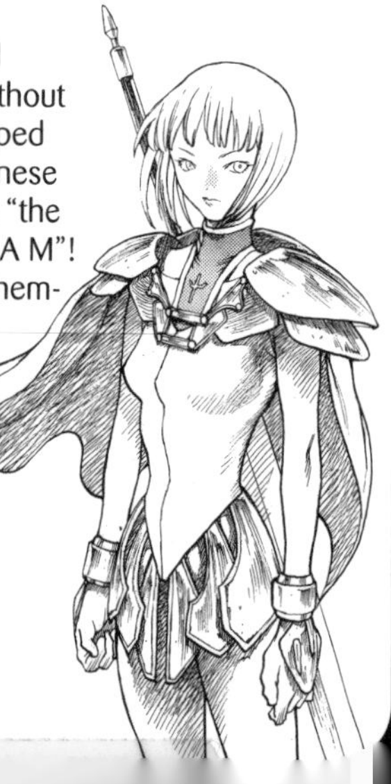

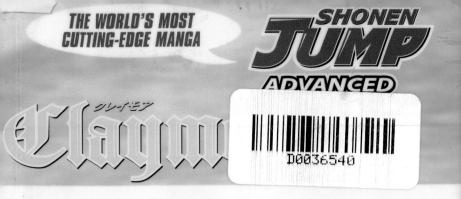

THE WORLD'S MOST CUTTING-EDGE MANGA

SHONEN JUMP ADVANCED

クレイモア
Claym

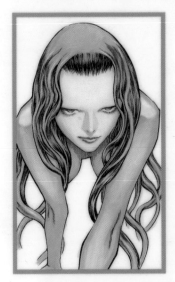

In a world where monsters called Yoma prey on humans and live among them in disguise, humanity's only hope is a new breed of warrior known as Claymores. Half human, half monster, these silver-eyed slayers possess supernatural strength but are condemned to fight their savage impulses—or lose their humanity completely.

GENESIS OF WAR

Galatea's plans to eliminate the Awakened former number 2, "Bloody" Agatha, have failed, but the arrival of Clare and her comrades turns the tide of battle. In the aftermath, Miria decides to finally share her shocking discoveries about the true nature of the Yoma, of the Organization and of the Claymores themselves.

www.shonenjump.com

$9.99 USA $12.99 CAN £6.99 UK

This book reads from right to left.

viz media

RATED T+ FOR OLDER TEEN
ratings.viz.com

ISBN-13: 978-1-4215-3149-6

E